3/89

B E A N

Coco
(Segovia)

A

Rio Grande

Rama

ondido

San Juan

A

SAN JOSÉ
☆ •Cartago

R I C A

E A N

AGONY IN THE GARDEN

AGONY IN THE GARDEN:
 A STRANGER IN

 EDWARD R. F. SHEEHAN

CENTRAL AMERICA

HOUGHTON MIFFLIN COMPANY · BOSTON

1989

For information about permission to reproduce selections from
this book, write to Permissions, Houghton Mifflin Company,
2 Park Street, Boston, Massachusetts 02108.

Library of Congress Cataloging-in-Publication Data

Sheehan, Edward R. F.
  Agony in the garden : a stranger in Central America / Edward
  R. F. Sheehan.
  p. cm.
  Includes index.
  ISBN 0-395-48906-7
  1. Central America—Politics and government—1979–
  2. Social conflict—Central America—History—20th
  century.   3. United States—Military policy.   4. Sheehan, Edward R. F.   I. Title.
F1528.S48   1989   88-39549
972.8'053—dc19   CIP

PRINTED IN THE UNITED STATES OF AMERICA

P 10 9 8 7 6 5 4 3 2 1

Endpaper map by Jacques Chazaud

Portions of this book have appeared, in substantially different
and briefer form, in the *New York Review of Books*,
the *Boston Globe*, and *Commonweal*.

The excerpt from T. S. Eliot's "Little Gidding" from *Collected
Poems, 1909–1962*, copyright 1936 by Harcourt Brace Jovan-
ovich, Inc., copyright © 1963, 1964 by T. S. Eliot, is reprinted
by permission of the publisher. Reprinted from *Four Quartets*
by T. S. Eliot by permission of Faber and Faber Ltd. The
excerpts from Roberto Sosa's "De Niño a Hombre" and "La
Ciudad de los Ninos Mendingos" from *Los Pobres* are reprinted
by permission of Editorial Guaymuras.

Por los niños de Centroamérica
To the children of the isthmus

Then cometh Jesus with them unto a place called
Gethsemane. . . . And being in agony he prayed
more earnestly: and his sweat was as it were
great drops of blood falling down to the
ground. . . . And while he yet spake, behold a
multitude, and he that was called Judas, one of
the twelve, went before them, and drew near
unto Jesus to kiss him. But Jesus said unto him,
Judas, betrayest thou the Son of man with a
kiss? When they which were about him saw
what would follow, they said unto him, Lord,
shall we smite with the sword? And one of them
smote the servant of the high priest, and cut off
his right ear. . . . And Jesus . . . touched his
ear, and healed him. . . . Then said Jesus . . .
Put up again thy sword into his place: for all that
take the sword shall perish with the sword. . . .
But all this was done, that the scriptures of the
prophets might be fulfilled. Then all the disciples
forsook him, and fled. . . . Then Jesus said unto
the chief priests, and captains of the temple, and
the elders . . . this is your hour, and the power
of darkness.

MATTHEW 26; LUKE 22

And what you thought you came for
Is only a shell, a husk of meaning
From which the purpose breaks only when it is fulfilled
If at all. Either you had no purpose
Or the purpose is beyond the end you figured
And is altered in fulfilment.

T. S. ELIOT, *Little Gidding*

AUTHOR'S NOTE

Central America is a garden. It abounds in beautiful vegetation, lakes, birds, valleys, and volcanoes; in forests I picked wild orchid and avocado pear. The isthmus is also a Gethsemane, where human agony seems to flourish in Biblical counterpoint to the luxuriance of the landscape.

This is not a travel book, a "news book," or an opus of political science. It is a personal impression of fragments of recent time: from late 1985 through most of 1986, nearly a year, when I wandered through the isthmus and noted what I saw, heard, and read. In 1987, I watched the unraveling of U.S. policy toward Central America and the initiatives for peace with peculiar interest, then returned to Nicaragua for several weeks in the summer of 1988. This is a story about human faces —children, women, guerrillas, colonels, traditional and Marxist ecclesiastics, amidst squalor, wealth, weapons, sorrow, humor, religious emotion, military dictatorships—nearer in geography to most of us than New York and Los Angeles are to each other.

In my journeys through five nations I followed a simple rule. I took up with anyone, high or low, who cared to talk to me. I accepted any invitation, from men who lived in palaces to women and children who barely survived in hovels. Remaining loyal to my rule was not always easy: my nature is somewhat misanthropic. However, for this experience I stepped out of character, and I found myself from time to time in absurd and dangerous situations. Luckily I had already spent large portions of my life visiting poor nations of the Third World, though this was my first exposure to Central America. Also I spoke Spanish, having learned it (imperfectly) in Spain when I was young, then I refreshed it in Puerto Rico and thereafter throughout the isthmus.

I do not try to be exhaustive about my subjects — the contras, Honduras, Nicaragua, El Salvador, and Guatemala. Panama — politically more a part of South America than of the isthmus — lies outside the scope of this book. Costa Rica, where I spent some time, is also beyond its scope except insofar as the country is blessed by having no army.

Save for those characters whose names are known internationally, I have — for their protection — given my characters fictitious names or none at all. To disguise the identity of some characters, and for literary economy as well, I have occasionally telescoped conversations or incidents with an individual into a dialogue with several individuals in a single scene. Similarly, once or twice I have created a composite character who represents the collective sentiments of several. All major facts and incidents, such as battles, tortures, statements by high officials, are documented in my notes. My gratitude to various friends and strangers is expressed in the Acknowledgments.

Graham Greene (among others) has suggested that in the end the coherence and success of any narrative is shaped by the writer's point of view. As this narrative unfolds, my own point of view will become more and more apparent. The reader will be at liberty to accept or reject it, though at the least I trust that he or she will find it provocative and controversial. André Gide once wrote that "what another would have done as well as you, do not do it; said as well, do not say it; written as well, do not write it. Be faithful to that which exists nowhere but in yourself." Gide's final phrase I really should not quote: "— and thus make yourself indispensable." To that, I have no pretense.

E.R.F.S.
September 1988

CONTENTS

PROLOGUE

I was young, not long out of school, when I discovered the tropics of the poor.

It was the spring of 1955. I had been traveling in Spain, spent Holy Week in Andalusia, and soon descended to the south where I climbed the ledges around the Rock of Gibraltar and gained my first glimpse of Africa. Across the Strait, jagged in the sunset, stood the mountains of Morocco. On an impulse next day I boarded a boat at Algeciras and crossed the narrow strait to Tangier.

Most of Morocco at that time was still a French protectorate, nominally governed by a puppet sultan and feverish with nationalists demanding independence. I remained in Morocco for many weeks, venturing further and further south, from Tangier to Fez, from Meknes to Rabat and Casablanca. At night, French paratroopers patrolled the boulevards of Casablanca and shot on sight Moors they suspected of mischief. Eventually I reached the Atlas Mountains and the seething casbahs of Marrakech, where in a medieval palace I met the cruel and legendary Pasha, another puppet of the French.

I had no clear idea of what I was doing or even of what I sought, but I recognized at once that I loved the labyrinthine alleys, the clandestine meetings with Moorish outlaws, and the game with danger. In Rabat, I became friendly with one Mehdi Ben Barka, the most brilliant revolutionary of his period and reviled by the French as "the Lenin of Morocco." Soon I discovered that I was being followed by the French police, and it became obvious even to a mind as innocent as mine that for my safety I had best return to Spain. About a year later, the French despaired of keeping Morocco in their empire and granted the kingdom its independence. A decade afterward, my old friend Mehdi Ben Barka was lured to Paris, where he was murdered by a Moroccan general with the connivance of the French police.

I mention these fragments of my young writer's life to explain that my taste for the intrigues and convulsions of the Third World began early and that such experience—combined with my classical education —largely shaped my conception of mankind. My addiction to the poor tropics became incurable, and it dominated my writings for three decades thereafter.

Not that I had to wait for Africa to discover the tribulations of the poor.

I grew up in an affluent suburb of Boston in a large wooden house with high ceilings and mahogany fireplaces, full of books and music lessons, at the top of a shady hill. My family (Irish-French-Yankee) was comfortable, my father did well in business, and in those days— the era of World War II—my mother was assisted by a succession of maids as she raised her five children. As the war ended and I entered adolescence, my father sent me to the Jesuits for a classical education.

The Jesuit high school at that time was a decrepit Victorian building in the South End. To reach it I had to rise early, hitch a ride out of the rich suburbs, take a streetcar past Symphony Hall to Washington Street—always night beneath the girders of the elevated railway —and skid row.

I remember a maze of rusting stanchions, decayed doorways, and grimy brick buildings, billboards, pawnshops, storefront missions, junk-littered empty lots, bars and liquor stores, vagrants queuing early on the snowy mornings blowing at their hands as they waited for the bars and package stores to open up. In the afternoons when I emerged from school, women stumbled from the murky bars, their children running after them, and even occasionally a woman pushed a baby carriage from bar to bar. Around the corner at Columbus Avenue or up the street near the hideous puddingstone cathedral in the shadow of the shrieking railway old women stood muttering obscenities to the wind or old men shouted blasphemies at Christ.

The squalor of skid row intruded on my lessons with the Jesuits, but the lessons redeemed the squalor. The windows rattled and the ancient building shook as we read—in Latin—Caesar and Cicero, and—in

Greek—Xenophon and Homer. Somehow I jumbled these ancients with the clatter of the passing trains, daydreaming they might transport me out of the slums, across the curvature of sky and ocean to the mansions of the Caesars and the temples of Troy.

Later in my youth, as I have told you, my fantasies of travel all came true. Throughout the tropics of the poor, the brown and black races were in revolt against the imperial domination of Great Britain and France, and—more and more—the power of the United States aroused similar passions of resentment. Over time, I grew ever more fond of writing of tribal wars in Africa, the intrigues of the CIA in the Middle East, and Palestinian guerrillas. In the 1960s, during the Nigerian civil war, by the side of a dirt road, I saw my first headless man. In Jordan two years later, during a Palestinian revolt against the king, a bullet pierced the window of my bedroom, missing my head by inches and covering me with glass. Eventually I despaired of solutions in the Middle East and wondered about Central America.

The conflict in Nicaragua beckoned to me. Here was an imperial power—the United States—scheming to overthrow the rulers of a tiny nation because their Marxism posed some sort of vague threat. The U.S. was supporting an army of guerrillas who hated the Sandinistas as much as the Americans did and who in the name of democracy raped women and murdered children as they waged a filthy little war. I imagined I might do well writing about the contras, and I resolved to meet them first. The Sandinistas I would meet soon thereafter. I thought: This war was made for me.

1/THE CONTRAS···HONDURAS

My keenest image of that contra camp is of young men running. One morning, unable to sleep, I rose before dawn and stood by my barracks in the darkness, waiting for the sun. Roosters crowed. In the first light, a thick mist ascended from the vegetation, enshrouding even the dirt paths of the camp. I heard a tramping of boots. Over a hill came about fifty men in T-shirts, olive pants, and heavy boots, running and puffing in measured gait. They dipped below me, in a gorge of mist, then emerged eerily up a hill in the feeble light.

Some of them were children. They ran to a hilltop and a long shack without walls under a plastic roof. There, at tables, they took their breakfast in silhouette against the dawn. Behind them, barely visible in the mist, stood La Tierra Prometida, the Promised Land —the steep mountains of Nicaragua.

From my journal

I

ON THE DAY I reached Tegucigalpa, I was invited to visit the contras.

Such visitations normally were not easy to arrange. However, not without adventure, I managed to elude the contra bureaucracy and establish contact with commanders of the field. On the morning after my arrival in the capital of Honduras, a dark stump of a man, in blue jeans and a green Oakland A's baseball cap, walked into my hotel. "Meester Edward? I am Comandante Aureliano. *Vamos.*"

He led me outside to a covered jeep, crammed with contras in civilian dress and a mysterious Canadian with a dark mustache and a British accent who introduced himself as "Pete." I sat squeezed in front as the comandante sped through the teeming streets of Tegucigalpa southeast into open country. For hours we drove on a hardtopped highway, through valleys covered with evergreen, until we reached Danlí, all shabby tile and plaster. Then the roadblocks started. "If the soldiers ask you questions," the comandante warned me, "don't tell them you're a writer."

My presence with the contras was indeed a delicate matter. Wary of reprisal raids into their territory from the Sandinistas, the Honduran military denied that the contras were operating against Nicaragua from Honduran soil. Officially in Honduras the contras did not exist, and the authorities were not eager for publicity that exposed their fiction.

We encountered half a dozen military roadblocks as we proceeded through the waning afternoon off the hardtopped highway onto dirt roads toward the border of Nicaragua. We were in lowlands now; beneath the mountains on the hairpin turns the terrain became gorgeously tropical, watered by streams and graced by orchid and palm. *Campesinos* (peasants) loitered in the doorways of their wretched huts. Twilight and darkness: at the roadblocks, the Honduran soldiers, many of them, seemed boys of twelve. As they emerged languidly from their bivouacs or from behind dancing flashlights in the darkness, they looked like beardless dwarfs.

"Why are they so tiny?" I asked Pete the Canadian.

"Malnutrition probably," Pete said. "They're not here out of patriotism. They've been press-ganged. The army rounds them up in cinemas, bars, and whorehouses. Honduras has never won a war."

We resumed our journey, over the twisting dirt roads, narrow, steep, almost impassable. Eventually we stopped. Uniformed contras emerged from the forest bearing automatic weapons. After a discussion by the roadside, Pete decided to continue on to the headquarters of Colonel Enrique Bermúdez, commander of the FDN, the Nicaraguan Democratic Force. With Comandante Aureliano and a band of contras, I walked through forest in the moonless night up and down hills until we reached the rushing of a stream. By flashlight I saw I was in some sort of camp, log huts in a wood by a river. Shadows moved, men and women, infants crying farther off. I was brought inside a hut.

Only a kerosene lamp lit that hovel; Comandante Aureliano presented his chiefs of personnel, logistics, and operations in this "Region of Segovia." We were in the Las Vegas salient, a protrusion of Honduras by the River Coco that juts into northern Nicaragua. As the comandante conferred with his officers over documents and maps, a toothless woman, her face as wrinkled as a mummy's, dressed in a khaki shirt and trousers, served me a supper of rice and beans. I said, "*Gracias, Señora.*"

"He's not a *woman,*" the comandante said. "He's a soldier. He fought fifty years ago with General Sandino — against the United States." Rebuked, I went to bed, lying in my clothes on a cot behind a partition of the hut. The comandante flopped down on the cot beside me. His stomach growled, and he kept rising in the night to swallow pills, cursing his worms from those long marches to the interior of his homeland. I lay awake from his moans and rainfall on the plastic roof.

At dawn, I walked about the camp, huts under roofs of green plastic in a forest of birch and palm. A hundred troops, in camouflage pants, their caps stamped U.S. ARMY, were lining up for a breakfast of rice and beans and coffee, served by women at open hearths under green plastic. Others bathed and washed their clothes in the river; women, bare-breasted, bathed and scrubbed clothes on rocks and hung them to dry on strings between stumps of trees. Above them on the slopes stood chaotic tents and lean-tos where the families of contras lived, peasant women, pubescent girls, and naked children bustling about, dogs and kittens foraging, the girls sweeping their hearths with twig brooms, all of these creatures subsisting, it seemed, at the harshest level of life. Wherever I wandered, Leonel followed me.

Leonel was my bodyguard, assigned no doubt by Comandante Aureliano to keep an eye on me. He was a slight, copper-skinned youth, perhaps eighteen, sensuous of face, with long black hair and the movements of a predatory leopard. He was clad in olive green U.S. issue —a visored cap, a T-shirt, trousers tucked above his ankles into dusty boots. He wore an ammunition belt around his waist and a dagger in the belt. A loaded Soviet AK-47 automatic rifle was slung over his right shoulder. An immense white rosary dangled from his neck. "I'm fighting for Jesus Christ and His Virgin Mother," he said. "For democracy, pluralism, and a free Nicaragua. I hate Marxism-Leninism." He repeated this, like a pop lyric.

Leonel had a potbelly, the result no doubt of his recent indisposition. Some weeks before, he had been wounded in combat with the Sandinistas inside Nicaragua, and he was still recovering. Proudly he rolled down his shirt to reveal an ugly perforation by his shoulder, inviting me to touch it. Like so many Nicaraguans, he was a chatterbox. "The Sandinista soldiers are on drugs. They're bad fighters, and they're all cowards. Did you know that girls march with us, and kill the Sandinista pigs?"

Back in the log hut, Leonel was cheerfully recounting more of his adventures when a girl walked in. She was Rocibel, seventeen, a bit wide at the hips, as Nicaraguan women tend to be, with a lovely, wide-eyed white face. She wore her brown hair bound by an elastic band, army pants, blue slippers on bare feet, and an AK-47 strapped to her shoulder. I asked her what she did.

"I'm a commando."

At the moment, however, Rocibel's mind was on guerrilla combat of another sort. She could not keep her hands off Leonel. She produced a comb, sat him on a log, and addressed his luxuriant black locks. He resisted, but as her combing progressed to fondling he seemed more pleased. She tickled and caressed him; he giggled constantly and sang out, "*Ro-cee-bel, Ro-cee-bel,*" as her ministrations grew more ardent. Beside each other on the log, they half entwined, their AK-47s still hoisted on their shoulders. Such beautiful children, I thought, as I left the hut.

Beauty and death. In the field, the contras showed less loving kindness. Numerous witnesses report that inside Nicaragua they were notorious for killing civilians whose only sin was support of the Sandinistas; members of their families were also killed. The contras seemed especially fond of torture and mutilation. The Americas Watch Committee has written:

> [Eleuterio Matute's] abdomen [was] slit open from the chest bone down. He had been punched with a knife or bayonet many times in the chest, and his tongue had been cut out.
>
> Gabriel Brenes, age 25, was picked up by the contras on the road between Los Angeles, where he lived, and Nueva Guinea, on October 30 . . . The contras tied him and four other men and took them away. The next day the army went looking for them and found Brenes's body full of knife cuts; the wife was told that he had been castrated.
>
> In Verdun, two brothers were found dead . . . : their ears and lips had been cut off, their nails pulled out and they had been castrated.
>
> At Nueva Guinea . . . [a] witness who recovered the body of Carla Reyes told us she was in advanced pregnancy, and that the body was on its back, with the legs apart, and no clothing from the rib cage on down. She had been bayoneted and the body had begun to decompose.

I wondered, were these contras, in whose camp I stood, butchers or liberators, true guerrillas or merely terrorists? Whatever their brutalities in combat, most of the foot soldiers were peasant boys from northern Nicaragua. They had migrated into the contra camps largely from the northern departments (provinces) of Estelí, Madríz, Nueva Segovia, and Jinotega and from the central departments of Matagalpa, Boaco, and Chontales. Some had fled with their families; many more had left their families at home. They were a hillbilly army, sprung from subsistence farms that patched the cruel and mountainous earth of their provinces. They were a simple, almost animistic peasantry, their reverence for the rhythms of nature mingled with a primitive devotion to the Roman Church.

In the formalities of doctrine they were often lax, but their basic faith was indestructible. Theirs was a landscape of itinerant friars on donkeys, church bells tolling out the Angelus across meadow and hill, rosaries mumbled at bedtime, intense veneration of the Virgin. As farmers, they were freeholders. Their values were not only mystical in religion but traditional in matters of property, rooted in land they considered their own. They looked aghast at the social experiments of the Sandinista Revolution, particularly collective ownership of the land. Above all, they feared that Managua would outlaw the Church and seize their farms.

These peasants had always been isolated from Managua, from the capital's intrigues and great affairs. It was for their very isolation that the Somozas in their day preferred peasants from the north as their pool for the National Guard. Peasant soldiers with no ties to the intelligentsia of the capital and the other cities of Nicaragua's western coast could be depended on to control the urban population, to shoot them when necessary. Indeed, almost to the end, such campesinos were savagely loyal to Anastasio Somoza.

The seeds of the counterrevolution were sown within weeks of the Sandinista triumph in July 1979. Some Sandinista guerrillas themselves, resentful of Cuban advisers and fearful that the Revolution was going communist, returned to their farms in the hills and within less than a year formed small roving bands called *chilotes* that harassed the new government. In 1980, bands of *somocistas* began guerrilla operations from Honduras; in 1981 they fused with the chilotes, forming the Legion of 15 September. The new army was advised by right-wing Argentine officers, who were preempted by the CIA in 1982. From this mixture, the command structure that emerged in the field was roughly 40 percent former National Guard, perhaps a quarter or more ex Sandinista, and the rest mixed. Comandante Aureliano boasted that he fought against Somoza, but in fact (I learned eventually) he had served Somoza in the National Guard. Sensing my disbelief, he protested constantly of his reverence for human rights, and he made human rights the theme of his contra graduation ceremony.

Before the ceremony, a dozen recruits gathered in a hut to read comic books and sing songs. The comic books showed contras in manly field combat with Sandinista troops, but they also stressed solicitude toward the civil population — pictures of warriors cuddling infants, offering milk to mothers, helping old women hobbling on their canes. I had read the notorious CIA manual that instructed the contras how to kill people, *Psychological Operations in Guerrilla Warfare*. Had the CIA, with sudden remorse, now produced the human rights cartoons as well? An older contra began strumming a guitar.

The insurgents sang ballads of the lush beauties of their homeland and of living free, redeemed at last from the lash of servitude and the heel of the oppressor's boot. They sang hymns. "*Juntos como hermanos, Miembros de una Iglesia, Vamos caminando, Al encuentro del Señor.* Together as brothers, Faithful of the Church, Onward we march, To a meeting with the Lord."

We adjourned to the graduation. Perhaps fifty contra novices, most under twenty, others no older than fifteen, clad variously in U.S. Army issue and bearing their AK-47s and Belgian FAL rifles, lined up in neat rows. Each wore an emblem with a peasant in his hut over a sword and a machine gun. Comandante Aureliano delivered a valedictory.

"Without discipline, we cannot win the war," he told them, standing on an embankment in the birch forest still wearing his Oakland A's cap. "You must maintain discipline and you must respect the human rights [*los derechos humanos*] of all — the civilian population and even the Sandinistas. You must not harm or steal property. As for women, you must respect their bodies and commit not the slightest violence against them . . . *Los derechos humanos* . . . When you take prisoners of war, you must treat them well and not kill them — they're our brothers . . . *Los derechos humanos* . . ." Did he intend the speech for the contras or for me?

The new contras marched off toward the river — singing more hymns, their rosaries bobbing about their necks — I assumed to battle inside Nicaragua. Indeed, that very day in mid-November, a comandante led two hundred fifty volunteers into the homeland. It was the season of the coffee harvest: these and other guerrillas would try to disrupt it in Jinotega, Matagalpa, and Estelí. They would attack collection points and burn down buildings, but the buildings would be defended by Sandinista militia and the encounters were certain to produce bloodshed.

I moved on to another camp in the Las Vegas salient. Still bearing their rifles, Leonel and Rocibel escorted me through the forest to the road and the comandante's jeep. As the jeep sputtered off, I leaned out of the window and looked back. Rocibel had her arm around Leonel's neck, fingering his white rosary. In the ensuing months, thousands of Nicaraguans, contras, Sandinistas, and civilians, were killed in this civil war. I assume that when Leonel recovered from his wounds he returned to Nicaragua and that Rocibel followed him into battle.

2

WITH COMANDANTE AURELIANO I drove several miles to Yamales, the main contra camp near the Nicaraguan border and the headquarters of Colonel Bermúdez. Passing by cornfields in the hot afternoon, I saw some Honduran peasants but no Honduran soldiers. Like an army of occupation, however, the contras were everywhere, ambling alone, jogging together on the roads, marching in columns with full gear, singing martial hymns. I remembered my visits a decade earlier to "Fatah Land," that enclave in southern Lebanon controlled by the PLO until the Israelis invaded and pushed the Palestinians out. Indeed, the hilly terrain was vaguely similar, Nicaraguans resemble Arabs — the likeness of ambience was bizarre.

The Yamales camp, or Jefatura, was a full-fledged military establishment. It had roads, jeeps, wooden barracks, command tents, tiny shacks, irregular bivouacs, and outhouses. In a deserted barrack, taking a siesta in a hammock, was Pete the Canadian. I sat on a dirty mattress and regarded him as he slept. He was a long, hairy man, perhaps in his midthirties, and he had changed his civilian clothes for olive military fatigues. For his siesta, he wore a floppy military hat, the string drawn tightly about his neck; even in repose, his mustachioed face seemed troubled. Clumsily, I dropped my cigarette lighter. Pete started, and woke up. "Oh," he said. "Edward."

He rose and took me on a tour of the camp. His full name was Peter Bertie; he had been born in Britain, had lived in France, had a daughter (I think) by his divorced wife, and he was a journalist of sorts, running out of money. "I'm a terrible writer," he said. "I write about the contras all the time, but nobody wants my stuff. I did get a piece into *Soldier of Fortune.*"

It seemed that Peter's true ambition was to be a soldier himself. "I'm only interested in the military side of the contras," he said. He had already spent five months on missions with the insurgents inside Nicaragua, trudging and running (under Sandinista fire) up and down mountains with a full pack on his shoulders, and he wanted to spend six months more. "I'm forty," he continued, "and each time with the contras I barely make it. My companions are lads of twenty and younger. Our long marches last for weeks, and the terrain is so rugged — not only the damned mountains but deep valleys, bush, brush, forest, and jungle. I don't carry a gun. It's so . . . frustrating to be with the comandante when the shooting starts. He won't let me near enough to all the action. I want to *be there* with the lads.''

He evoked the killing he had seen inside Nicaragua. What American liberals called atrocities, Peter called necessity in a savage civil war. The contras killed civilians because they had to: the civilians were ''spies'' for the Sandinistas, and in any sort of war spies got shot. ''They're not all shot. Sometimes the contras knife or bayonet them to save ammunition.'' And yes, the contras attacked civilians in collective farms, but only because the Sandinistas forced the farmers to defend themselves. The Sandinistas committed the true atrocities. They skinned people alive, injected babies with blue poison, bashed them to death against the trunks of trees, then raped their mothers: the campesinos of Zelaya had told him so.

I had met people such as Peter all over the tropics of the poor: troubled aliens, discontent with their native cultures and hungry for heroism, who drift into exotic wars and soon are true believers. Peter's conversion, almost mystical, began in 1968, when Soviet tanks rolled into Prague, and he consecrated his life to fighting Marxism-Leninism. So devoted was he to the contras that he had even gone to Washington to plead their cause with U.S. senators and to mingle with kindred spirits in the anticommunist brotherhood, the likes of General John Singlaub, the former Green Berets who published *Soldier of Fortune,* and Lieutenant Colonel Oliver North of the staff of the National Security Council.

Near the command tents we sat for coffee at a picnic table, where we were joined by Mike Lima, the chief of contra operations, another veteran of Somoza's National Guard. He held up a wired plastic contraption instead of a right hand, and I shook his stainless steel claws. The missing arm, the right and left legs both wounded in combat did not dishearten him: his craft was killing Sandinistas. ''. . . one hundred fifty, two hundred, two hundred fifty dead . . .'' he reminisced. ''. . . I was stumbling over bodies of young conscripts . . . Nicaraguans . . . my brothers . . . I wept . . .'' Three more guerrillas approached and asked me for cigarettes. Politico, all bushy hair and bad teeth, was over thirty, but the other two were children barely entering adolescence — Conejito, Baby Rabbit, and Bodoque, Half Wit. Both wore olive green U.S. issue and giggled as schoolboys do. Schoolboys? They were killers. Half Wit had long hair beneath his visored cap, full Mayan lips, and a Band-Aid on his forearm. Baby Rabbit was even smaller and more cuddly.

Politico fondled Baby Rabbit incessantly. Cooing "*Conejito, Conejito, mi cariño* — Baby Rabbit, Baby Rabbit, my beloved," he tweaked the boy's ears, pinched his hairless cheeks, tickled him beneath his shirt. "He's only fooling," Peter said. Baby Rabbit laughed and loved it.

Half Wit, it turned out, was the grandson of a Nicaraguan hero who had fought with General Sandino against the United States Marines. However, after the Revolution the Sandinistas seized his great farm in Nueva Segovia. "When Grandpapa protested, he was taken away," Half Wit said. "His body — but not his soul — was given back to us with marks of torture and a leg missing."

How many Sandinistas had Half Wit killed?

"A lot. I never kept count."

And why was Baby Rabbit a guerrilla?

"The Sandinistas killed my father."

How many Sandinistas had Baby Rabbit killed?

"Three or four that I know about."

In how many battles had Baby Rabbit fought?

"More than twenty."

Sweet Mother of God. How long had he been a guerrilla?

"Since I was eleven."

PETER: Twelve-, fourteen-, fifteen-year-olds do fight in the field if they want to. In Nicaragua, I met an eleven-year-old contra who began fighting when he was ten.

HALF WIT: The Sandinistas do the same.

BABY RABBIT: Girls, thirteen years old, fight with us, too.

POLITICO (*hugging Baby Rabbit*): *Conejito, Conejito, cariñ-o-o-o-o.*

I wondered, could Mike Lima pull a rifle trigger with his claw?

MIKE: Of course. We like a mixture of Kalashnikov AK-47s, Belgian FALs, and German G-3s.

P: The Kalashnikovs are no good for sniper fire, but good enough for reasonably close combat.

HW: The FALs are bigger than Kalashnikovs. Both automatics, but the FAL is a real submachine gun.

BR: The FAL is my favorite.

POL: It's too heavy for you. Stick to Kalashnikovs.

HW: We capture ammunition for Kalashnikovs from the Sandinistas.

M: A mixture of weapons is the best of worlds.

BR: The FALs and G-3s pack more punch.

I wondered, could Half Wit and Baby Rabbit read and write? The sun set. In the twilight I was summoned to the presence of 380, code name of Colonel Enrique Bermúdez, commander of the Nicaraguan Democratic Force, Número Uno, the Counterrevolution Himself. I walked up to the command tent, a stretch of white canvas on the crest of a muddy hill.

Inside, a young woman in khaki sat at a desk, tapping documents on an old typewriter. Nearly everything she used was stamped MADE IN THE U.S.A., even her bottle of correction fluid. The tent had a long conference table covered with green cloth, on which lay documents and books and an ancient American field telephone — the kind you cranked, World War II vintage. On the wall was a poster of a contra protecting children and an old woman above the legend RESPETA A LAS PERSONAS CIVILES. Behind a partition, a radio crackled and a man's voice rasped commands.

Eventually the man emerged — Colonel Bermúdez. He was a stocky, trim soldier in camouflage fatigues. He had a full head of black hair and wore horn-rimmed glasses. As he perused a document he seemed almost pedagogic. His mouth was a straight line, and his dark face seemed faintly cruel. "I'm sorry," he said. "I've been talking to my units in Nicaragua."

I knew something of his past. He had headed the National Guard's constabulary in Managua in the 1960s and into the mid-1970s. Corruption had flourished in that constabulary, but U.S. diplomats claimed that the colonel was clean and also that he had no connection to Somoza's torture apparatus. The worst outrages were not committed until late in Somoza's reign. By then Bermúdez was in Washington as military attaché, so supposedly little blood stained his conscience.

And after that — with the rise of the contras? His alliance with the Argentine colonels, who tortured and murdered "subversives" in their homeland and had helped Bermúdez organize the contras? And what about the colonel's intimacy with the CIA, his tolerance of atrocities by his insurgents, the dollars intended for supplies he was accused of diverting to his own pocket? I was wary of him before we exchanged a word. We sat at the head of the green table, and as the night descended he rose often to receive more radio messages in the room beyond.

I asked, "*Mi comandante,* have you any serious chance to win this war?" Bermúdez responded, "Not only have we a chance, I'm *sure* we can win this war. This is the first opportunity to defeat a Marxist-Leninist regime. No guerrilla movement can succeed without the population, but we are supported by the Nicaraguan people, and the morale of our troops is high. Our only problem is that we've not enough resources to win the war in a very short time. U.S. aid is not sufficient. We're fighting with rifles, machine guns, very few rocket-propelled grenades, very few 60 mm mortars. We're fighting an enemy with MI-24 helicopters, BM-21 rocket launchers, 152 mm artillery units, PT-76 amphibious tanks, BTR-60 armored personnel carriers . . .''

An old song: give us more guns and victory is ours. What guns did he want? "We don't want a U.S. invasion of Nicaragua. We want to fight our own war. Look, our product is much *cheaper* than a U.S. military intervention." Soviet helicopters were slaughtering his men, and he needed better missiles to shoot them down. The contras had SAM-7s, but often they didn't work; he wanted shoulder-held Stingers, the kind the U.S. sold to Israel and Saudi Arabia. How about the Redeye? Oh, that was obsolete. He wanted an air force, too, however small — any little planes that could shoot down Soviet helicopters — and special radar equipment for night drops to supply his troops. I said, "I assume you'll get some of it. What are you doing now?"

The comandante continued, "We're paralyzed by lack of supplies, and we're fighting at forty percent capacity. Not our fault, but the war doesn't wait. The Sandinistas are gaining time — they have helicopters, ammunition, better recruiting, and better defense. They have cruelly relocated the population from parts of Nicaragua and mounted terrible reprisals against peasants they suspect of sympathy to us — so we've lost some civilian support structure. Still, we're operating in almost half the country."

He produced a map of Nicaragua. "We monitor Sandinista communications all the time," he said with satisfaction. "Here, in Chontales, for example." He pointed to the center of his homeland, handed me a batch of Sandinista intercepts, and withdrew again to his radio room. FROM JUIGALPA TO SANTO DOMINGO. TAKE CARE, COUNTERREVOLUTIONARIES CUTTING TELEPHONE LINES AND SETTING AMBUSHES . . . SEND PATROL TO RIVER BUT DON'T CROSS UNTIL WE COLLECT FURTHER INFORMATION . . . NRO. 680 A BOACO DE BLI F. MARTI PTO. NECESITO MAS TROPAS PORQUE ES DEMASIADA LA CANTIDAD C. R. PARA LA GENTE QUE YO TENGO. PTO. 0727. I NEED MORE TROOPS, TOO MANY COUNTERREVOLUTIONARIES FOR THE MEN I HAVE . . . Reply from headquarters: SPOKE WITH CHIEF, SAYS YOU HAVE TO REPULSE THEM. SENDING REINFORCEMENTS. COUNTERREVOLUTIONARIES INTEND TO CAPTURE ROAD . . . Body counts: WE'VE FOUND NINE COMRADES DEAD AND WE'RE LOOKING FOR THE OTHER LOST . . . As I scribbled on, a shadow fell across my page. The colonel said, "So?"

"Your men seem very active, *mi comandante,*" I said. "These body counts . . ."

"I've just received another report from Boaco," he rejoiced, waving a piece of paper. "We've captured an 82 mm gun, one AK-47 rifle, four thousand rounds of ammunition, ten grenades, ten hammocks, and sixteen mules."

Later, over my supper of rice and beans, I reflected on the prospects for contra success. The insurgents so far had won but minor battles, and I wondered whether more weaponry from the United States would make much difference. The counterrevolutionaries yearned for an insurrection in the cities, but would that ever happen or would the war drag on and on? I was calmer than Peter. Next afternoon, waiting to see the colonel again, I stood with Peter near the command tents as he cursed the contra bureaucracy. His heart was with the troops, he said — with the lads twenty and younger who did the fighting. Their comandantes in the field were young as well, but they lacked experience in managing a war, so most of the administrators were hacks from the National Guard. "Bermúdez is the only one with brains." Without him the war might collapse.

Peter pointed down below, to an open tent where a gray-haired officer was shuffling papers and dictating to a secretary. "Look at that idiot. The Exec."

I asked, "If you're so fed up, why are you here?"

"I'm torn, Edward. I want to fight communism. The Sandinistas are so evil. Marching with the troops is a matter of conscience. The lads are my way of life. I hang on through sheer stubbornness. I can only get to Nicaragua if Colonel Bermúdez himself sends me in. I won't let the clerks ruin my dream."

My conversation with the colonel that afternoon did not go well. I challenged him about contra atrocities, but he turned my questions around and blamed the Sandinistas. Why, they even shot prisoners of war. He handed me another intercept. NRO. 617. 20/11. PTO. FROM JUIGALPA TO SANTO DOMINGO. WHEN THE CHIEF COMES I WILL BRIEF

HIM ABOUT THE FOUR COUNTERREVOLUTIONARY PRISONERS. WE HAVE
ALREADY KILLED THREE AND OTHER STILL ALIVE. PTO. 1123.

A commotion with the guards, and Peter burst in. At the green table,
he exhorted the comandante to allow him into Nicaragua with the guerrillas and a German photographer. "He's a first-class photographer, world
famous. His pictures will tell your story to the world, and I'll be there
to guide him. We want to go in."

Colonel Bermúdez took off his spectacles and pondered, as though
puzzled by the ardor of this tormented Briton. "I'll do what I can,"
he said.

In the barracks, before retiring, I told Peter, "I'm returning to Tegucigalpa tomorrow. Perhaps we'll meet again in Nicaragua. You'll be
with the contras, I'll be with the Sandinistas. I'll wave."

"If they give me a gun," Peter said, "I promise not to shoot you."

I slept badly. I did not much care for the comandantes, including
Colonel Bermúdez, but I felt some sympathy for these peasant troops.
They were not National Guardsmen, but simple bumpkins, on fire with
honest grievances, void of ideology save their fervid Catholicism. Were
they, after all — if the Sandinistas were so repressive — an authentic army
of national liberation? I had arrived in Central America with the conventional liberal wisdom that the contras, through their links with the
Argentine colonels and the CIA, were a reactionary right-wing force.
Was I modifying my preconception?

An army of peasants. An army of children. The Children's War. The
Children's Crusade. True, most contra troops were eighteen and older,
but some were children, and in facing such superior Sandinista firepower
so many of these children would be killed.

Could I espouse the contras' plea for more U.S. weapons? Did not
history show that arms races, once unleashed, were impossible to control, and in Nicaragua would not more arms for the contras provoke
the Russians into giving more guns to the Sandinistas, resulting at
last in tens of thousands more fratricidal deaths? To what purpose?
Tossing there fully clothed on my bare mattress in the Las Vegas
salient, I felt rumpled and confused, like a letter delivered to the wrong
address.

I rose before dawn to meet a truck for my return to Tegucigalpa.
In the dark I flicked my cigarette lighter and glimpsed Peter in his
hammock, still wearing his floppy military hat, but I did not wake
him.

Sixteen months later, early on a Saturday morning, I sat in my study in Massachusetts placidly writing this book, half listening as I wrote to the radio and Mozart's Mass in C Minor. During the news break, somewhere between the Credo and the Agnus Dei, a report was read from the UPI wire that "a Canadian journalist traveling with the contras has been killed by the Sandinistas in Nicaragua."

I rummaged among my photographs and found one of Peter at the Jefatura, in his fatigues and floppy hat, sitting at the picnic table between Half Wit and Baby Rabbit. He was staring into space, his mouth open, in midsentence.

A later broadcast confirmed my fear: "Peter Bertie, a Canadian journalist, died when a Sandinista helicopter hit a West German film unit somewhere in northern Nicaragua." Next day, Reuters reported that "Mr. Bertie was believed to have been traveling with a sixty-member Democratic Force column when it attacked a Sandinista force. First reports indicated that Mr. Bertie and four rebels assigned to protect him had been killed by a rocket." In Miami, a contra bureaucrat promised that Peter's body would be recovered "so he can have a Christian burial."

3

IN TEGUCIGALPA, I visited the United States Embassy—third largest on earth, in a nation the size of Ohio, population five million—on the Avenida de la Paz. That Sunday, Honduras was to hold a presidential election; the embassy, anxious for its success, offered elaborate briefings. The chancery was immense, concrete and glass and ivy, steel doors and combination locks within, a fortress the size of a city block, with an annex opposite. Security: the same metal detectors as used at an airport, briefcases emptied and probed by a beeper, marine guards, identity checks, bulletproof windows.

Some years before I had served as an attaché in the U.S. embassies in Cairo and Beirut, where visitors simply showed up at the gate and blithely entered for their appointments. Today, however, was the age of terrorism, so diplomats are sealed inside these bastions. Are their emotions and their minds sealed there as well?

The briefings: A USAID (United States Agency for International Development) official: "macroeconomic" versus "microeconomic"

. . . "health variables" versus "demographic variables." Family planning: we don't finance abortions, but we do favor voluntary sterilization. Infant mortality: one hundred eighteen Honduran infants per thousand dead in 1970 versus ninety per one thousand in 1980 versus seventy-nine now. No, it wasn't true that corrupt Honduran officials drained off U.S. aid: 95 percent of the aid was properly, productively spent. "We do rigorous audits." . . . "Total activity portfolio . . . rural infrastructure . . . macroeconomic . . . microeconomic . . . impact upon . . ."

I yearned for the contras.

The military briefing: a pair of U.S. colonels sounding alarums about the military threat to Honduras from Sandinista Nicaragua. Inventories of Sandinista weaponry: one hundred ten T-55 battle tanks, thirty PT-76 amphibious tanks, two hundred armored personnel carriers, HIP helicopters, HIND helicopters, howitzers, sixty thousand active troops with another sixty thousand in reserve. Much discussion of conventional military threats and unconventional military threats, of an expansionist communist regime just across the border bent on aggression and infiltration through insurgency. Flagrant, indiscriminate shellings from Nicaragua into the Las Vegas salient; no mention that the contras were the target. Inadequate Honduran defenses, only twenty thousand troops, no tanks; the Hondurans needed more effective firepower. Their Super Mystères from Israel and their A-37s from the United States were antiquated. They also feared the Cubans, who could send MiGs to Nicaragua overnight and overwhelm their air force.

Someone asked, "Will the United States send F-5 aircraft fighters to Honduras?" Answer: "No. We've promised only to maintain Honduran air superiority." This was a lie, or at least it proved to be. The public U.S. commitment of F-5s came a little later. I soon got used to the lying. In subsequent conversations with U.S. officials, I protested, "Come now, aren't we mounting a major military build-up in Honduras?" *Oh no.* I sensed a state of mind that echoed the official wisdom of the Reagan White House and suggested a metaphysics of the world composed in varying measure of hysteria and self-hypnosis. The Sandinistas posed a military threat not merely to Honduras but northward to Guatemala, Mexico, and Texas; Honduras was infected with communist subversives in league with the Sandinistas, the Cubans, and the Russians.

I had luncheon conversation with Fred, a U.S. Information Service officer, in an expensive restaurant down the avenida from the embassy.

Fred had previously served in Poland. Wasn't it possible, I wondered over the hors d'oeuvres, that the Polish government was as nationalist as it was communist, that it had to repress Solidarity and other liberal phenomena in Poland to prevent a Soviet invasion? Oh no, said Fred, the Jaruzelski regime was not nationalist, it was the Kremlin's creature root and branch. Then what of Poland's primate, Cardinal Glemp, and his compromises with the communists? Cardinal Glemp was too soft. But the Polish Pope had appointed Cardinal Glemp. The *Pope* was too soft. I thought of Norman Podhoretz and the night on public television when he had protested his despair over President Reagan for not being anticommunist enough.

Over the paella, I asked Fred about Honduras. What of Dr. Ramón Custodio López, the eminent human rights activist, who accused the Honduran military of torture, murder, and disappearances of civilians? Dr. Custodio was a communist. Fred had secret documents to prove it. I thought of Fred's opposite number at the U.S. Embassy in Costa Rica, who had told me a weird tale of being spied upon by the KGB during a visit to Nicaragua: "He was a fair-haired man. East European type. He wore a T-shirt marked 'San Francisco State College.' I was in an embassy car, riding to the airport. He drove a jeep in front of me, and kept staring at me through his rearview mirror." I wondered, *where on earth do we find these people?* Fred let me pay for the lunch.

4

HONDURAS WAS the original banana republic. During the first third of this century, the United Fruit Company (now United Brands) wielded such power, making and unmaking governments, supported at intervals by direct U.S. military intervention, that Honduras richly deserved that contemptible title. Indeed, during those ardent days of America's "manifest destiny" United Fruit seemed to govern Central America in all but name. The company was a superstate; Latins called it "the octopus." Within its enclaves it installed its own infrastructure of roads, schools, warehouses, hospitals, and housing on millions of acres from the islands of the Caribbean across the isthmus down to Ecuador; it owned its own fleet, railroads, airline, and telegraph company.

As United Brands, the company is much less powerful, and more benign, today. United Brands, and Standard Fruit, the other main multinational, now pay their nearly twenty thousand workers the highest agricultural wages in Honduras. Their direct influence over Honduran politics has ceased. Yet bitter memories linger; Honduras was traumatized by the "banana enclave economy." Successive Honduran governments handed over the economy of the country to the banana companies, binding Honduran political institutions and internal security to the vagaries of the superstate. The state put all the necessary natural resources at the companies' disposal, while the companies built an infrastructure to serve the growth of the enclave, unrelated to the economic development of Honduras as a whole. By holding massive areas of the country's best land, by using up much of the available labor supply, by expanding into all other sectors of the local economy — banking, fishing, industry (such as it was), agriculture on a broad scale — the companies effectively smothered most other sectors of the economy and their aspirations for development. The banana enclave inflicted a permanent wound on the history of Honduras.

This economic servitude, accomplished not least by the corruption of Honduran politicians and military, was robustly supported by the armed might of the United States government. Not only U.S. ambassadors and ministers but even consuls had the privilege of calling in the fleet. Willard Beaulac, U.S. consul at Puerto Castilla on Honduras's banana coast during the 1920s, recalled in his memoirs that "marines were landed on several occasions while I was in Honduras . . . When things looked especially threatening, I would call a warship." Such landings not infrequently happened during local revolutions; their purpose was not only to protect American lives and property but to prevent bloodshed among the civil population. Nevertheless, though such "interpositions" (the U.S. euphemism) were sometimes requested by the Hondurans themselves, they were also loathed as an affront to their sovereignty. Between 1913 and 1924, Cuba, Mexico, Haiti, the Dominican Republic, Nicaragua, and Honduras were occupied by the U.S. Marines at least once, in some instances often. Blithely peeling their bananas, ordinary citizens of the United States seemed unaware of these adventures undertaken by their government for the sake of their nutrition or, if aware, seemed not to care. Yet in recent decades, American liberal intellectuals have produced a revisionist literature of anger and remorse for the country's long history of bullying its hapless neighbors to the south:

> Around the turn of the century, a man named Lee Christmas went to Honduras from New Orleans looking for a little action. He was a tough retired general, and he proved it to the awed locals by chewing on

glass. Soon he had his own little band of devoted followers. At that time the Honduran government was as honest as it ever had been, which wasn't very, but Christmas overthrew it anyway, in 1911. In the only remark of his to survive that turbulent era [also attributed to other American adventurers], he is alleged to have summed up the U.S. view of Central America thus: "A mule costs more in Honduras than a congressman."

Yankees have been walking . . . all over Central America since our mutual history began. In the depths of our unacknowledged national prejudice, the region has been the other side of the tracks, the place to go for some cheap adventure, a little sweaty self-indulgence and maybe some big bucks — if you could stand the climate. We have considered it ours; not a very attractive possession, perhaps, and certainly rambunctious, but a place where we set the limits and a place where we could do business. The Monroe Doctrine spelled this out in 1823; this is U.S. turf, it said, and other nations had better stay away.

The Monroe Doctrine is often misunderstood: it is more the accretions and corollaries of the doctrine that deserve censure. Latin, European, and American intellectuals rage against it constantly, yet few of them seem to know what it said.

President James Monroe proclaimed the doctrine in a message to Congress on December 2, 1823. The key clauses declared that "the American continents, by the free and independent condition which they have assumed and maintain, are henceforth not to be considered as subject for future colonization by any European power." The United States would regard any attempt by European nations "to extend their system to any portion of this hemisphere as dangerous to our peace and safety . . . We could not view any interposition for the purpose of oppressing [the former colonies of Spain or other powers or] controlling in any other manner their destiny by any European power in any other light than as a manifestation of an unfriendly disposition toward the United States." Reciprocally, the U.S. would stay out of European politics.

The doctrine was rooted in the broad principle — fundamental to American thinking since the Revolution — that Europe and the Americas embodied utterly distinct spheres and that politically they should remain as distant as the sea had made them distant physically. The principle was expounded by Tom Paine and John Adams and assumed rudimentary doctrinal form when President George Washington warned against "entangling alliances" with the European powers. President Thomas Jefferson reiterated the principle in his first inaugural address, and it had become almost conventional American wisdom by the time of President Monroe's elaboration to Congress.

The Monroe Doctrine originally had as much to do with Alaska as it did with the tropical Latin republics. Tsar Alexander I had forbidden foreign vessels to sail within one hundred miles of territories claimed by Russia in the Western Hemisphere (the modern Alaska), and it was to preclude further tsarist imperial pretensions on the northwest coast of the Americas that Monroe spoke. Additionally, Monroe was concerned that the continental European powers, acting in concert, might move to restore to Spain her former colonies (many of them by now independent republics) in Central and South America.

The doctrine was received with contempt in Europe, with satisfaction in Central and South America. Taken in the context of its time and circumstance, it seemed a reasonable manifesto of American interests from a weak and fledgling democracy in fear for its future safety. Far from intending imperial domination of the tropics, for some years the United States avoided entanglements and even cooperation with the new Central and South American republics.

As the decades passed, however, the doctrine evolved in theory and was distorted in practice by successive interpretations, extensions, accretions, and corollaries. As the United States grew stronger and larger, it felt justified in asserting its hegemony to the south. Texas was annexed in 1845. In 1881, all European powers were warned off from any project to dig an isthmian canal in Central America. Various disputes ensued with Great Britain and Germany over Venezuela.

Invoking the doctrine, Secretary of State Richard Olney declared in 1895 that "the United States is practically sovereign on this continent, and its fiat is law upon the subjects to which it confines its interposition."

This delicious bombast was soon dubbed "the Olney corollary." After war with Spain, the U.S. annexed Puerto Rico in 1898 and imposed a protectorate on Cuba three years hence.

In 1904, the doctrine assumed its most exuberant form in the proclamation of a corollary by President Theodore Roosevelt. The U.S. interventions elsewhere in the Caribbean, in Mexico, Nicaragua, and Honduras were yet to follow, but they were justified and inspired by the Roosevelt corollary, which — even considered in the context of that time — was magisterial in its arrogance:

If a nation shows that it knows how to act with reasonable efficiency and decency in social and political matters, if it keeps order and pays its obligations, it need fear no interference from the United States. Chronic wrong-doing, or an impotence which results in a general loosening of the ties of civilized society, may in America, as elsewhere, ultimately require intervention by some civilized nation, and in the western hemisphere the adherence of the United States to the Monroe Doctrine may force the United States, however reluctantly, in flagrant cases of such wrong-doing or impotence, to the exercise of an international police power.

That was yesterday; today there are three main power centers in Honduras: the United States Embassy, the military, and the presidency — roughly in that order of importance. After 1930 the power of United Fruit gradually gave way to a succession of (mostly) military dictatorships until the early 1980s, when Roberto Suazo Córdova, a portly country doctor of the Liberal party, was constitutionally elected civilian president. Possibly to enshrine his victory, Dr. Suazo built a stadium at La Paz, his native town, population six thousand, with a capacity of thirty thousand seats. The grandiose stadium was not the monument of his reign, however, but rather the rise of an ugly thug — General Gustavo Alvarez Martínez — to supreme command of the armed forces.

Dr. Suazo played no role in General Alvarez's promotion; the army chooses its own commanders. Alvarez had been trained at the Military College in Argentina, where his mentors included officers who later abducted, tortured, and killed thousands of "subversive" Argentines. In the late 1970s, as a colonel in charge of public security, Alvarez brought to Honduras a number of these Argentine zealots to teach Honduran officers the macabre arts of selective disappearance, torture, and murder of Hondurans (particularly peasant agitators and leftists suspected of insurgency) nebulously considered "subversive." He forged a close alliance with the U.S. ambassador, John D. Negroponte, who knew something of counterinsurgency from lengthy experience in Vietnam as a diplomat in that country during the height of American military involvement in the 1960s. Negroponte was by common account arrogant and clever, and he made it his business to insert himself into nearly every sector of Honduran society. He was, said the eminent Honduran author and intellectual Victor Meza, *"el americano feo* — the Ugly American." Gazing down upon the squalor of Tegucigalpa from his mansion high on a mountain, riding about the capital in his limousine surrounded by armed guards (a prudent precaution), seeming almost a chief of state, the ambassador appeared to revel in his role as "*el Proconsul norteamericano.*"

The general and the ambassador consolidated real power in their own hands, with Negroponte the senior partner. A Honduran writer who knew them both described Negroponte as "God the Father" and Alvarez as "His Divine Son." Poor President Suazo was only "God the Holy Ghost." Soon Alvarez received the Pentagon's Legion of Merit. Rarely bothering to consult President Suazo, he dealt with the Pentagon, the CIA, and Negroponte directly, consenting to the ambassador's de facto mission of turning Honduras into a U.S. military base.

Suddenly, in 1984, General Alvarez was sacked by his fellow officers and — at gunpoint — exiled to Miami. He had favored too many of his cronies, threatened the power of other senior officers, and conspired to make himself president of Honduras. Besides, he was too corrupt, even by Honduran standards. In 1985 Negroponte also was reassigned (to Washington), perhaps partly due to the disgrace of General Alvarez.

Alvarez was succeeded as commander in chief by a handsomer and milder man, air force general Walter López Reyes, who appointed a commission to investigate charges of human rights abuse by the Honduran military. General López did not, like General Alvarez, rule the military with an iron hand but rather by a consensus in which colonels of the far right enjoyed the privilege of veto over his own more liberal inclinations. The colonels remained a caste apart, as distant from the squalor of Honduras as was the U.S. Embassy and, like the embassy, a sealed fortress unto itself. Under General López, adolescent youths continued to be press-ganged into service, while the officer corps drank Johnnie Walker Black Label and lived as princes. In 1985 López's commission completely absolved the military of any guilt for killings, tortures, or disappearances.

Yet the Reagan administration insisted that whatever the tribulations of the past, Honduras now was irrevocably "on the road to democracy." Thus the presidential election that late November was a showpiece of U.S. policy: not only had the election to be credible and free, it had to be perceived so by the world beyond. Numerous complications loomed. Dr. Suazo loved his little office, decided to retain it (legally he could not succeed himself), and maneuvered to remain in power. Angrily, the embassy intervened, warning the colonels that they might not get their new military toys (the F-5 aircraft, for example) unless the election were held on schedule.

It was. An enemy of Dr. Suazo, José Azcona del Hoyo—a civil engineer of the Liberal party—was elected to succeed him. Rarely has a foreign power been so conspicuous in promoting elections in a client state. Journalists arriving at Tegucigalpa airport were greeted by an enormous sign: USIS PRESS CENTER, SALON DEL NORTE, HOTEL HONDURAS MAYA. Bushels of briefing papers were handed out; USIS computers and Telex machines were available to any correspondent who cared to use them. The United States paid for the election's ballot paper, ballot boxes, ballot machines, and even for the ink into which Hondurans were obliged to dip their fingers to ensure against fraud. On election eve, the new U.S. ambassador convened a crowded press conference at the Honduras Maya in which he pretended that the contras were not operating from Honduran soil. The United States spent by its own admission nearly $1 million in financing the election, though irreverent people said $3 million.

Was the election free? Yes. Credible? In a way. Fair? Not quite. Under complicated rules, Señor Azcona was chosen president with less than 30 percent of the popular vote. It seemed to me, however, that it hardly mattered who took possession of the pink Presidential Palace. Señor Azcona was said to be honest, but his party, like most Honduran parties, was corrupt, the army and the embassy were certain to retain ultimate power, and little seemed destined to change. Honduras, though not as poor as India or several countries I had seen in Africa, was— after Haiti—the poorest nation in the Western Hemisphere.

I concluded that despite the legitimacy of the election, given the atrocious condition of the country the election was largely meaningless, divorced from the tragic reality of nearly five million Hondurans. It would be impossible for President Azcona to act independently of the army, which would continue to do as it pleased internally, to dominate foreign and military affairs, and to control relations with the United States. The preeminence of the army was Honduras's foremost unwritten law. Surely Hondurans should have elections, but elections that would portend some choice in changing the condition of the country. This election seemed like political theater, staged to edify an audience far away.

Finally I had to juxtapose that theater with the languor of the Honduran character, with a rate of unemployment and marginal employment that exceeds 50 percent, and illiteracy even higher, with the slums that surround Tegucigalpa, where hundreds of thousands live in shacks by open sewers, in garbage dumps where they breed multitudes of bastard children, then starve them, beat them, and send them out to beg. In time I would learn something of those children, but first I went to Comayagua.

5

ON THE WAY to Comayagua, I stopped at Palmerola, the chief American military base in Honduras. The base stood on a hot plain amid mountains fifty miles northwest of the capital, and the Americans shared it with the Honduran air force. The Honduran half loomed behind barbed wire and troops with submachine guns, but once inside I was impressed. Honduras has the strongest air force in Central America, much of it trained in the U.S., and its officers and cadets are the elite of the military. They live in pretty stucco buildings; assisted by Chilean mechanics, they maintain their American A-37s, Spanish Casa 101s, and French Super Mystères in neat rows upon the ground, impeccable formations in the air, and proudly display a huge sign boasting of their efficiency: DIAS SIN ACCIDENTES — 299.

The Hondurans shared with the Americans an 8,005-foot airstrip, built by the United States, where regularly landed America's largest transports, UH-1 and CH-47 helicopters, and occasionally air force attack planes. Indeed, the Palmerola airstrip was the nucleus of the immense American military base much of Honduras has become, of the U.S. strategy to surround Sandinista Nicaragua with armed and hostile states.

The United States had spent unknown tens (possibly hundreds) of millions of dollars on joint maneuvers and the improvement of Honduran facilities for its own use. Operation Big Pine II, from August 1983 to February 1984, mobilized six thousand American soldiers, sailors, marines, infantry units, amphibious forces, combat engineers, and communications specialists, who participated in artillery, naval and field training maneuvers, parachute landings, and practice air strikes.

U.S. Navy ships maneuvered off the Honduran coast and called regularly at Honduran ports on the Caribbean. The vessels included submarines, destroyers, cruisers, guided-missile frigates, and battleships. Besides Palmerola, the U.S. had military landing rights at the Honduran bases of Trujillo, La Mesa, and La Ceiba. From San Lorenzo, near the Nicaraguan border, it released drones to intercept Sandinista communications and photograph their military movements. Throughout much of 1986, the U.S. Army Corps of Engineers conducted a joint road-building exercise with the Hondurans over tropical and mountainous terrain similar to the topography of Nicaragua. Since 1983, these joint maneuvers with the Honduran military had been nearly constant, and by 1987 the number of Americans participating in such exercises had risen to seven thousand.

Anxious to prove the "impermanent" nature of its presence at Palmerola, the Pentagon had made the American side of the base positively ramshackle — in bleak contrast to the elegance of the Honduran establishment on the other side of the barbed fence. Since 1982, about a thousand American troops had been rotated at brief intervals (exactly 179 days for the army, 89 days for the air force) in Joint Task Force Bravo, established to assist the influx of other American military participating in the nearly continuous combined training operations with the Honduran armed forces. The Americans, officers and men, lived in crude canvas tents, in "hootches" of rude wood and galvanized metal roofs without air conditioning, and trudged over dirt trails to communal showers and latrines where they urinated into lead pipes covered with wire mesh. Even the base commander had no private toilet. Yet, however crude, this gringo base kept growing larger. The gringos' only creature comforts were old video tapes of professional football games and gallons of alcohol. Bored to the bone marrow, the officers killed the hot evenings guzzling beer, gin, rum, and Chivas Regal.

I killed an evening with them, at some picnic tables under a hazy moon. Some lady sergeants were there, blond and big, without brassieres in peach T-shirts and army pants. They swore less, and drank less, than their male companions. Early, still sober, Major Joe told me, "We're here to defend democracy. The Hondurans are gung-ho." Major Joe was the public relations officer. Major Jim, still half sober, had a different opinion of Honduras: "It sucks." Major Jim was the security officer, a career man with a beer belly, a southern drawl, and a confiding tongue. "The Honduran army sucks. They hoard ammunition like food, so it rots and doesn't work. Not much initiative. Ossified command structure. The younger officers, trained in the States, are better. But what can you do with an army that press-gangs fifteen-year-olds in whorehouses? I'm frustrated as fuck-all. In Honduras, Easter lasts two weeks."

The commanding officer was away that night, but a senior colonel in Bermuda shorts staggered up and said, apropos of nothing, "Jimmy Carter was an asshole. Human rights. A fucking asshole. The United States, greatest goddamn country ever was. Ronald Reagan, greatest president since JFK. The only way to deal with communism in Central America is to kill it."

Kill people? I wondered.

"Social and economic progress. Elections. We can't have a communist regime on the American mainland. Freedom Fighters. Kill it."

MAJOR JIM: I'm right-wing, anticommunist, and pro-Reagan. A Honduran was caught last week on our side of the base, stealing.

AUTHOR: What did you do about it?

MJ: Turned him over to the Honduran military.

A: What did they do about it?

MJ: Took him out and shot him.

A: After a court-martial?

MJ: No. They just shot him.

A: Did you witness the execution?

MJ: I stay away from those things.

Next morning, in the public affairs office, a wooden hootch of fans, electric typewriters, the U.S. Armed Forces Radio blaring the Grateful Dead, I met Captain B. He was a West Point graduate, fluent in Spanish, young, clean-cut, soft-spoken, in starched fatigues, of a breed very different from the drunken rednecks of the night before. He was civil affairs officer, assigned to maintain good relations between the base and the people of Comayagua and anxious I should not depart with any wrong impression.

In a pickup truck, Captain B drove me into town to show me his projects; on the way, he said, "We spend half a million dollars a month on the local economy, which means jobs for Hondurans. Our Honduran workers on the base are not lackeys. We train them to be mechanics, carpenters, cooks, and plumbers." We bumped over some dirt roads on the outskirts of Comayagua. "See this road? We have an informal agreement with the town of Comayagua to provide dump trucks, gravel, and a grinder—to improve their dirt roads. Over at the fire station, we're upgrading their equipment."

These seemed to me modest investments, considering the reciprocal benefits to the United States. I asked, "Why are you doing all this, Captain?"

"We have a philosophy," Captain B said, "to enhance U.S. security in the communities outside the base and to improve popular perceptions of the U.S. presence. This has intelligence ramifications."

Intelligence ramifications?

"Well, we're helping these people. We're hoping that, when individuals approach them from dubious organizations, they will identify the individuals and inform the Honduran authorities."

"Do you mean, Captain, that when some Honduran complains about your base, you want him handed over to the police?"

"To protect, to enhance, to heighten the security of the U.S. forces — that's our whole objective."

"Have you any idea, Captain, what happens to these Hondurans once they're handed over?"

He seemed distressed. I recalled what Victor Meza had told me of the Palmerola base: "We get no benefit from the American military. All we get is *cervezas y putas* — beer and whores." I asked the captain to take me to Rosie's Whorehouse.

"The prostitution in town has been exaggerated," Captain B objected. "It's inevitable. We have a thousand men between the ages of nineteen and twenty-five." I repeated my request. Silently, he drove past the cathedral onto the dirt roads among the tumble-down adobe buildings, the gray palm trees, and shabby bars and discos to the Combat Zone. I knew already that the U.S. base had attracted a plague of prostitutes to Comayagua, that on nights and weekends the troops poured out of Palmerola into this sad town, where their dollars were the prey not only of harlot women but roving bands of begging children. Apparently not all of the troops were heterosexual. "I guess some of the guys have taught the kids in Comayagua to give them good blow jobs," a soldier at Palmerola joked. One heard rumors of local youths with AIDS.

Rosie's, however, was supposed to be special. The Americans had designed Rosie's themselves. The women there, as at other brothels, were injected regularly against infection, but Rosie's by reputation had the prettiest girls, the best bar, the most American disco, the cleanest rooms, the whitest linen, the softest beds, private showers, and a parking lot. When Captain B pulled up in front, I suggested that we look inside.

"I'm in uniform," he said. "This is an official U.S. Army vehicle. I'm expected back at the base." As I reached over to shake his hand farewell, again I was struck by his West Point poise, perfect teeth, decency. "Take care," he warned me. "Prostitution has made Comayagua violent. At the hospital, most of the emergency cases are from stabbings."

He screeched off, in a puff of dust, leaving me alone in front of Rosie's. It was midday; I knocked on the door, but the brothel was shuttered and silent, apparently not yet ready to receive callers. So I wandered the dirt streets, amidst old men, old women, bands of children, youths drinking beer at open bars and loitering outside of discos, as though yearning out of boredom to be press-ganged at any moment . . . until I came to the White Elephant. By the doorway, beneath a plaster elephant, lay a young man in a filthy shirt and blue jeans, clutching a bottle of *guaro,* the local firewater, a clear liquid distilled from sugar cane. He had evidently passed out, not an uncommon sight. The sun beat upon his face, so with my boot I turned his body over, to save him at least from sunstroke, and I went inside the White Elephant.

The place was dark and empty, save for an aging woman behind the bar; Julio Iglesias sang a recorded soft ballad. I ordered a bottle of Cerveza Nacional, the Honduran beer. I remembered William Faulkner's dictum that a whorehouse was the ideal place to write a book because it's so quiet in the mornings. Eventually from one of the cubicles along a long corridor a younger woman emerged and approached me. Would she like a beer? No, but she would love a coffee; she had just got up. She was thin with very pale skin, her hair dyed strawberry, and she was without make-up. She wore sandals and a fading floral dress and was almost pretty in the way of her wilting flowers. She did not look like a puta, and I told her so.

She giggled; I should see her at night, she said. I liked her tremulous, distant voice, her unsure hands as she rattled her coffee cup against its dish, even her vapid eyes. Where was she from? San Pedro Sula, on the banana coast. "There's no work there. My husband abandoned me. I have three small children. I left them with my mother in San Pedro Sula. They have to eat." She hated her work, but the gringos paid good money. "*Donde hay norteamericanos hay siempre pesos.*" How many Americans did she handle on a given night? "A dozen, maybe, on a good night." She had pictures of her children on the wall of her room. Would I like to see them? I'd love to, I said, but I was late for an appointment with the Bishop of Comayagua. I gave her ten lempiras for the children. I kissed her hand, and her face was blank.

I had no appointment with the Bishop of Comayagua: the man had never heard of me. Yet soon I found myself on the steps of his white cathedral, its carved saints and Corinthian pilasters shimmering in the sun. I stepped inside. Ah, inside it was so cool. This early-eighteenth-century cathedral, like so many cathedrals, churches, and chapels of the isthmus, abounded in enormous statues of Christ, robed in real velvet, bearing a cross of real wood, His head crowned with real thorns, His brow sprinkled with drops of painted blood.

Or He is recumbent in a glass sarcophagus, His eyes closed but still weeping tears of blood, His head still crowned with real thorns, a gash of purple in His side where the Roman soldier thrust a lance, His body otherwise enshrouded in linen, lace, or diaphanous muslin. And there were towering statues of the Virgin, too, likewise gorgeously vested, standing among the moon and stars. For the Honduran Church remains traditional, and, though nominally it accepts the progressive social doctrines of the modern popes, in practice it prefers such ancient icons to console the poor.

And so it was here, in the cathedral of Comayagua. Beeswax candles sputtered before the statues of the saints. I sniffed traces of burnt frankincense. I imagined the bishop, a plump Hispanic in full pontificals, purple soutane, French lace, a golden miter atop his head, one hand gripping a golden crosier, the other, gemmed, scattering benedictions. The cathedral echoed with wails and lamentations. Before the high altar, of baroque carved gold, a group of old women, old men, young children, kneeling on stone, clutching rosaries of wood, chanted the Litany to the Virgin.

Santa Virgen de las Vírgenes
Madre purísima
Madre castísima
Madre sin mancha
Madre sin corrupción
Madre inmaculada . . .
Trono de sabiduría
Causa de nuestra alegría . . .
Rosa mística
Torre de David
Torre de marfil
Casa de oro
Arca de alianza

Puerta del cielo
Estrella de la mañana
Salud de los enfermos
Refugio de los pecadores
Consoladora de los afligidos . . .

Holy Virgin of virgins
Mother most pure
Mother most chaste
Mother Inviolate
Mother Undefiled
Mother Immaculate . . .
Seat of Wisdom
Cause of our joy . . .
Mystical Rose
Tower of David
Tower of Ivory
House of Gold
Ark of the Covenant
Gate of Heaven
Morning Star
Health of the sick
Refuge of sinners
Comfort of the afflicted . . .

They were still wailing as I walked out of the cathedral. I looked across the street to the bishop's palace, a white building the length of a city block. People were passing in and out of a great wooden door; I decided to join them. The vestibule was large, full of old men, old women, laughing children; some of them seemed to live there. Beyond, a lovely courtyard and a lush garden, a glimpse of chamber after adjoining chamber, sixteenth-, seventeenth-century baroque chambers full of oil portraits of saints and of ancient bishops in purple mozzettas framed in rococo gilt, statues of the Virgin in silken robes and golden crowns, walls and chairs of red damask, torn and fading. Somehow I thought of Tyrone Power, of a movie he made set in the era of the Spanish Inquisition.

Now from one of the damask rooms, the Bishop of Comayagua emerged, yet he was not some plump Hispanic from, say, Valladolid, but a diminutive American from Watertown, Massachusetts. He wore no purple, but a simple white soutane. I genuflected to kiss his ring: if I could kiss a whore's hand, I could kiss a bishop's. He recoiled; evidently such obeisance had gone out of style, even in Honduras. He said, "Ay-yay-yay."

The bishop was a Franciscan, a homely, balding little man in his middle fifties, full of cares and troubles. People continued to appear from the vestibule, many of them women and small children, all beseeching him for favors. He gave money to some, made promises to others, told others still to come and see him another day. "Ay-yay-yay," he said. "Everybody with a problem in Comayagua expects me to solve it." A bearded youngish man in a sport shirt, black trousers, and wooden sandals came clip-clopping down the long stone courtyard. "This is Father Brian," the bishop said. Father Brian was from Brooklyn. He was leaving presently for his parish of El Rosario in the interior, thence to the mountains to visit his more remote flock by mule. I had visions of Graham Greene, atop a mule, wandering among the ruins of churches in the wilds of Mexico in the 1930s. "Would you like to come along?" Father Brian asked.

Night had fallen when we set out, in Father Brian's Toyota pickup, over bumpy dirt roads. Once out of Comayagua, electric light ceased. When finally we reached the pueblo of El Rosario, two youths appeared in the glare of the Toyota's headlights, standing by the padre's adobe wall. These were Bruto and Feo, Father Brian's parish helpers. Inside the primitive parish house, under a kerosene lantern as we drank warm Pepsi Cola, I asked Bruto in Spanish about his parents. A gangling boy in blue jeans, he stammered something unintelligible and left the room.

"Better stay off that subject," Father Brian admonished me in English. "Bruto's father is an army officer, but he's never met him. His brothers and sisters all have different fathers. Most Honduran couples are not married. Legal marriage means paying taxes, and Honduran peasants are too poor." He laughed, a quick, high-pitched laugh, not quite a giggle, that punctuated his conversation. "My three predecessors as parish priest of El Rosario, all Honduran, all had concubines. They all had children, quite a few of them, but today the children never come to Mass."

Father Brian gave me his own bedroom, and I slept comfortably between clean sheets. The padre, Bruto, and Feo slept on a couch and chairs in the front room. At dawn, I walked about the pueblo, built up and down hills and gullies, dirt ways, and cobblestones. Five thousand souls lived in these environs. The church, high on a hill, built by Spanish Franciscans in the early seventeenth century, was adobe white with a gilt gold altar, almost a miniature of the cathedral of Comayagua. The houses were of red-tiled adobe plaster, wood, stones, and mud white-washed with the local calcite. There were Mayan ruins, too, almost interred beneath neglect and vegetation. On the side of a hill, at the outskirts of the pueblo, stood the remnants of a gold mine, abandoned since 1902 when a gringo company exhausted its treasure and left the pueblo to its misery.

Presently a toothless campesino appeared at the parish house and saddled two white mules. We set out for the mountains, the padre and I astride the mules, Bruto, Feo, and Miguel, a child, following along on foot. Just outside the pueblo, we passed a graveyard and a soccer field. "The two essentials," said Father Brian. "Death and football."

Soon the dirt roads ran out; the terrain grew more and more rugged. We climbed up and down ridges, escarpments, the sides of mountains; occasionally we crossed streams. The vistas were noble — a necklace of mountains, stretching to El Salvador, in a mauve haze. Pine in the highlands, jungle on lower ground, clusters of poinsettia, brilliant hibiscus, and white orchid. Here and there grew wild oranges, banana, pineapple, mango, avocado; cultivated patches of corn, coffee, rice, and beans — but the steep earth was poor. Not as poor as the campesinos, who emerged at intervals from the bush to beg the padre's blessing. They had no roads, no physicians, no medicine, no electricity, few mules, few cows, few schools, and much disease. They lived in hovels, without potable water. Malaria is common, thus apathy; they work little. The children are infested with parasites that stunt their growth.

It occurred to me that I was glimpsing the peasantry as it must have lived under Louis XV in prerevolutionary France, except that these peasants were surely worse off. And, I thought, when the Spaniards conquered this territory in the sixteenth century, they showed a weird prescience in choosing its name. In Spanish, after all, honduras means "the depths."

We passed through a luxuriant grove of banana and palm. As our mules struggled upward, more children stepped out of the jungle and escorted us on our steep journey. Soon we were surrounded by a band of boys and girls, some of them barefoot, chattering and scrambling over rocks and thistles, some running ahead, others struggling to keep up. "It's a local custom," laughed Father Brian. "Wherever the priest goes, his parishioners must escort him." At midday, we approached our destination, San Francisco de Loma Larga, Saint Francis of the Long Hill, an *aldea,* or hamlet, atop a mountain. The scent of coffee buds filled the air, then the sight of green coffee strewn across a hillside drying in the sun, then peasants waving palm branches as we mounted the hillside toward the white chapel at the top. The whole hamlet, half the populace of these mountains, had come out to welcome us. Father Brian, in his red beard, black pants, and white sport shirt, was Christ, astride His ass, entering Jerusalem.

In fact, today was the feast of Francis Xavier, the patron saint of that mountain. As Father Brian vested in his white robe and a bright Mayan stole, the faithful thronged into the chapel, festooned with flowers and crackling beeswax, to shower him with petals of wild orchid, peals of guitar, and song: *Gloria, Gloria, Aleluya, en Nombre del Señor,* to the tune of "Battle Hymn of the Republic." Honduras is short of priests, and the padre came here only a few times a year. Father Brian retired to a wooden stool outside the chapel to hear confessions, but even as they waited for him to celebrate the Mass the faithful inside continued their hosannas and their songs.

Celebradóres de la Palabra — lay Delegates of the Word who preach the Gospel, read the liturgy, and deliver homilies in the absence of priests — led the people in constant supplications to the Virgin. *Madre inmaculada, Trono de sabiduría, Rosa mística* . . . Sickly dogs wandered in and out, sniffing and yapping. The faithful all wore their Sunday best, but the women were too poor to own mantillas, so they covered their heads with bath towels. I felt pangs of contempt, not for these faithful but for my well-fed friends at home who presumed to be certain that religion was the opium of the people. Religion was all these people had.

As the father heard confessions, the village elders and the children flocked about me. What was America like? they asked. "Greedy," I said. What was Honduras like? I asked. "Hard," they said. "*El gobierno no hace nada . . . la Iglesia no tiene nada . . . no tenemos nada . . . yo soy nada*": the government does nothing, the Church has nothing, we have nothing, I am nothing — phrases of incantation I heard everywhere. The favorite Honduran word is *nada* — nothing. An air of hopelessness, of the futility of human effort, of ever truly changing anything, pervades the whole country, suggestive of Lampedusa's nineteenth-century Sicily in *The Leopard.*

Yet the celebradóres did try. There were eight of them in that parish, and they advocated modest social change—potable water, a few more roads, farming cooperatives. Occasionally the government grudgingly gave them a little potable water, but otherwise for their pains the delegates were considered communists by the security forces. During the last year in that district several had been picked up, beaten badly, and imprisoned; others had been killed or vanished in the night.

Father Brian finished hearing his confessions, then entered the chapel to baptize two infants and welcome ten children, eleven adolescents, and two men to their First Communion. In his homily he said, "This is the holy season of Advent. Christ is coming. Be prepared. Live your faith. Live the life of the Church. Christ will come finally on the Day of Judgment to judge us all, but He comes today as well, in His body and His blood, in the Holy Eucharist. In the hard struggle of your daily lives, remember that He cares for you, He loves you, He is forever at your side."

After Mass, Father Brian and I repaired to a delegate's house for luncheon. As in Islam, the women kept to themselves—to the kitchen and to serving the men and boys a greasy meal of chicken, fried eggs, rice, beans, and warm Coca-Cola. As we ate, a column of soldiers trooped through the hamlet. Bruto and Feo bolted from the table and hid behind the outhouse. I asked Father Brian, "Why are the soldiers here?"

"We never know," he said. "Maybe because I'm here, or you're here. Maybe they're looking for someone. I don't think they're press-ganging today, but Bruto and Feo aren't taking chances. When they press-gang they usually come in trucks. The boys hear the trucks and head for the mountains. Look at them, kicking the dogs and poking into people's houses. We never know."

He laughed his sudden, high-pitched laugh again. In the late afternoon we mounted our mules and headed back down to El Rosario, our escort of children still with us. As the sun lowered over the escarpments and wild mango, Father Brian mused, "You know, in confessions this afternoon, so many of the women told me they had sinned by dancing. Some of the boys said they'd sinned by playing soccer."

Soccer? Dancing? *Sins?*

"Honduras has been invaded by fundamentalists, many from the States. Evangelicals. Jehovah's Witnesses. Seventh-Day Adventists. Moonies. They're all over Central America, and they have loads of money. No booze, no dancing, no soccer. I said, 'Dancing and soccer are not sinful. Keep dancing and playing football.' "

I wondered, how many Honduran couples were unmarried?

"I'd say eighty percent. In Honduras you need a civil marriage before a church marriage, and you can't have a civil marriage unless you pay income taxes — say, fifteen to twenty-five dollars a year — and most campesinos can't. So the men take common-law wives and breed many bastard children. This wreaks havoc when the parents die, and drunken quarrels over land and cattle can lead to fratricide. The delegates and I urge our couples to pay the tax, get married civilly so I can sanctify the unions and legitimize the children, but so few can pay the tax. Of course, I never refuse the sacraments to common-law couples or baptism to their children.

"That's how I see my job — bringing the Word and sacraments to the people, educating them in their faith. I'm not a social worker. I dislike it when strangers say, 'All these poor, poor peasants.' They have more dignity and self-respect than many people I know in Brooklyn. I do wish I had some medical training — I can hardly give first aid. Just in the last week, I've taken half a dozen infants, children, and young adults to the hospital in Comayagua. Consumption. Malaria. Malnutrition. Bowel parasites. The hospital sent them home to die. The worst disease, I'd say, is fatalism. Death, like football, is a given."

He laughed again, a little. "As long as I can remember, I wanted to be a priest." He said this as a matter of fact, without piety. It seemed to me that this sandy-haired young celibate was very happy.

We reached El Rosario in darkness. At a *pulpería* (general store), we each drank a beer. By the counter lingered an angelic child. "*¿Tienes diez años?* Are you ten years old?" I asked him. "*Tengo quince.* I'm fifteen," he answered resentfully. Afterward, Father Brian told me, "His name is Sixto. He's full of worms."

6

LATER THAT EVENING, Father Brian drove me back to the bishop's palace in Comayagua. I found the bishop in a monastic room off the courtyard, sitting at a wooden desk, rummaging through the drawers, pulling out papers and photographs, sorting them out, tearing them up. He was close to tears.

One of his young priests, whose room this was, and a young nun had just been killed in a car accident. "I have so few priests," the bishop mourned. "Padre Raúl was in charge of our youth apostolate." He shuffled about the room, removing posters and photographs from the walls, went into the bathroom, flushed the toilet, and emerged laden with shampoo, toothbrushes, and dirty linen. "Ay-yay-yay. What will I do with all this stuff? O Raúl, Raúl, why did you have to die on me?"

He invited me to pass the night. I slept in the dead priest's bed. After breakfast with the bishop, I settled into the lively routine of his palace, sitting in an armchair in the courtyard as people came and went. The interior of the palace was cloisterlike, a quadrangular patio framed by arched pillars surrounding a garden full of palm, scarlet hibiscus, the songs of exotic birds. The bishop was harassed. There was but one telephone in that large establishment, mounted in a niche of the cloister wall. It rang constantly, and the bishop kept rushing out of his office to answer it. Evidently many of the callers needed money, for often after hanging up he repeated, "Ay-yay-yay. Everybody with a problem in Comayagua expects me to solve it." Whenever the bishop withdrew to his office, a strange young man appeared from the shadows, from behind a pillar or a palm tree. He was a mulatto, with unfocused eyes, an unkempt goatee, a curled Rastifari coiffure. When he passed me on the patio, I addressed him in Spanish, but he did not seem to understand. He said, in English, "Hey, baby, I'm a seminarian."

Conversation was difficult. I gathered he was from Jamaica, but otherwise his English was unintelligible. He lolled his head; his sentences were disconnected and dreamy. The telephone rang again; when the bishop rushed out of his office the young man retreated to a far corner of the cloister, took out a tin of something, and rolled a cigarette. As he crouched there, surrounded by smoke, the bishop hung up and went to him. They exchanged angry whispers. The bishop returned to his office muttering "Ay-yay-yay."

At luncheon, in the episcopal refectory, the bishop asked me, "You, ah, talked with that black fellow?"

"I tried to, Monseñor. He seems . . . odd."

"Odd? He's a dope fiend."

"He said he's a seminarian."

"He wants me to ordain him."

"Just what the Church needs. A priest on grass."

"He says it's part of his religion."

"Why don't you send him back to Jamaica?"

"He won't leave. He's been living in my house for weeks. I just told him, 'Tomorrow morning, and out with you.' "

Hard to consider that ultimatum seriously: the bishop was too kindly. I imagined that weeks hence, the mulatto would still be there, drinking the bishop's beer and getting stoned. Over the soup, the bishop poured out his other troubles.

He was miserably short of priests and money. He had a thousand lay Delegates of the Word, but since they advocated social change they were harassed by the police, who favored the Evangelicals, Mormons, and Seventh-Day Adventists because they preached acceptance of the status quo. The Honduran priests of this diocese were so destitute they kept all of their collections and could share none of their pittance with the poor. Besides, some of the priests had their own children to support. The bishop told a curious tale of John Paul II's treatment of this problem.

The nine Honduran bishops had gone collectively to Rome to render their visit *ad limina apostolorum,* reporting in person to the Supreme Pontiff on the condition of their dioceses. The audience took place in the Apostolic Palace, in one of those marble chambers full of frescoes by Fra Angelico. The Pope, in white, sat on a damask armchair; the bishops, in purple, on lesser chairs around him. The Pontiff had recently returned from a foreign journey and seemed exhausted.

"Yet he was very cordial," the bishop said. "He gave each of us ten minutes to speak. We told him of the terrible poverty of Honduras. This seemed to move him. Finally, he shifted in his chair and asked, with some embarrassment, 'I am told that some Honduran priests take concubines and father children. Could this be so?' "

"*Sí, Santísimo Padre. Así es.* Yes, Most Holy Father, it is so," the bishops answered.

"*Debilidades humanas*—human frailties," the Supreme Pontiff said, sighed, and changed the subject.

The bishop seemed less equable about the matter. "I have a priest, right here in Comayagua, who is living openly with a young woman. A scandal, Edward, a scandal! He has kids all over the place. I'll have to crack down." I wondered if he ever would. More troubles poured forth. Comayagua was swarming with whores and corrupted youths. He had complained to the American commander, who said, "Bishop, if this keeps up, I'll declare the town off limits." Ah, that he would, but he never had. The troops kept pouring in, the whores increased, and the begging boys were an epidemic. And, "Listen. I've lived here thirty years. Let me tell you something about Hondurans. They're *lazy*. By nature. They never do anything. You'll find, practically without exception, that a Honduran with drive has mixed blood. He's either part Salvadoran—they're real go-getters—or Guatemalan. This includes the politicians and practically all the priests. Ay-yay-yay."

Again, I did not take him entirely seriously. When I asked him to arrange a meeting for me with two of his "radical" priests, both young and both Honduran, he said, "Oh, I don't approve of their ideas. If I let them, they'd start a revolution. I'd rather you didn't meet them." Then he went to his telephone and summoned the priests to see me.

They were quiet but angry young ecclesiastics. They sat with me in the cloister amidst the trilling of the birds and politely made it clear how much they loathed the United States. The bishop kept out of the conversation, appearing on the patio only when he hastened from his office to answer the telephone. Both of the priests wore polo shirts, black boots, and blue jeans. Padre Tito, intense with black eyes and a black beard, was pastor of a destitute parish in the countryside. Padre Antonio was tiny, with copper skin and a shaven Mayan face, thirty-nine but looking nineteen. He worked in the city with the poor, including whores and abandoned children.

PADRE TITO: I have thirty thousand people in my parish. Ninety percent of the children suffer from malnutrition and intestinal parasites. We have one medical center, and one doctor, but no medicines. The government has built some schools, with U.S. aid, but few have teachers. When we have teachers, we have no books. U.S. aid is planned in air-conditioned offices in Tegucigalpa with the bureaucrats of the Ministry of Natural Resources without any sense of the reality in the countryside and with terrible corruption.

AUTHOR: How do you cope?

PT: I've formed cooperatives for our campesinos to do away with middlemen, to raise their income a little bit. The government is constantly obstructing us. The Civil Defense Committees—they're illegal, by the way—accuse me and my celebradóres of being communists. They persecute the delegates and lock them up. Five of my delegates are in jail now, without formal charges. The Civil Defense Committees are directed by the military. They see all social progress as a form of communism.

A: I understand that you advocate the Theology of Liberation.

PT: I advocate a Theology of Liberation that is pure in the principles of the faith. I advocate social action without violence or revolution. I advocate agrarian reform that really responds to the needs of the peasants — and which until this moment has not been touched by U.S. aid.

PADRE ANTONIO: I read the liberation theologians — [the Peruvian Gustavo] Gutiérrez, [the Brazilian Leonardo] Boff — and I agree with them. Social action against the established order is essential. I believe in Jesus Christ, Liberator.

A: What of the Marxist element?

PA: I accept Marxist analysis, including class warfare.

A: Do you advocate violence and revolution?

PA: I'm not saying I advocate them, but the people are so poor and the system is so unjust.

A: Frankly, I don't see a revolution happening in Honduras. The people are too passive.

PA: They *are* passive. We must raise their consciousness.

A: That, it seems to me, will take a long time.

PA: *No importa.* It doesn't matter.

A: The Honduran Church is passive, too.

PA: *La Iglesia no hace nada.* The Church does nothing.

A: Well, *you're* doing something. John Paul II has denounced Marxism and the doctrine of class warfare, but his social encyclicals are very progressive. He has condemned the greed of capitalism as he has the cruelty of communism.

PA: I admire Paul VI's and John Paul II's progressive social doctrines, but John Paul II doesn't really understand Central America, Latin America, or liberation theology. He's a well-trained theologian, but his experience is with communist Poland, and it colors his outlook on every problem.

A: I keep hearing that.

PA: We are as doctrinally pure as the Holy Father is. We believe in the Incarnation, the Resurrection, that in the consecration of the bread and wine the body and blood of Christ truly come to life. We believe that Christ is the Son of God.

A: But you don't believe in the United States.

PT: How can we?

PA: The U.S. is building roads here, not to help us, but to turn Honduras into a U.S. military base against Nicaragua. How does that help us?

PT: How does your air base help us? People who ask such questions, people who work to change conditions in the country, can disappear, be tortured, or be killed.

Not long after I left Comayagua, Padre Tito was arrested by the antiterrorist Cobra police, who had been partially trained and financed by the United States. He was blindfolded, shackled, and tortured — for a short while. His parishioners rioted, and the bishop raised a storm, venting his holy wrath on high authorities. Padre Tito was released — but the message was clear.

That, however, was yet to come. Once Padre Tito and Padre Antonio had departed the cloister, I bade good-by to the bishop. He escorted me to the street. In the vestibule, the mulatto was crouched in the middle of a mob of children, still lolling his head. "Ay-yay-yay," the bishop said.

7

LATE THAT AFTERNOON, I took the bus back to Tegucigalpa.

Usually at day's end I took a beer at the Brik Brak, a noisy café near the cathedral, then at dusk I strolled across the plaza past the equestrian statue of General Francisco Morazán, the martyred father of isthmian unity. (Legend said that Honduras had been too poor to cast its own statue, that the hero on the horse was really Marshal Ney, one of Napoleon's generals.) Occasionally beneath the statue a demonstration would be taking place, a cluster of women, Families of the Disappeared, shouting into loudspeakers about their sons and husbands abducted and murdered by the police and army. At dusk the Parque Central in front of the white cathedral was thronged with the poor, sprawled on the benches, munching tortillas, the children jumping and playing games. The tropical trees were so luxuriant on top they formed a canopy, a leafy ceiling that covered the park and obscured the stars. Always at twilight a multitude of invisible birds settled in the trees, and as darkness fell the birds screeched in a chorus so shrill and eerie they muffled the conversation of the poor.

My hotel was situated around the corner from the cathedral. One evening as I returned from dinner, I noticed a tiny child, almost an infant, crouching in a dark crevice of the cathedral wall. He was three years old perhaps, no more than four. He held up his little hand to grasp my coins, and I could see his fear. When I spoke to him, he cried.

I had read of such abandoned children, of the multitudes of that young subproletariat cast so quickly upon the mercy of the world, prone to hunger, sickness, lice, worms, drugs, tuberculosis, begging, picking pockets, prostitution, living in abandoned buildings, empty lots, beneath bridges, in sewers, along railroad tracks, teeming in the streets and gutters of Bogotá, Mexico City, Lima, La Paz, São Paulo. So it was as well in Tegucigalpa, cursed in proportionate measure with orphaned toddlers, rapacious youths, prepubescent girls forced into whoredom at the age of twelve. Like the Brahmins of Calcutta who simply do not see the squalor of the casteless, prosperous Hondurans seem as collectively blind to this tragic theater that meanders through the streets of their capital. Yet the verse of Roberto Sosa, Honduras's foremost poet, is a photograph of such misery.

> Es fácil dejar a un niño
> a merced de los pájaros
> Mirarle sin asombro
> los ojos de luces indefensas . . .
> ¿De donde vienen estos niños
>   mendigos
> y que fuerzas multiplican sus harapos?
> ¿Que humano no ha sentido
> en el sitio del corazón
> esos dedos
> picoteados . . . ?

> So easy to leave a child
> to the mercy of the birds
> Watch without surprise
> his eyes of dimming light . . .
> Whence are born these beggar tots,
> in whose garden grew their rags?
> Who human has never felt
> at the bone of his breast
> those fingers
> pecking . . . ?

I had discovered Sosa's verses that morning. They pecked at my emotions as I took the tot by the hand and led him across the street toward the cafeteria of my hotel. As my little charge toddled before me, I saw the seat of his pants, worn away, revealing shitty drawers across his tiny bottom. Inside the cafeteria, I told the waitress to fill a paper bag with milk, bread, and bananas. Back on the street, I was at a loss for what to do with my orphan next. Should I find him an orphanage? Should I take him to Comayagua and pay for his lodgings in the bishop's palace? The tot was more confused than I; he would not touch his food, and when I asked him his name he sobbed. Two girls strolled by. Observing our distress, they offered to take the child and place him in an orphanage in the morning. A young man stepped forward, took me aside, and said, "Don't give the child to those girls. They're *putas*. They'll sell him. Such things happen in Honduras."

I chased the whores off, then soon out of the shadows an older child appeared. My tot stopped crying and grasped his hand. "*Es mi hermanito*. He's my little brother," the bigger boy said. "Mama will be very mad. You took Rogerio away from his spot. When he gets home, if he has no money, Mama will beat him." I led Hermanito — I remember him thus — back to his crevice in the cathedral wall. Still he would not eat or smile.

I mounted to my room. From my window I could see the cathedral in the moonlight. Hermanito crouched in his dark crevice; occasionally a girl or an older woman would pause to hand him a coin, but not a single man. I arose at three, and he was still there. At daylight, he was gone. Thereafter, for as long as I remained in Tegucigalpa, each evening after dinner I visited Hermanito in his niche and gave him a bag of food. He would not even nibble on a crust of bread. "Why don't you eat something?" I asked. "*Es por la casa*. It's for the house," he said.

On my final evening in Honduras, I bade him good-by, gave him his food and a little money, and told him he would not see me again. Hermanito's tiny face was vacant. I crossed the street and glanced back. He smiled.

8

SOON AFTER I MET Hermanito, I called on Dr. Ramón Custodio López in his shabby clinic down the street from the cathedral. Dr. Custodio catered to the poor, charging them low fees or none at all. He was also president of CODEH, the Commission for the Defense of Human Rights in Honduras. He was an elegant gray man who spoke perfect English, unusual here. I had been told that he was wealthy.

"Yes, I am one of the privileged," he said. "My family gave me a first-class education. I studied medicine in El Salvador and here in Honduras. I wanted to take my postgraduate degree in the United States, but those were the McCarthyist 1950s, and I was being harassed by your embassy, so I studied in England instead. You see, as a student I had condemned the CIA's invasion of Guatemala in nineteen fifty-four. The embassy accused me of attending a communist meeting in Mexico even though I had never set foot in Mexico. I have been refused a visa to the U.S. on the basis of that false accusation. Am I of the left? I believe in law and social justice. I suppose I'm a Christian humanist.''

The Honduran army, Dr. Custodio continued, began its surveillance of the population in 1982, coinciding with the rise to power of General Alvarez. The Committees for Civil Defense were the army's instrument of terror, though they were unconstitutional. The committees had waned since the fall of Alvarez, but now they were being revived. Again, throughout the country, defenseless Hondurans were being arrested and "disappeared." Nobody was secure. Idle gossip, anonymous denunciations to the army were enough to cause a knock on the door at midnight. Men and women were dragged away, dumped into the hands of the police or the National Directorate of Investigations, held incommunicado for months, with no word to their families even of their whereabouts. Torture of the prisoners was routine and systematic. These outrages were happening even as we spoke. Dr. Custodio had documentary proof. He handed me a sheaf of papers.

I examined the papers, petitions and testimony to the Supreme Court. They seemed authentic. Yet I objected, "You say that one hundred thirty-eight people are still unaccounted for. That is deplorable, but it's mild compared to El Salvador and Guatemala. Surely since the fall of General Alvarez, things have gotten better in Honduras?"

Dr. Custodio became quite angry. "I hate it when someone says, 'Things are better.' I am telling you the facts *right now*." More calmly: "I feel myself in danger. I get telephone calls threatening my life. The U.S. Embassy says I make things up. They say that human rights are improving in Honduras. They say that I'm a communist."

"They told *me* you're a communist."

"Because I condemn the presence of U.S. troops and the contras in Honduras! The contras are involved in disappearances and assassinations of Hondurans who oppose their presence in our country. You didn't know? The contras have death squads in Honduras."

I had drinks that evening with a young Spanish diplomat, in the cool air beneath the stars, on his terrace on a mountainside overlooking the lights of Tegucigalpa: "Look down there. In darkness, don't the slums seem pretty? The United States is the enemy of change. Don Eduardo, let me explain.

"The Honduran military are a caste apart. Their economic privileges are enormous. The officers have high salaries, Mercedes, Black Label whiskey, women, foreign currency for their holidays in Miami. They no longer need a coup d'état: they're perfectly happy with the façade of civil democracy the United States has given them, because they are free of the messy details of civil administration and they keep all their privileges anyway. They know better than anybody the horrible reality of Honduras, but above all they know that they can keep their privileges only if Honduran society stays as it is. Everybody is afraid of them.

"With a larger middle class, with a less apathetic and more educated population, Honduran society would not tolerate the greed and corruption of the army. The officers would lose their privileges, so they do not want development. Every nation, every elite, is governed by its own fear — the Honduran military by its fear of change — things they call 'communist' — the United States by its obsession to retain control of Latin America. Like most Hondurans, the military here suffer from low self-esteem and have a mythic reverence for the immensely efficient and powerful United States — a society that works. Conversely, the Americans recognize that they cannot keep Honduras as a de facto colony, they cannot continue to build up the country as a base against Nicaragua, if the nature of Honduras changes in any basic way. The U.S. needs a corrupt and cruel army here as much as the army needs the United States."

Next evening, I met a friend in the bar of the luxurious Honduras Maya. She was an attractive, dark woman, an accomplished cellist, and, like her cello, tautly strung; she kept a shapely foot in either culture and knew everybody of importance in Honduran society, Honduran politics, and the United States Embassy. Over our tumblers of gin and tonic water she said, "Don't believe the conventional wisdom that the U.S. ambassador is the proconsul of Honduras. The State Department has been pushed aside. The real proconsul is the CIA, or at least various occult characters from Washington who seem to be spooks and may be sent by the White House. I'm not sure. It's all wrapped up in whispers, gossip, and mystery."

This was nearly a year before the Iran-contra scandal broke and Lieutenant Colonel Oliver North became famous, but now — vaguely — she alluded to his name. "There are rumors that he runs things, but I'm not quite sure how. I know that he's Mr. Big with the contras, and if you promote the contras you put your finger into every pie. He has a brash young man — *Bob* Somebody? — who comes down here with satchels of cash and hands it out to the contras and — I've heard — to Honduran colonels. Anyway, if you ask me, Honduras has become one big spook operation, and there are deals going on all over the lot. You know the official Honduran line, of course?"

"I hear it every day," I said. "That no contras are operating against Nicaragua from Honduran soil."

"A very clever ploy. The Hondurans played this sort of haggling game for centuries with imperial Spain. Now they're playing it with the United States. The longer the contras stay here, the more the U.S. will have to pay."

"Ah. The tyranny of the weak. So?"

"So, the deals, the payoffs, the kickbacks, the money laundering, the front operations for the Honduran politicians and colonels, to keep them happy and cooperative. I even hear of drug deals."

"By whom?" I asked. "The contras or the colonels?"

"Both. I'm not sure."

She left her drink unfinished, protesting that she must be off to another dinner party. I watched her drive away in her BMW, then decided to walk the mile or so back to my hotel. At the bottom of the steep hill, by the bridge over the Río Chiquito, I stopped at an open food stand to have my shoes shined. At once I was besieged by several children, barefoot and in rags, begging for money. One of them, in a nervous tic, kept squeezing an empty plastic bottle of Resistol.

Resistol. I had heard all about Resistol. It was a glue, the angel dust of Honduran orphans. The street children sniffed it. The glue produced a trance that helped them forget their misery; they preferred it to food, though it damaged their brains and before they reached twenty turned them into walking zombies. In Tegucigalpa, their addiction had become so common they were known as *los Resistoléros*.

Originally I was told that Resistol was made in Guatemala, but upon inquiry I discovered it was manufactured in each of the Central American republics under license of Kativo Chemical Industries, S.A., and its parent company, H. B. Fuller of Pompano Beach, Florida, and Minneapolis, a major American corporation. As I write I have Kativo Chemical's annual report for 1985 before me. Under "Adhesives Division" the report states, in Spanish and English, "We can affirm that our H. B. Fuller industrial adhesives are leaders in all the countries in which we operate. Besides, Resistol is the leading trademark in Central America . . . in the following segments of the market: artisans, educational, office and domestic. Our philosophy is oriented to servicing our customers and to offering them the best quality through our postulate of excellence . . ."

Under "Financial" the report states, "Consolidated net sales reached $63.7 million, an increase of 5.7% over last year's $60.3 million . . . On a product-line basis, paints continued to be the major contributor to sales volume, but adhesives showed the highest growth."

Already in Tegucigalpa I had discussed the Resistol-sniffing plague with various Honduran luminaries. Did the manufacturers know of the epidemic? I asked a former cabinet minister.

"Of course they know," the ex-minister said. "So does the government."

Then why didn't they put some controls on the glue to keep it from street children?

"Are you crazy? The profits are too enormous. If anybody tried that, they'd call him a communist."

Later, in Guatemala, I had a similar discussion with the local director of H. B. Fuller. "What can we do?" he asked. "The sniffing is a social problem we can't control. Look, there's a warning on the bottle." True, there was a warning against inhalation, and the glue did have legitimate industrial and domestic uses. Yet I imagined a warning on each packet of cocaine: THE SURGEON GENERAL HAS DETERMINED THAT COCAINE SNIFFING IS DANGEROUS TO YOUR HEALTH. The advice on Resistol had as much chance of being heeded. In central Africa once I heard of a naked tribe that lived in trees and for food survived by following baboons, whose droppings they ate. That menu was at least more nutritious than Resistol. Now at the food stand, as a boy shined my shoes, I was surrounded by begging Resistoléros.

Fearing they would spend my coins on glue, I fed a few of them on chicken and fried potatoes. An old hag showed up, so I fed her, too. Other children converged on us, and all began to fight over the food, tearing the chicken and potatoes from each other's mouths and leaving the old hag hungry. A riot was starting. I got out of there.

In my half sleep that night I heard the verse of Roberto Sosa. *So easy to leave a child to the mercy of the birds . . . Whence are born these beggar tots, in whose garden grew their rags? . . . those fingers pecking . . .* ? In the morning, I returned to the food stand in the shadow of the Honduras Maya to look for Carlos, the shoeshine boy, and his companions Javier and Ernesto, all about thirteen, though from undernourishment of stunted growth. I found them fighting over a flask of Resistol.

I took them to the smoky, labyrinthine popular market not far away and fed them a breakfast of eggs, rice, and beans. As they ate it, slopping hot coffee on the table and each other, I thought of Half Wit and Baby Rabbit in the contra camp on the Nicaraguan border. For all their traumas, they were better clad and better fed than these Resistoléros. They wielded guns; these three, flasks of glue, just as deadly. Half Wit and Baby Rabbit killed brother Nicaraguans; Carlos and his companions were killing themselves. I wondered, why am I doing this? Do I truly care about these children, or am I just taking notes? They demanded second helpings, then as they served themselves with bare hands I struggled to recall the children in Francis Thompson's *The Hound of Heaven:*

> I sought no more that after which I strayed
> In face of man or maid;
> But still within the little children's eyes
> Seems something, something that replies,
> *They* at least are for me, surely for me!
> I turned me to them very wistfully;
> But just as their young eyes grew sudden fair
> With dawning answers there . . .

Fair eyes? Dawning answers? These urchins were gutter garbage, lower on the human scale than those tribesmen in central Africa who tracked baboons. Carlos seemed to be the *jefe;* he wore a filthy white shirt, and his straight black hair reached nearly to his nostrils. He was slightly older and bigger than the other two, and when he shouted they deferred to him. Besides, inside his box, among the brushes and dirty rags, reposed the bottle of Resistol. Javier had thick lips and curly hair and kept begging me to buy him a new pair of pants. Ernesto, the smallest of the three, bore a wound on the heel of his bare foot and kept scratching his scalp: did he have ringworm? They spoke a rough, illiterate Spanish I could barely understand; they lived under the bridge of the Río Chiquito; their matted locks were alive with vermin; their bodies smelled of mud and smegma. Thereafter I saw them nearly every day, but only to give them food: I could not bear the smell.

"I'm finding you a home," I told them. "You'll have a bed at night, a bath in the morning, and three meals a day, but no Resistol."

They giggled and said, "*Sí*." We agreed to meet some evenings later on the steps of the cathedral.

Meanwhile, not without difficulty, I arranged their placement in a primitive, overcrowded orphanage run by the American Episcopal Church on the outskirts of Tegucigalpa. Besides bed and board, they would learn carpentry, bricklaying, or some other useful trade: eventually they would lead productive lives. I would pay their inexpensive lodgings for three months while the orphanage sought other sponsors in the United States.

I remained curious and fascinated by the reputed trance of Resistol. I had never tried cocaine, but in Egypt and in Paris I had smoked hashish and hated it: hashish gave me horrible nightmares. Resistol, I understood, produced marvelous hallucinations. And I wanted to know what my urchins were going through. I bought a bottle and one night was about to sniff when my lady cellist told me, "You're already insane enough. If you sniff that glue, you'll suffer additional brain damage and your condition will be clinical." I bowed to her better judgment, but when she cautioned also against high hope for my Resistoléros, I shrugged her off.

9

DURING THOSE DAYS I heard constant rumors of dissension in the army, of officers chafing under the (relatively) liberal rule of General López, of his mild efforts to deossify the upper command structure, above all of the military's dissatisfaction with the United States. The high command, exposed to so many sophisticated American weapons during years of joint maneuvers, wanted more of these lethal toys for their own arsenal, not just updated F-5E aircraft and helicopters but bigger guns and modern tanks. They had turned their nation into an American military laboratory. They felt the price the U.S. was paying — not only for the contra presence but for the blemish on their sovereignty by allowing the laboratory to exist—was not nearly high enough.

On Armed Forces Day on December 11, I drove out to the base of the Second Airborne Infantry Battalion at Támara, north of the capital. During the ceremonies I saw the assembled high command, portly men in sunglasses, immaculately uniformed, splashing in ponds of gold braid and bright ribbon, as they watched their jets fly by in flawless formations. Then came their cadets, dressed like toy soldiers in an operetta, goose-stepping. At the center of the reviewing stand, beside General López, stood fat, lame-duck President Suazo, his conspiracies to cling to office now all aborted. A toy cadet handed me a tiny card, which read ARMED FORCES OF HONDURAS. ARMED ARM OF THE PEOPLE. DEFENDER OF DEMOCRACY. MAY THE SWEET WORDS OF JESUS, "LET US LOVE ONE ANOTHER," LIVE IN OUR HEARTS DURING CHRISTMAS AND THE NEW YEAR. Sublime counterpoint to Roberto Sosa: *"La Historia de Honduras se puede escribir en un fusil, sobre un balazo, o mejor, dentro de una gota de sangre.* The History of Honduras can be written with a rifle, above a bullet wound, or better, inside a drop of blood."

General López, more svelte than his fellows, strode to the lectern and delivered a speech. His rhetoric, elegant and floral, had a Spartan, martial resonance as well since he spoke without emotion. Obviously referring to the reports of divided counsel in the military, he condemned the "idle gossip, wild judgments, absurd speculations, and unscrupulous lies" spread by "those enemies of democracy" bent on "provoking disorder and anarchic outrages."

His brother generals applauded robustly, then in several weeks fired López as supreme commander and replaced him with a portly colonel who had been running the navy. Later, in the backwash of the Iran-contra scandal, General López appeared on American television and provided a version of Honduran reality rather different from his oration at Támara. The CIA, he said, was bribing half of the Honduran establishment—bureaucrats, businessmen, members of parliament—to keep the contras and U.S. bases on Honduran soil. As supreme commander, he, López, had resisted, of course, but the CIA was so rich . . .

10

ON MY LAST AFTERNOON in Honduras, I walked up the Avenida de la Paz to the concrete, glass, and ivy fortress, the United States Embassy. A secretary guided me through the metal detectors, marine guards, bulletproof glass, steel doors, combination locks into the presence of the ambassador. He wore spectacles, a thatch of brown hair, and a face that reminded me of rice pudding. His conversation was less bland. He contradicted every conclusion I had reached about Honduras.

Elsewhere, I had heard him speak fluent Spanish; he had long served in Latin America and had headed the U.S. mission to Havana. Fidel Castro was his favorite subject. He knew Fidel fairly well. Fidel was shrewd but off his rocker. As for Honduras, no, the ambassador was not the American proconsul. "I regret that perception. U.S. policy toward Honduras is based totally on respect for Honduran sovereignty and the independence of Honduran institutions. That's not pap. It's a *fact*." No, the presidential elections were not political theater. "*Emphatically* not. The Honduran people demonstrated they understood what representative democracy is all about." No, Honduras was not all that poor. "Most houses I've seen here are made of tin roofs, lumber, and cement floors. Any house here in Tegucigalpa is made with purchased materials, indicating that the owner is in the money economy." Moreover, "The American military presence in Honduras is *small*." Furthermore, "There is no human rights problem in Honduras today. I'm not aware of any disappearances or arbitrary arrests. The only human rights violations I'm aware of came from the extreme left."

The sun was setting, but I descended the Avenida de la Paz in a midnight mood. I was sick of being lied to. (So, apparently, was the ambassador. Within some months of our conversation, he was summarily recalled. Washington was dissatisfied with his tepid support of the contra war, and he supposedly was fed up with the ascendant power of the CIA in Honduras and the fiction that the White House sought a diplomatic solution in Nicaragua.) Had the ambassador and I been discussing the same country? I felt ashamed of the United States. My country was turning Honduras, once only a banana republic, into a brothel. I was, I felt, somehow an accomplice.

I turned south from the Avenida de la Paz, crossed the Río Chiquito, and walked through the dusty, twisted streets toward the cathedral. At dusk, I reached the Parque Central, as ever milling with the poor under the canopy of tropical trees and that eerie chorus of screeching birds. On the steps of the cathedral, I waited for my three Resistoléros: I would take them tonight to their new home.

I waited nearly an hour, more and more unsure they would show up. At last I glimpsed Carlos, bearing his shoeshine box, milling in the crowd. I called out to him, but he kept circling the park, as though undecided whether to approach. He vanished into the crowd. Eventually Javier and Ernesto climbed the steps of the cathedral.

"What's wrong with Carlos?" I asked them.

"He says you're lying," said thick-lipped Javier.

"Lying?"

"He says you're going to sell us," said little Ernesto.

"*Sell* you? To whom?

"*El ejército.*"

"The *army?* You're all too young for the army."

"Carlos says you work for the army."

"Carlos is crazy. Are you coming to your new home?"

"*He vivido en un centro, y no me gusta.* I've lived in an orphanage, and I don't like it," Ernesto said.

"But don't you want food and clothes, a place to sleep?"

"*Prefiero vivir en la calle.* I'd rather live in the street."

Yet they seemed reluctant to leave me. Now Carlos hovered at the edge of the park, watching us. They wanted money — to eat, they said. I surrendered. I led Javier and Ernesto across the park to a cheap restaurant, Carlos following not far behind. At the restaurant, I fed the three of them for the last time and left them to their lives of begging coins and sniffing Resistol.

I returned to the cathedral, immensely sad. The birds screeched.

> But just as their young eyes grew sudden fair
> With dawning answers there,
> Their angel plucked them from me by the
>   hair.

The cathedral was crowded with the poor — men, women, and children muttering the responses as a lay celebrador in soiled trousers led them in the Sorrowful Mystery of the Rosary. He stood before an altar, two centuries old, of priceless rococo gilt. The altar soared from the floor to the dome with niches, pediments, and ornate swirlings. As my eyes ascended I saw Saint Michael Archangel with his avenging spear, then the Virgin Triumphant, then the Risen Christ, Saint Thomas the Doubter probing His wounds. Soon the faithful began to wail *"Ruega por nosotros*—Intercede for us" as the celebrador chanted out the Litany to the Virgin.

Madre inmaculada . . .
Trono de sabiduría
Rosa mística
Torre de David
Torre de marfil
Casa de oro . . .
Estrella de la mañana . . .
Consoladora de los afligidos . . .

Mother Immaculate
Seat of Wisdom
Mystical Rose
Tower of David
Tower of Ivory
House of Gold
Morning Star
Comfort of the Afflicted . . .

A young woman stood beneath an immense statue of Christ, robed in real velvet, His head crowned with real thorns, bearing His heavy cross. She raised her arms aloft to Him, pleading for some silent favor. I stood behind her, praying for my Resistoléros. I prayed that somehow His wooden hand might come alive, reaching down to rescue them: no one else's would.

I emerged from the cathedral to the Parque Central and the screeching birds. A barefoot filthy child, one hand clutching a flask of Resistol, the other extended for my coins, approached me with dull eyes.

"*No tengo nada.* I've nothing," I told him, and fled—across the mountains—to Nicaragua.

II / NICARAGUA

Adelante marchemos compañeros
Avancemos a la Revolución
Nuestro pueblo es el dueño de su historia
Arquitecto de su liberación.

Combatientes del Frente Sandinista
Adelante que es nuestro el porvenir
Roja y negra bandera nos cobija
Patria libre, vencer o morir.

Los hijos de Sandino
Ni se venden ni se rinden
Luchamos contra el yankee
Enemigo de la humanidad.

Adelante marchemos compañeros . . .

Forward let us march, comrades
Onward we march to the Revolution
Our people are the masters of their history
Their liberation they made themselves.

Fighters of the Sandinista Front
Forward to what is ours, the future
Wrapped in the banner red and black
Free fatherland, victory or death.

Sons of Sandino
Don't sell out, don't surrender
Fight on against the Yankee
Enemy of mankind.

Forward let us march, comrades . . .

From the Sandinista hymn

I

Sons of Sandino, Don't sell out, don't surrender, Fight on against the Yankee, Enemy of mankind. I confess that the first time I heard the Sandinista hymn sung at a rally in Managua, I felt saddened and hurt. In retrospect, I should not even have reacted. For nearly thirty years, since youth, I had traveled widely in the Third World. From almost the first moment, I was exposed to verbal violence against the United States, to rhetoric against American imperialism so blood-curdling that in the beginning I was outraged. After all, I had been brought up to believe that America was practically the Kingdom of Heaven on earth. Yet in time I grew so accustomed to such outbursts that I often found them funny.

I first visited Egypt in May of 1956, about two months before President Gamal Abdel Nasser nationalized the Suez Canal, igniting a firestorm of anti-Western, anti-American hysteria in the Arab world and the invasion of Egypt by Britain, France, and Israel the following October. The United States opposed that invasion and rescued Abdel Nasser by reversing it, but President Eisenhower's refusal to finance the Aswan high dam provoked the nationalization in the first place and set in motion the chain of inevitable results. "America, may you choke on your fury," Nasser raged as he nationalized the canal, but that language was mild compared to the anathemas that were to come.

In 1957, I returned to Cairo as a junior attaché at the United States Embassy. It was one of my tasks to monitor the Egyptian press and radio and to summarize the content in cables to Washington. In the wake of the Suez war, despite Eisenhower's undoing of the British-French-Israeli aggression, U.S.-Egyptian relations were envenomed by Washington's refusal to release Egyptian assets frozen in American banks and by its general opposition to the anti-American thrust of Arab nationalism propounded by Nasser throughout the Middle East. In his public speeches, Nasser became a past master of anti-American invective, but he was irenic compared to the diatribes of the Egyptian press (which he controlled), and particularly to the bombast of his radio station, Sawt al-Arab, Voice of the Arabs, which reached every corner of the Arab world from Morocco to the Persian Gulf.

The star of Sawt al-Arab was one Ahmed Saïd, a shrill ventriloquist who according to the season told his brother Arabs that the Americans were dogs, jackals, snakes, lice, leeches, vampires, toads, cockroaches, chimpanzees, hyenas, whoremasters, and much worse. Riots against the United States erupted regularly in Amman and Damascus; in 1958 the pro-Western monarchy of Iraq was overthrown in a carnival of bloodshed; King Faisal, the rest of the royal family, and the prime minister were butchered. Ahmed Saïd was a ventriloquist because his voice really belonged to Nasser. In private, Nasser boasted to a former CIA agent that "Sawt al-Arab is my baby. Not a word is broadcast that I don't approve beforehand." Nasser's army, after all, despite its Soviet weapons, was a joke. His radio transmitter was his real cannon; he knew it, and so did the United States. Paradoxically, Nasser rather liked Americans personally. He admired the United States or at least was in awe of American power in a love-hate complex.

Despite his rhetoric, for a full decade following the Suez war I admired Nasser. I knew of Egypt's mythic poverty and corruption under the monarchy and believed that Nasser's revolution was not only inevitable but necessary. I made an act of faith in Nasser's sincerity, in his palpable commitment to assuage the disease and penury of the Egyptian peasantry and to improve the lives of the millions who barely subsisted in Egypt's fetid cities. True, I always harbored reservations about the Egyptian army, about the incompetence and self-enrichment of its ascendant officer class, but I accepted the argument that in such a poor country only a robust army could serve as the locomotive of social change. I was also distressed by Nasser's mendacity, by his conspiracies and interference in countries not his own, but again I dismissed these doubts by reasoning that the Arab world was in upheaval anyway, that Nasser was essentially benign, and better his milder form of revolution than something bloodier or even communist. In admiring his ends, I absolved his means.

Moreover, essentially I sympathized with Arab nationalism, with the right of Arabs everywhere to assert their own cultural, religious, and national identity free of bondage to the West. I was angry at the West (and especially at the U.S.) for its shabby treatment of the Palestinians during the creation of Israel. I supported the Palestinians' right of return to Palestine or the establishment of their own homeland on the West Bank of the River Jordan—and I still do. For the decade following Suez, Nasser was the paladin of Arab unity, Arab nationalism, and Palestinian rights; for all his flaws I preferred him to such prigs as John Foster Dulles, Eisenhower's secretary of state and Nasser's devil. I resented American pressure on Nasser, particularly the intrigues of the CIA to weaken him. In fact, I admired him so much that I made him the protagonist of my first novel, drawing a satirical but sympathetic portrait that I rather regret today.

For in 1967, my perceptions of Nasser began to change. In June of that year, Israel—seizing on Nasser's bluster, on his threats to close the Straits of Tiran and to remove Israel from the map—invaded the Sinai desert, destroyed the Egyptian air force within hours, and within days crushed the Egyptian army. Nasser blamed the defeat on the United States and then on his own military, specifically on Marshal Abdel Hakim al-Amer, a hashish addict who had been Nasser's boon companion in military school and commander of the Egyptian forces in the defeat of 1956 and again in 1967. The marshal eventually committed suicide, yet it was clear that the real architect of the disaster was Nasser himself.

The defeat exposed all the weakness and error of Nasser's system, not only in a flaccid army but in Egyptian society at large. It was a country still burdened by backwardness, a slothful and bloated bureaucracy, and it was governed by the secret police. Fifteen years after the revolution, the Egyptian people may have enjoyed some marginal social progress, but generally their condition seemed no better—it may have been worse—than at the hour the monarchy was overthrown. For fifteen years Nasser had fed his people—and the Arab world—a daily meal of bombast, fantasy, and lies. The defeat of 1967 left the Arab world in shambles. The fault was chiefly Nasser's. He seemed to recognize this privately, or at least his sons did, and they told him so. He died only three years later, possibly of a broken heart.

In late 1958, I was posted from Cairo to the U.S. Embassy in Beirut, where I caught the tail end of the Lebanon's first civil war, then watched with fascination as seeds were sown for the next, much bloodier, one.

In the early 1960s, eager to write, I resigned from the embassy and traveled throughout the incipient nations of East Africa.

These compulsive peregrinations resumed again and again as over a decade I returned to the Middle East and visited much of black Africa for the *New York Times Magazine* and other publications. As a sort of hobby, I collected the gems of various Arab and African demagogues (some on the CIA's payroll) screaming imprecations from their balconies against the treacheries of imperialism and the rapacity of the United States. I always listened for new cadenzas and twirls, but the most common metaphor was of a ravished maiden. Often I was amused by these orations, a kind of rhetorical, liturgical masturbation. Juxtaposed with such oratory, the Sandinistas' *"el yankee, Enemigo de la humanidad"* seems like schoolboy teasing. When not visiting the Middle East or Africa, I resided for nearly nine years in France, where anti-Americanism was also intellectually fashionable though not nearly as erotic.

I came to know many of the leaders of the Third World. Over time, I developed perhaps a certain imperfect instinct for the dynamics and sorrow of the poor tropics. I was also exposed, in some detail, to Arab socialism, black African socialism, and North African socialism as solutions to the suffering of those regions. My experience in Egypt and elsewhere in the Third World conditioned me for my encounter with Sandinista Nicaragua.

2

I BELIEVE in literary balance but not in literary objectivity. The most scrupulous of writers are subjective, and all have bias. It is only fair that I admit mine.

The struggles and contradictions of my social conscience were born not only beneath the ugly girders of skid row but—during adolescence—by my reading of the *Catholic Worker*. I was enchanted and disturbed by Dorothy Day's anguish for the poor, by her simple, terrifying descriptions of New York's slums, her humble ministrations to homeless vagabonds, her call to Christians to live up to the papal social encyclicals and practice the compassion of the Gospels. Growing older, I was devoted to the ideals of Catholic distributism advanced in the *Worker* by Miss Day and the French peasant-philosopher Peter Maurin. I was confused by the indifference of the official Church to

Dorothy Day's apostolate, though later I learned that even Francis Cardinal Spellman — urged by his minions to crack down on her — hesitated and refused. "I can't," the Cardinal said. "She may be a saint."

The Jesuits, who were responsible for my education, scared me then, and they still do — for different reasons. The Jesuits taught me how to think. They were superb and learned teachers, dogmatic, and — many of them — arrogant. They drenched me in logic, traditional theology, scholastic-Thomist philosophy, classical literature, epic poetry, more Latin and Greek. They were very papist, very Marist, and very anti-communist. In high school I studied hard, but in college I became a mediocre pupil distracted by foolish things. Yet their indoctrination marked me for life, to my rejoicing and regret.

In my late twenties I became mildly rebellious against the traditional encrustations of the Church, but I rejoiced (as did the Jesuits) in John XXIII and the reforms of the Second Vatican Council. Gradually I was disenchanted with the results of that assembly. It did not, as so many hoped, produce a millennium of faith but huge confusion. Throughout, I have remained a Roman Catholic. I agree with Wilfrid Sheed that the Roman Church would be intolerable were it not so interesting.

As I approached middle age, my disquiet about the Church mingled with my distress for the Third World. My theology became more conservative — a reversion to my old Jesuit values — as my convictions on foreign policy remained liberal and I clung to the progressive papal declarations on world poverty and nuclear war. I was horrified by the election of Ronald Reagan, by his harangues against "the evil empire" and his ignorance of most of humanity. On the eve of my departure for Central America, I had settled on an unsatisfying, perplexed Christian humanism, ideologically neither left nor right. Was I merely jaded, too diffident, lacking serious commitment or concern for human suffering?

3

I ARRIVED IN Nicaragua with considerable, if qualified, sympathy for the Sandinistas. As in Egypt years earlier, I believed that the Nicaraguan Revolution was not only inevitable but probably necessary. I had read a lot about it; if I harbored reservations about the communist nature of the government, I nursed much deeper grievances about the American response. Only two months before, on October 15, the Sandinistas had suspended civil liberties. That bothered me, but it seemed quite understandable in context, given the onslaught on their tiny nation by American brute force.

I felt that the Reagan administration was guilty of war crimes against the Nicaraguan people. The CIA's association with sadistic Argentine colonels early in the contra movement, then its embrace of bloodthirsty thugs from the Guardia Nacional, were chilling enough. The destruction of infrastructure, the blowing up of power lines and bridges, mining of harbors, attacks on civilian buses, atrocities against defenseless peasants, the macabre techniques of the assassination manual, all this by the contras or other allies of the CIA; the economic embargo, even to depriving the Nicaraguan populace of food; the various other facets of William Casey's "covert war" — I found unconscionable.

So was the Orwellian Newspeak of President Reagan's speeches: "They [the contras] are our brothers, these freedom fighters, and we owe them our help . . . They are the moral equivalent of the Founding Fathers and the brave men and women of the French Resistance. We cannot turn away from them. For the struggle here is not right versus left, but right versus wrong." In a press conference, the President added that he was going to make the Sandinistas cry "Uncle." I squirmed. ". . . el yankee, Enemigo de la humanidad."

Commander of the Revolution Daniel Ortega Saavedra, in an address to the General Assembly of the United Nations on October 7, 1981, two years after the Sandinista triumph, accused the United States of "more than seven hundred eighty-four acts hostile to the sovereign rights" of Latin American nations since 1840 "and more than one hundred since 1960.

"Why were our countries insulted, invaded, and humiliated on more than two hundred occasions from 1840 to 1917? Under what pretexts, since at that time there was not a single socialist state in the world and the Tsar ruled over all the Russias? Treaties and loans were imposed on us, we were invaded, we were given the status of protectorates under that same thesis of American national security, which was first called the Monroe Doctrine and later Manifest Destiny and still later the Big Stick or Dollar Diplomacy . . . At this time it is necessary to remember the history of aggression against Central American countries throughout more than a century.

"1855. The William Walker filibusters landed in Nicaragua with the purpose of annexing the whole of Central America to the southern states of the United States. Walker proclaimed himself president and restored slavery in Nicaragua . . .

"1867. The United States affirmed its ownership of Nicaragua through the Dickinson-Ayon Treaty, which gave it the right to build [an] interoceanic canal.

"1896. United States military forces landed in Nicaragua, at the port of Corinto.

"1899. More United States military forces landed in our territory, in San Juan del Norte and Bluefields.

"1900. The United States imposed on Nicaragua and Costa Rica the Hay-Corea and Hay-Calvo treaties to acquire control over the canal route through the Central American isthmus . . .

"1909. The United States intervened in Nicaragua to overthrow the government of General José Santos Zelaya through the infamous 'Knox Note.'

"1910. The Marines landed in Corinto, Nicaragua, and attacked our shores until they imposed their own oligarchic government.

"1911. The United States again landed its Marines in Corinto, imposed presidents on Honduras and Nicaragua; and compelled Costa Rica and Nicaragua to accept onerous debt consolidations and new loans.

"1912. The Marines landed yet again in Honduras and the United States began its military occupation of Nicaragua which was to last until 1925.

"1914. The United States imposed on Nicaragua the shameful Chamorro-Bryan Treaty, which divided our sovereign territory . . .

"1926. After leaving the country for many months, the Marines returned to occupy Nicaragua. That military occupation was to last until 1933, when the Yankee troops were compelled to withdraw in the face of the heroic resistance of the army, headed by General Sandino, defending our national sovereignty . . .

"The United States . . . tries to use Central American territory — as it did in the 1960s to attack Cuba — to attack Nicaragua now.

"Acts of aggression, interference, pressure, and blackmail never cease. Respect for the sovereignty of our countries has never been obtained from the United States. The expansionist thinking of the last century, the gunboat treaties, the big-stick policy have emerged again . . .''

Making prudent allowance for rhetoric and exaggeration, essentially it is not easy to disagree. Following the independence of Central America from Spain in 1821, Nicaraguan politics was dominated by warfare and bloodshed between two parties—the anticlerical, entrepreneurial Liberals and the proclerical, landholding Conservatives. In 1855, the Liberals hired the legendary Tennessean freebooter (*filibustero*) William Walker, and his mercenaries, to help them crush the Conservatives. General Walker, whose previous adventures included an abortive conquest of northern Mexico, soon seized control of the army and all of Nicaragua. He decreed slavery, made himself president, declared English "the official language," and even expropriated the railroad that Cornelius Vanderbilt had built across Nicaragua connecting the Atlantic and Pacific oceans.

A fabulous figure, General Walker aspired to rule all of Central America, and his Nicaraguan government was recognized by President Franklin Pierce. Understandably upset by the seizure of his railroad, Vanderbilt conspired with the British and Costa Ricans to depose him. Walker was eventually shot by a Honduran firing squad at Trujillo on the banana coast in 1860.

Walker's demise was followed by more than three decades of comparative peace under Conservative presidents, but in 1893 a Liberal, José Santos Zelaya, established a rapacious dictatorship. In 1909, disaffected Liberals joined forces with Conservatives, and a civil war erupted. The bloodshed invited the first direct intervention by United States Marines, under President William Howard Taft.

"The primary intentions of the United States," Shirley Christian has written of the cycle of intervention throughout the 1920s, "were to protect foreign holdings, those of Americans and others, and keep the ports and customs houses open, but Washington was also nervous about [the Liberal pretender to the presidency, Juan Bautista Sacasa, and his] ties to Mexico, which had recently taken a leftward turn under its revolutionary government."

Now two extraordinary men entered Nicaraguan history—General Anastasio Somoza García and General Augusto César Sandino. Both were Liberals, but they had little else in common. Anastasio Somoza was not much of a general, he had failed repeatedly in business, yet he was descended from a picturesque family of Liberal soldiers, was shrewd politically, and understood power. General Sandino, the bastard son of a rich landowner, had worked as a car mechanic in Honduras and as a clerk for an American oil company in Mexico, where he became a bookworm and read much about the struggles of the young Mexican labor movement. Back in Nicaragua, working his way up in the army, he is remembered by contemporaries as a tiny, frail man, remarkably nervous. His speech seemed full of tics, but it was effective. Like so many Nicaraguans, he was not only voluble beyond control but very persuasive. "Sandino," remembers an old adversary, "could stand on a tree stump and talk and talk and send his men off to fight." When he became a general he acquired a long whip, which he carried everywhere and snapped constantly. With the whip came the famous hat, sort of a tall, ten-gallon hat, rather like the one John Wayne wore in his early Westerns.

In 1927, President Coolidge sent Henry Lewis Stimson — past and future secretary of war and future secretary of state — to mediate the war in Nicaragua. General Somoza, who had studied in Philadelphia and spoke fluent English, somehow became Stimson's interpreter. In the Peace of Tipitapa — so called because Stimson and the Liberal leader General José María Moncada signed it under a blackthorn tree at Tipitapa near Managua — the Liberals agreed to stop fighting in return for political control of several of Nicaragua's provinces. The Conservatives, exhausted on the battlefield, accepted. Many Liberal politicians resisted, but Stimson threatened an invasion by U.S. troops, and they finally acquiesced. Moreover, the United States would supervise the next elections in 1928. That intervention, however, was not as crucial as the last — the decision to establish a "nonpolitical" National Guard under American officers.

All of the Liberal generals accepted the peace, save one — Sandino. Supported by a handful of loyal troops, Sandino took refuge in the mountainous northern department of Jinotega, denounced General Moncada for treason to the Liberal cause, and vowed to continue the war. Above all, he would not agree that a Conservative should continue as president of Nicaragua until 1928. Curiously, Sandino did agree to stop fighting if the United States would establish its own military government and rule Nicaragua until the next elections. The United States refused. For nearly six years thereafter, U.S. Marines and their disciples in the new National Guard pursued General Sandino through the mountains of northern and central Nicaragua.

In early July 1927, from his hiding place in an abandoned mine, Sandino dispatched his first political manifesto.

> My greatest honor is to have emerged from the bosom of the oppressed, who are the soul and nerves of the race . . . My insignificance is surmounted by the loftiness of my patriot's heart, and so I pledge before

my country and before history that my sword will defend the national honor and will be the redemption of the oppressed.

I accept the invitation to the struggle and I myself will provoke it, and to the challenge of the cowardly invader and the traitors to my country I answer with my battle cry. My chest and that of my soldiers will form walls that the legions of Nicaragua's enemies will crash upon. The last of my soldiers who are soldiers for Nicaragua's freedom, might die, but first, more than a battalion of you, blond invader, will have bitten the dust of my rustic mountains . . .

Come, you gang of morphine addicts. Come, murder us in our own land. I am awaiting you, standing upright before my patriotic soldiers, not caring how many you may be. But bear in mind that when this happens, the destruction of your grandeur will shake the Capitol in Washington, reddening with your blood . . . your famous White House, the den where you concoct your crimes.

According to Sandinista legend, Sandino had embarked on a war of national liberation. According to his victims, he was a common bandit, raiding plantations, sacking towns, allowing his men to burn, rape, and murder. When Sandino withdrew to the forbidding mountains of Nueva Segovia, the marines sent a small expeditionary force to capture him. Captain Gilbert Hatfield, commander of the town of Ocotal, telegraphed Sandino with an offer to negotiate. Sandino replied with a proposal "to put you in a handsome tomb with beautiful bouquets of flowers." Captain Hatfield answered that "if words were bullets and phrases were soldiers, you would be a field marshal instead of a mule thief." Following further pleas from Hatfield to "surrender with honor," Sandino responded with his famous vow, *Patria Libre o Morir* — Free Fatherland or Death — which on any given day one can hear or read a hundred times in contemporary Nicaragua.

In midsummer of 1927, Sandino and a small army attacked Ocotal. The marines and National Guardsmen might have been slaughtered were it not for the appearance of five de Havilland aircraft piloted by marines. They dived low, strafing Sandino's men with machine-gun bullets, and dropping bombs that killed civilians and many of Sandino's troops, driving the general back to the mountains.

After the battle of Ocotal, Sandino's clashes with the marines and National Guard ended indecisively. Eventually, he went to Mexico to seek money and weapons. His secretary for a time was Agustín Farabundo Martí, the (later legendary) Salvadoran communist, and while in Mexico Sandino was courted by international communists. Sandino himself, however, was not a communist and showed no zeal for conversion. Over time he called himself a socialist, but he rejected the doctrine of class warfare. Frustrated by his failures in Mexico, he returned to Nicaragua in 1930 but was soon wounded in an air raid. Hors de combat, he continued to direct what was now a desultory war in which the main strategic target was U.S. property.

Meanwhile, in the United States, the marine war in Nicaragua had become unpopular, and enemies of the entanglement in the Senate nearly succeeded in cutting off its funding. In 1931, President Herbert Hoover decided to withdraw the marines within a year. First, however, a Nicaraguan had to be found to replace the retired marine officer who headed the National Guard. What better choice than Anastasio Somoza, Henry Stimson's old interpreter and friend, by now foreign minister and a man of proven competence, charm, and sangfroid?

Shirley Christian — at pains to correct official Sandinista mythology — has stressed the nuances of the marine wars in Nicaragua: "The presence of the Marines had been prompted [largely] by the U.S. desire to establish a constitutional system [to] halt the warfare between the political parties. [Also] there was concern about influence from Mexico . . . then emerging from its own revolutionary period and . . . interested in controlling Central America since its independence from Spain . . . There was concern about the possible spread of Bolshevism . . . Of more immediate importance . . . was the need to collect customs duties . . . to pay Nicaragua's debts to European bankers and . . . keep Europeans from intervening. Several European nations had earlier [sent] gunboats to collect debts. [Moreover] Nicaraguan politicians and warlords regularly sought . . . help from the U.S. . . . to support their own cause. Those who complained about such interventions usually did so because the intervention of the moment happened to be working against them."

Nevertheless, for whatever complex motives, the United States bears a major responsibility for the modern course of Nicaraguan history, not least as an efflorescence of the Monroe Doctrine or rather of its oppressive corollaries.

After several abortive attempts at reconciliation with the national government, in 1934 General Sandino was lured from his mountains in Jinotega to Managua. There, National Guardsmen detained him, drove him to an airfield late at night, and shot him. By prearrangement, General Somoza attended a poetry reading as the execution took place, but earlier in the day he had authorized the murder in an operation called "The Death of Caesar."

César Sandino was dead, but his martyrdom in the fullness of time would transform Nicaraguan history. A liberal American journalist who had known Sandino had written in *The Nation* that "he had fired the imagination of the humble people of Nicaragua. In every town Sandino had his Homer. He was of the constellation of Abdel Krim, Robin Hood, Pancho Villa, the untamed outlaws who knew only daring and great deeds, imbued ever with the tireless persistence to overcome insurmountable odds and confront successfully overwhelming power. His epos will grow — in Nicaragua, in Latin America, the wide world over."

The United States was not involved in Sandino's murder, except by indirection in having helped to raise General Somoza to his eminence as commander of the National Guard. Two years later, Anastasio Somoza García deposed the constitutional chief of state and rigged his own election as President of Nicaragua. The Somoza dynasty was born.

For the next forty-three years, from 1936 until 1979, the Somozas ran Nicaragua as a family business. Anastasio Somoza García and his wife, Salvadora Debayle, produced two sons, Luis — who was reared to succeed his father as president — and Anastasio II — "Tachito" or "Tacho" — who was trained to command the National Guard. Luis was rather a weak sister, but Tachito was a bull. Educated on Staten Island and then at West Point, Tachito learned to speak colloquial American English more fluently than his native Spanish. Later on, as I toured the interior of Nicaragua, I met an elderly merchant in Estelí who had known the Somozas well. "They were insatiable," he told me. "Their corruption, kickbacks, estates, companies, their fingers in every pie, *Madre de Dios,* Mother of God. But if you didn't mess with them, if you stayed out of politics and didn't scream too much about their stealing, they left you alone. They left the campesinos alone, so the campesinos, most of them, didn't care. If you steered clear of the Somozas, they never bothered you. The Sandinistas bother everybody."

The United States saw no reason to bother the Somozas. Reciprocally, the Somozas were loyal vassals of American foreign policy not only in the Western Hemisphere but in the world at large. In a famous remark, repeated since about many other disreputable U.S. allies, President

Franklin Delano Roosevelt said of Somoza García, "He's a son of a bitch, but he's our son of a bitch."

In 1956, at a dinner party in León, Somoza García was assassinated by a deranged poet. The assassin, Rigoberto López Pérez, had already versified, "The seed of Sandino's blood / lashes the murderous rooftops . . . / It will exterminate all of the murderers / and each and every one / of the murderers' seed." Luis Somoza became president, Tacho commander of the guard. Luis, however, had little stomach for the brutality of power, passed the presidency to a minion, and died of a heart attack in 1963. In 1967, Tacho assumed the presidency.

As President, Anastasio Somoza Debayle proved even greedier than his father, snatching more vast landed estates, acquiring factories, a shipping company, an airline. (In the 1970s, he was accused of stealing much of the foreign relief money after Managua's earthquake.) Though indulgent in allowing his critics within Nicaragua some political space, much like his father, Anastasio II intimidated, tortured, or killed those enemies he felt went too far, and he never countenanced the notion of sharing power. Six years before Tacho assumed the presidency, the FSLN, the Sandinista Front of National Liberation, had been founded in Honduras by three young Marxists — Carlos Fonseca, Tomás Borge, and Silvio Mayorga — much impressed by Fidel Castro, Ernesto (Che) Guevara, and the triumph of the Cuban revolution.

During the 1960s, the Front's minuscule endeavors at armed insurrection inside Nicaragua were disastrous and pathetic. In 1967, during an engagement with the National Guard in the central department of Matagalpa, Silvio Mayorga was killed. Yet the movement itself survived, and in 1969 the FSLN proclaimed its Historic Program, the first coherent declaration of Sandinista objectives. The Historic Program opens:

> The Sandinista National Liberation Front (FSLN) arose out of the Nicaraguan people's need to have a "vanguard organization" capable of taking political power through direct struggle against its enemies and establishing a social system that wipes out the exploitation and poverty to which our people have been subjected in past history.
>
> The FSLN is a politico-military organization, whose strategic objective is to take political power by destroying the military and bureaucratic apparatus of the [Somoza] dictatorship and to establish a revolutionary government based on the worker-peasant alliance and the convergence of all the patriotic and antioligarchic forces in the country . . .

The program went on to promise the Nicaraguan poor not only all of Nicaragua but implicitly the moon, Mars, Jupiter, and the Milky Way for good measure. Among many other goals, the program pledged the creation of a revolutionary government that would guarantee all citizens full freedom and respect for human rights; the free exchange of ideas; freedom for worker-union movements; the expropriation of all properties plundered by the Somoza family; the nationalization of all banks, external commerce, and exploitative foreign corporations; industrialization and electrification; "massive distribution of the land"; a "massive campaign to wipe out illiteracy immediately"; "free medical assistance"; and "adequate shelter." Prostitution and "the humiliation of begging" would be abolished. Women would enjoy complete emancipation. The Revolution would guarantee "the population of believers the freedom to profess any religion . . . It will support the work of priests . . . who defend the working people."

In foreign affairs, the Revolution "will eliminate the . . . policy of submission to Yankee imperialism, and will establish a patriotic foreign policy of absolute national independence . . . It will expel . . . the so-called Peace Corps — spies in the guise of technicians . . . It will actively support the struggle of the peoples of . . . Latin America against . . . the common enemy: Yankee imperialism."

Finally, the FSLN would create "a patriotic, revolutionary, and people's army" with "obligatory military service" inspired by the "veneration of our martyrs." All new generations of Nicaraguans would be educated in "eternal gratitude . . . toward those who have fallen in the struggle to make Nicaragua a free homeland."

During the 1960s and early 1970s, various Sandinista leaders studied in the Soviet Union and undertook political and military training in Cuba and North Korea. Yet their armed attacks inside Nicaragua, such as they were, invariably were thwarted by the National Guard. In November 1976, during one such clash in the northern mountains of Zinica, Carlos Fonseca, first among equals of the FSLN's founders, was killed. Now the Sandinista leadership was riven with violent ideological quarrels. All the leaders were professed Marxists, but by the mid-1970s they had splintered into three factions.

The first was the Proletarian Faction, headed by Jaime Wheelock Román, a handsome intellectual who had spent more time in Chile and in West Germany studying Marxism than he had on the field of battle. Wheelock argued that the only true path to revolutionary power — no matter how long it took — was by organizing the masses, in the cities and countryside, raising their consciousness, preparing them for insurrection through indoctrination in proletarian ideals. The second tendency was the Prolonged War Faction, headed by Tomás Borge, one of the FSLN's three founders. Borge had spent years in the mountains of Nicaragua battling the National Guard, and he was subsequently tortured in Somoza's jails. He despised Wheelock, and for a time had him expelled from the Sandinista Front. Borge argued for a strategy of prolonged peasant war, based on the principles of Mao Tse-tung.

The third tendency was the Tercerista Faction, or advocates of "the third way," headed by the Ortega brothers, Daniel and Humberto. The Ortegas argued that the FSLN should mute — but not abandon — its Marxist principles as a method of reaching out to Somoza's noncommunist opponents now so numerous throughout Nicaraguan society in the bourgeoisie, business, industry, and the Roman Church. The terceristas sought an alliance with the bourgeoisie as the only swift strategy to ignite a mass insurrection and to overthrow Somoza. The Ortega brothers won the strategic argument, and — in July 1979 — the war against Somoza.

This was a revolution that many Christians had embraced and of which I wanted to be fond. Before I left Tegucigalpa, over breakfast at the Honduras Maya, a senior Western correspondent, full of experience and wisdom, offered me his counsel. "Don't be too influenced by what you've read," he said. "Trust your own instincts. Judge the Sandinistas for yourself. Nicaragua today is not another Iran or Libya. There are opposition parties and an opposition newspaper. The Church still functions. The Sandinistas do things in a strange way — repress in a strange way. So many Nicaraguans resent the Sandinistas, but they have no sympathy for the contras. I've accompanied the contras in battle. Yes, they have real grievances, and, yes, the troops are a peasant army, but their commanders are thugs. The contras suck."

I was excited by the saga of the struggle, of the wars that had waxed and waned for over a century, as I approached my first encounters in Nicaragua. I kept thinking of the Sandinista Front's founder, Carlos Fonseca, and his killing by the National Guard about a decade earlier on a steep mountain.

The guard brought Fonseca's severed head to Tacho Somoza as booty. Somoza (so a Sandinista told me) took the head in his hands and stared at it. Fonseca's brown eyes were still wide open. Gazing into them, could not Tacho have glimpsed his own future—his own assassination in his Mercedes-Benz several years hence on a busy street in Paraguay? There must have been at least a gleaming, some tiny glint. After all, Fonseca was still wearing his eyeglasses.

4

MANAGUA WAS HOT. It is an ugly capital of broken buildings, empty lots, and no center, facing Lake Managua and volcanoes distant in the haze. It mingles the scent of human sensuality with lingering devastation from the earthquake of 1972 that destroyed or damaged most of the homes and buildings and killed ten thousand people. The streets and sidewalks crumble in the tiny tornadoes of dust and terrible humidity.

Whole sides of buildings, deserted or still in use, were covered with revolutionary art or slogans, the portraits mostly of General Sandino in his John Wayne hat and of Carlos Fonseca in his Vandyke beard and eyeglasses, on a background of rifles, books, campesinos, volcanoes. These enormous, bright, vivid paintings were, I supposed, a sort of art gallery for the proletariat. They were less offensive to an esthete's eye than the proletarian art gallery of the United States—Holiday Inn, Burger King, Pizza Hut. In a huge square, deserted save for thin, barefoot boys peddling newspapers to passing cars, was a muscular Sandinista cast in bronze, a dagger in one hand, in the other a rifle raised to heaven.

Here are the ubiquitous slogans: NICARAGUA VICTORIOSA—NI SE VENDE NI SE RINDE: NICARAGUA TRIUMPHANT—NO SELL OUT, NO SUR-RENDER . . . HOY TENEMOS EL PODER: TODAY WE HOLD POWER . . . In the Plaza de República, the white portico of the National Palace—made famous in 1978 when a handful of Sandinistas seized it and held fifteen hundred people hostage—is today mounted with immense por-traits of Sandino and Fonseca. Diagonally across the plaza stands the shell of the National Cathedral, its roof caved in, all of it still a ruin from the earthquake, though on the front steps outside is a towering billboard of a Sandinista soldier gripping a rifle and raising his Sandino hat against an orange sun. Beneath him, ¡SEGUIREMOS CUMPLIENDO! LET'S FOLLOW THROUGH TO THE END! At the large bakery near the Plaza de España, an endless line of the proletariat is waiting to buy bread.

I did not stay at the "de luxe" Hotel Intercontinental — the high, white eyesore, shaped like the pyramid of Cheops, that survived the earthquake — but at the much smaller Nuevo Siete Mares (New Seven Seas) not far away, near Lake Managua. The Siete Mares was a villa, really, of white plaster with rooms for rent upstairs and out in back, owned by a Chinese and with a Chinese restaurant. My fellow lodgers were mostly East Europeans, and at luncheon the restaurant filled up with Sandinista soldiers. I came to know many of these habitués. I was prepared for dire shortages from the contra war and the U.S. embargo, but my crude bathroom at least had toilet paper. There were cigarettes for sale as well, Alas, a Nicaraguan brand that cost nearly nothing, though as soon as you touched them they crumbled.

Shortages there were, however, and hard. Electricity was often cut throughout Managua for hours at a time, shutting off my air conditioner and turning my tiny room into a humid oven. Two days a week, there was no water; on other days, water was interrupted unpredictably. In the restaurant, there was usually no bread for breakfast, no fruit juice, not even bananas. (The Belgians were eating Nicaragua's bananas: foreign exchange.) Sometimes I was lucky and was served scrambled eggs. My normal breakfast was dry crackers and black coffee, rich and delicious.

At midday the menu promised a cornucopia of Chinese cuisine — chop suey and chow mein, exotic soups and seafood — but all the dishes were much the same: a portion of rice heaped with cabbage and bits of tough beef, chicken, or (sometimes) shellfish. The exotic soups were concocted by adding hot water to these mixtures. There were no desserts, not even fruit. Sometimes we had beer and sometimes we didn't: Victoria beer, which when cooled really wasn't bad, and Toña, weak as water. I learned later that the Ministry of Tourism determined the provisions and the prices for each restaurant. For my evening meal, Los Antojitos, a garden restaurant a block away, offered guitar music, grilled chicken (sometimes), shish kebab (sometimes), and a hideous brown mush of mashed beans always. The cafeteria at the Intercontinental was more expensive, the food much worse. After a week or so, I began to eat less and live more on coffee, crackers, and beer when I could get it.

Often when I walked from the Siete Mares to Los Antojitos or the Intercontinental, an elderly bourgeois woman would rush out of her villa and beg me to exchange cordobas for dollars. She offered seven hundred cordobas to the dollar (under Somoza the ratio was *seven* to one), but I knew that elsewhere on the black market I could get eight hundred or (soon) nine hundred. (At the airport, entering Nicaragua, I was obliged to change $60 for only 27.5 cordobas to the dollar, but this was a disguised tax.) As a foreigner, I had to pay my hotel bill in dollars: by government decree, Nicaraguan currency was refused. The cordoba was weakening day by day, and only dollars counted. Inflation was a pox on the lives of the poor, but again I blamed the perversity of Ronald Reagan and his aggression against the Nicaraguan people.

At the Siete Mares, beneath a painting of the Sacred Heart and a large photograph of Pope John Paul II enthroned in white and scarlet, the restaurant each noon began to throng with Sandinista military, young men and women, many of them officers, in starched khaki or camouflage fatigues, most bearing sidearms, from a command post around the corner. They were handsome, the men lithe with copper skin and lush mustaches, the women supple, of generous breasts and mouths too sensuous. They reminded me of contras, their brothers and sisters, grown up, even to the uniforms and guns. The air conditioner in the restaurant worked poorly or not at all, and in the wet air the odor of the women's young bodies added to their allure.

Over my several visits to Nicaragua, I broke bread (when there was bread) and drank beer (when there was beer) with some of these martial Sandinistas. They were gracious, as most of their compatriots were gracious: that is the Nicaraguan nature. For all the shrill attacks on the United States in the Sandinista press, they were at pains to protest their love of the American people, and they pleaded with me to change American policy, as if I could. Sometimes an East European sat with us. For example, Dimitri, a Bulgarian journalist based in Havana, who had been waiting for weeks for an interview with Tomás Borge, sole surviving founder of the FSLN, now the powerful minister of the interior and chief of the security police.

Borge, I knew, liked to keep his petitioners waiting, especially if they were not young, blond, and female. For all his Marxist credentials, Dimitri was middle-aged, balding, and unmistakably a man. The Siete Mares had only one telephone, perched atop the cashier's counter, and half the time it did not function. Yet Dimitri spent half his days there, vainly trying to get through to Borge's secretary or alternately climbing into a taxi and riding up the hill to the government press office to urge his request for the—hundredth?—time. Eventually he was fobbed off on some insignificant policeman. He left Managua in disgust, never having glimpsed his Hero of the Revolution.

And there was Viktor, a Czech technician who spoke bad Spanish and broken English. Viktor worked on a mysterious Sandinista hydroelectric project in the interior, but he got away whenever he could and kept a room upstairs at the Siete Mares. He was tall and very blond, but his fine face was flushed from drinking. He bought Johnnie Walker Black Label at the Supermercado Internacional, the International Supermarket, much like the one in Moscow, open exclusively to selected foreigners and eminent Sandinistas, where only dollars were accepted. But Viktor seemed to prefer Flor de Caña, that clear, sweet sugar-cane brandy distilled in Nicaragua, as potent as whiskey, which he drank by the gallon.

In the evenings Viktor took young girls to his room, then came downstairs and played cards with them and with Camilo, the hotel manager, getting very drunk. Before midnight he was screaming and could barely stand. Viktor was delighted when I boasted of being an *"imperialista norteamericano"* and made me repeat the remark to his girls again and again. He was by nature so generous that whenever I walked in the door he would stumble upstairs and return with packages of Parliaments and Kents, which he gave me for nothing. I would sit at his table, tease the girls, then go off to bed. In the backwash of my departure, I could hear Viktor muttering of me, *"Buen hombre."*

One evening, I dined at the Mirador de Tiscapa, a garden restaurant, with several young women from an American television network, a British journalist, and a Canadian engineer. During the meal, Omar Cabezas marched in. Cabezas was vice minister of the interior, a Comandante Guerrillero, which ranked him just below the nine Comandantes de la Revolución who sat on the National Directorate and ruled Nicaragua. More, Cabezas was not only a poet (most of the comandantes are poets, half of all Nicaraguans are poets) but a gifted author who had written a famous book about his life as a guerrilla, risking mountain leprosy and living on monkey meat. He seemed about thirty-five, with feral movements, a thick mustache, and a hard physique, yet he was well fed with a bearish quality. He wore the military uniform of his rank, but his physical presence was not what struck me.

He was surrounded by military bodyguards bearing AK-47s as he dined with some women and a burly East European type, possibly a Russian. The bodyguards, fair enough: after all, Nicaragua was at war.

But the guards would not allow the waiters to approach the comandante's table and insisted on serving him themselves. I had the impression that one of the guards tasted the comandante's food before passing it to his master. I excused myself briefly and went out to the street. Here stood several military vehicles and more troops, all waiting on the comandante. When I returned to my table, one of the young women, a Nicaraguan, told me, "All the comandantes do this. It impresses their girlfriends."

I was bemused, but our conversation turned to other things. Michael, the Canadian engineer, described his work in helping the Nicaraguans to build a power plant somewhere in the interior. "Everything is politicized," he said. "You don't get a big job unless you've proved your loyalty to the party. So they have Sandinista big shots managing the operation, most of them incompetent, and other Nicaraguans sweeping the floors. In between, building the plant, are the foreign technicians. A few Canadians, like me. On other projects, some Frenchmen. A lot of East Europeans. Czechs, Bulgarians, East Germans. Cubans, too. Everything is so screwed up. I wonder if my plant will ever get built.

"Listen. These foreigners are ripping off the Nicaraguans. They get huge dollar contracts, do shoddy work, then keep the difference. Sure, the Russians give some aid, but nothing like the U.S. pours into the rest of Central America, and for the Russians this is a low-risk war. The Russians ship in lots of vodka, some merchants with Sandinista connections buy it up at low prices, then sell it in Europe at high prices. The ministries are being run by sociologists with fancy degrees, but they all have Cuban and Bulgarian advisers, and none of them know what they're doing. I came to Nicaragua as a friend of the Revolution. Now I'm not so sure. Listen—"

We were interrupted by an earthquake. Not an earthquake really, but an eerie tremor that lasted less than a minute, rattled the teacups, and spilled my beer. From his private fortress, Comandante Guerrillero Omar Cabezas released a bluff laugh and slapped his Russian (?) on the back. Oliver, the British journalist, exclaimed, "Now an earthquake. A bloody *earth*quake." He turned to me. "Not a bad first week for you in Nica-land, eh, old boy?"

5

CHRISTMAS WAS COMING: a notion hard to grasp for all the heat. Not long before the feast, I called on Dr. Alejandro Bendaña, secretary general of the Foreign Ministry.

Don Alejandro was young, almost dashing. He was tall, with a generous mustache and touseled hair, and spoke colloquial American English. He had spent years at Harvard pursuing his doctorate in history and had an American wife. In fact, he had attended Harvard during my own residence there as a Fellow in international affairs, though in Cambridge we had never met. "I miss the Widener Library," Don Alejandro said wistfully. "I'd get lost in it. I'd linger there all day long, and I never wanted to come out." He sighed. "Now . . . reality . . . finally."

His arguments were as urbane and nuanced as the books he had read in the stacks of Widener. He was an expert on the inner mechanics of Washington politics and not ashamed to show it. "Take the Boland Amendment," he said. "Despite those congressional restrictions, Colonel Oliver North and the National Security Council are maneuvering around them and providing the contras with advice and money. The CIA's hands are hampered but not tied. They are resorting to all kinds of stratagems and tricks to escape the watchdog eye of Congress and the General Accounting Office. North and his people are waltzing around congressional oversight and the GAO now that the Boland Amendment is law." That shadowy Colonel North again.

I objected that Congress had authorized "humanitarian assistance" to the contras. Don Alejandro laughed. "Are guns humanitarian?" he asked, noting that Colonel North and the NSC had illegally arranged the delivery of arms to the contras through third countries. "When the U.S. military stage maneuvers in Honduras, they bring tons of equipment that never goes back. It goes to the contras. From El Salvador — from Costa Rica, too, though less — there are airplanes and supply drops to the contras taking off against Nicaragua all the time. We have the United States on our borders north, south, and west. On the east, U.S. ships sail the Caribbean monitoring our communications. The Pentagon sends aircraft over Nicaragua to photograph our territory two or three times a week. All this intelligence — this 'humanitarian aid' — is shared with the contras . . . These are U.S. invasion rehearsals."

I objected further that a U.S. invasion seemed unlikely — American opinion was against it, and even the Pentagon, fearful of the cost and of high casualties, had qualms. "Reagan," Don Alejandro rejoined, "has made a commitment to get rid of the Sandinistas in 1986. [This was December 1985.] He's preparing a strike if he can get away with it. We must measure the content of his rhetoric. Reagan is the radical. We are the victims, and we are the moderates."

Had the Sandinistas made no mistakes? "Our mistakes? We're not saying none were made. Have we been too harsh — or too lenient? No doubt the U.S.-contra war has increased tensions in Nicaraguan society, placing a terrible strain on our meager resources. To fight the war, we've had to reach deeper into our primary base of support — the poor. We've accelerated land reform — and some of the former landlords are not happy."

Did that mean that Nicaragua was headed more and more toward the model of Castro's Cuba? "Look, a pear tree can't grow apples. That won't and can't happen. This is not nineteen fifty-nine. We've much to learn from Cuba, but in our Revolution we're trying to create something *unique*. It must be *Nicaraguan*."

Apropos I digressed and related to Don Alejandro the story of my visit to Granada the previous Sunday.

Granada — about an hour's drive south of Managua, built at the base of a volcano on the shores of Lake Nicaragua — was once the bastion of the Conservative party. General Walker fought a famous battle there and burned much of the city down in 1856. Today, driving into the city, one passes an extraordinary outdoor mural of revolutionary art, peasants pointing submachine guns at Uncle Sam's skeletal head, that sort of thing, then some dreary slums, but finally one emerges onto the most beautiful Castilian plaza in all of Central America. The white, neoclassical cathedral, the stately, pillared arcades, surrounded a park of towering palms, shady walks, horse-drawn carriages, a fountain of sculpted nymphs, and a bandstand of balustrades and a marble dome. This could have been a movie set of what Latin America was supposed to look like, and in fact an American film company recently made it one.

The park was thronged with people, young and old, soldiers, adolescents, a mob of children, for across the street — on the steps of the town hall — an important ceremony was taking place. The ambassador of the Czechoslovak Socialist Republic was the guest of honor — surrounded by local Sandinista officialdom — there to receive the keys of the city. A brass band played flourishes, the Sandinista notables pronounced lengthy allocutions, more flourishes from the orchestra, applause from the crowd, and finally the ambassador of the Czechoslovak Socialist Republic — silver-haired, florid — rose to reply.

"*Estimado Señor Alcalde,*" I think he said, "*. . . estimados comandantes, estimados compañeros . . . la lucha socialista . . . la democracia socialista . . . la hermandad socialista . . . la hermandad marxista . . . la hermandad leninista . . . la hermandad comunista . . .* Distinguished Mr. Mayor . . . distinguished commanders . . . distinguished comrades . . . the socialist struggle . . . socialist democracy . . . socialist brotherhood . . . Marxist brotherhood . . . Leninist brotherhood . . . Communist brotherhood . . ." His Spanish was nearly impenetrable. The heat was stifling, and I was hungry. As the ambassador droned on, I went into the Hotel Alhambra, next door to the town hall, and ordered lunch.

It was not a bad luncheon, indeed the best I had eaten so far in Nicaragua: fresh prawns, grilled beef, white rice, vanilla ice cream, and several bottles of cold beer. I had a book with me, so after the meal I lingered over my literature and beer. When I returned to the portico of the hotel, the Czech ambassador was still talking. "*. . . la lucha socialista . . . la democracia socialista . . . la hermandad leninista . . .*" Most of the Sandinista notables, after what I assumed was an epic struggle, had dozed off in their chairs, and one was snoring. But it was the comportment of the crowd that I found remarkable.

They were getting smashed. Just across from the ambassador, five young men, in folk costume, sat at a wooden table strumming their guitars, singing ballads, guzzling guaro and Toña beer. Gorgeous, giggling little girls and boys ran up and down the bandstand steps, swung from the balustrades, then played tag almost between the ambassador's legs. Vendors hawked tortillas and soda pop at the top of their lungs. The crowd milled, growing noisier. In the terrific heat of the afternoon, in their drunken haze, young men began to quarrel over women: a fist fight broke out.

The Czech ambassador did not seem to mind. He kept talking. "*. . . la lucha socialista . . . la hermandad marxista . . .*"

When I finished my story, Don Alejandro smiled. Tentatively I added that the Nicaraguan people were perhaps not yet quite ready for the discipline of socialism. His answer disappointed me: I expected some flash of pedagogic wit. "Yes, you'll find a Latin American product here," he said blandly.

The rest of his remarks were more vigorous: "You'll find no decapitated bodies in Sandinista Nicaragua. We have no death squads. We don't gun people down. We respect human rights. We have no political prisoners — unless you call ex-somocistas political prisoners.''

But what of all the political prisoners in Tomás Borge's jails?

"Look, we have laws. They're stringent laws, because we're at war. People have been warned. If they're in jail, it's not for their beliefs but because they've broken the *laws*. We'll show them the same leniency that you Americans showed to Nazi sympathizers during World War II. And *we* have no concentration camps — as you did for Japanese Americans in California. How can we be totally normal when war is waged on us? Do you see the deadly effects of U.S. policy? You talk of refugees from Nicaragua. That is normal, let them leave the country — it's the surest proof of social change. Under conditions of war, can you expect us to act as Gladstonian liberals?''

6

OVER DRINKS that evening in a moonlit garden I spoke with a West European diplomatist and with Oliver, the British writer. Like myself, the diplomatist had served in Egypt. Oliver, it turned out, was a Tory with not much taste for Sandinistas. He was a devout High Anglican, a conservative Anglo-Catholic in the mode of T. S. Eliot, and he loved in his pink-gin way to debate about politics and religion.

DIPLOMATIST: How do you find Nicaragua so far?

AUTHOR: Kafkaesque.

D: Frightfully so, with an element of Greek tragedy. I mean, the inevitability of it all. In your country, Nicaragua has become an obsession — this nation of three million people, if that, so many have fled. I see an escalation, inexorable really, toward open conflict between Nicaragua and the United States. I ask you, is this tiny backwater so worthy of such lavish attention?

A: I'm not sure. The Falkland Islands have only forty thousand people. Mrs. Thatcher sent the fleet. I don't know the Falklands, but Nicaragua reminds me a bit of Egypt.

D: True, the Sandinista revolution is reaching the Nasserist phase. Borge's police are opening mail, tapping telephones — they get the equipment from the Cubans — hauling people in for interrogation and roughing them up. The Sandinistas are sorry now they suspended civil liberties in October—too much bad publicity—but the decision was dictated by its own logic. The Sandinistas fear growing social discontent on all levels. Suspending civil liberties allowed them to strengthen their internal front.

A: How?

D: These Sandinistas are like poachers turned gamekeepers. They were guerrillas themselves, remember, and they know the guerrilla game. They have good security, they know all about "safe houses" and the other tricks of clandestine agitation, and they will do anything to stop subversion before it starts. Under the new rules, the police can call in anybody, scare the blazes out of people before they get naughty. Then, of course, there's the Church.

A: You mean Cardinal Obando.

D: He's far too popular. When he was raised to the Sacred Purple, and returned to Managua last June in his triumphal progress, the Sandinistas took fright. They can't coexist with a cardinal who opposes them so deeply. So, more and more, they'll force him out of public view, confine him to the pulpit.

A: Of course, the Sandinistas have their "Popular Church."

OLIVER: Bloody awful. Graham Greene loves them.

A: I'm not surprised. On his eightieth birthday, Greene told the *New York Times* that the present Pope is a horror.

O: I think the Pope is marvelous.

A: How close are the Sandinistas to the Cubans?

O: Too blasted close.

D: Come off it, old man, it's more complex than that, and you know it.

O: Cuba is their model. Their fucking *prototype*.

D: That's true, in the sense that Cuba is the only other country where the Sandinista leadership have *lived*. But the comandantes here are not campesinos, they're petit bourgeois—the Ortega brothers, for example. Fidel has warned the Sandinistas to avoid his mistakes.

O: Was Fidel a peasant? *Fidel* was bourgeois.

D: You're missing my point.

O: I'm not missing anything. In Nicaragua the ruling class of the Somozas has been replaced by a new oligarchy of communist bureaucrats—as in Cuba when Fidel chased out the Batista family. Have you read Djilas's *The New Class,* Edward?

A: Years ago.

O: Then you know it's all in there. The same fucking phenomenon — Yugoslavia, Hungary, Romania, Bulgaria, East Germany, the Soviet Union. Whenever the Reds replace a dictatorship or a royal family, they create their own royal family — themselves. Have you seen how these comandantes *live?* Their Mercedes-Benzes, their palatial villas? Go look at the private residence of Humberto Ortega [the minister of defense]. It's surrounded by a wall a mile high, and it covers four city blocks. Go to the Supermercado Internacional, where the comandantes throw around their dollars. Chivas Regal, French wines, French perfumes, French hosiery, Russian caviar, designer jeans, Gucci boots! While the Nicaraguan people queue up at the single bakery in Managua [at the Plaza de España] and find no bread! Furthermore —

D: Oliver, old cock, if I may finish a phrase, or even a sentence, I was trying to make a point to Edward. Fidel has been here several times and urged the Sandinistas not to repeat the errors of the Cuban revolution. "Avoid the traps I stepped into just after my triumph," he keeps telling them. "Avoid international isolation. Don't reject foreign capitalist investment — you'll need it. Pursue a moderate, nonaligned foreign policy — and links to Western Europe."

O: He tells them that in public. In *private,* he gives them all kinds of spook gadgetry and tells them how to entrench their police state.

D: The Sandinistas want to create another Cuba, but without the dreadful mistakes of Castro over a quarter of a century. A "Cuba Without Warts."

O: Talk to ordinary Nicaraguans, Edward . . .

A: Oh, I've started to.

O: . . . they'll tell you all about the warts.

7

I WAS STILL suspending judgment about the Sandinistas, however. Shortly before Christmas, I went one evening to the poor Barrio Maximo Jerez to attend a public "dialogue" between the Sandinista leadership and La Marcha por la Paz.

La Marcha was an international peace march, hundreds of men and women, young and old, who were advancing up the isthmus on foot, through heat, dust, and rain, to protest U.S. policy and through their presence and solidarity with the poor to plead with the leaders of Central

America for an end to bloodshed. Many of the marchers were Americans, but the group included Canadians and numerous West Europeans, particularly Scandinavians. They had been taunted and attacked by right-wing hoodlums in Costa Rica, received warmly in Nicaragua, and were soon to be refused admittance to Honduras.

To the naked (cynical) eye, most of these marchers appeared to be hippies, and aging hippies at that. The men wore long hair, headbands, funky hats, beards, dirty jeans, and sandals. The women wore long hair, headbands, funky hats, dirty jeans, and Mother Hubbards. (The description is not meant to be pejorative: after all, they were hiking through the tropics, not touring the Sistine Chapel.) The Nicaraguans called such activists *internacionalistas,* which does not translate easily and carries a peculiar connotation. In Nicaragua an internationalist is a foreigner who has chosen sides — the Sandinista side — and has come to the country to lend his (or her) talent to the success of the Revolution in the face of U.S. aggression.

Tonight the meeting was taking place on an open dirt field, in a poor barrio, ablaze with the lights of television crews. As I stood near the front awaiting the arrival of President Ortega, I chatted with friends from the world press. Near me stood a wrinkled blond woman in a Mother Hubbard — a flower child of the 1960s, twenty years later — impatiently eavesdropping. Possibly I made some comment mildly critical of the Sandinistas. Finally, quite agitated, she interrupted me.

MOTHER HUBBARD: Sir, do you represent CBS?

AUTHOR: Madam? No, I don't.

MH: The *New York Times?*

A: Not at the moment.

MH: It's the world press's fault. If you'd give Nicaragua a fair hearing, there wouldn't be a war.

A: The world press has been much harder on Reagan than on the Sandinistas.

MH: I mean the establishment press in the United States. It's fascist.

A: Oh, come now. The *New York Times,* the *Washington Post* —

MH: They won't *choose sides.* Whose side are *you* on?

A: I'm just taking notes, Miss.

MH: Fascist pig.

We were interrupted by the arrival of President Daniel Ortega. He sat down in a fire of flash bulbs and applause, at the center of a long wooden table, accompanied by much of his cabinet and surrounded by a small army of bodyguards. He was a slight man, just forty, in mustache, spectacles, a khaki tunic open at the neck. Beside him the vice president of Nicaragua — Sergio Ramírez Mercado, a civilian intellectual — towered. Also present were several justices of the Supreme Court and three defrocked priests — Father Miguel D'Escoto Brockmann (ex-Maryknoll), minister of foreign affairs; Father Fernando Cardenal Martínez (ex-Jesuit), minister of education; and his brother, Father Ernesto Cardenal Martínez (ex-Trappist, ex – secular priest, active poet), minister of culture.

As pleased as I was to witness these illustrious Sandinistas, I kept looking for two Comandantes de la Revolución who did not show up. The first was Bayardo Arce Castaño, the dashing (some said reckless) erstwhile guerrilla who was now in charge of party affairs and was by reputation one of the most radical Marxists on the National Directorate. The second was Tomás Borge, who shared Arce's ideological passion. Borge fascinated me. Not only had he been tortured by Somoza's police, the National Guard had tortured and murdered his wife. Moreover, he was not merely a masterly policeman and the sole surviving founder of the FSLN but an eloquent poet.

While still in prison, Borge wrote of the Nicaragua he wished to create: "Today, for us and for our people, the dawn has ceased to be a temptation. Tomorrow, some day soon, an unknown sun will shine to illuminate the land that our heroes and martyrs promised us. A land with rushing rivers of milk and honey where every fruit will flourish, except the fruit of discord, and where man will be the brother of man. Where love, generosity, and heroism will reign, and at whose doors our people will be a guardian angel, who with a flaming sword will prevent the rebirth of egoism, arrogance, pride, corruption, violence, and the cruel and aggressive exploitation of man by other men." Throughout my visits to Nicaragua, I battled ceaselessly to be received by Comandante Arce and Comandante Borge.

Compared to them, I found Daniel Ortega boring, and he particularly lacked Promethean sparks tonight. As the peace marchers rose one after the other to ask him questions, he did not reply but simply wrote the questions down or referred them to individual members of his government. What a dull, dull man, I thought again. Look at him there, like a little clerk in his glasses and mustache, hunched over his legal paper, punctiliously writing the minutes down. This is a former mountain guerrilla, the President of Nicaragua, Sandinista Número Uno, a threat to Ronald Reagan and the great state of Texas? Suddenly Ortega rose, and—surrounded by his bodyguard—disappeared into the night.

I turned to the CBS technician standing next to me. "Has the President left for the evening?" I asked.

"He's gone to take a piss," the technician said.

Within twenty minutes or so the President returned, and the questions resumed. Not all of the questions were fawning. One woman wanted to know why Nicaragua always voted with the Soviet Union in the United Nations and had failed to condemn the Soviet invasion of Afghanistan. The President referred her to the foreign minister. Father D'Escoto took half an hour to answer in perfect English, then we waited another half-hour while he repeated every word in Spanish.

The UN resolution condemning the Soviet Union was "unbalanced," Padre D'Escoto said. Of course Nicaragua opposed all armed interventions, but what of armed interventions by the United States? He went on to quote, at numbing length, Mahatma Gandhi, Martin Luther King, Jr., Jesus Christ, and the doctrine of St. Thomas Aquinas on just and unjust wars. On American television I had found Father D'Escoto a pithy and persuasive advocate of his country's cause, but here I found him pathetic. He had endured a "fast for peace" the previous spring, but now his belly popped between the buttons of his tropical shirt, and he seemed very stout.

A young man from Berkeley, California, asked the President what Nicaragua was doing to control poisonous fertilizers and chemical pesticides, as if Nicaragua could afford any. Ortega wrote the question down. Someone was disturbed that Nicaragua had suspended civil liberties. Three justices of the Supreme Court took an hour to lead us in Spanish, then in English, through a jungle of judicial verbiage. Someone asked if communism and Christianity were truly compatible. The President motioned, and the minister of culture rose to reply.

From afar, in the United States, I had admired Father Ernesto Cardenal. I had read his poetry. I knew that he had studied literature at Columbia University and that afterward he had entered a Trappist monastery in Kentucky, where he became close to Thomas Merton, one of my favorite mystics. I knew of Ernesto's famous declaration, "Christ made me a Marxist." Even if that frightened me a little, I rather resented Pope John Paul II for wagging his finger at Ernesto at Managua airport in 1983, warning him to get out of the government or out of the priesthood.

Now here Ernesto was, at last, not ten feet from me, in his odd black beret, blue jeans, and white beard, about to explain how he had reconciled Marx with Christ.

I could not make sense of a word he said, either in Spanish or in the interminable translation to English afterward. He began in a high-pitched shout, then screamed and in his fury drooled. He raved, like King Lear, something about Pope Pius XII and bishops who opposed socialism and revolution and social democracy and French bishops who favored social democracy but Pius XII favored Social Christians but many bishops condemned Social Democracy as a mortal sin and on and on. Something must be wrong with *me,* I thought. From some flaw in my character, I find this man repulsive.

Of all the speakers, Vice President Sergio Ramírez seemed to me the most intelligent. In his blue jeans and brown shirt, he was the briefest, clearest, most straightforward. Someone asked when Nicaragua would pay its foreign debt — by now at least $6 billion, the highest in Central America. "When we have the means to care for the Nicaraguan people first," he said.

Finally a young woman rose and in English implored President Ortega to speak. "We've waited so long," she said. "Won't you please answer us?" The President waited for the translation, then scribbled on his pad. He put aside his pen and looked at her.

"You will receive your answers in due course," he said. "Please continue your questions."

It was nearly midnight. I went home. Walking to my taxi in that poor barrio, I noticed that except for the presidential party and the peace marchers, it was deserted. Hardly a Nicaraguan had waited up to hear Daniel Ortega speak.

Perhaps eventually around midnight, the President did answer some of the questions. *El Nuevo Diario,* a Sandinista newspaper, reported next morning only that he had attacked Ronald Reagan and the "genocide" of Nicaraguans by the United States government.

8

MY FIRST IMPRESSION of Miguel Cardinal Obando y Bravo, Archbishop of Managua, Primate of Nicaragua, was also unfortunate. At his Sunday High Mass, the Cardinal appeared in full robes, but his orthodox liturgy was corrupted, I thought, by a band of youths with electronic guitars, synthesizer, and drums blaring out ecclesiastical rock.

"*Gloria a Ti, Señor,* BOOM-BOOM. Glory to Thee, O Lord, BOOM-BOOM." Besides, His Eminence was too rotund.

Watching him as he intoned the liturgy, seated on his throne in purple chasuble and white miter, he seemed to embody the old cabal of Church, state, and army that by legend had kept Latin America in ignorance and bondage for four centuries. Moreover, his rotundity made me think of a film of Fellini's I had seen in Rome — the one with the ecclesiastical fashion show. Acolytes, priests, then obese bishops and cardinals in full pontificalia advanced toward the camera — on roller skates. I pictured Cardinal Obando in his sacred purple, roller-skating.

Such fantasies aside, it would be false to suggest that His Eminence pontificated in surroundings of opulence. On the contrary, with his grand cathedral downtown in ruins still from the earthquake of 1972, his procathedral was a humble white church, Santo Domingo de las Sierritas, indeed hardly larger than a chapel, miles from the center of the city. To reach it one drove south on the highway toward Granada almost into open country, then at a huge sign erected by the opposition Social Christian party, REVOLUCION SI, PERO CRISTIANA, turned right onto a narrow road that led eventually to Santo Domingo on the summit of a little hill. Yet however remote, the procathedral was thronged each Sunday with the bourgeoisie, who came in rusty, dented cars, and with the poor, who came on rusty, dented motorcycles or on foot.

Inside, the church was an esthetic disappointment: no enormous statues of Christ robed in real velvet, crowned with real thorns; no life-sized recumbent Christs in glass sarcophagi, wrapped in precious lace, weeping tears of painted blood. No high altar of carved rococo gilt, no Saint Michael Archangel and avenging spear, no Virgin Triumphant, Tower of David, Tower of Ivory, House of Gold, standing amidst the moon and stars. Instead, the altar was of cheap brown wood, the saints figurines of chipping plaster painted red and blue. Even the Cardinal's throne was a creaky armchair, barely able to withstand his weight. And that rock orchestra, howling of freedom and justice and other code lyrics against the Sandinistas. "*La libertad . . . la justicia . . . Gloria, Gloria, Aleluya, en Nombre del Señor.* BOOM-BOOM." The congregation rocked with them, singing and clapping, stomping their feet. This noisy, tawdry chapel seemed unworthy of a prince of the Church.

Yet maybe such modesty was suitable after all, since it mirrored so clearly the current condition of the Roman Church in Nicaragua and the wobbly posture of the Cardinal himself. He was at war with the Sandinistas, and not doing well. Not least of his recent battles, which he had lost to the overwhelming compulsion of the state, were the harassment and imprisonment of some of his priests, the drafting of seminarians into the Sandinista army, the expulsion from Nicaragua of foreign priests considered hostile to the Sandinistas, the silencing of his newspaper, the seizure by armed security forces of his Social Pastoral Office. Now, despite his popularity with the Nicaraguan poor, he was even forbidden to conduct processions in the street or to celebrate Mass in open fields, where invariably (especially since the bestowal of his Red Hat) he attracted multitudes. More and more the Sandinistas were confining the Cardinal to the closed pulpit and (they hoped) to obscurity and impotence.

It was not always so. The Sandinistas once loved Miguel Obando. Indeed, they encouraged the epos of his popularity, for in his own way he opposed the Somoza dictatorship as ardently as they did. Partly Indian on his mother's side (his face is dark and Mayan), sprung from the steep earth of Chontales in central Nicaragua (his town was La Libertad, or Liberty), formed by the Salesians (who taught the poor, unlike the Jesuits, who taught the rich), Monseñor Obando had entered the episcopacy as an auxiliary bishop of Matagalpa, near Chontales in the hinterland. There, he became a mythic figure as he wandered by oxcart and pack animal to the remotest of his parishes to preach the Word. He was, in figure and in fact, one of those itinerant friars on donkeys so beloved of the peasants, a dark dot creeping across the landscape as a bell tolled out the Angelus over meadow and hill. He was of the earth, earthy, not sophisticated (never will be) but shrewd in the way of the wise peasant, steeped in Scripture and traditional theology and a Latinist as well. When, two decades ago, Paul VI removed him from obscurity and sent him to Managua, the faithful rejoiced for their first native archbishop. Anastasio Somoza II, not yet aware of the primate's spine, began to call him "my little Indian."

Somoza soon knew better. When he sent the archbishop a Mercedes-Benz, the archbishop sold the limousine for charity. His offers of cash were likewise refused. In December 1974, a squad of Sandinista guerrillas stormed a Christmas party in Managua, seized illustrious citizens as hostages, and barely missed the United States ambassador (who had just left the party). The guerrillas demanded the release of fourteen political prisoners. Monseñor Obando was called in as mediator. Somoza capitulated, exchanged the prisoners for the hostages, and allowed the Sandinistas to fly to Cuba. Again, in 1978, when Sandinista insurgents seized the National Palace and more than a thousand hostages, the archbishop mediated the exchange for Sandinistas in Somoza's jails — including Tomás Borge. The dictator accused Monsenor Obando of provoking rebellion.

For the year before, under the archbishop's leadership, the Nicaraguan episcopacy declared in a pastoral letter that "repressive forces" were poisoning the nation's life — a clear condemnation of Somoza. More and more priests, encouraged by Monseñor Obando's militance, actively embraced resistance to the dictatorship. In spring 1979, as thousands died in fighting throughout Nicaragua in revolt against Somoza, the bishops in another pastoral letter condemned him as a tyrant, not least for "routine disappearances of people, jailings without cause, onerous fines, tortures, murders of innocent people, killing of prisoners, abuse of corpses, invasion of homes, hospitals and schools, arbitrary closing of radio stations, and persecution and defamation of bishops, priests, and lay people." The letter so alarmed the U.S. Congress that it discontinued financial and military aid to the Somoza government. With such a severance of American support, the Somoza dictatorship was doomed. Monseñor Obando and the bishops — quite as much as the guerrillas — were responsible.

The bishops were acting palpably in the spirit of the conference of Medellín, that assembly of the Latin American episcopacy in Colombia in 1968 that resolved to shed the ancient image of the Church as the accomplice of the rich and powerful and declared instead its "preferential option for the poor." A consequence of Vatican Council II, Medellín embraced a "liberating Gospel" for the Western Hemisphere and gave birth to the most remarkable trend in Roman Catholic thinking during this century — the Theology of Liberation, which mingled the mystical message of Christ with the political agenda of the left and in its more radical efflorescence attempted a marriage between Christ and Marx.

Monseñor Obando had always embraced the poor; his archdiocese struggled to address their misery through hospitals, schools, orphanages, the distribution of food and clothing, and by other good works. Yet throughout, his theology remained traditional: one did all one could in the name of Christ to assuage human suffering, but essentially men and women would remain forever flawed by Original Sin, poor banished children of Eve, sighing, mourning, and weeping in this vale of tears — until the Day of Judgment. He regarded Tomás Borge's prophecies of a Heavenly Kingdom here on earth — that "land . . . where every fruit will flourish, except the fruit of discord," where "egoism, arrogance, pride, corruption, violence" will cease even to exist — as poetic nonsense. Could not the social order at least be made more just? Of course it could, and should, but the world itself and all its woes could only be redeemed in Christ. The Cardinal was too shrewd a witness of human nature, too much the peasant realist, to expect such regeneration in his own lifetime or in the lifetime of his archiepiscopal successors into indefinite perspective.

Thus he was skeptical of messianic, utopian political movements and shrank, half in laughter, half in horror, from the Marxist Jesuits, Franciscans, and Maryknollers who had proliferated throughout Latin America in the decade since Medellín, aspiring to redeem the poor by preaching for revolt against oppressive social structures and for the creation of the Kingdom of God on earth. For Monseñor Obando, the Kingdom of God could never exist on earth, only in Heaven. The Marxist Jesuits were certain they had Scripture on their side and at any instant of the day or night could produce quotations from Matthew, Mark, Luke, and John that justified their fixation of "Jesus Christ, Liberator." The archbishop could quote Scripture as copiously as they, and often did: "My Kingdom is not of this world."

He had the Pope on his side. John Paul II, addressing Latin American bishops at Puebla, Mexico, in 1979, questioned the very core of liberation theology: "This idea of Christ as a political figure, a revolutionary, as the subversive man from Nazareth, does not correspond with the catechesis of the Church." Christ was not crucified in a political conflict: He delivered Himself to redeem fallen men. Monseñor Obando felt likewise. In the meanwhile, until the Heavenly Kingdom, throughout our terrestrial journey, Catholics did the best they could, if they were wise immersing themselves in Christ Redeemer and in veneration of His Mother, Queen of Heaven.

Nevertheless, the archbishop had helped to lead the struggle against Somoza, and once the Sandinistas triumphed in July 1979 he did try to live with them in harmony and even in cooperation. He celebrated a festive Mass, sanctioning their victory. Soon he and his fellow bishops, in a pastoral letter, attempted to define what sort of socialism they could bless. Again, they swore their solidarity with the poor, even as they warned against constraint of political liberty and the loss of "revolutionary creativity." What could *that* be? Revolutionary creativity meant that the Nicaraguan people would truly rule, that in their socialism the poor would enjoy authentic dignity and the fruits of a "progressively participative" planned economy, that they would be empowered to shape their own destiny free of victimization by any regime that in the name of a bogus socialism sought blindly to submit them to manipulation and dictatorship. Obviously the bishops were advocating a Christian socialism free of the usual bonds imposed by a communist despotism in thrall to ideology.

"Christian Socialism," wrote Karl Marx, "is but the holy water with which the priest consecrates the heartburnings of the aristocrat." The coexistence of Church and Revolution, from the first moment full of wariness on either side, was doomed to collapse. The archbishop by degrees came to be certain of what the Sandinistas were really up to, of their true intentions for the long term. Within months of victory the Sandinistas made it clear they would reach into every nook of Nicaraguan life, into the Roman Church itself, and what they could not control they would eliminate, preempt, or push to the margins of society and reduce to impotence. The Ortega brothers' tactical alliance with the bourgeoisie began to crumble before the year was out, prompting prominent non-Marxists to resign from the revolutionary government and eventually provoking several into exile and leadership of the counterrevolution.

The phenomenon was repeated in the regime's relations with the official Church. The Sandinistas favored priests who professed Marxism and vocally endorsed all of their social experiments, not only their laudable initiatives in literacy and health care but their collectivization of the economy, control of the media, and their embrace of Cuba and the Soviet Union. Above all, the Sandinistas resolved to remake the Nicaraguan character, to raise its revolutionary consciousness, by indoctrinating the young. Monseñor Obando recoiled when, with his blunt, peasant fingers, he turned over the pages of the children's new textbooks. They were drenched with juvenile renditions of Marxist materialism, class warfare, Sandinista militarism. "Two Sandinista rifles plus three Sandinista rifles equals five Sandinista rifles . . . All those who oppose the goals of the Revolution are enemies of the people . . . Who are the natural enemies of the people? The rich . . . Who is the greatest enemy of human progress? The Yankee . . . Who is the greatest hero of the Soviet Revolution and thus a great hero of the Nicaraguan people? Lenin . . ." And so on. This seemed a naked attempt to sever the Church from the next generation. Within a year of the Sandinista triumph, it was clear to the archbishop that the marginalization of the official Church was as essential to the Sandinistas as mastering the secular opposition.

More than in any other sector of the social order, the Church's abiding conception of the citizen—bound umbilically to the Church in sacrament, education, family ethics, in the whole body of traditional moral and social values—was incompatible with the Leninist vision of the Sandinista vanguard. As if this philosophical clash was not enough, with the rise of the contras in the early years of the Revolution, Monseñor Obando adopted an attitude toward the counterrevolution that was so vague, ambiguous, and elusive that in Sandinista eyes it amounted to complicity. He refused to condemn the rebels, claiming that he had insufficient evidence of their operations even when accounts of their atrocities were called to his attention. He spoke obliquely instead of "dialogue" and "national reconciliation"—code words for negotiation between the government and the counterrevolution that enraged the Sandinistas. *They* accepted only "a dialogue of rifles." Was the archbishop secretly in sympathy with the contras? Surely they shared a common interest—the undoing of a revolution that Monseñor Obando increasingly considered diabolical.

Moreover, the peasant army of the contras were the kind of Catholics closest to his heart—of the earth, earthy, devoted to the ancient rubrics of the faith, to the recitation of the rosary at bedtime, and above all to the veneration of the Holy Virgin. He had sprung from contra soil in Chontales and had ministered to the mothers and fathers of the contras and even to the insurgents themselves in their infancy as he wandered while a young bishop throughout Matagalpa province on his donkey, a church bell tolling out the Angelus across meadow and hill. They were *his* people, however violent. How could he condemn them? The insistence of the government and the Sandinista priests of the "Popular Church," or "People's Church," grew ever more shrill. Should he condemn the contras, the archbishop answered, his condemnation would be "manipulated" by the Sandinistas and place him publicly in their camp. Irrevocably, there he would never stand.

The regime increasingly circumscribed and harassed the official Church. The archbishop's inexorable response was to question the very legitimacy of the Sandinista state. He attacked the institution that embodied their power and their deepest values—the Sandinista army. In August 1983, the Nicaraguan episcopal conference released a public letter that vented the archbishop's bitter thoughts: "In all countries with totalitarian governments, a highly politicized army has been created in defense of its own ideology and . . . to force people to undergo political indoctrination . . . This juridical-political system identifies the State with the Party and the Party with the people . . . This absolute dictatorship of a political party, established by force and at the sole discretion of the State . . . raises the problem of its very legitimacy, together with the legitimacy of its institutions, including the army."

Furthermore, an "armed authority" in the service of a political party made a democratic and pluralistic state impossible. To force citizens to enlist in a "political-party army" when they disagreed with its ideology was an attack on their freedom of thought. Thus no citizen was in conscience bound to bear arms to defend an ideology he opposed in a political army that the government had converted into "an obligatory . . . indoctrination center for the Sandinista party." The episcopal letter then explicitly endorsed "conscientious objection."

This declaration was explosive—an open encouragement to Catholic youths to shirk obligatory military service in the Sandinista war against the contras. By its own lights the government was introducing conscription in legitimate self-defense, and Monseñor Obando's defiance reeked of treason. As head of the Nicaraguan Church, the most popular man in the nation, the archbishop could not, of course, be made a martyr, shot, or dragged off to one of Tomás Borge's jails, but the full thrust of Sandinista propaganda now portrayed him as an agent of U.S. imperialism and the CIA. Borge called him "the Antichrist." The episcopal declaration on military service created a terrible chasm between the Roman Church and the Sandinista state. Worse, less than a year later, in a joint pastoral letter, the Nicaraguan bishops publicly called for negotiations between the government and the contras. Thus John Paul II's decision in the spring of 1985 to pass over the heads of other worthy Central American archbishops and to raise Monseñor Obando to the Sacred College of Cardinals was rich in symbolism. It meant that Rome endorsed the archbishop's intransigence and perhaps even questioned, as he did, the very legitimacy of the Sandinista state.

Not long before he received the Red Hat, Monseñor Obando reminisced about the Revolution and his disenchantment: "I had hopes that this would be a good process, that it would benefit the great majorities, that there would be great respect for human rights and the dignity of the human person, that people would have more housing and better living conditions. I dreamed about that. Well, as time passes, we all make mistakes. Even bishops are human.'' As for the Theology of Liberation, so associated with the Sandinista cause, ''I was enthusiastic at the beginning. I thought that liberation theology could help people and play a role in reducing the enormous gap between rich and poor. But now, watching it in practice, I think this is unlikely, because I see that it foments class hatred . . . You know a tree by its fruit, and this tree has produced bad fruit. If you absolutize an ideal, as liberation theology does, then man returns to slavery. If you fill people with hatred, then you have not liberated them.''

By the time of my arrival in Managua, the Sandinistas' harassment of the official Church was escalating day by day, the focus of their assault more and more the charisma and mystique of the contumacious Cardinal. In October, the St. Louis Cardinals had won the World Series, so *La Prensa,* the newspaper of opposition, ran a headline, CARDENALES CAMPEONES — CARDINALS CHAMPIONS. No, said the government censor, that headline is subversive! The headline was changed to ST. LOUIS CAMPEONES. In the same month, over Radio Católica, paraphrasing the New Testament, His Eminence declared that ''Liberty is the dearest gift of God to man, and when liberty disappears so all joy is lost.'' Radio Católica was silenced for several days. But the Sandinistas could not silence the Cardinal in his own procathedral, and at each High Mass that I attended again he spoke out.

He spoke without notes, yet he was clarity itself, his phrases beautifully organized and crafted, above all pithy, ascending from a quiet exordium through rich references to Scripture to a vigorous peroration. He began obliquely with code words. ''. . . *Jesús de la Cruz . . . Jesús de la luz . . . Jesús de la justicia . . . Jesús de la paz . . . Jesús de la reconciliación''* — incanted shorthand meaning that the government must negotiate with the contras, a notion that was anathema to the Sandinistas. Alluding to the Gospel, the Cardinal noted that Christ spoke of ''justice toward the nations.'' Yet the Saviour did not traffic in demagogy of the streets (*''la demogogia por las calles''*). Christ was not a demagogue who deceived and tricked the common people when He promised them Eternal Life. The Redeemer made no distinction between the rich and poor: all were washed and saved by the sacramental water of baptism. Moreover, once baptized, all men should show no fear, even of other men who would ruin them, destroy them, and — because they denied God — bring down terror on their heads. The Church had no fear, only the sacred vocation to defend the rights of men and preach the Word of God (*"la palabra de Dios"*). Yet here in Nicaragua the state was choking off the Church, denying her right on radio, television, and in the press to preach the Word of God. This was the heaviest cross to bear — the sufferance of the state, its pretense that the Church's preaching of the Word was a privilege that depended on the mercy of the state. No, and no again a thousandfold. "This is not our privilege but our right."

The congregation erupted in applause, clapping rhythmically, stamping its feet. The drummer boy added his little bit. BOOM! I thought: this man is the only credible figure of peaceful opposition to the Sandinistas. He stands almost alone between the Sandinistas and exclusive power. I must come to know him well.

After the Creed, Cardinal and congregation petitioned Heaven for the success of the Church, Pope, and nation, omitting mention of the nation's rulers. Prayers for the sick and suffering, for all victims of injustice, *"Roguemos al Señor,* We beseech the Lord." Individual men, women, and children rose in their pews and called out their personal petitions. A man: "For a free Church . . . and for my beloved wife, dying of cancer." A child: "For my grandmother, dearest in the world to me, dying of tuberculosis." Cardinal and faithful. *"Roguemos al Señor."*

Finally, a middle-aged bourgeois woman, well groomed, her voice trembling with anger: "We pray for our sons, who are forced into military service and die without need for this government that we all detest."

Silence throughout the church. For an instant the Cardinal hesitated, as though not quite sure he should echo such frank defiance. After all, there were Sandinista agents present who would report his every word to Tomás Borge. Swiftly all doubt vanished from his fleshy Indian face: *"Roguemos al Señor."*

9

ON THE EVENING of that Sunday, I sought out the Sandinista Popular Church. The high temple of that communion was Santa Maria de los Angeles, an octangular building of brick and concrete in the Barrio Riguero of Managua. The barrio, home to the poor and the lower bourgeoisie, had been a hotbed of violent resistance to Somoza before the Revolution. The church was a marvel of revolutionary esthetics — far more interesting for its modern religious art than anything Cardinal Obando could offer. Here, Jesus Christ and César Sandino were intermingled.

The paintings, from the hands of Sergio Michilini and other Italian artists, blended the deepest symbols of the Christian legend with the beatification of *sandinismo*. In one mural, Carlos Fonseca and General Sandino are depicted not only as heroes and martyrs but as saints, their halos the flags respectively of the FSLN (red and black) and Nicaragua (blue and white) against a heaven bright with the aurora borealis. In another mural, *Los pobres reconstruyen La Iglesia de Dios,* The Poor Rebuild the Church of God, St. Francis of Assisi toils as a bricklayer while campesinos carry lumber and cultivate the fields; in others, David (Nicaragua) confronts Goliath (the United States); Christ relives His Passion in the body of an oppressed campesino.

The altarpiece was surreal, shaped like an immense, twisted mushroom growing from the floor into steel girders at the roof. Here, as in a dream, the mythology of sandinismo and the promises of its Historic Program were made flesh. At the center of the painting the crucified Christ became the Nicaraguan people, campesinos, women, and children, a Sandinista soldier at the forefront, bearing a heavy brown cross. Floating above them was the risen Christ, a campesino boy in headband, shirt, and trousers, his limbs still bleeding from the stigmata of his crucifixion. Swirling around cross and Resurrection were the Mothers of Heroes and Martyrs, bearing pictures of their murdered sons; four allegorical women arising by degrees from bent servitude to the arm-waving Liberation of Woman; dancing, joyous children; lush tropical vegetation; workers harvesting sugar cane; crops of coffee, corn, and cotton; huge, disembodied eyes; the brilliance of day, the darkness of night, the Holy Spirit embodied by the hovering dove of peace.

The pastor of this Sandinista shrine was Padre Uriel Molina Oliu, officially a mere Franciscan friar but in fact the unconsecrated archbishop — indeed, the uncrowned pope — of the People's Church. Scholarly, comely, and fair-skinned, with a doctorate from the Pontifical Institute of Biblical Studies in Rome and further studies in Jerusalem, Father Molina carried authentic revolutionary credentials as well. He had befriended and influenced such Sandinista luminaries as Tomás Borge and Carlos Fonseca during their shared childhood and youth in

Matagalpa, contributing to their intellectual formation and to the formation of several of their fellows who were later to govern Nicaragua.

Eight years before the Revolution, in this parish of Santa Maria de los Angeles, Father Molina began to give spiritual retreats to university students (most of them bourgeois, some of them rich) that soon evolved into political seminars, mixing Biblical exegesis with revolutionary analysis of history and society. The students formed a commune, living together in makeshift quarters behind the church. There they were joined clandestinely by Sandinista guerrillas who recruited them for the anti-Somoza underground. The neophyte insurgents moved out of the parish to embrace armed struggle against the dictatorship, but Father Molina continued to offer sanctuary to several eminent Sandinistas during the darkest hours of bloodshed before their victory in 1979. He was a major intellectual force in the Revolution before it had any prospect of success, he preached the gospel of liberation theology and the right of violent resistance to dictatorship before such ideas were widely fashionable, and he enjoyed the satisfaction of seeing his protégés assume the seats of power.

Padre Molina was at once the apostle and the incarnation of two of the Sandinistas' favorite slogans: ENTRE RELIGION Y REVOLUCION NO HAY CONTRADICCION — between religion and revolution there is no contradiction — and SER CRISTIANO ES SER REVOLUCIONARIO — to be a Christian is to be a revolutionary. His convictions sometimes compelled him to deeds that might have shocked more conventional Christians. In November he had celebrated a commemorative Mass for the M-19 guerrillas who, the week before, had seized the Ministry of Justice in Bogotá. During their battle with Colombian troops, nearly one hundred people were killed, including most of Colombia's high court. Yet Padre Molina draped an M-19 banner across his altar, hailed the guerrillas who perished in the carnage as "martyrs," then turned over his pulpit to an envoy of the M-19.

His Mass that warm December evening was also unsettling, as it was meant to be. Shortly before the service, several brand-new government buses pulled up before the church, disgorging dozens of North American tourists. (Managua has little public transport; such buses as exist are falling apart; the poor hitch rides or walk. Yet the government reserved its decent vehicles for excursions such as these.) The tourists admired the outside murals, then I chatted with several as they milled on the church steps. Most of them had come to Nicaragua to protest U.S.

policy and were embarrassed they could not speak Spanish. A dentist from Idaho, dressed in string tie and pinstripes (open necks, since the Revolution, are de rigeur), confessed his anguish. "He's going to say Mass? Should I go in? I'm not a Catholic. I'm nothing. I used to be a Reagan Republican. I voted for Reagan the first time. What Reagan's doing is just plain wrong. I hate Reagan. Aren't the contras awful? I don't know much about the Sandinistas. I wish I could speak Spanish. By the way, this is my wife." I shook hands with a large woman in a green dress. She smiled, showing her bad teeth. "I learned Spanish in high school," she said. "Great Falls. We're here as witnesses for the Nicaraguan poor."

We went inside for Mass. An orchestra was playing revolutionary hymns, nine young men in brown Levi's and silken shirts, arrayed on the platform between the altar and the immense mushroom with its floating campesino Christ, the Mothers of Heroes and Martyrs, the canoe in the rushing stream, the Sandinista soldier bearing his heavy cross, the disembodied eyes. Guitars and drums, saxophone, xylophone, and synthesizer: the best pop orchestra I ever heard on the isthmus, so much superior to Cardinal Obando's callow youths and their code lyrics *Jesús de la libertad, Jesús de la justicia, Jesús de la reconciliación.* Here in Padre Molina's shrine the hymns of praise were to *Jesús de la lucha* (struggle), *Jesús de la liberación, Jesús de la revolución.* Guitars, saxophone, and xylophone converged. The music and the voices soared. *Jesús de la revolución.* Despite me, my flesh tingled. Cardinal Obando offered only ecclesiastical rock. This was ecclesiastical theater.

The church filled up, roughly half with tourists and half with Sandinista officialdom, well dressed, some in uniform, with their well-fed wives and children. Father Molina appeared in the sanctuary wearing a sport shirt, which he covered presently with a white, hooded habit and a brilliant red stole. I had attended Masses in the Netherlands where radical priests celebrated the holy sacrifice in overalls and consecrated the wine in brandy snifters, and now I wondered what sort of liturgy to expect from Padre Molina. The Supreme Pontiff could not have complained. Father Molina's liturgy was wholly orthodox, and during the petitions he even prayed for Cardinal Obando. His homily was more remarkable.

It was a performance, like the pop orchestra's, Bishop Fulton Sheen in Spanish, whispers one moment, shouts the next. At his office in Managua, Father Molina displayed a huge cross, twenty feet high, listing the contras' crimes against the civil population, noting the year of the attack and the number of victims killed. Above the necrology a bomb bright with the Stars and Stripes fell on a flaming hut with a crucified mother inside, her dead children stabbed in their hearts with daggers of red, white, and blue. Put that painted crucifix to words, interweave a dozen references to the Nativity and the Prince of Peace, and many allusions to the poor, and there is his sermon that Sunday night. The poor, the poor, the poor. *Los pobres, los pobres, los pobres.* Let Reagan rain his bombs: the Revolution had brought the poor to life, and when the bombs stopped, which the poor would see to, the poor in their revolution would create the Kingdom of God on earth.

Los pobres. I could picture him as a young monk during the days of Somoza, in sandals and a coarse brown habit, instructing his guerrilla disciples, beneath a dim electric light bulb, on holy violence. *Los pobres.* He preached tonight at least an hour. I looked about at the tourists' faces, mostly blank. He was preaching to the converted in a tongue they did not grasp. Perhaps he sensed this. Finally, in broken English, he invited the tourists to join him in the sanctuary to sing *Silent Night*. Embarrassed, the tourists flocked about him, beneath the twisted mural and the campesino Christ. *Si-i-lent Night, Ho-o-ly Night. All is calm, all is bright. Round yon Vi-i-rgin Mother and Child. Holy Infant so tender and mild* . . . He resumed his liturgy. The orchestra resumed its odes to liberation and the revolutionary struggle, Padre Molina singing with them: he was a fine tenor, too.

Later, I met the padre privately in a conference room behind his church. Wearing casual secular dress, he was bookish in his eyeglasses and pale skin, and wary, armed with a Bible and a tape recorder. I was wary also: I knew that for all his attachment to the poor the father was handsomely financed by the World Council of Churches, liberal American Methodists, and — according to Cardinal Obando's senior clergy — by the Sandinista government. His ecumenical center in Managua, his magazine of liberation theology — *Amanecer,* Dawn — steadfastly produced panegyrics to the Sandinistas in the guise of religious revelation. Unkind bourgeois critics of the father claimed that, like his friend Tomás Borge and the other comandantes, he lived in a fine house behind a high wall. "What is your book to be about?" he wished to know. "What is the title?" Clearly, Padre Molina was feeling me out, probing for hints of where I stood. I told him directly that I was liberal in foreign policy, opposed President Reagan's military solutions for Central America, and tended to be traditional in theology. He said, "Ah," and turned on his tape recorder.

Would the father kindly explain how he came to combine Christ and Sandino? He had, he said, received his first revolutionary ideas in Italy, when he studied theology at Rome and at Assisi during the pontificate of Pius XII. Saint Francis of Assisi, his model, cast off his very raiment, rejected the right to private property, and refused all notions of superiority and titles in the Church. Padre Molina could not reconcile Saint Francis's theology of poverty with the Thomistic doctrine of private property imposed from above upon the whole Church: "I refused to submit to this authoritarian theological uniformity." God had revealed Himself in history through the poverty of Saint Francis: Christ liberates by lifting from us the burden of property and the enslavement imposed by unjust law.

And no, he did not muddle this with confused analogies to Marxism: "My exposure to Marxism came not in Italy but here in Nicaragua, and it's been very superficial. I don't have a solid philosophical foundation to defend the Marxist thesis. Hegel's dialectic — thesis versus antithesis equals synthesis, and the rest — I can't do it. It's a big zero for me. Class warfare — in Assisi I was afraid of it. So it's false to say that I'm a Marxist. I'm a student of the Church — of Scripture, Hebrew, Greek, and theological problems. I *am* a revolutionary."

In rejecting private property, Saint Francis was a revolutionary. He was more than the founder of an order, he established a grand movement that revolted against feudalism and the dictatorship of the Pope. Padre Molina did not quarrel with the essential doctrines of the Church — for example that Christ is the Son of God — but within the Church his theories were violently resented. Yet when he brought his ideas on Saint Francis and revolutionary poverty back to Nicaragua and to his young bourgeois disciples, "The impact was magnificent. Many of my pupils were anticlerical. The Church was identified with Somoza. I told them, 'No, the Church is the *poor*.' " His eyes shone. He relived the moment when he opened Saint Paul's First Epistle to Timothy, verses six through ten and seventeen through nineteen. We had been conversing in Spanish: now he opened his Bible and read to me in halting English:

> For we brought nothing into this world, and it is certain we can carry nothing out. And having food and raiment let us therewith be content. But they that will be rich fall into temptation and a snare, and into many

foolish and hurtful lusts, which drown men in destruction and perdition. *For the love of money is the root of all evil:* which while some coveted after, they have erred from the faith, and pierced themselves through with many sorrows . . . Nor trust in uncertain riches, but in the living God, who giveth us richly all things to enjoy; That they do good, that they be rich in good works, ready to distribute . . . that they may lay hold on eternal life.

The Franciscan closed his Scripture and gazed at me: " 'And having food and raiment let us therewith be content.' I told my students, 'If we analyze the society of Nicaragua, Latin America, Central America, we see that the poor are deprived even of these necessities.' I asked, 'Why does there exist in our society such difference between rich and poor?' The answer was in the text: *'For the love of money is the root of all evil.'* This was an explicit condemnation of capitalism. 'Rich in good works, ready to distribute . . .' We closed the Bible and began our discussion." The text, directly inspired by God, was an instrument to forge a new reality to the benefit of the poor. Henceforth, "The Church must be the agent of social change." Liberation theology would confront and vanquish "the scandal of social misery."

I was moved. This was not mere pious bombast. I recognized this obsessed Franciscan's historical achievement. His Biblical seminars had directly inspired many bourgeois and wealthy disciples to join the Sandinista underground, to suffer imprisonment and torture by Somoza's police, to kill and be killed to redeem the poor.

Los pobres. Only recently, Comandante Tomás Borge had written to Padre Molina to hail his silver anniversary as a priest.

Uriel:

Recuerdo nuestros primeros encuentros . . . I remember our first meetings in the dark days of December during our childhood, and the days we shared under the brilliant sun of Holy Week. We took part . . . in a Christian feast, and in acknowledging the word of Jesus Christ we put aside the cruelty of hell as incompatible with the boundless generosity of God . . . The struggle has led us, after all these years, to common cause with the poor, granted that we each of us are called to different paths. Were we to compare our separate lives, dear brother, I believe that yours is the fuller and more whole . . . Your exemplary life of daily identification with the poor, which fills your parish with psalms and hopes, is not far from your Franciscan heritage of humility, which if you reflect upon it is not so very different from—what must be—revolutionary humility as well . . . Twenty-five years of spiritual life, of sorrows and expectations shared with your people, are summed up in . . . the way of combat and in the people's victory that passed through your parish, in your secret meetings, in the valiant words of joyous Masses and processions . . . full of burning faith in God and the Revolution . . . *en Dios y en la Revolución . . . Fraterno,*

TOMAS BORGE

As I left the shrine after that evening Mass, the rock orchestra's recessional still pulsating—*Jesús de la revolución*—I thought I understood the comandante's zeal for this priest. I had written for the stage, and I recognized good theater. Yet as I watched the tourists return to their shiny buses and the Sandinista families to their fine cars, I wondered: where are all the poor?

10

NUMEROUS POOR were in Tomás Borge's jails. This according to Dr. Lino Hernández, who ran the independent human rights commission. Foreign priests and bourgeois intellectuals picked up by Borge's secret police at least could benefit from international publicity, but the poor enjoyed no such protection. Dr. Hernández meant the poor of Managua's endless foul slums, but even more the campesino poor in the remote provinces of the interior, whom Borge's men accused of collaborating with the counterrevolution. Such poor, sometimes guilty, sometimes not, were imprisoned indefinitely in bleak conditions, interrogated harshly, sometimes tortured.

Throughout my various visits to Managua, I grew quite fond of "Dr. Lino." I assume that the security police became aware of my visits to his office and, if so, were not pleased. Borge hated Lino, accused him of working for the CIA, and, so I was told, became even more enraged at the mention of his name than at Cardinal Obando's. Later on, Lino seemed to compromise himself when he allowed his human rights reports to be translated into English and distributed worldwide by friends in Costa Rica. His friends, it turned out, were partially financed by a procontra committee in Washington. Lino loathed the Sandinistas and belonged in effect to the political opposition; he was oddly bland about the contras and seldom condemned their violence.

Yet, as I toured the interior of Nicaragua, talking to a variety of persons, especially to the common people, Lino's data on Sandinista excess rang true in general terms and often in detail. I came to admire him considerably, wondering whether even Tomás Borge must not also have recognized his courage.

In fact, Lino had defended Borge in the late 1970s when Somoza's goons were torturing the future minister; Lino helped to mount an international campaign to remove him from solitary confinement, to feed him properly, to stop his torture. After the Triumph of 1979, when Lino began to condemn the abuses of the Sandinistas, Borge paid him back. Borge's comrades threw him in jail (briefly), painted "CIA" on the front of his building, beat him up at the airport. How sad, unsettling were my visits to Lino's shabby building. Those enormous slogans, spray-painted in rainbow hues all over the exterior: CIA. ¡A 50 ĀNOS SANDINO VIVE! ¡MUERTE A LOS VENDEPATRIA! CIA. Inside, as I wait downstairs for Lino to receive me, I am surrounded by poor and wretched women. No matter my foreign accent, my flawed grammar, the women refuse to believe I am not some sort of high official.

A dumpy woman from Matagalpa presses a typed petition into my hand. Her husband, Francisco, a born-again Evangelical, has recently been sentenced by a Tribunal Popular Antisomocista to twenty-three years at hard labor. With her coarse fingers she points out to me a passage in the petition for his release: ". . . *ninguna vinculación con Organizaciones políticas y Militares que estén encontra del proceso Revolucionario*" — in other words, he had no links to the contras.

I ask, "Have you seen your husband lately, Señora?"

"Here in Managua. They kept him at El Chipote [the state security prison] for two months."

"How is he?"

"Oh . . ."

"Don't cry."

". . . badly treated . . . terrible conditions . . . very sick with stomach trouble . . . lost so much weight . . ."

"Where is he now?"

"Las Tejas."

"Where's that?"

"The state security prison in Matagalpa. Are you the North American ambassador?"

"No. If I were, I could not help you as much as Dr. Lino can."

"Dr. Lino cannot help us. He has recorded our petition . . ."

"Why don't you go to the government with your petition?"

"I have. They sent me home. These are my children. Will you help us, Ambassador?"

Other women tell me stories just as sad: their men have been arrested and not heard from since, their men are still awaiting trial, their men have been condemned to sentences that range from several years to thirty years. Finally I am summoned by a secretary to see Dr. Lino upstairs. He sits in a dark, cavelike office surrounded by heaps of documents, a portrait of Beethoven, and a deafening air conditioner. He is quite young, with a square brown body, luxuriant black hair, and the wide nostrils of a noble Indian.

Lino tells me a little of his life. "I was born in Managua. My family is of *la clase proletaria,* the lower class. My father was a car mechanic, and my mother worked beside me in a textile factory to pay for my education. I studied law at the Jesuit university before the Jesuits embraced Marxism. I was graduated a year before the Revolution, and I went straight into human rights work. Nicaragua was coming apart, and I wanted to help people. My inspiration is Christian. I have a wife and two sons.

"My work has always been difficult, full of danger. I was put in jail for a week under Somoza, and then for three days in 1980 by the Sandinistas. This was a detention only, supposedly a 'confusion of identity.' Intimidation, obviously. Then *Barricada* and *Nuevo Diario* [Sandinista newspapers] falsely accused me of beating a woman. In 1981, I was attacked by a Sandinista *turba*, mob, at the airport. Later that year, I was attacked again, by the Sandinista Youth, and they beat me much harder. Then this building was attacked, and splashed with all those slogans. My telephones are tapped by the Ministry of Interior and their friends of the East German security. I receive death threats by mail and on the telephone.

"Yet in spite of all the pressures and the threats, we continue to seek justice. During the last years of Somoza, as bad as he was, there were six hundred political prisoners in Nicaragua. Today — my estimate is conservative — there are between fifty-five hundred and six thousand political prisoners, not counting the twenty-three hundred who served Somoza in the National Guard. Two hundred thirty-five Nicaraguans have 'disappeared' since 1983. All this in a country with a population of only three million — extraordinary."

Political prisoners, Lino continued, were nonpersons and nonpersons had no rights. They could be detained for over a year without recourse to habeas corpus. True, some prisoners were held only for brief periods — a few days or weeks — but many were held for longer periods or indefinitely. The Sandinistas boasted of their "revolutionary mercy," of their *granjas abiertas* or "open farms," model jails with low security where conditions of life were mild and political prisoners were "rehabilitated." But these open farms were mostly a show, staged by Tomás Borge to dazzle pro-Sandinista North Americans and other tourists of the leftist international, enabling them to return to their societies praising the marvelous compassion of "revolutionary justice."

Amnesty International and the International Red Cross were permitted to visit the open farms, but were never allowed inside the jails where the horrors happened. These were the nine prisons of the state security, scattered throughout the provinces, where suspected "enemies of the people," "enemies of the Revolution," collaborators or sympathizers of the contras, men and women who refused to serve in the militias or the Vigilancia Revolucionaria, were locked up and interrogated. Of the nine security prisons, the one in Managua, the infamous El Chipote, crouching behind the Hotel Intercontinental, was the most benign. Usually, only *psychological* torture was practiced there. El Chipote had its special charms.

From his heap of testimonies and petitions, Lino extracted some diagrams: "Look here, Edward. Chipote is subterranean. The cells are tiny, and ideal for solitary confinement. Inside a cell, a man can barely lie or stand. See the locked window in the metal door. The only ventilation is a tube from the ceiling to outside, and — in our Managua heat — you can imagine the air in there. Each prisoner is known by number. The prisoners are kept in darkness. They have an open pipe for their sanitary needs, but they have to feel in the dark to find it. Sometimes the pipes are clogged, and the prisoners are forced to live in their own urine and excrement. There's a water pipe, too, but on some days — as punishment — the water is shut off. Some prisoners go mad.

"We don't deal in rumors, Edward. We have thousands of testimonies from witnesses and victims, and we only publish what we can document. Inside Nicaragua, we live on local contributions, and we're practically broke. I have trouble paying my secretary. That should be enough for Tomás Borge, but it's not. Every day he applies more pressure, threatening to censor our reports, to jail us again, to close us down. Will we survive? How can I tell?

"More and more activists from the opposition parties and the independent trade unions—middle-class people—are being put in jail. Most of them are held for short periods, from weeks to several months. But the campesinos? When the doors close on them, they can close for a long time. They are arrested on the merest suspicion, without any proof. In Estelí, at the Barranca prison of the state security, the campesinos are hung by their hands from the walls. They're deprived of food and drinking water. They're beaten . . ."

And they were tortured with ice. Officials of CUS, an independent trade union, claimed that a member, jailed for sixty-three days and never accused, was forced to sit naked on a block of ice. Later on, when I toured the provinces, I met a poet who had spent some months in El Chipote: ". . . Imagine yourself, Don Eduardo, sitting in a dark, stinking cell, hour after hour, week after week, until a guard comes. He clanks his keys. He opens your little window. You think he has come to say, 'Don Eduardo, you are going home.' Instead he says, 'Don Eduardo, your mother is dead.'

"He leaves you in your cell, sitting in your shit, to think about your dead mother. You wonder, 'Is my mother really dead?' That night— or is it noon?—you hear a woman screaming in a distant room. You wonder, 'Is *she* my mother? Is my mother still alive? What are they doing to my mother?' . . ."

I I

FROM MY JOURNAL: Talks today at *La Prensa,* with Virgilio Godoy (for five years minister of labor in the Sandinista government and now leader of the Independent Liberal party), and with Ambassador Z.

La Prensa oozes hatred of the Sandinistas. The newspaper is at the mercy of a woman captain in Borge's ministry, one Nelba Blandón, the official censor. She slashes their columns with such obstinacy that for three days last week they could not even publish. The bulletin board outside the building is plastered with articles—many about the harassment of the Church—that the public never saw. *La Prensa* is the forum of Cardinal Obando and the entire conservative establishment, but the editors say that at any moment now Captain Blandón will forbid them even to mention the Cardinal's name. Odd, the caprices of fortune. It was the assassination of Pedro Joaquín Chamorro, publisher of *La Prensa,* that ignited the general insurrection against Somoza and brought the Sandinistas to power.

The editors/writers are nakedly pro-U.S. and pro-Reagan. Make that they *barely bother to conceal* their admiration of U.S. power and their clandestine sympathy for our reigning president: some are more subtle than their fellows. Editor X: "The Sandinistas say that Reagan is attacking Nicaragua because it's independent. That's false. The Sandinistas have a political goal — to turn this country, and the rest of Central America, into a communist state modeled on Cuba and the East bloc, with some differences. They're not doing it in one leap, because they know they could lose a lot. They don't have the absolute backing of the U.S.S.R. The Russians won't give them dollars. So the Sandinistas make the right noises for solidarity with Western Europe, Latin America, and the U.S. Congress — to neutralize them and because they're desperate for West European money. They boast that Nicaragua is democratic, pluralist, with a mixed economy, but that's all a show. The Sandinistas control everything, or they will quite soon."

Next, Y, a personage who dropped by: "Reagan's policy in Nicaragua is a classical confrontation between East and West, between communism and democracy. The great majority of Nicaragua's people don't want a communist government. They want the Reagan administration's help against the Sandinista Revolution. This is accepted by everybody. The United States is not attacking Nicaragua but helping our people who want democracy. The counterrevolution is asking for outside help — that's a tradition in Nicaragua. We don't want a U.S. invasion, but we have the right to help. Without help, it's impossible to achieve democratic change. The Sandinistas promised us a pluralistic regime, and we have the right to that since we all fought Somoza for it. So, a civil war. We're not fighting Nicaragua, we're fighting the Sandinistas . . . I think that in private Cardinal Obando approves of the contras."

I was astonished by such reckless candor. Upon reflection, I assume that Ortega and Borge — with their telephone-tapping machinery from Castro, East German expertise, and network of informers — know the private indiscretions of each *La Prensa* personality in rich detail. When will Borge pounce? Already, President Ortega has condemned *La Prensa* as the mouthpiece of U.S. hegemony *("la voz de la hegemonía norteamericana").*

I saw a fascinating crucifix on *La Prensa*'s wall: the body of Christ *has no arms*. Does this symbolize His mutilation by the Sandinistas? I thought again of Tomás Borge, who collects rare crucifixes as a hobby. He displays them on his office wall.

Next, a chat with Virgilio Godoy. Supposedly Cardinal Obando is the only credible leader of the opposition, but now I am not so sure. Within ten minutes of talking to Godoy, I sense that somehow some day he might become the chief of state. An intellectual, a professor of sociology, he is an elegant man with silver hair and his face pitted by a childhood disease. Certainly he knows more about the secret councils of the Sandinistas than does any other figure of the opposition.

He says, "I resigned my ministry because there was nothing further I could do. The Sandinistas are, shall we say, *inefficient?* The Ortega brothers at the presidency and Ministry of Defense, Borge at Interior, and Jaime Wheelock at Agriculture each run separate empires. There is no coordination and no coherent economic policy. A minister can't make decisions without the blessing of the Sandinista party. When approval comes, it's so late it makes no difference. There are two governments — the state and the party. Yes, there are other parties such as mine, but the Sandinistas are the party of hegemony. Daniel Ortega talks of 'limited pluralism' and what he means is that no other party will ever be allowed to threaten his. The official party must have total control. Nicaragua is headed toward the Bulgarian model.

"We're partly there already. The comandantes are the New Class. Their latest thing is video machines. The brand name is Betamax. Expensive. Foreign exchange. Another status item. All the comandantes have them."

He chuckled, remembering a droll incident. "When I was a minister I sat with the comandantes one evening while the president of the Central Bank told them that our foreign exchange reserves were minus thirty-six dollars. One of the comandantes made a sharp remark about another comandante's grandmother. Something to do with her role during the Revolution. Minus thirty-six dollars in the treasury, and they spent the rest of the evening fighting over the grandmother. A week later, Colonel Qaddafi sent one hundred million dollars."

From Virgilio Godoy to dinner with Ambassador Z, a Western diplomat, and deep. I am puzzled that he entered diplomacy at all, since he is too intelligent for that profession. An amateur musician, a novelist manqué, he consoles his lost dreams by reading verse in seven languages. He has served in the Orient, Paris, Eastern Europe, and in the capitals of various Hispanic despots. He has made it his business to be intimately informed about the vicissitudes of the Sandinistas in the drama of human rights. I believe he senses that I admire him, but on several matters we disagree. I tell him of my talks with Dr. Lino, Virgilio Godoy, and the dissidents at *La Prensa*.

AMBASSADOR Z: I admire Lino, but you have to put his data in perspective.

A: How do I put such horrors in perspective?

Z: I agree it's sad, but as compared to what? As communist governments go, this one is mild. I lived in Eastern Europe for several years. If you wish to see serious state terror, go to Bulgaria, say, or Prague. Go to Havana. In at least two thirds of the world, torture is a growth industry. Most of Sandinista torture is psychological. "White" torture, they call it. From their perspective, they have to practice it because they're at war, they're fighting for their lives, and they need information about the enemy. If they weren't at war, they wouldn't torture people. Have you noticed how freely people talk to you in Nicaragua? Loose tongues do not prosper in your typical tyrannical totalitarian state. Do you think the kind of reckless talk you heard today at *La Prensa* would be tolerated in Cuba or Bulgaria? They'd be in cement. And wait until you reach El Salvador. For the fine arts of horror, the extreme right will never fail you.

A: I'm fascinated by Tomás Borge. I *must* get to him. How well do you know Borge?

Z: Rather well.

A: His character . . .

Z: He's half mad, but brilliant. His mind was somewhat warped, I think, by his torture in Somoza's jails and the murder of his first wife. An anointed Marxist zealot, much more gung-ho than Danny Ortega or Jaime Wheelock. Takes long vacations in Cuba, and he's thick as thieves with Fidel. At his ministry, according to his mood, he can be merciful one moment and cruel the next. At home, he lives well, but so do all the comandantes.

A: I still have no focus on his person.

Z: Oh, he's nearly a dwarf. I'm only an inch or so above six feet, but whenever I talk to him his nose is in my bellybutton. I enjoy his poetry; it's not inspired, too political, but it's lyrical and rich and rather good. He can be brusque or charming as the spirit moves him. I've seen him bark orders at his girlfriends. He can't keep his hands off pretty blond women, and I wonder if that upsets his present wife. I'm not sure. Borge's biggest defect, he exudes deceit. In fact, he's a shameless liar. In Mexico City, about six or seven months before the Triumph, when the Sandinistas were trying to convince the bourgeois world they were only social democrats, Borge publicly denied he was a Marxist. For Borge, for all the comandantes, the name of the game is to get power and to stay in power. That means never sharing power.

A: So, once Borge had power, he had to consolidate it.

Z: First priority of any revolution. That meant, among other things, killing a few people. During the first two years after the Triumph, certain people had to be eliminated. From Borge's perspective, he had no choice. As a doctrinaire Leninist, he anticipated the counterrevolution. Certain enemies of the Revolution, if allowed to live, might coalesce and reverse it. Borge and his cohorts designated selected targets under a dossier of "special measures" — a hit list, if you like.

A: How many victims?

Z: I've heard various estimates of victims, from a few hundred to fifteen hundred. Again, as revolutions go this one is not bloodthirsty. Compared to the Cuban executions in the first years of Fidel, the Sandinistas are Boy Scouts.

A: Maybe it's because Borge found religion.

Z: Isn't that amusing? The crucifixes on his wall? The way he massages the People's Church? He's the ultimate cynic, and probably an atheist, but he's so eccentric one can't be sure.

A: When will he kill *La Prensa?*

Z: At the opportune moment. He'll have to consult the other comandantes. They only take decisions of that magnitude by consensus. They'll need a pretext.

A: And one to get the Cardinal, too?

Z: They won't *kill* him. Conceivably, the Cardinal could create his own pretext. His Eminence is not very subtle. In Washington recently, he met secretly with high officials of the Reagan administration.

A: Elliot Abrams? George Shultz?

Z: Oh dear. Perhaps I've been indiscreet.

A: Colonel North? The President?

Z: I'll have a bit more of that Bulgarian butter, if you don't mind . . .

12

THE UNITED STATES in effect was at war with Nicaragua, but neither side wished to rupture diplomatic relations. It served Washington's purpose to maintain a listening post and intelligence agents under diplomatic cover in the enemy camp; reciprocally the Sandinistas used their embassy in Washington to influence American opinion against Reagan's contra war. The U.S. Embassy at Managua was under siege, but more from dissident American citizens than from the Sandinistas. True, the Sandinistas did harass and interrogate the embassy's Nicaraguan workers, tapped the embassy's telephones and applied various other minor pressures and vexations. But the American ambassador enjoyed a cordial rapport with the Sandinista leaders, became a personal friend of Tomás Borge (who sometimes called on him at home and used his swimming pool), and he was the safest man in Nicaragua. The ambassador traveled all over the country, seeing whatever and whomever he liked, often without guards. His personal liberty was extraordinary, whereas the U.S. envoys in the American client states of Honduras and El Salvador, for fear of assassination, only ventured out when surrounded by small armies. Similarly, the ambassador's aides (even his military attaché) were free to visit most of Nicaragua without impediment.

The result, it seemed to me, was the best-informed and least paranoid U.S. Embassy in Central America. The embassy enjoyed no influence on Sandinista or U.S. policy; its major function was to provide data to Washington about Sandinista rule. Washington then used the data to justify its hostile policy, interpreting and distorting as it pleased in pursuing its military and propaganda offensive against the comandantes. What Washington thought was one thing, the mind of the diplomats inside the embassy quite another. Not that any were pro-Sandinista, to the contrary, only that their minds were cool, without hysteria and delusions.

The ambassador was a humorous and learned man, a career diplomat loyal to his President in the venerable tradition of his service but with a mind very much his own. He had been posted to Managua against his better judgment, was diffident about the policy he had to defend, and yearned to be somewhere else. The ambassador was a historian by avocation and tended to the long view. He was, shall we say, bemused by the *Weltanschauung* of the Reaganites. Had Washington instructed him to work out an accommodation with the Sandinistas he might well have done so, but Washington wanted no such accommodation. Thus the continued presence of the embassy at Managua was paradoxical.

The embassy was an undistinguished white building, one story high, surrounded by a barbed-wire fence and situated by a highway at the outskirts of Managua. Its embellishments made you smile. The sign at the entrance: SOLO A LA DERECHA: RIGHT TURN ONLY. The sign at the exit: PROHIBIDO GIRAR A LA IZQUIERDA: NO LEFT TURN. As though not to be outdone, the Sandinistas had thoughtfully erected a huge sign of their own on the other side of the road facing the embassy gate:

CAMPAMENTO DE EL CHIPOTE VIA SAN FERNANDO
12 DE JULIO DE 1927

AL CAPTAIN G D HATFIELD
COMANDANTE DE LOS MARINES YANQUES
EL OCOTAL

RECIBI SU COMUNICACION AYER Y ESTOY ENTENDIDO DE ELLA
NO ME RENDIRE Y AQUI LOS ESPERO   YO QUIERO PATRIA
LIBRE O MORIR   NO LES TENGO MIEDO   CUENTO CON EL
ARDOR DEL PATRIOTISMO DE LOS QUE ME ACOMPAÑAN

PATRIA Y LIBERTAD

A   C   SANDINO

YOUR TELEGRAM OF YESTERDAY RECEIVED AND UNDER-
STOOD I WILL NOT SURRENDER COME AND GET ME   I SEEK
A FREE FATHERLAND OR DEATH AND KNOW NOT FEAR   I
COUNT ON THE FIERCE LOVE OF FATHERLAND OF MY COM-
PANIONS

FATHERLAND AND LIBERTY

A   C   SANDINO

Every Thursday morning at 7:30, the police halted traffic on the highway, and American citizens in Nicaragua displeased with U.S. policy demonstrated between General Sandino's billboard and the embassy gate. I arrived early, finding myself alone before the embassy with a bohemian young American in a beard and a denim jacket. Clustered behind the gate were several guards; when the youth noticed them he raised his fists in rage. "You bastards! You cocksuckers! You moth-erfuckers! Are you proud of your country?" He grabbed the locked gate, shook the iron bars, raged on. "Are you proud of your fucking country?'' The guards were not North Americans but Nicaraguans, a detail that seemed to elude my slovenly compatriot. Other North Americans assembled, many of them nuns and clergy, and by their faces I knew they did not intend that kind of uncouth disturbance.

On the contrary, their mood seemed a mixture of Christian concern and sorrow. Numbering now about two hundred, they did not even call this a demonstration but a "vigil." Here were not only clergy both Catholic and Protestant, but many earnest young men and women in blue jeans and brown corduroys, cotton shirts, sunglasses, baseball caps, not all of them tourists but many *brigadistas* as well, volunteers who toiled for no pay with coarsened hands harvesting coffee and sugar cane, building houses and water systems, contributing whatever they could to the success of the Revolution in the remote and dangerous provinces of the interior. They were mostly white Americans, with one or two blacks. Gently they sang hymns, marched in circles before the gate, hoisted signs and banners: REAGAN: STOP THE DISINFORMATION. ¡NO A LA GUERRA DE REAGAN! PEACE! ¡QUEREMOS LA PAZ! ¡BRIGADISTAS DE EEUU CONTRA LA AGRESION! ¡CONTRA NO PASARAN! NO VIETNAM WAR IN CENTRAL AMERICA! US CITIZENS: BEWARE OF WASHINGTON'S LIES ABOUT NICARAGUA! STOP U.S. AID TO THE CONTRAS!

A young woman in jeans and sunglasses spoke into a loudspeaker. "Good morning. I'm Sister Susan. Welcome to the one hundred fourteenth consecutive Peace Vigil outside the United States Embassy to protest the immoral policy against Nicaragua Libre [Free Nicaragua]." (*Applause.*) "Please remember that this is not a vigil against the U.S. Embassy or embassy personnel, but against President Reagan's immoral policy. Please respect all United States symbols and the American flag." (*Applause.*) "We are here to bear witness to the noble struggle of Nicaragua Libre to build a just society of pluralism, democracy, and diversity, where all men and women are free to practice their religion, and to contradict the lies and delusions of aggressive U.S. policies." (*Applause.*) "We want to welcome all the ecumenical groups and the tireless working people, the brave young men and women of the Woody Guthrie Brigade." (*Applause.*) ". . . organizing in the States . . . thousands of leaflets throughout America . . . police brutality under Somoza . . . police brutality in the United States . . . the people of Nicaragua Libre wield the most powerful weapon in the world—the Truth." (*Applause.*)

An elderly Presbyterian pastor read an open letter to President Reagan, something about the thousands of innocent Nicaraguans, including eleven-year-old girls, killed by his cruel choice, something about the Gospel according to Matthew and a speck in our neighbor's eye but a log in our eye and contra terror. "Stop the war." Then somebody else hailing "one hundred and twenty university students cutting coffee in Jinotega, living on rice and beans, protecting themselves at night against terrorist attacks," then a Liverpudlian accent and "we're the British coffee-cutting brigade. We're the first but not the last . . . inoculations . . . literacy crusade . . . agrarian reform . . . Nicaragua Libre will not be crucified . . ." Someone handed me a newsletter.

It was called *Nicaragua: Through Our Eyes,* published by the Committee of U.S. Citizens Living in Nicaragua. Written for distribution in the United States, the newsletter justified the Sandinistas' suspension of civil liberties. Almost all Nicaraguans who opposed the government, even peacefully, were directly or by innuendo linked to the counterrevolution. The letter spoke darkly of "networks of conspirators . . . disseminating counterrevolutionary religious propaganda . . . youth wings of several opposition political parties . . . reactionary elements in the business sector . . . trade unions pushing inflationary wage demands" who by design or not were doing Reagan's work. As for the Sandinistas, their human rights record was "among the best in Latin America" and everything they did "in accordance with law . . . Abridgement of civil liberties such as freedom from arbitrary arrest and search, and of procedural rights such as habeas corpus, applies only to persons suspected of counterrevolutionary activity." Habeas corpus was a mere "procedural right"? In my innocence, I had thought it essential to any civilized legal system.

I sympathized with the anticontra sentiments of the vigil. But could not one condemn Reagan's military solutions without blessing everything Sandinista? Must one embrace the Sandinistas with no reservations about their system? This vigil, full of pastors, priests, and nuns, was telling me with the certitude of dogma that morally I must choose. It was either . . . or. There was no middle way, American policy was so heinous. I refused and took refuge in detachment.

On Christmas Eve, I left Managua for León.

13

I HAD HOPED León might be cooler. León was hotter. Nicaragua's second city, though nearer the breezes of the Pacific coast sixty miles northwest of Managua, languished in a debilitating moist heat at midafternoon before the feast. And this was still the city's "cool" season. The celebrations had already started. A bazaar was laid out in the terrific sun along a side of the cathedral: women and children sold bright cloth, straw baskets, wooden sandals, plastic toys, and bric-a-brac and such sweets and food as they could muster to a mob of people. In the marketplace behind the cathedral campesino men and women drank guaro from clear bottles and vomited on the pavement.

The cathedral was enormous, the largest on the isthmus, and it seemed almost the size of Saint Peter's. The style was Spanish baroque, begun in the middle eighteenth century and so elaborate that the building took a century to complete. Now the outside walls and crenelations, the domes and life-sized crouching lions, are black with decay, but the interior remains a marvel, all marble, mahogany, and whiteness, topazes from Philip II, ivory Christs and bronze Christs, gilded choirs and altarpieces. At the feet of an apostle lies the tomb of Rubén Darío, Nicaragua's renowned poet, guarded by a weeping lion.

Two hours before Midnight Mass, the cathedral was full. Everybody was talking; the place was loud. Children ran everywhere, along the aisles, into the sanctuary, screaming, rolling, and playing tag. The adults ate sandwiches. Vendors refreshed them as money, food, and drink passed in the pews from hand to hand. The scene was wild. More lights came on, illuminating the cathedral brilliantly, to thunderous applause. The vicar general appeared and chased the children from the sanctuary. By the marble altar rail, on the marble step, a drunken youth lay fast asleep. The Bishop of León, a portly Italian in lace and purple, descended the altar, shook his head, and said, "Psst! Psst!" The youth would not wake up. The bishop returned to his throne to begin the Mass.

The music, from a small organ and choir near the front, was disappointing. After the Gospel, the bishop sat in an armchair before the high altar, in a golden chasuble and miter, and delivered his Christmas homily. No Theology of Liberation here; he spoke in traditional pieties of the coming of the Christ Child and the meaning of His birth in times of want. Stabbing the air with his ringed hand, repeating his pieties a hundredfold, he droned on. I slipped out of the cathedral for a cigarette.

The Parque Jerez, the vast plaza in front of the cathedral, was deserted. No, there was a woman in the park, selling soft drinks. Suddenly thirsty, I descended the cathedral steps and asked for a cola. In destitute Nicaragua a vendor never hands you a bottle. Bottles cost money and there are too few of them. She empties the bottle into a tiny plastic bag, adds ice, then ties the bag at the top. You shake the bag to cool the cola, bite a tiny hole from a corner, then suck at the bag. Even plastic bags are scarce because they are made with American machinery, and under the trade embargo the Nicaraguans cannot buy spare parts.

As I sucked my cola, I could hear the bishop through the loudspeakers going on and on about the Christ Child in the manger and I regarded the woman. She seemed well enough fed, but she was very pregnant and already gray, no more than thirty and old before her time. I heard a child, crying softly. I turned to a wooden pushcart, almost full of empty bottles, and there, squeezed among the bottles, was a naked child, an infant girl perhaps a year or more old.

I caressed her auburn filthy hair, and it fell out. At the roots, only very slightly, were tints of orange. Her stomach was distended, and as I felt her little ribs they stuck out.

I had seen such phenomena years before, in Nigeria during the Biafran civil war. The children of Biafra suffered from kwashiorkor, a chronic deficiency of proteins. They had the same wrinkled faces and haunted staring eyes, the utter apathy of aged men and women. They looked like macabre witchcraft dolls, their bald heads tufted with halos of white or reddish hair, their huge eyes popping out from hunger. I did not know whether this naked infant in the pushcart before León cathedral was suffering from incipient kwashiorkor, though the symptoms appeared similar. I picked her up, touched her head and sick body again. She was confused, but not so apathetic she could not whimper. The bishop droned on about the Christ Child. I turned to the woman.

"*¿Es su niña, Senora?* Is this your child?"

"*Claro que sí.* Of course."

"Why don't you feed and clothe her?"

The mother shrugged.

I hesitated. My emotions had been burned in Tegucigalpa by my failure with the orphans who sniffed glue. I wished to take this child from her indifferent mother, pay for her care in some shelter. No, I was a foreigner and a transient, I foresaw a hundred complications from the woman, and I feared that my good deed would be wasted. Good deed? Was my generosity largely literary? I was writing a book: was I simply searching for vivid experience? An elderly French Cardinal once told me, "Never probe too deeply into human motivation, which is always mixed. When one man helps another, *mon cher Edouard,* it is usually to satisfy himself. What matters is the generous act, for regardless of the motivation it causes joy."

Still I had no confidence that my selfish generosity would feed the child or cause her joy. I returned the infant to the pushcart, fumbled in my pocket, and took out five thousand cordobas — barely five dollars on the black market. I handed the money to the mother, said "Feed her," and returned to the cathedral steps. In the days that followed, I noticed the pregnant woman again, in the park with her bottles and plastic bags, and the pushcart. The child was never with her, and I wondered if she were dead. Soon there would be another.

That Christmas, I did not return to Midnight Mass. Instead I lingered on the side porch of the cathedral, pondering the architecture. There was no moon, but even in the dim glare of the street lamps the architecture awed me. The crouching lions, the crenelations, two Corinthian pillars forty feet high embracing the side portal, even in their blackness and neglect, hinted of a lost, rich culture. I thought of the planning that must have been spent on this cathedral, of the decades that architects from Castile or Andalusia must have labored over their drawings, of the kings of Spain who sent treasures and craftsmen, of the monks and common people who raised the stones with their sweat. Suddenly, from inside the cathedral, the whole congregation, those thousands, so irreverent and noisy before the Mass, sang their lungs out. *Gloria, Gloria, Aleluya, en Nombre del Señor.* At my hotel, I fell asleep thinking of the naked child.

14

MY HOTEL was the América, near the cathedral, shabby on the outside, primitive within, no hot water or air conditioning, but the most luxurious that León could offer. At the clandestine exchange rate, meals and lodgings were laughably cheap; for the best room I paid hardly more than a dollar a day. The América was owned by a bourgeois family that had seen better times. They all lived there—parents, children, and grandmother. The hotel was an old, large house, and like all such houses in León it was built around a lovely courtyard full of flowers and palm.

As the days passed I became friendly with R, the owner. He was a becoming, well-read bourgeois, graying at the temples, who also worked in a bank. On days off, he played with his little son, sank into apathy, and let his beard grow. Though he stammered slightly and showed reserve, clearly he was miserable with conditions in Nicaragua and anxious for the future of his class. His friends were voluble. Lawyers, intellectuals, gentleman farmers visited him at night, gossiping on the patio in rocking chairs. When they learned of me, they sought me out. "We're all dying," a landowner said. He had once bred bulls, taken holidays in Andalusia. "There's no credit from the banks because the currency has no value and the farms do not produce. What little we produce, we must sell to the state. I fill out a dozen government forms, then wait a year for a bag of cement." Though not yet old, he was lame from his encounter with Borge's justice. "Ration cards, work, and privileges are in the hands of the state. If I don't do as the state says, I get nothing. When I do as the state says, I get less and less. They'll take my farm next."

These bourgeois sought my company because I was American. Throughout Nicaragua I never ceased to marvel at the ardent pro-Americanism of the middle class, or what was left of it. American blunders and interference in Nicaraguan history made no difference; the United States remained for them the citadel of a free economy, a focus of their values. Though few of them (in León at least) expressed overt sympathy with the counterrevolution, running like a barely visible thread throughout our conversations was their guarded wish that in the end American naked power would save the middle class from the rapacity of the Sandinistas. Not that the Sandinistas, with their rule entrenched, cared any longer for what the middle class thought. They could, if it ever came to that, crush the middle class completely. The idea was part of their poetry:

> We will be new, love
> We will wash away with blood
> the old and depraved,
> The vices, the tendencies,
> The putrid petite bourgeoisie.

These conversations occurred after Christmas. For most of Christmas, I was alone. I sat in the courtyard with a heap of American newspapers, missing my family and our festive meal. Trying not to be homesick, I put aside the newspapers and scribbled in my journal about the Americans I had met in Nicaragua, dividing them into four types.

The first type I thought was mine, people who came to Nicaragua dubious about U.S. policy but otherwise uncommitted, with a wish to be empirical about the Revolution and to judge it on its own merits. This type was not numerous. The second type were the tourists, the confused dentists, aging hippies and Mother Hubbards, the flower children of the 1960s twenty years later, enamored of Sandinista mythology, eager to be deceived, ready to rationalize all of the Revolution's warts — if they noticed any. For them this was a simple struggle of good and evil, and for one's personal credentials Nicaragua was the place to be. This type was very numerous, perhaps tens of thousands over the course of a year. Even diplomats friendly to the Sandinistas mocked them: "They're members of a cult," mused a European ambassador. "They've failed to find a moral center in their own country, so they come to Nicaragua to fulfill their religious aspirations." Tomás Borge laughed at them. He called them "useful idiots."

The third type were more serious. They were the genuine internacionalistas, men and women who made no bones about their commitment to the Revolution and proved it by working in the fields, often near the front lines. They got their hands dirty. One must respect anyone who suffers hardship for a cause. Moreover, since they lived in Nicaragua they knew the country, and as their knowledge grew some became less naive and more critical. This group, numbering over a thousand at any given time, sought, as it were, to be baptized in blood, craving the same kind of sacrament Americans found in fighting fascism during the Spanish Civil War. The Nicaraguans called them "Sandalistas."

The final type was the hard-core left. Evelyn Waugh's description, written of revolutionary Mexico nearly fifty years ago, applies as well to modern Nicaragua: "Besides the holidaymakers and the sentimentalists, there . . . are the ideologues; first in Moscow, then in Barcelona, now in Mexico these credulous pilgrims pursue their quest for the promised land; constantly disappointed, never disillusioned, ever thirsty for the phrases in which they find refreshment." For these Americans in Nicaragua the United States was the enemy and always wrong. Not only Reagan's ephemeral policy but the very nature of the American system itself was evil. They admired Cuba and were convinced that only a full Cuban model in Nicaragua, with all its constraints, could achieve social transformation. Their vocabulary was studded with Marxist code words, they offered their services and advice to government ministries, and they overlapped with types two and three. Yet so far as I could tell these pure ideologues were not numerous.

Generally the American internacionalistas lacked experience of the world, particularly the Third World, outside of Nicaragua. They seemed unknowing that the Sandinista experiment had been attempted, in greater or lesser degree, time and again, in other impoverished nations and had largely failed. Yet even if they knew this I doubt it would have mattered. They were lugubrious with guilt and remorse, without the faintest hint of humor, especially the nuns. For them the heart of the matter was Reagan's policy, which had to be expiated.

Trendy Nicaragua. As I closed my journal, I still did not believe that the drama of Nicaragua could be as intense to young Americans as Spain in the 1930s. Why, that was the time of the Abraham Lincoln Brigade, when Americans fought fascism by laying down their lives, and whoever heard of an Abraham Lincoln Brigade in Nicaragua? I returned to my newspapers; eventually two young Americans approached me on the patio and asked to read them. I asked, "What are you doing in Nicaragua?" They said, "We're with the Abraham Lincoln Brigade."

They were brothers, Lev and Rick, on holiday from building houses for campesinos in Matagalpa. Their father had fought fascism in Spain; they were fighting it in Niacargua, yet with few illusions. Lev said, "I'm pro-Sandinista, but everything at our cooperative is screwed up. The bureaucracy you wouldn't believe. I wonder if they care."

Rick, though more reserved, was as troubled. He admired the Sandinistas for their achievements in public literacy and health — "There's an old man in our cooperative, illiterate before the Revolution, and now he's reading Shakespeare in Spanish" — but land reform was not working. Lev said, "For over a year now, the Abraham Lincoln Brigade has been trying to get ambulances into Nicaragua to carry the sick and wounded. Every day, for the import license, more red tape. Christ, what chaos. Do they care?"

That evening, I invited them to dinner; then we walked to a rock concert at the Institute of Heroes and Martyrs. On the way, in the dim streets, we passed through another art gallery of the proletariat. ¡NO LE

FALTES A LA PATRIA! ¡EL SERVICIO MILITAR ES TU OBLIGACION! ¡A 50 AÑOS SANDINO VIVE! Not a soul seemed to notice those huge billboards: they were part of the landscape, like dead trees.

15

LEON IS an ancient civilization, buried above ground, long the bastion of the Liberal party, and once the capital of Nicaragua. This made the Conservatives of Granada quite unhappy, and they fought León in civil wars which even transfer of the capital to Managua could not solve. The city was the scene of barbaric fighting between Somoza and the Sandinistas in 1979. At least five thousand civilians died, bodies littered the streets, and the stench of death lingered even into peace. Somoza's makeshift air force, having no more bombs, dropped immense Molotov cocktails on the civil population, incinerating parents and their children. With the Triumph, the Sandinistas dragged National Guardsmen and other somocistas from their redoubts and shot them.

León has an old university and is still the intellectual capital; elderly people seldom venture from their antique houses of white adobe and red tile during the heat of day and remain in their gardens reading Cervantes. This is a city of churches, of a dozen fantastic temples— El Calvario, La Merced, La Recolección—whose crumbling baroque grows tawny in the sunset. The church of the Subtiava is nearly five centuries old, built over Indian catacombs. Inside, men and women mournfully chant responses of the rosary to the music of clarinet, accordion, and trumpet; on the porch, their children merrily explode firecrackers, for that is the rubric. A moment: a priest in his undershirt arrives on a bicycle at El Calvario. He pauses; a woman nearby is screaming at a policeman: "For you Sandinistas misery is a business!" Impassively—has he heard it before?—the priest rolls his bicycle into the vestry. The Mass is crowded, for León is seized by a religious revival. The poor look to heaven to soothe their hardship; urchins wear rosaries on their necks. Another moment: in a bookshop, an old woman, her body covered with boils, buys a tiny flask of Resistol. She leaves, and I tell the lady that her customer will sniff the glue. The lady sighs: "Isn't that a shame?"

The lady, well groomed and pregnant, sells more bric-a-brac and glue than books. She has few books, or, rather, the shop is stacked with Sandinista books by Sergio Ramírez and Jaime Wheelock and books printed in East Germany full of Marxist exegesis and Lenin's childhood but little else. I ask her how they sell. "Nobody buys them," she answers. Did no one from the university still write books? "I haven't seen any." And what of the great Rubén Darío, who was of León? Had she none of his poetry? "No." I sighed. At last she sympathized with my frustration: "Isn't that a shame?"

Luckily R, my landlord, had all of Darío's verse. For several days, too intimidated by the heat to go outside, I sat in the courtyard and read Darío's poetry and his life. He was born in 1867 in poverty at Metapa (now named Darío, after him), outside León. He lived most of his life in Argentina, Paris, and Madrid but returned to León to die before he reached fifty. His bohemian youth confirmed him in habits of wine and satyriasis, and his early verses are odes to Eros. Much influenced by the French symbolists, he was nonetheless a genius of new word forms, labyrinthine singsong rhyme schemes, and his innovations prefigured Ezra Pound: *month of roses. My poems / wander through the vast forest / to gather honey and fragrance / from the half-opened flowers.* Darío's influence on modern Spanish verse has been unrivaled; he is acknowledged now as probably the greatest poet Latin America has produced. Indeed, it was his example and success that turned Nicaragua into a nation of poets.

For all his obsession with lust, with bucolic nymphs and Aphrodite, with *"el abrazo imposible de la Venus de Milo,"* the preposterous embrace of the love goddess, Darío to his last breath was intensely Catholic, forever brooding on the mystery of God and over his own dual nature. In a timeless essay, Pablo Antonio Cuadra (possibly Nicaragua's greatest living poet) identifies Darío's duality, the unceasing war between soul and flesh, as the core of his poetry and of the Nicaraguan character itself. In one of his poems, Darío laments that *"siempre quiero ser otro, / y en que, dos en mi mismo, triunfa uno de los dos?"* He wished always to be other, and being two in himself, he wondered which of his two would conquer. Cuadra seizes on this lament, this *"dos-en-mi-mismo"* — two-in-myself, as opening endless doors into the "fused contradictions" and mysterious duality not only of the poet but of the Nicaraguan people.

Even before I read Darío, I brooded on this duality. How could a people so ardently religious be so wildly sexual? All religious men are dual, they have their human nature; a man without passions is not a full man, but in Nicaraguans such ambivalence is raised to the twelfth power. The more I considered the mystery the more, and the less, I understood. Lust touched all levels of society, but among the poor its consequence was tragic. It seemed to me that the greater blame belonged to the men, not only to their natural machismo but to their reckless insouciance as fathers. They seduced women maniacally, with no heed to the number of their bastards. Yet the woman was complacent, too, pleading she needed a lover to survive but knowing he would walk out.

The sexual life of poor girls often begins with puberty. Girls and boys, brothers and sisters, cousins, parents, uncles, aunts, grandmothers live together in tiny shacks and share the same beds. In the country they have no electricity, so when the sun sets they go to bed because they have nothing else to do. Or the adolescents slip out of the house and meet in darkness by the river, where their bodies join. When the girl is with child, she and her beloved, both penniless, may go to the city in search of work. There is no work, they live with relatives in an open-sewer slum, and the cycle resumes. Christopher Dickey describes it well: "Each morning you wake to the grit of dust on your body that seeps into your bed through the wide cracks between the rough boards that make your walls. Sweat turns the dust to rivulets. Sex turns the dust to mud. The men who live in the slums are used up by their work and if they don't work, they're used up by the bottle. And the women are used up by the men. Sex most often begins as rape, and it begins young. A woman looks for a protector. Relations are informal, brutal and one-sided. Marriage is rare and largely irrelevant. Children are everywhere."

Hungry children are the saddest result of Rubén Darío's mysterious duality. As in Honduras, in León also my life intersected with street children — but in a happier way.

Each evening when the sun was down and the streets a little cooler, I left the América and walked to Sesteo's, a café-restaurant facing the cathedral. El Sesteo was the watering place of *le tout León*. The food was meager and always terrible, but the beer, when they had it, was ice cold. Within a few nights my presence was anticipated, and as soon as I sat at my sidewalk table people were asking permission to join me.

Nicaraguans love to meet strangers, and they love to talk. Many of my table guests were soldiers, either in uniform or in mufti for Christmas leave. A few recited the standard speech about U.S. aggression, but most did not bother. I cannot remember a conversation with those young men that they did not eventually bring around to the same subject: *la miseria*. The army fed the soldiers well enough, but their families were barely managing to survive. "When will the misery end?" one soldier asked me, as though certain I knew the answer. He had no arm. I said nothing. The lights, all over León, went out again. We sat in darkness for a while, sipping our beer, and when electricity was restored my armless friend was gone. A child approached me, with a white begging bowl for scraps of food. I invited him to dinner.

His name was Armando, barefoot, with a dirty headband, about eight years old. He did not want to eat at Sesteo's: the owner knew him and would throw him out. He led me down the street, past the fire station, past a high wall covered with a looping snake labeled "CIA," to another restaurant. This was the Coronado, but Armando and all other children called it the "Azul y Blanco," blue and white. It was almost open air, with wide doors and grilled walls painted blue and white. I ordered dinner, *bistec encebollado*, a beefsteak heaped with onions and shreds of raw cabbage, but the meat was as tough as wood and as usual I barely touched it. Other children, barefoot boys and girls, stared with envy at Armando through the grilled walls. I invited them to join us, and by the end of the meal there were half a dozen children at my table.

Thereafter, I returned to the Azul y Blanco every night, looking for the children. As the afternoon ticked by I grew impatient: my meal with the urchins had become my feast. *What matters is the generous act, for regardless of the motivation it causes joy.* Reconciled at last with my imperfect motivations, I made a new rule: You can't save them, but at least you can feed them. *Get them through today.*

Armando had many friends. One of them, Enrique, who said he was eight but looked six, might have been one of Botticelli's cherubs had he ever washed. Enrique was brash and sly, in the way of the street. He was a businessman. He sold newspapers. Every night he dashed barefoot into the Azul y Blanco balancing a pile of newsprint on his head and a dirty little bag around his shoulder in which he kept rolls of worthless cordobas. He sold *Barricada, El Nuevo Diario, La Prensa,* and the tabloid of the Sandinista Jesuits, *El Tayacán.* He loved to haggle on the price, claiming he had half a dozen mouths to feed. I believed him: invariably he was followed by a small army of hungry children, Sergio and José and Antonio and Rosita and Carmen, whom he intro-duced as his brothers and sisters. Despite his tiny size, Enrique was clearly the king. They imitated everything he did.

One night Enrique appeared at Azul y Blanco with his whole court, demanding to be fed. I was about to leave and told him that I could not feed so many children. Just then a soldier dropped a coin in the juke box: a samba. Enrique put down his newspapers and danced. Ah, the twirls, the rolling eyes, the movements of his chubby arms and bare feet, the giggles as he grabbed his little "sister" and did turns around my table. Now all the children, maybe nine or ten, were dancing. I had seen Nureyev in Paris: he was less pleasing. Later, as the children munched on their tortillas, I asked Rosita, no more than seven, where she lived. "In the park," she said.

16

AFTER THE NEW YEAR, I traveled throughout Nicaragua's northwestern and central provinces — the departments of León, Chinandega, Estelí, Madriz, Nueva Segovia, Jinotega, and Matagalpa. I paused at La Trinidad, in Estelí, to visit the public hospital.

Only months before, the contras had invaded La Trinidad, shooting up the town, attacking the health center, killing civilians, until the Sandinistas sent in helicopters and chased them out. Today, even in tranquillity, the hospital was overcrowded with the sick and bereft of equipment, antibiotics, morphine, even of pillows. Chips of paint and plaster were flaking from the walls and ceilings and dropping into wounds; men, women, and children gazed forlornly from their untidy beds; in the operating chamber the patients had to be strapped down and the Cuban surgeon coped as best he could without benefit of anesthesia.

An American worked here as a nurse, one Joe Poe, a slight bald man in a beard and plastic eyeglasses as thick as milk bottles. He had studied epic poetry at Columbia University; here he dressed wounds, bathed the elderly, dumped bedpans for no salary. In journalism I learned to ask dumb questions: "Why are you doing this, Joe?"

"To make a statement."

"To whom?"

"Ronald Reagan."

"Do you think he's listening?"

"If only we had *pillows*."

For my conscience I contributed to his pillow fund. In his room, Joe

Poe kept a large portrait of Lenin and he was more Christian than I could ever be.

My next days were a fugue through the provinces: visits to schools, clinics, churches, private farms, collective farms, bean crops, coffee crops, cotton growers, cattlemen, a bishop, the bourgeoisie, campesinos displaced by the contras, Sandinista officials high and low, and many of the common people. The landscapes were sublime: rolling plains with fruit trees in León and Chinandega, deep valleys with parched earth, sacks of coffee brought in for harvest, cool rain forest in the highlands and jagged mauve mountain peaks the farther I ventured north. Everywhere soldiers were on the roads, walking or hitching rides. I picked them up. A soldier near Totogalpa: "My salary is six thousand cordobas a month [about six dollars]. I have a wife and two children. The army gives me nothing, except my uniform. I can't feed my family." A recurring image of Nicaragua: dark men with rusty crowbars changing tires as smooth as marble. In Estelí, I must sleep in the same room with my driver Julio at a hovel called the Mira Flor. He snores, but he is not my sole companion. Before taking to his bed Julio removes his best tires (as smooth as marble) from the wheels of his taxi, and I sleep with the tires against my feet.

It is fashionable among the Reaganites to belittle the achievements of the Sandinistas in public literacy and health as mythical or at most inconsequential. The facts favor the Sandinistas. In the early years of the Revolution, their campaigns of "alphabetization," vaccination, and preventive medicine throughout town and country yielded real results. The official claim that more than four fifths of the populace learned to read and write may be inflated, but the crowded schools and courses for adults are evidence that more than half the poor have learned the rudiments. Health care was even better. The Sandinistas inoculated children against diphtheria, whooping cough, measles, tetanus, tuberculosis, poliomyelitis, and the rate of infant deaths dropped dramatically. They established a network of urban and rural health clinics that now have no medicine, but the infrastructure exists should the war end and Nicaragua know a better time. It is more on the mark to ask whether a communist dictatorship is necessary to teach reading and arithmetic and to vaccinate poor children. The right-wing governments of El Salvador and Guatemala, whatever one thinks of them, also vaccinate their young and teach their citizens to read, though in literacy they have been less thorough.

Walk into any Nicaraguan primary school. The first-grade writing text, printed (with an acknowledgment) in East Germany, is an unabashed indoctrination pamphlet. One of the first phrases any child must copy out is *"niños sandinistas"* — Sandinista children. *"Toño es un niño sandinista"* — Toño is a Sandinista child. *"Carlos Fonseca nos enseñó el camino* — Carlos Fonseca taught us the way . . . FSLN." And, naturally, *"Sandino combatió a los yanquis"* — Sandino fought the Yankees. *"El FSLN guió y guia las luchas del pueblo"* — the Sandinista Front led and leads the struggles of the people. *"¡Vivan los heroicos guerrilleros!* — Long live the heroic guerrillas!" As the child advances through higher grades, through mathematics, history, and geography, the drumbeat grows more shrill: all disciplines are made to correspond with the loves and anathemas of the party. By the time Toño reaches high school, he is ready for the unexpurgated *Fundamentos de filosofía marxista-leninista: materialismo dialectico, materialismo historico, critica a la filosofía y la sociología burguesas contemporaneas.*

Sandinista luminaries never hid their purpose to turn all education to the service of the party. Father Fernando Cardenal, the Jesuit who was first director of the national literacy crusade and is now minister of education, announced soon after the Revolution that he saw the crusade as a "great schoolhouse for political formation." Tomás Borge added that "we must educate the new generations in determined values, not vague and abstract, but the values of the Revolution . . . without any concessions . . . and [with] adequate mechanisms of control."

It has been done. *Control* is the obsession of sandinismo, in education, commerce, agriculture, religion, all sectors of human life. A nun in Estelí: "This is a religious school, but we can teach religion only two hours a week. The rest of the curriculum is controlled by the state, the books are provided by the state, the salaries of teachers, lay and religious, are paid by the state." A priest in Estelí: "Our bishop tries to get along with the Sandinistas, but the state has taken away all our social services to the poor. We are confined exclusively to evangelization." A coffee farmer in Nueva Segovia: "Look there, that's all my farm, from here in the valley to the foot of the mountain. Do you like Nicaraguan coffee? It's the richest in the world, and I'm going broke. In theory, this is a pluralist economy and more than half is private enterprise. In fact, all our production, export, and prices are controlled by the state. The state pays me nine thousand cordobas per quintal [about 100 pounds] and five American dollars as an incentive. It sells the coffee for two hundred twenty-five dollars a quintal to the Europeans, and Nicaragua is going broke. The coffee crop's not bad this year, but the rest of agriculture is disastrous.''

Sandinista officials in the rural areas received me graciously. They took me to their cooperative farms, explained patiently how land reform, liberal credits, and Russian tractors had improved the life of their campesinos, but everywhere I looked I saw only familiar poverty. These campesinos, too, were ''as poor as the needle which clothes the people but which itself remains unclad'' (Egyptian wisdom). Land reform, so noble to the Sandinista soul, seemed too hurried and ambitious on the land itself, relying on resources that did not exist.

Peasants were given land titles that their children often could not inherit, making the family in effect tenants of the state. The prices of their crops were theoretically negotiable, but in practice the prices and the campesinos' salaries were fixed by the state. With the cordoba almost worthless the campesinos both on state and private farms had no incentive to produce. So, passively they resisted the state, growing only enough food to feed their families. Peasants who worked six hours a day under Somoza worked less than three now. With so little foreign exchange, the Sandinistas' economy had descended into a vicious spiral. They could not earn foreign exchange because their exports were declining. They could not increase exports because they had no hard currency to buy tractors, fertilizers, spare parts. Thus, the harvest each year was more meager still, and their foreign earnings tumbled. A campesino in Madriz: ''Under Somoza we were poor. Under Sandino, we are miserable.'' A clerk in Matagalpa: ''Ten years ago, when I got a dollar, I hung it on the wall. Today, if I get a dollar, I buy food.''

Mismanagement, ideology, inflation, a debased currency, flight of capital — at least $1 billion since the Revolution — the effect is palpable as I progress from province to province. In Matagalpa, the private association of farmers and cattlemen keep symbols on their walls — pictures of John Paul II, Cardinal Obando, and Dr. Lino's testimonials on human rights. Symbols of protest, badges of the bourgeoisie, but pictures of the Cardinal and the Sovereign Pontiff are as common in the hovels of the poor, and rarely do I see a portrait of Sandino.

Occasionally I see some housing projects, but most new housing seems to be reserved for members of the party, that elite vanguard of twenty-five thousand faithful. The ''masses'' and ''the poor'' are abstractions to the Sandinistas as they are to the rest of us. The ''good'' masses and the "good" poor support the Revolution; the poor who oppose the Revolution are not the "real" poor. In Jinotega, I visit some campesinos relocated by the state from contra country farther north. My Sandinista host exhorts me: "See how happy they are in their new homes. Before they had nothing, now everything." The campesinos live in communal shacks without clean water and scratch out a new life on the side of a hill, planting potatoes and cabbage. They wear white rosaries on their necks.

Another sign, spray-painted in Matagalpa: ¡YANQUI LES RESPONDER-EMOS COMO EN VIETNAM! A dissident journalist in _____ whispers to me which of the comandantes on the National Directorate are homosexual and which members of the cabinet, including which priests. I had heard such gossip in Managua. Sandinista officialdom, high and low, ask me in so many words, "What is Ronald Reagan *really* like?" I develop a standard answer: "He sleeps a lot. He gets up, has breakfast, goes downstairs to his office. He sees a few people, has lunch, takes a nap, sees a few people, watches television, and goes to bed. He's very ideological, but sometimes he bends. He dictates the outlines of policy but hates details. He's a good actor and has great presence. He was formed by Hollywood and tells very funny Hollywood stories. He's ignorant but not stupid. He sleeps a lot." They seem delighted to have this information.

From the displaced campesinos in southern Jinotega I drive farther north in the direction of the Honduran border. The roads become ever more impassable, and Julio resists going on for fear that his rusty Datsun will break down. Besides, we are nearing contra country. We pass cooperatives that have been attacked, and campesinos tell us that roads ahead are mined. Minor battles rage from time to time along the border, but as I creep northward the army intercepts me and turns me back. I retrace my route, wander in circles, proceed eventually to Ocotal, near Honduras in Nueva Segovia, the scene of Sandino's famous battle with Captain Hatfield.

At dusk I sought out the pastor of the Parish of the Assumption, a Spanish Jesuit educated in Madrid, a Basque I think. This encounter was eerie. I looked through a wooden fence and in the fading light saw the padre crouched in his garden, pulling weeds from a patch of squash and cabbages, wearing a campesino's wide straw hat. The scene seemed out of Georges Bernanos, from his portrait of a rural priest. Bernanos begins: "Mine is a parish like all the rest. Good and evil are evenly distributed. I look out over the village, from the road to Saint Vaast along the hillside — miserable little houses huddled together under the ugly sky. This village was my parish. I stood there watching it sink into the dusk . . .'' Through the wooden fence I call into the garden. "Padre? Padre?"

Padre T rises from his cabbages, walks to the fence. "Who are you? What do you want?" I explain. He invites me inside his cement house, but his hospitality is cool. He is a big, rawboned man, maybe forty, with a red-brown beard. He wears rough blue trousers and a white shirt rolled to his sleeves. He explains that he cannot offer me anything because his cupboard is bare. I reply that I did not come for food or drink. He lifts a large glass jug and says, "See? Not even water." I believe him that he lives in holy poverty, but I wonder why he boasts of it.

"This is a society of peasants," he begins. The peasants were very traditional, hidebound by the customs of clan since the reign of Philip II. They hoped always for a better life but had no confidence before the Revolution. Padre T was the only priest in a poor parish five hundred miles square. "We used to have two other priests," he said mournfully. "Spanish like myself. One went away, and the other — he was too friendly to the Revolution — was expelled by the Bishop of Estelí."

I objected that the Bishop of Estelí was known as more sympathetic to the Revolution than was Cardinal Obando. "There is no unity in the Nicaraguan Church," Padre T said bitterly. "It is deeply divided." Cardinal Obando and the other bishops were trying to turn Nicaragua into another Poland, to establish the Church as a base of resistance to the Revolution. The People's Church, of which Padre T was proudly a member, wanted a dialogue with the bishops, but the bishops refused.

I interjected, "I've been traveling through Nicaragua. I've found little support among the people for the People's Church. They flock to the ancient mysteries of the official Church."

Padre T sighed. "That's true," he said. "The people prefer the traditional faith." Yet the Popular Church offered hope to future generations. "I help the government to help the people. I get aid from the Catholic Church in England. We've installed potable water systems, bought small trucks, we manufacture clothes, for the people's cooperatives. This is Christ in action. However, the economy is low. We're in a state of war. Do you want a list of the contra atrocities I've seen with my own eyes?" He recounted stories of children, old women, pregnant women dispatched horribly to the next life within the boundaries of his parish. The true mission of the Church in Nicaragua was to support the Sandinistas in their struggle against aggression, to support Christ against violence.

"But Cardinal Obando and the other bishops refuse. They've never condemned the counterrevolutionaries, or spoken in favor of *el servicio militar patriótico*, patriotic military service, against contra massacres. The Pope doesn't understand Nicaragua or the needs of the Nicaraguan Church. The Pope and the bishops have committed a sin in Nicaragua in not condemning the counterrevolution. In effect, the Pope and bishops are sending arms to the contras. They are accomplices of the United States and the counterrevolution by their *silence*. They are guilty of vertical authoritarianism. This does not conform to the will of Christ, *no conforma a la voluntad de Jesucristo.*"

He paused. We were sitting in darkness now at a rude table, and Padre T did not rise to turn on the light. Perhaps there was no light; maybe the electricity was cut again. In the gloom he raised the empty jug another time. "So sorry I can't offer you anything to drink." I respected him because he was helping people and lived in holy poverty; like Joe Poe, in practice he was more Christian than I could ever be. Yet his statement that the Pope and bishops did not conform to the will of Christ bemused me. I wondered, *How does he know?* Could anyone on earth be certain of the will of Christ? Yet as he talked on, extolling the love of Marxists for the poor, quoting Gandhi that "Christians don't believe in Christ," insisting that the masses must be leavened and that many Marxists of his acquaintance were more Christian than the Christians, I thought I understood. I was back in my Jesuit high school. I sat across the table from a stern Jesuit about to discipline me for some boyish infraction. He spoke in disappointed tones of my refusal to obey the Sacred Heart of Jesus and the Heart of His Immaculate Mother. Padre T was just like that. Ever arrogant, the Jesuits, ever certain. The old dogmas they had sworn oaths to us would never change they had dumped for new ones just as hard. But if the sermon now was different, the method was the same.

I am too harsh. As Padre T talked on in the darkness, my resentment was mastered by my emotions of respect. He loved Christ, he lived in holy poverty, he helped the poor. In the end, what more could I ask of any priest? Bernanos ends: "*He did not seem to hear me. But a few minutes later he put his hand on mine, and his eyes entreated me to draw closer. He uttered words. 'Does it matter? Grace is every-where . . .' "*

17

FROM OCOTAL I returned to Matagalpa en route back to the capital. Radio Sandino, amplified in the Parque Central, blared constant warnings against "speculators," with a telephone number to report such criminals of the black market. This city in the heart of Nicaragua teemed with soldiers and military trucks. In a murky restaurant where I went for breakfast, nearly all the tables were taken by young soldiers consuming black coffee and hot beans. As I waited to be seated, five soldiers in green camouflage, bearing Kalashnikov automatics, entered and waited with me.

From their shoulder patches I knew they belonged to a BLI — Batallón de Lucha Irregular, elite troops who specialized in search-and-destroy missions against the contras. These were the best troops in a defense force that was named not for the nation but for the party — Ejército Popular Sandinista, the Sandinista People's Army. That army numbered perhaps sixty thousand men, with as many again in reserve, remarkable for such a small country. The BLI troops were renowned for their flair in killing. One of them here, very young, dark, and too handsome, oozed killing. You knew that from his movements, as he fingered his sheathed knife in impatience for his breakfast, then bounded, foxlike, predatory, to his table when the waitress summoned him to eat.

The road from Matagalpa to Managua was crowded with East German IFA military trucks, transporting soldiers and equipment. Soldiers, in clusters or alone, stood along the highway, hitching rides. I had picked up enough soldiers in the provinces; now I had my pick of pregnant women.

It seemed to me that half the women over sixteen years in Nicaragua were with child. So many of these women were beautiful when very young, but constant childbearing decayed their beauty much too soon, turning them into dark and formless shapes. They stood along the highway in the shadow of a far volcano, laden with bags of clothes and vegetables, hitching rides, shouting curses at the cars that passed them by. A pregnant woman on the highway curses me, so I tell Julio to stop and pick her up. She is on her way to the market in Managua to sell cheap sandals; her bundle takes up half my tiny taxi. She has green eyés, is plump for all the food rationing, and turns out to be a flirt. She calls me "Señorito."

"How gracious of you, Señora," I reply. "No one has called me *señorito* since I lived in Spain, and I was very young."

"You're still young, Señorito."

"That was nearly thirty years ago."

"*No puede ser*. It can't be ten."

"Are there no buses from Matagalpa to Managua?"

"They're so old and crowded. I'd lose my child."

"How many children have you?"

"Four."

"How old are you, Señora?"

"Your age, when you lived in Spain, Señorito."

Signs along the highway: ¡TODAS LAS ARMAS AL PUEBLO! . . . ¡VEN-CEREMOS! . . . ¡NO PASARAN! . . . ¡SANDINO VIVE! At the crossroads, mobs of campesinos rush at my car, waving cabbages, bananas, mangoes, and fresh pineapple, desperate for my worthless cordobas. Stupidly I buy no fruit, and in Managua back at the Siete Mares I curse my improvidence. There is no water, no jam, no beer, no telephone, and no fruit. This in a country whose trees drip with fruit. Could the Sandinistas blame Reagan and the contras for no fruit in the capital? This I ask of Viktor, my Czech friend, who says, in halting English, "Fuck the communism." He is on his way to his room upstairs with two very young girls, and already he is very drunk. I walk to the Intercontinental to take my dinner.

In the bar, I run into Oliver, the Tory writer, large, bespectacled, faintly florid, curious about my trip to the interior. I tell him, "The campesinos, everybody, are on the edge. I saw a daily struggle to survive. Not much food, but no famine. Enormous discontent with the Sandinistas, but not much sympathy for the contras either. The whole country is in a state of torpor, waiting for the war to end."

Oliver says, "It won't end, and can't end, until the Sandinistas are chucked out. Ah, Nica-land. Have you ever seen a worse government?"

"In many places, and much worse. The Congo, Nigeria . . ."

"Chucked out!"

"Come on, Oliver. You've seen the suffering. Communism left in peace is preferable to this. The Sandinistas spend half their resources on the war. Some of the suffering is due to them, to their ideology and mismanagement, but the rest is Reagan's fault."

"You mean the trade embargo? If the Sandinistas didn't have the embargo, they'd invent it. The blockade's a godsend to absolve them of their economic wreckage and stupidity.''

"Oliver, one way or another, my country is starving Nicaragua. Have you no compassion for the people?''

"More than you do. I'm looking to the great future, to the long gray night of another poor nation condemned to the preposterous solutions of Marxism. Furthermore . . .''

18

IN MATAGALPA, I had called on the bishop of that province, a gracious Franciscan who told me he would not talk politics. We spent two hours talking politics. In Sandinista Nicaragua, politics clings to religion as lice cling to the scraggly beards of troglodytes. Religion obsesses Nicaraguans, Central America at large: one cannot begin to grasp the agony in that garden unless one glimpses the various versions of Christ reliving His passion, His "sweat as it were great drops of blood falling down to the ground.'' The battles between the Sandinistas on the one side, their feeble internal opposition and the armed counterrevolution on the other, all the acrid polarization of the secular society, were reflected and magnified in the de facto schism between the Nicaraguan bishops and the Sandinista priests within the Roman Church. The Bishop of Matagalpa coped with the government as best he could; he had his woes, but he was less anathema to the Sandinistas than was Cardinal Obando and not nearly as embroiled. On the morning after my return to Managua, I called on the primate at the Curia near his procathedral on the outskirts of the capital.

I had no appointment. Early that Thursday morning the Cardinal's antechamber was already crowded with men, women, and children; priests, monks, and nuns; the poor and the better off; a mother with a deaf daughter whom she hoped the Cardinal could somehow help. On the wall was a photograph from the *New York Times* that suggested the Cardinal's sense of irony: the front page of the *Times* of December 30, 1974, showing Monseñor Obando, much leaner then, leading to safety the hostages whom the Sandinistas had seized in their renowned Christmas raid. The release of the hostages liberated Sandinistas in Somoza's jails; dryly the Cardinal was wont to tell visitors that without his mediation Nicaragua's present rulers might be dead. Now, in a black clerical short-sleeved shirt, swinging a thick black briefcase, the Primate of Nicaragua bounces into his office: "*¡Buenos dias todos!*"

I waited for him several hours. During my absence in the provinces, Tomás Borge's censor, Captain Nelba Blandón, had permanently shut down Radio Católica. Now the official Church was silenced in its last public forum. The Holy See uttered cries of pain and outrage. Captain Blandón explained that the radio had failed to broadcast President Ortega's New Year message. Furthermore, Radio Católica had persisted in its fictitious allegations of religious persecution in Nicaragua, inciting the populace to disorder and disobedience, aligning religion with the aggression and the counterrevolution. I mulled over the incanted rhetoric in *Barricada* as I cooled my heels in the Cardinal's antechamber. Finally, Josefa, the Cardinal's matronly secretary, says I might see His Eminence for five minutes.

I enter a dark, monastic room with a dripping air conditioner. The primate sits plumply behind a simple desk beneath an oil copy of Velázquez's *Crucifixion*. I greet him in Latin: "*Benedictus qui venit in nomine Domini . . . sit nomen Domini benedictum.* Blessed is he who cometh in the name of the Lord: blessed be the name of the Lord." I kiss his ring: he seems pleased.

"*Ex hoc nunc et usque in saeculum.* From now until the end of time," he answers, in the Latin rubric he knows so well. In Spanish: "*¿Usted es sacerdote?* Are you a priest?"

"*No, Eminencia, soy escritor.* No, Eminence, I'm a writer."

We talked for nearly an hour. The Cardinal, who can bubble with irony and wit when the spirit moves him, was mournful this day to the point of anger. "We are being silenced," he said. "We can no longer preach the Gospel. The state is monopolizing all instruments of communication." I agreed that his situation was sad, but wasn't the Church in other countries much worse off, the victim not simply of such harassment but of violent persecution? "It's a *form* of persecution," the Cardinal continued, compounded by other strategems of the state, the imprisonment of laymen, the drafting of seminarians, the expulsion of priests, the prohibition of Masses and processions in the open air. The state could not tolerate a popular cardinal surrounded by multitudes of his people: such fervor was "subversive." Indeed "the faithful are like a bunch of matches: the state is not breaking us together, but in pieces, one by one." That was the tactic of the state as the harassment turned to open persecution, and the persecution worsened.

But the state's most treacherous stratagem, His Eminence suggested, was its promotion of the Popular Church. Here was the timeless tactic of divide and rule. In *Barricada* and other organs of the party, the official Church, including the august person of the Sovereign Pontiff, was incessantly mocked, but the Iglesia Popular, the so-called Church of the People, was exalted as the voice of God. Here was the cynicism of Tomás Borge and the other comandantes in its most naked form, for these men were implacable Marxist determinists and, in a word, atheists. Yet the priests of the Popular Church, protesting they remained in communion with Rome, were all too eager to dance to the music of the comandantes. The comandantes rewarded them, giving them money, privileges, generous access to radio and television that was now denied completely to the Cardinal and his steadfast faithful. The Popular Church was an arm of the state created to infest the body of Christ with insurrectionaries and spies, to proclaim the propaganda of the state, to twist the Gospel of Christ into slogans for the state. For the state would tolerate only a Church that served its purpose of violence, hate, and class warfare. Juridically the priests of the Popular Church were in communion with Rome, but in practice they were schismatics.

The Nicaraguan people in their wisdom were not deceived. Support among the masses for the Popular Church was pathetically small. Nor was Rome deceived. The Holy Father had suspended the disobedient priests in the cabinet *a divinis,* from all their sacerdotal faculties, and Heaven bless him, for he had done well. And, "No, no, I've nothing to do with the contras. I'm against all violence. I favor dialogue, civilization, reconciliation, and pardon. It doesn't depend on me. Nicaragua has become a Ping-Pong ball between the superpowers. I oppose all violent solutions. It doesn't depend on me."

Josefa entered, reminding the Cardinal of other visitors. I rose to leave, asking in my farewells about the supposed six thousand political prisoners in Borge's jails. The Cardinal leaped to his short legs. "¡Hay al menos *seis mil presos políticos!* There are *at least* six thousand political prisoners!" he said, nearly shouting. In a torrent of Spanish he acted out their plight, pressing his palms against his temples, hurling imaginary men to the floor. "They squeeze their heads like this and beat them on the ground. They give them no food or sleep for three or four days. In Managua, too, they torture them psychologically and physically . . ." I withdrew, touched by the primate's bucolic force.

Soon I visited UCA, the University of Central America, bastion of liberation theology and the Sandinista Jesuits. UCA was financed by the state, not only for its budget but the salaries of Jesuits and lay professors alike. The mood of that modern campus, full of airy cement buildings that in the wet air were beginning to erode, differed little from party headquarters. ¡MUERTE AL YANQUI INVASION, MAS DISCIPLINA EN EL COMBATE MILITAR, MAS ESFUERZO EN EL TRABAJO DIARIO! Beneath the red and black flag of sandinismo, beneath an entire wall splashed with the portrait of Comandante Julio Buitrago Urroz, PADRE DE LA RESISTENCIA URBANA 1944–1969, clusters of young men and women bandied Marxist phrases back and forth like tennis balls: ". . . *la lucha de clases . . . la explotación del hombre por el hombre* . . ." This seemed a parody of Cardinal Obando's jeremiad but days before.

I was not, however, prepared for my encounter with the rector. I have rarely met a stupid Jesuit, and in Padre César Jerez I recognized at once a deep intellect and a learned theologian. Padre Jerez was Guatemalan, Indian of aspect, with copper skin and white hair, indifferently dressed in a sport shirt and khaki slacks. Once the provincial (superior) of all Jesuits in Central America, he had probably studied in the United States and he spoke perfect English. He was one of those Jesuits whose talent was detected early in seminary and destined from the first for advancement in the Society of Jesus. In his office, he kept an oil portrait of Saint Ignatius Loyola gazing at bookshelves crammed with the works of Karl Marx. "Marx wrote fifty books," the padre told me later. "I have only twenty-one of them."

I hoped for a fencing match: expecting nuanced answers, I began deliberately with dumb questions. But the father's sword was blunt. I asked, "Have you ever met the Pope?"

"Three times," he said. "I don't want a fourth meeting."

"Why?"

"He's *suspicious*. He receives all his information on Nicaragua from Monseñor Obando, but Nicaragua is not Poland and Cardinal Obando is not Cardinal Wyszynski. We all respect the Holy Father, but his analysis of Nicaragua is bad."

What a sad turn events had taken when the Pontiff studied his dossier on Central America, the learned Jesuit continued. What Nicaragua needed was a Church that would adapt to revolutionary change and remain united in its purpose, but the Pontiff chose division and confrontation when he raised Miguel Obando to the Sacred College. Cardinal Casaroli, the secretary of state, was as dismayed as the Jesuits, and other cardinals at the Holy Roman Curia shared his distress. When the Pontiff pronounced his will, the Cardinal Secretary visited the Nicaraguan ambassador to the Holy See, shaking his head. "He's *done* it," he sighed. "He's created Obando a cardinal." The Jesuits, from the moment of their foundation by Saint Ignatius in the sixteenth century, took a special vow of obedience to the Pope, but it was no secret that their relations with the Pontiff now were extremely strained.

Nowhere was this truer than in Nicaragua. The position of the Jesuits there might be easier were His Eminence more direct with them, but the man dissembled. "In the past he has been friendly and thanked us for our work, but in the meantime he was writing to Rome denouncing us. Communication must be *honest*. I do not enjoy good relations with him now. He's suspicious." Cardinal Obando had convinced the Pope that the Sandinistas were a danger to the Church and must be confronted by a strong leader at the top. He was obsessed with the notion that Nicaragua would become a Marxist-Leninist dictatorship on the Cuban model, but that was a delusion. Christianity and Marxism had already been reconciled: this university was proof. One could never reconcile the *atheism* of Marx with belief in Christ, but the most devout Christian made the truest revolutionary. The heart of the matter was that the official Church was losing its old privileges. For Padre Jerez, it was essential for the future of the Church to avoid confrontation with the state, to evangelize the new Nicaragua not by yearning for the past but by creatively forging a theology that would "meet the new things."

I objected that I found no interest among the Nicaraguan poor for the Theology of Liberation: "They don't understand it, don't want it, or have never heard of it." Like Padre T, the Sandinista Jesuit of Ocotal, Padre Jerez astonished me by responding, "I agree. The people don't care about liberation theology. But they're less enchanted than you think with the political position of Cardinal Obando." And yes, the Sandinistas made mistakes. Sometimes they used religion as a political weapon, but they were politicians, after all. Dialogue between Church and state might heal many wounds, but how was that possible when His Eminence so clearly favored the contras? Why, in Miami, he had even met with Adolfo Calero and other leaders of the counterrevolution. Was it unreasonable to ask the Nicaraguan bishops to condemn the contra-U.S. war when the Roman bishops of Europe, Canada, and the United States had themselves so forthrightly condemned it? Alas, His Eminence saw the Sandinista Revolution as intrinsically evil: and intrinsic evil had to be expunged.

I emerged from this conversation considerably impressed. Padre Jerez had deciphered my predilections moments into our encounter and had adroitly wielded all of his Jesuit craft (positive sense) to win me to his view. I could never follow him into his Marxist thicket, but at least he mildly criticized the Sandinistas, and I admired his immense learning. Yet I was not done with Sandinista ecclesiastics. Soon I saw the defrocked Jesuit, Padre Fernando Cardenal, minister of education, and his defrocked brother, Padre Ernesto, minister of culture.

Reaching the minister of culture was an ordeal. In their ponderous bureaucracy the Sandinistas insisted that all appointments with luminaries of government be arranged by INTERPREN, their office of foreign information. The mills of God grind slowly, but they are swift compared to the gears of a people's republic. Finally, I took the matter into my own hands, rose at dawn, and drove out to Padre Ernesto's ministry to ambush him as he arrived for work.

The Ministry of Culture turned out to be Anastasio Somoza II's old Managua estate, a sort of Deer Park in decay. Here were high walls, fruit trees, almond, cacao, and banyan trees, a tiny stream run dry, Mayan idols chipping off, tottering amber lamps, vast lawns that in their halcyon-sculpted time the dictator must have strolled upon in the mist of similar mornings. I imagined Tacho's goons lurking in the rhododendron, fingering their automatics against phantom assassins. I walked about at leisure, retracing dead Tacho's steps. Behind the rambling white villa was a disused tennis court and an empty swimming pool. I pictured obese Tacho, naked, splashing in the pool with half a dozen lithe, nude women, very young, very blond.

How fitting that Ernesto Cardenal should have this deer park as his ministry, since it was to destroy forever such exotic privilege that he had devoted his priesthood and his poet's life. Paradoxically, the Cardenal brothers were themselves of a privileged family of Conservative Granada. Ernesto's bishop later told me that in Granada the Cardenal brothers "aspired to be noblemen. That could never happen, so they became cabinet ministers instead." Ernesto began his intellectual pilgrimage as an esthete and a pacifist, attending Columbia University in the 1940s to study American literature and poetry. In the 1950s he experienced a profound religious conversion and entered the Cistercian monastery of Gethsemani in Kentucky as "Brother Lawrence." There he grew close to his fellow Trappist and fellow poet Thomas Merton. Father Merton, in his mysticism and contemplation that shut him off so long from the world, knew little of politics. Ernesto set out to educate him, reminding him constantly that the misery of the poor was the product of violence and capitalist exploitation. Eventually Ernesto's health suffered from the rigor of Cistercian observance and he left Gethsemani, but he and Merton corresponded. In the 1960s he tried without success to persuade Merton to come to Nicaragua to live at the monastic commune he had founded on Solentiname, an island in Lake Nicaragua. (Later, Ernesto told me that "Merton was the most important religious influence of my life, but not in poetry. Ezra Pound influenced me most in poetry." Father Merton never lived to witness Ernesto's fame as a revolutionary. In 1968 he died in Thailand.)

As Ernesto's fame in poetry grew in the great world, he underwent a second conversion as powerful in its mystical resonance as his exposure to Thomas Merton and the Cistercians of Silence and the Strict Observance. After founding his commune on Solentiname, he visited Cuba, and in the early 1970s he went to Chile, where he mingled with Marxist Christians. These experiences converted him irrevocably to Marxism. Typically — for Ernesto is that kind of poet — in embracing Marxism he did not abjure his priesthood, he passionately combined the two.

This synthesis was historic, for, more than any other personal act, it created the ideological convergence between Catholicism and sandinismo. From his commune at Solentiname, Ernesto wrote page after page radically reinterpreting Scripture, transforming the four Evangelists into tractarians for political revolution. He seized on Matthew 10:34: *Think not that I am come to send peace on earth: I came not to send peace but a sword.* David Nolan has vividly described this period of Ernesto's development: "In Cardenal's theology, the growth of revolutionary consciousness was the second coming of Christ, the armed struggle represented the Battle of Armageddon, and the communist society, like that of the early Christians, constituted the Kingdom of God on earth . . . Jesus had come, sword in hand, to liberate the oppressed, not to defend the peace of apathetic exploitation, and . . . the will of God demanded armed revolution against the capitalist system."

In Cuba, Ernesto was so touched by the social achievements of Castro's revolution, he declared that if Fidel could avoid bureaucratization the Kingdom of God was at hand on that island. By now Ernesto had abandoned the pacifism of Thomas Merton and the Cistercians of Silence and the Strict Observance, embraced violence in the name of love, and — from the early 1970s until the Triumph — clandestinely harbored

Sandinista guerrillas in the nooks of his island commune. For Ernesto, all of these experiences were deliciously Hegelian: thesis (Christ) plus antithesis (Marx) equals synthesis (sandinismo). At random I choose a passage from one of the four volumes of Ernesto's *El Evangelio en Solentiname,* The Gospel in Solentiname:

> PANCHO: Excuse me, then do you mean that if we follow the word of God, we're communists?
>
> I [ERNESTO]: In that sense yes, because we seek the same perfect society. . . .
>
> REBECA: If we unite as God wills, yes. To be a communist means a society of equals. "Communist," the word, means community. Thus if we unite as God wills, we are all communists, all equals.
>
> WILLIAM: That's what the first Christians practiced, since they owned everything in common. . . .
>
> REBECA: It's community. Communism means community.
>
> TOMAS: This communism says: Love thy neighbor as thyself.

This sort of passage, on page 95 of volume one, continues with variations for another 493 pages. Ernesto's *Gospel* has been much admired throughout the world. I wondered what it might resemble were it applied to real life. Ernesto, who is famous for never altering his dress — blue jeans, white jumper, the black beret I am told he even wears to bed — gives us a hint of how all of us will dress in the Kingdom of God. This is from a book he wrote on Cuba:

> Everybody dresses the way I like to dress. And the way that poets, artists, intellectuals, and students like to dress. And the way Fidel Castro likes to dress. And the way everybody ought to dress everywhere.

However, that is Cuba. Here is Ernesto in the real Nicaragua:

> Comandante [Tomás Borge?], when we went to visit the Sandinista Children's Association
> and in one line of your speech
> was a simple phrase
> "now we are free"
> (it was among other phrases)
> at that very moment
> I saw movement in the stands
> some climbing up and others, very small, working their way down
> one eating an ice cream
> there was movement and even disorder in the happy crowd

of children and young people
hearing the voice magnified by microphones and the loud echo
and I felt that all those children were free, and knew it,
the seven-year-old licking his ice cream, free forever
they will grow up free.

Ernesto wrote that for him the Revolution was "obsessive, like love. The Revolution is like love in that one surrenders oneself to it; the Revolution possesses one more and more. Better yet, revolution *is* love." This passion, the identification of revolution and love, was ardently shared by Ernesto's brother, Fernando, at the Ministry of Education. To the union of revolution and love, Fernando the Jesuit — borrowing language from Saint Paul — added his own obsession of the Nicaraguan "New Man." The New Nicaraguan Man, born of the marriage of revolution and love, rejected "individualism, egoism, materialism, consumerism" (Fernando's words to me) for the "new revolutionary values of love, sacrifice, and justice. The New Man is animated by devotion to the masses and the common good. He seeks above all love and peace. Love and independence are the foundation of the New Man and the New State."

In the United States, I had enjoyed some of Ernesto's earlier poetry, though I recognized his strong reliance on Pound's techniques, but his revolutionary poetry is so political it is almost unreadable. During my tour of the provinces, I met a traditional Jesuit who knew Ernesto and wondered whether an artist who used *mierda* (shit) and *culo* (asshole) in his verse could be seriously considered either a poet or a priest. The Bishop of Matagalpa told me that Ernesto "*toma mucho,* drinks a lot." Cardinal Obando told me Ernesto was "*poco serio*" — a joke. I was dying to meet him.

Finally, at about half-past eight that hot Friday morning, Padre Ernesto arrives for work. He penetrates the high walls in an open jeep, sitting in the front seat beside his bodyguard, a Sandinista soldier. As the jeep approaches, through the fruit and almond trees, past the neglected lawns and the tottering amber lamps, I am astonished. *He is not wearing his beret.* He has a full mane of flowing hair, like his beard as white as a cloud. Am I one of the few ever privileged by this vision? He alights from the jeep, thrusts on his beret, and walks toward me as I wait by the huge poster on the façade of his ministry: portraits of Rubén Darío and General Sandino: A 50 AÑOS SANDINO VIVE. MINISTERIO DE CULTURA.

AUTHOR: "Padre, may I speak to you?"

ERNESTO: "*Sí.*"

A: "I've been trying for five weeks to see you." I explain who I am. "Have you received my request from INTERPREN?"

E: "No. I've never heard of you. I cannot receive you without the authority of INTERPREN."

A: "I am devoted to the memory of Thomas Merton. In his name, Father, would you make this one exception?"

Ernesto pondered, and I noticed then in his bespectacled eyes that Nicaraguan essence that transcends all ideology: he was gracious. "Come in," he said.

I followed the minister and his bodyguard through the rambling villa, up the stairs past an immense portrait of Karl Marx, into his humble office, full of portraits of Carlos Fonseca and other Sandinista martyrs and wooden sculptures, crucifixes, geese, and such, that Ernesto had wrought with his own hand. Even at his desk, he wore the beret.

Surprisingly, his English was halting, so we spoke in Spanish. "I'm still a priest," he said. "The Pope has forbidden me to celebrate the sacraments, but I remain always a priest." The Pontiff had told him at Managua airport, "Choose your priesthood or your political ministry." Ernesto had defied the Sovereign Pontiff, but he remained serene. "Now I achieve the will of God because I serve Him by serving my people." Yet didn't Ernesto resent the Pontiff for wagging his finger at him as he genuflected in respect?

"The Pope humiliated me in public. I don't resent him. I don't resent anybody. He has his own *esquema político*, political agenda. John Paul doesn't understand Nicaragua, our Revolution, or Latin America. He thinks Nicaragua is another Poland."

I winced. If I heard that phrase — "He thinks Nicaragua is another Poland" — another time, I feared to go off my head. I remained calm: "Surely, Padre, you admit that John Paul's social doctrines are progressive?"

"In some respects, but he's not a revolutionary. I'd like him to be a revolutionary. The Pope and the bishops don't want us precisely because we are revolutionaries." How sad this was, because "ours was the first revolution in history made with the massive participation of Christians. It set an example for future revolutions where the population is Christian. The Christian role can be historic in the making of these new revolutions — not against the Church but with the Church.

"There is no contradiction — there never was — between Marx and

Christ, because you can be a Marxist and not an atheist. I declare myself a Marxist Christian. Saint Thomas Aquinas integrated the philosophy of Aristotle into his own philosophy — and Aristotle was a pagan. Thus we can practice the philosophy of Marx without being atheist . . .''

He elaborated variations on this melody, repeating essentially his famous manifesto to a Spanish newspaper in 1978, about a year before the Sandinistas overthrew Somoza. A clear correspondence existed between the classless society of Marx and the Kingdom of God as promised by Christ. Violence was a proper and sadly essential weapon to create the New Society, the New Man, and the Kingdom of God. Ernesto had embraced the Revolution not by reading Marx but by reading Christ. The Gospel made him a Marxist. "Marxism" — I cite the Spanish interview— "is the sole solution for the world.

"True Christianity not only can be — but must be — Marxist . . . The spirit of God is the spirit of liberation, of the revolution . . . Outside the Church there is no salvation, and outside Marxism there is no liberation . . . The revolution and the Kingdom of God of which the Gospel speaks are the same thing . . . God does not want rites, nor prayers, nor incense, what He wants is that the oppressed break their chains and end their exploitation . . . Christ was a revolutionary, and for that he was crucified . . .''

I mentioned Dr. Lino Hernández's documented accusations of Sandinista abuse of political prisoners. "These accusations are false," said Padre Ernesto. "There is no systematic abuse. Isolated cases, perhaps, but the offenders are punished by the police.''

I was tempted to challenge him, but I knew it would be futile. Ernesto *believed* there was no abuse of human rights in his Kingdom of God. If such abuse did not exist, he had no duty to defend it or absolve it.

Tomás Borge, the master policeman, wrote letters to Ernesto as he did to Padre Uriel Molina:

Padre Cardenal:

. . . *Nosotros hemos renunciado a todos los placeres* . . . We have both renounced all the pleasures of life: we cannot even satisfy the elemental need of seeing the street and the incomparable spectacle of human beings coming and going. In a certain sense we are monks, with the difference that death haunts us always. But we are happy . . .

I have seen born [a] new God inside myself — I don't know why He reminds me of my mother — and I see how He grows . . . It will depend on the attitude of the Church, or at least on that part that is honest and progressive, whether this God will grow strong. Or whether on the contrary He will die anew of starvation. If He dies, He will never return to rise again . . . *no volverá a resucitar jamás* . . .

TOMAS BORGE

P.S. The bearer of this letter does not know my identity.

For some days I meditated on the People's Church. I had mellowed toward Ernesto Cardenal: I no longer found him repulsive. He was not King Lear, he was Falstaff and one of the very few of the Sandinista clergy with a sense of humor. He was a screwball, an ecclesiastical hippie, a buffoon who perhaps wore his silly hat to bed, a Marxist poetaster, but rather fun. His eye twinkled when he hurled his thunderbolts, equating Christ and Marx. He contributed to the People's Church at large a faint scent of lunacy.

19

ANOTHER NOCTURNAL CONVERSATION in a vast garden of Managua. The air is warm and moist, there is a half moon, the sky is ablaze with stars. The wives and others are inside the villa, leaving Oliver, Ambassador Z, the West European diplomatist, and me to quarrel, over tumblers of gin and tonic, on deck chairs by a mango tree.

AMBASSADOR Z: When are you leaving, Edward?

AUTHOR: At dawn.

DIPLOMATIST: Will you return to Managua?

A: Definitely.

OLIVER: When, old boy?

A: In several months, maybe. I *must* see Borge. For now, some writing to do in San José, then on to El Salvador.

D: When you come back here, you can compare the then and now.

A: Can the future be worse? The economy, I mean? When I arrived, eight hundred cordobas to the dollar. Today, twelve hundred.

O: Under Somoza, two, five, seven to the dollar. Oh, it will get much worse.

D: You seem to look forward to it, Oliver.

O: Is it my fault if this bloody government collapses of its own weight?

z: It's not going to collapse. With all the pressures, it's stable.

d: Quite. Like it or not, Oliver, Marxism-Leninism is in Nicaragua to stay.

a: Cardinal Obando told me almost the same. He said, "Indefinitely."

d: How did your meeting go with Padre Fernando Cardenal?

a: He dissembled to me.

o: You mean he lied to you.

a: He challenged me to show him, page by page, where Nicaraguan education is Marxist. He grants that Marxism is studied in university but denies it is studied in the high schools. In León, a high school girl showed me her *Fundamentos de filosofía marxista-leninista* . . .

z: Oh, that's a basic text, published in Moscow. Many of the Nicaraguan high schools use it.

o: So there we are!

a: Marxism *should* be studied in high schools, Oliver, including our own, but it's the only philosophical system the Sandinistas teach. Nicaraguan parents complain it's turning their children against them.

o: That is the Sandinista *intention*. Go out to the airport any Saturday morning. You'll see Nicaraguan children being put on airplanes for special indoctrination in Cuba.

I observed that the Sandinista indoctrination and the slogans seemed weirdly disembodied, divorced from the ebb and flow of real life. I found the Marxists in the Popular Church especially puzzling. They seemed obsessed with tearing down bourgeois social structures, but they ignored human nature.

Some years ago I had gone to Bavaria to meet Konrad Lorenz. Lorenz studied aggression in geese, but his analogies with the human condition revolutionized anthropology. He had dazzling insights into human nature, and he was very hard on Marx. He said that Marx disastrously misunderstood the instinctive side of human nature. Marx thought in a strait jacket of stimulus and response, convinced that if only we could remove cruelty, oppression, exploitation, greed—all the pangs that supposedly produce aggression—man would turn into an angel.

d: Borge's rhetoric is drunk with that notion.

a: Maybe that's my point. Lorenz thought that Marx was crazy, because aggression doesn't depend on stimulus or environment. It's built in. Man is programmed that way.

o: You and I, Edward, would call it Original Sin.

I said, "I'm afraid so." Everybody called the battle between Cardinal

Obando and the Popular Church a pure power struggle, but it was much more. It was a savage civil war inside the Church for possession of the body of Christ. The official Church was the traditional, superstitious, poetic, bleeding Christ—which the people preferred because it looked to eternity but comforted them today in their pain. The Popular Church was the demystified, rational, practical, liberating Christ—which promised the people a tomorrow here on earth where there would be no pain. Oliver said that the Popular Church had made Sandino the Fourth Person of the Holy Trinity. I said, "Then Fonseca must be the Fifth." Z (laughing): "Borge will be the Sixth." Somehow Oliver and I began debating various heresies about the nature of Christ.

o: Under the Docetist heresy, Christ did not even have a body.

A: Under Arianism, He was inferior to the Father.

z: You left out the Pelagians.

o: Ah, they denied Original Sin.

D: So we're back to Karl Marx.

z: Where you err, Oliver, is in considering Nicaragua another Afghanistan. The Soviets moved into Afghanistan, just as they moved into Prague—and would have gone to Warsaw if things got bad enough—because they had to. All those countries are contiguous to the Motherland, they're embraced by the Brezhnev Doctrine, and they fall within the vital sphere of Soviet interest. Nicaragua doesn't come close. Where their vital interest is not involved, the Russians *never* take risks.

o: Then why are they sending the Sandinistas the bloody HIND helicopters? They'll send MiGs next.

D: I do rather doubt they'll send MiGs. Washington has drawn the line at MiGs, and the Russians take such warnings seriously.

z: They'll always make mischief for the Americans anywhere. For them, Nicaragua is a nice little toy, a funny little chess piece. If they can give Reagan a black eye, make the United States bleed a little, splendid. But they won't spend any *money*. They got burned in Cuba, and they learned that lesson. No more Fidels. Too expensive.

D: The Sandinistas get about half a billion dollars a year in foreign aid, but the hard currency is from Western Europe. The Russians send guns, oil, and vodka, they help service Nicaragua's debt, but otherwise they give little cash. For them, this war is cheap.

A: I saw the same in the Middle East. The Russians used Egypt as a geopolitical chess piece against the United States, but they never pushed their luck. They gave the Egyptians defensive weapons—SAMs and such — but not the kind of sexy offensive aircraft the U.S. was giving Israel. I agree with Z. Unless it's a crucial interest, the Russians are never reckless.

o: It's not only guns and vodka, it's fucking ideology. The Reds ship that in by the metric ton, and the Sandinistas ship it out to the rest of the culture, infecting a whole hemisphere.

z: Oliver, what danger do the Sandinistas really pose to anybody when their revolution has so starkly failed?

d: Hear, hear.

a: The Sandinistas resemble the Egyptians more than they do the Russians.

o: You mean *physically*.

I acknowledged, naturally, the vast differences between Egypt and Nicaragua. Egypt was a large place, twice the size of France, with a populace (today) of perhaps fifty million. Nicaragua was a small place, a speck compared to Egypt, with a populace of perhaps three million. Yet the resemblance between Nasser's earlier revolution and the Sandinista Revolution now had begun to haunt me.

The revolution that Abdel Nasser led in 1952 erupted not from the peasantry but from army officers of the petite bourgeoisie: first parallel to the Sandinistas a quarter century later. Egyptian society was also similar, with a sad history of public corruption, private greed, an economy dominated by foreign powers. The Nasserist revolution, like the Nicaraguan, confronted a high birth rate, an inert bureaucracy, a national character as languid as it was endearing. Undaunted, Nasser promised that a young, robust, idealistic army would henceforth, as the locomotive of revolutionary change, redeem society.

Nasser dithered for some years before inventing "Arab Socialism," but in 1961 he did so with a fury. He defined his socialism as "simply the act of taking from the rich and giving to the poor — shaking society to its very foundations." He vowed reforms that would turn the bureaucracy "to the service of the people" and introduced a pervasive state capitalism with allowances for a "mixed economy." At first he struck at the upper class, and then, failing to fulfill his promises, at the bourgeoisie, shifting the base of his support to the hopeful proletariat.

Nasser was much less Marxist than the Sandinistas, but — while most of the comandantes were still in high school — his slogans foreshadowed theirs. In fact, Nasser in his turn borrowed many of his slogans from the Soviet Revolution. All those who opposed or even questioned his innovations were "capitalist reactionaries" and "enemies of the people." Himself a target of the CIA and of U.S. intrigues to weaken if not to topple him, he plausibly could blame the remainder of his woes on the machinations of American imperialism. Moreover, the philosophy of his socialism in some respects was uncannily similar to the effusions of sandinismo.

For example, all the rhetoric about "the New Man" and "the Revolution is love." Nasser, too, confessed that he was trying to "remake" the character of his people. Padre Fernando Cardenal's remarks to me at his Ministry of Education — of this new creature, born of the marriage of revolution and love, who "rejected individualism, egoism, materialism" for the "revolutionary values of love, sacrifice, devotion to the masses" — could have come from Nasser's mouth. Indeed, I heard Nasser and Nasser's men say much the same in speeches from various balconies when I lived in Egypt. In Islam, there is no division between temporal and celestial power, so in the mosques the sheikhs simply parroted whatever Nasser said, much as in Nicaragua the court theologians of the People's Church incensed all that the Sandinistas said.

Here, in Nicaragua as in Egypt years before, one heard the same poetic wish, that millennial intention to remake human nature. The consequence in Nicaragua, as in Egypt, was massive flight of capital, social and economic failure, a nasty little military dictatorship — though (as in Egypt) by no means the world's worst. Mirror images of soldiers teeming on the roads, of military bureaucrats stamping documents, imposing ever more labyrinthine rules on a confused and hungry populace. As rulers, the comandantes were incompetent, but in this corner of the world incompetence was the norm. That the standard of Nicaraguan life had regressed under the Sandinistas was perhaps as much the fault of American persecution. More difficult to forgive was the Sandinistas' invincible ignorance, their refusal to learn from the errors of their forerunners elsewhere in the Third World, their delusion that the deeds they were attempting in Nicaragua were somehow unique.

Next day, as I flew out of Nicaragua, I felt not so much disillusion as déjà vu.

III / EL SALVADOR

We do not seek peace in order to be at war, but we go
to war that we may have peace. Be peaceful, therefore, in warring, so that you may vanquish those
whom you war against, and bring them to the prosperity of peace.

Saint Augustine

A tyrannical government is not just, because it is directed, not to the common good, but to the private
good of the ruler . . . Consequently there is no sedition in disturbing a government of this kind, unless indeed the tyrant's rule be disturbed so inordinately that
his subjects suffer greater harm from the consequent
disturbance than from the tyrant's government. Indeed
it is the tyrant rather that is guilty of sedition, since he
encourages discord and sedition among his subjects,
that he may lord over them more securely; for this is
tyranny, since it is ordered to the private good of the
ruler and to the injury of the multitude.

Saint Thomas Aquinas

General Ochoa made all who had been captured crawl
on their knees to him seated in the courtyard of the
fort. He said to them: "Come here and smell my
gun." The prisoners pleaded in the name of God, for
they had heard shots. But the General insisted: "If
you don't smell my gun then you are a communist
and afraid." The campesino smelled the barrel of the
gun . . .

From an account of the Matanza,
the massacre of 1932

I

I RETURNED to Costa Rica, where I kept my things, to write of the contras, Honduras, and the Sandinistas. I had lost at least fifteen pounds: the night clerk at my hotel in San José told me I looked unhealthy. Eventually I flew to El Salvador.

With so much of the world's attention now focused on Nicaragua, El Salvador's civil war had of late been overlooked. Yet there it was, in its seventh year, being waged in a dwarf nation, smallest of the isthmus, eight thousand square miles, and the most densely populated, with nearly six million souls. When the death squads of the extreme right were committing eight hundred political murders a month and the Salvadoran army was massacring civilians in its pursuit of leftist guerrillas, people paid more notice. Now, under U.S. pressure, death-squad atrocities were much diminished and the army with its American advisers was more discreet, but dreadful suffering was still inflicted on the populace.

The Salvadoran army and the insurgents of the FMLN, the Farabundo Martí National Liberation Front, fought on without issue, endlessly. More than half a million people, a tenth of the population, had been displaced; perhaps sixty thousand civilians had been killed, many of them by death squads. People were still mutilated and tortured and some death squads went on murdering, but today the horrors were of a lesser scale and the American television networks had lost interest. I spent two months in El Salvador. The horrors were quite enough for me.

I paused in San Salvador, then flew from the capital—over a landscape like the moon's, pocked with volcanoes—to San Miguel in the east. My destination was Morazán, the province farther north, where the guerrillas were very active. In San Miguel, I met Padre F, an Irish

Franciscan with an Isuzu pickup. He drove me the twenty miles to San Francisco Gotera, the capital of Morazán. The padre had lived in Morazán for many years, including the years of the horror. His sweet brogue dripped detail. "Along this stretch of road," he said, "during six months of nineteen eighty-three, I counted one hundred sixty-one headless bodies."

I noticed, along the road, corn and sisal crops burned out and, in the valleys and along the sides of mountains, clouds of smoke and fires raging. "That's the army," Padre F said. "Burning again. Flushing out guerrillas, depriving them of food and cover. The water table has dropped disastrously. In a few years, Morazán will be a desert." In San Francisco Gotera, at the door of my hotel, he gave me good advice: "Don't go on operations with the army. On no account. The guerrillas ambush the armored trucks and convoys, and they shoot at helicopters. You'll get killed."

I rose at dawn and walked to the *cuartel*, army headquarters beside the Franciscan church, looking for Colonel E. He was commander of the Fourth Detachment of the Third Brigade, in effect the military governor of Morazán, and by reputation a humane man. Yet that very day, in late March, he was (I learned later) launching his Operación Héroes de Joateca, a major campaign to crush the guerrillas and (he hoped) chase them out of Morazán. Not easy: the Ejército Revolucionario del Pueblo, People's Revolutionary Army, one of the five fighting branches of the FMLN, held half the province north of the River Torola to the Honduran border. I loitered by the gate of the cuartel, waiting for the colonel to come out.

American jeeps and trucks, protected with armor plate and mounted with machine guns, line the plaza facing the Franciscan church; troops in berets and olive combat uniforms, bearing American automatic rifles, loll in the turrets and atop the hoods, laughing lewdly about women. Young soldiers, youths, beardless boys almost, hobble on crutches in and out of the garrison, their feet and legs blown off by guerrilla land mines. Now, still early in the morning, from the courtyard of the cuartel, a dozen armored trucks roll out, full of other youths with whole bodies en route to search-and-destroy missions in the countryside, where they will set more fires, step on more mines, lose more limbs. Or they will be ambushed, and some of them will return to Gotera dead. A commotion at the gate, youths saluting, presenting arms, snapping to attention. A cohort of officers streams out: at the center is my prey. I approach him: "*¿Mi coronel?*"

Colonel E is a young man with pouting lips and a Mayan face, clad in combat fatigues and a floppy hat. I present my official letter of recommendation from army headquarters in San Salvador, stamped DIOS, UNION Y LIBERTAD and TODO POR LA PATRIA, JUNTOS PUEBLO Y FUERZA ARMADA. Colonel E does not seem impressed. He ponders and, with a bored expression, finally says, "I'm leaving for my units in the field."

"Where?" I ask.

"North of the Río Torola."

"That's guerrilla territory."

"Who told you so?"

"Radio Venceremos."

Guerrilla radio. He smiles. I have, however slightly, challenged him: government propaganda makes no admission of sequestered territory. "*Sí,*" he says. "*Puede ser un poco peligroso,* it can be a bit dangerous. Are you coming with me?"

I remembered the Franciscan's warning. Minutes later I was aloft, seated near the colonel on the floor of a UH-1 helicopter. The hatch was wide open, and were I not strapped down I would have fallen out. By the hatch sat a soldier in a helmet, fingering his mounted pair of M-60 machine guns and scanning the landscape underneath. I thought: Vietnam. We banked and turned. Soon we crossed the Río Torola and flew northeasterly into the guerrilla enclave toward the Honduran border. The terrain was brown, parched, hilly, with escarpments eventually and purple mountains far off. It seemed depopulated; I saw hardly a soul beneath, only once or twice a man on a bare patch. Fires were burning the sides of hills, and everywhere was ash, bare patches burned out. Yet even in such devastation shoots of trees and green bush struggled to grow anew. We landed near Honduras at the foot of a hill black with the skeletons of trees still smoldering from a fire, where Colonel E and I were greeted by about forty of his soldiers.

We trod up and down the blackened hills, the colonel conferring with his junior officers, examining his field maps, talking with nearby units on an American PRC radio, scanning the next hills with his high-powered "mil-scale" binoculars and seeing no guerrillas. He turned to me.

"We had a battle here yesterday," he said.

"How many guerrillas did you kill?"

"We captured one."

"Where is he?"

"Undergoing interrogation."

I had heard accounts of what "interrogation" meant and was glad I was not the guerrilla. Where were the other guerrillas? With his field glasses, the colonel scanned the hills again. "They're out there somewhere," he said. "Hiding in the ground. We'll find them." I borrowed his binoculars and sat down to smoke a cigarette. The colonel and his officers drifted off, reading their maps, planning their operations, talking.

I was seated by a hut, built into a hole, where guerrillas had lived till yesterday; the tin roof was bashed in by army shells. Peasant soldiers — press-ganged? — gathered around me, carefree outside the colonel's presence, asking for cigarettes. Again, they were mere boys, not long into adolescence, equipped with M-16 rifles, American fatigues, American boots, American water bottles, American bullets, American bazookas, American knives. They asked me who I was, where I came from, and when I told them the United States, they laughed with delight. They had brothers and sisters there; they wanted to join them.

A soldier offers me his water bottle, another asks if I own a swimming pool. With the cigarettes and water bottle and dreams of swimming pools we have a little party. A soldier tells an obscene joke, something about a *piscina,* swimming pool, and a *puta,* whore. Laughing, I lift the colonel's binoculars to scan the next hills. For an instant I glimpse three or four young men in civil dress with rifles dashing through a patch of burned-out trees. I say, "Oh."

"Did you see somebody?" a sergeant asks.

They're guerrillas, I think. *They'll die tomorrow. Why should they die today?*

I say, "*Ninguno*. Nobody." I hold on to the binoculars, and to distract the soldiers I hand out more cigarettes and tell a bad joke about a crocodile in a swimming pool, *cocodrilo en la piscina*. Boyish laughter.

2

EVENTUALLY I FLEW BACK to San Francisco Gotera with Colonel E. I knew by now that the guerrillas, depleted by years of carnage, avoided major battles with the army, preferring to ambush small government columns and above all to maim and kill by planting land mines. Yet my glimpse of them through the colonel's binoculars was not enough:

I intended to visit the fiefdom of the ERP, People's Revolutionary Army, north of the Río Torola.

I asked the colonel for a laissez-passer, but he was loath to oblige me. Too risky, he said. When the bastards shot me, he'd get blamed. Besides, there was no bus. I'd ride a truck, I said. *"Tampoco.* I've stopped the trucks.'' I persisted, visiting the cuartel every day, and finally received permission when I signed a scrap of paper absolving the army of responsibility for my safety.

The proprietor of my hotel drove me to the crossroads at Osicala — the scene of savage battles before and since — and the last army check-point. Once past it, in no man's land, I was seized by doubts. There was no trace of transport. My destination was Perquín, a guerrilla town ten miles beyond the river, high in the hills more than halfway to the Honduran border. Though early morning still, it was hot and I would have to walk.

In my usual confusion I had brought no water, only two large satchels packed with personal effects and books. The two miles or so in no man's land were not bad: they wound along a mountain, downward. At the Torola, the bridge was blown up, so I hopscotched on stones across the river, balancing my bags and forgetting to drink the water. Once over the Torola, inside the guerrilla enclave, my journey was uphill.

For a while, I managed. Though full of potholes the road was paved, and I maintained a steady pace. For mile after mile, I saw not a soul, but in my creeping paranoia I was certain I was being watched. The land, hills and valleys here, seemed less burned out, but for months no rain had fallen and the trees and grass were parched. Here was a different kind of devastation: the road was strewn with bullet shells from auto-matic rifles and the houses alongside had been gutted in the fighting. It was noon now. In a cloudless sky the sun blazed; my bags seemed heavier, like rocks; I was thirsty. I called out at the ruined houses, the parched hills, the eyes I knew were watching me: *"¡Hola! ¡Hola! ¿Alguno? ¡Agua!"*

No answer. I resumed my upward march, shifting my bags from hand to hand, then strapping them to my shoulders. For a mile, perhaps two miles, three miles, I persevered, hating my folly for ignoring Colonel E's advice. Now beneath every pothole I knew a land mine lurked, so I zigzagged between the holes, then in the shade of a tree sat down, gasping. My mouth was dust; I called out: *"¡Hola! ¡Hola! ¡Agua!"*

Beneath my hand, I felt something, a glass bottle, clear with a rusty cap, empty, but I knew I had to fill it. Nonsense, there were no streams. I resumed my climb, sat down again as the landscape whirled.

Somewhere in my delusion descended a dark spot, a formless shape that wavered to and fro and became a man carrying a hen. No, he was true, and the hen. He stood over me asking "*¿Está bien?*"

He was a young campesino. I handed him my bottle and begged him to find me water. He handed me his baby hen and sprang into a ravine. He was, like that soldier in Matagalpa, foxlike, predatory. In a while he returned, with a tiny portion of dirt and water at the bottom of my bottle. I drank and we walked on, he uncannily knowing just where to stop to look for water. In a while the bottle was full.

"What's your name?" I asked him.

"Cristián."

"Will you carry my bags to Perquín?"

"Will you pay me?"

We settled on thirty colons, about six dollars, and I would have paid much more. Refreshed and cheerful, I resumed my climb, still carrying the hen, Cristián bounding ahead of me with my bags. In the waning afternoon, by the side of the road, a fat girl with a rifle sat tilted on a wooden chair reading a book. At last. Perquín lay not far beyond. Other guerrillas emerged from the jungle.

They were mostly very young, a mixture of boys in baseball caps and more fat girls in khaki slacks, all bearing captured American M-16 automatic rifles. Other, older guerrillas wore mustaches, mufti and military dress, and various nationalities of gun. The jefe appeared to be a senior guerrilla, nom de guerre Luis, who wore a cocked safari hat and had no front teeth.

"Where are you going?" he asked politely.

"To Perquín."

"We must ask permission of the comandante."

I was escorted to another post farther up the road, where a message would be dispatched to guerrilla headquarters in Perquín. Cristián still bore my bags, but he seemed nervous now and anxious to be gone. I gave him back his hen. "*Adios.*" He dropped my bags in the middle of the road and ran away. Luis opened up the bags, spreading all of my possessions across the road, examining them microscopically. My letter from army headquarters to Colonel E bothered him, or it did when he asked the fat girl to explain it. Now several guerrillas hovered over his shoulder, repeating the phrases. "... *a fin que se le autorice el acceso a dicho lugar, siempre y cuando no vulnere las normas de seguridad y usted se lo permita* ..." —routine bureaucratic jargon requesting Colonel E to allow me to visit Morazán provided no prejudice to security. "... *normas de seguridad* ... rules of security ... *usted se lo permita* ... with your permission ..." They passed the letter from hand to hand. Fat girl said, "*Espía.* Spy."

"Colonel E is not in charge here," Luis said finally. "Why did you come?"

"To visit Perquín. May I go now?"

"We must wait for *la respuesta,* the response."

Several guerrillas escorted me into the forest, perhaps a quarter of a mile, to a tiled and gutted farmhouse, where I was told to wait. Two guerrillas were assigned to guard me, an older man with a mustache and a gun and a young woman with braids and a gun. If the road was reserved for fat girls, the jungle was reserved for lithe ones. My keeper wore a denim blouse and American camouflage pants; her olive skin was smooth, her eyes black, and she called herself Dalila. She smiled, showing full white teeth. I asked why so many of the guerrillas had no teeth.

"Because we have no dentists," she said. "We have no doctors. The army bombs our hospitals, and our people bleed to death."

She told me the story of the farmhouse. A family of eleven had lived here, growing a little sisal, tending a little corn, minding their own lives. One day the army came and killed them all because they lived in the wrong place. Mother and father, grandparents and children, babies, chickens, pigs, and a cow. It was a large house, with a shattered roof on mud brick, shards and bullet shells and vegetation where the floor had been, open beneath the sky. I pictured infants playing in the corners, the mother cooking dinner, the father drinking too much guaro. I did not care to pass the night with those ghosts, but as the sun went down it occurred to me that I was the prisoner of these guerrillas and that this abbatoir was my jail.

Dalila brought me supper, a G.I. ration can of rice and tomato, and a fresh pineapple. I lay down on bullet casings and tile shards, beneath the shattered roof and stars, and tried to sleep. In these highlands, the night was cool. As I shivered in a thin jacket, I rejoiced for my insanity in coming to this place. I loved the guerrillas, the game with danger, and Dalila, my pretty one of night. I remembered my father's death, a slow death not so much of the body as of a spirit once robust. I prayed: "Lord, when my hour comes, let it come like this. No lingering, no decay: a guerrilla's bullet through my skull, Beatitude."

I could hear Dalila, still watching me, whispering in the bush with Mustache, my other guard. I slept badly, and at daylight when I got up my back ached. More guerrillas, fingering their guns, their faces hidden behind dirty handkerchiefs, came into the forest to stare at me. I knew something of their history.

For six years they had been waging war against the central government, surviving incessant onslaughts of superior armor and aircraft, at high cost. The ranks of the guerrillas in this enclave had been reduced to two thousand troops; the towns and countryside, once overcrowded and mildly prosperous, had been ravaged and largely depopulated.

Hidden somewhere in the enclave was the headquarters of Joaquín Villalobos, founder of the People's Revolutionary Army and the senior comandante of the Farabundo Martí Front. Child of a bourgeois family, a pragmatic Marxist who had dropped out of university for the armed struggle, Villalobos led a magic life. As a student in San Salvador he had barely escaped the death squads; as a guerrilla in Morazán he taunted the government with his Radio Venceremos and with military tactics so elusive that the army could never kill him. "I'll wage war for thirty years," Villalobos promised. I hoped somehow to meet him.

Late that afternoon, Luis returned. He said, "You have till sunset to be on the other side of the Torola."

"You're kicking me out?" I protested.

"Sunset. Otherwise we cannot be responsible for your safety."

"I want to stay."

"The army will attack this sector tomorrow."

"How do you know? Does Colonel E inform you of his plans?"

"Sunset. The Torola."

"I'll never make it by sunset. How will you know I've crossed the river?"

"We'll know."

I collected my bags and ran. My flight now was downhill, but I was sure I would fail the deadline. Past the ruined houses, over the potholes and the bullet shells, I had never been so swift. Once or twice I stumbled, scraping my bad knee. I reached the riverbank just as the sun, its last rays, vanished. In the twilight, laden with my bags, I leaped from stone to stone to the river's other bank in no man's land. There, I threw down the bags and collapsed on them.

In the murky light a man in a straw hat, bearing a huge machete, walked up and stood over me. To the guerrillas I pretended never to be afraid, but now fear seized me. I imagined a chop of the machete into my neck for my money. Quickly I stood up, my body trembling but my hands ready to defend my life. The campesino was tiny, half my size, and now he trembled, too. O God, I thought, he's afraid of *me*. I took his free hand and shook it.

"I'm Edward. Who are you?"

"Paco. What do you want?"

"It's getting dark, and I'm too tired to climb the mountain to Osicala. A place to sleep?"

"You could sleep in my house."

"I'd pay you well."

"*Es igual*. Doesn't matter."

From the riverbank in the faint light I followed Paco through a settlement of hovels perhaps half a mile to his own hovel. It was a large hut made of sticks and covered with a corrugated tin roof held down by sticks and stones. Poultry and pigs mingled in the yard, and inside the hut with its earthen floor Paco's woman and their children were preparing supper—some sort of mush, cornmeal and millet, I think. I pleaded nausea and passed my portion to the children. But for the hearth fire it was pitch black now, and in the *campo* when night falls everybody goes to bed.

As they prepared for bed, stringing up hammocks, unfolding blankets, chasing out the pig, I observed the family at their most natural. Paco's children were a girl and four boys, in age perhaps between eight and fifteen. Francisca, his wife in common law, though already wizened and hunched from a life of poverty, seemed slightly more refined than he, and she had teeth. Their little girl, not yet in puberty, was lovely, and the boys were handsome. Though respectful and affectionate to Paco, the children seemed to favor Francisca. Any deed she wanted done, hardly were the words from her mouth, they did. Their reward was a kiss—whenever one of them passed near her she was hugged and then her kiss was granted. Paco appeared to accept, without rancor, his wife's primacy of the heart. His worldly wealth was a tiny plot of corn and sisal that he tilled as a tenant farmer and of course his hens and pigs, but he seemed to understand that his real riches were this hunched woman and their splendid issue.

I was given the best hammock, where I lay fully clothed. The girl slept in the same large bed with her parents by the hearth, the boys in hammocks and, in a smaller bed near me, two of them together. I tried to sleep, but my back still hurt and the pig kept wandering in and out, oinking and brushing beneath my hammock. As the night passed it turned to chill. Two of the boys emerged from their places and took refuge in their parents' bed, crying "*Mamá, mamá, tengo frío* . . . I'm cold." They huddled to their mother, beneath her blanket, hugging and kissing her.

Toward three o'clock, still bothered by the pig and despairing of sleep, I rose from the hammock and tried to tiptoe outside without disturbing the family. I knocked over a jug; everyone woke. They rose also and sat with me by the chicken coop to await the dawn. One of the boys, Diego, was not, it turned out, Paco's and Francisca's real son, but Paco's nephew, about thirteen. He came from Cerro Pando, not far across the river. Only several years ago, his whole family — parents, siblings, grandparents — had been massacred in an army sweep. Diego escaped by hiding in a hole.

Dawn, and time to go. Paco carried my bags up the side of the mountain to the bus stop at the Osicala crossroads. Along the way, children were spinning rope from hemp of the sisal plant, the rope strung out over hundreds of yards between great wheels. In the fresh day, the children were mythically beautiful and the scene was pastoral, medieval, there in no man's land. On and on they spun, turning the wheels with their busy hands, laughing, without cares, as though spinning out the very woof of time.

At the crossroads, waiting for my bus to San Francisco Gotera, I looked up to the sky. Colonel E's helicopters flew over, toward the Torola, in the direction of Perquín.

3

SAN FRANCISCO GOTERA was a garrison town of white adobe and red tile, swarming children, a white statue of Saint Francis of Assisi preaching to a wolf. It had three thousand troops, five thousand natives, and fourteen thousand refugees of war. My hotel was the Arco Iris, Rainbow, on the main cobblestoned street. At the entrance was an inscription:

GOD IS WITH US, BECAUSE: WHERE THERE IS FAITH, THERE IS LOVE, WHERE THERE IS LOVE, THERE IS PEACE, WHERE THERE IS PEACE, THERE IS GOD, Y DONDE ESTA DIOS, ¡NO FALTA NADA! — AND WHERE GOD IS, NOTHING'S LACKING! Alas, save for the dubious presence of Deity, the Arco Iris lacked rather a lot.

José, the owner, ran a grain and feed business from the front rooms and kept his trucks parked in the courtyard. He lived above the business with his large family and was perhaps the most prosperous merchant in Gotera, not least for his friendship with Colonel E. Behind his business along the courtyard and the trucks were the guest rooms, austere, hot, and dirty. Sanitary arrangements were a tub of water and a toilet that could be flushed only between four and six in the morning because the rest of the time in Gotera the water was shut off; throughout the day and night electricity was often cut for lengthy periods. This was Holy Week. During the heat of afternoon, when I took my siesta, I could hear military helicopters chopping incessantly across the sky and Ramón, the boy who ran the hotel for José, constantly opening soda pop and tossing the metal caps on the cement ground. At night, officers and sergeants brought women to the Arco Iris, and through the open windows I could hear them laughing and making love.

I ate well enough in San Francisco Gotera, at a pulpería with tables and chairs, down the street from the Arco Iris: fresh meat and poultry, plenty of imported fresh fruit, grapes, melon, pineapple; no alcohol, not even beer, because Colonel E wisely forbade the sale of alcohol in this *"zona conflictiva."* Otherwise in Gotera — throughout most of El Salvador — you could get anything you wanted if you could pay for it. Here was the keen difference between the Nicaraguan economy of scarcity and the capitalist economy of El Salvador even during war.

In San Miguel, I had been astonished that a hardware store sold the same merchandise — garden hose, hedge clippers, Black & Decker household machinery — available in the United States. The major cities had luxury hotels, and despite the economic sabotage wrought by the guerrillas the infrastructure of the country — roads, bridges, electrification, even transport to an extent — was sophisticated. Resplendent with shopping plazas and high-rise buildings, parts of San Salvador resembled Miami. As a people, the Salvadorans were intelligent, industrious, compulsively clean. In San Salvador, even the *slums* were clean. In Gotera, campesinos in the tiny Franciscan sisal cooperative honorably, promptly, whatever the hardship, paid back their loans.

However, most of Gotera's people did not have money — unemployment was 80 percent—because most of them were refugees relocated by the army from towns and villages north of the Torola. They lived in squeezed camps, short of water, profuse with infant children, their huts as hot as fever under the noon sun. Whenever I visited the camps I found it hard to move about because men and women blocked my path, beseeching me to find them work. They did not seek charity, only honest work, yet to survive they lived on handouts of food from the government, the United States, and the army. If they wanted more than meager handouts—medicine, a health center, a schoolhouse, cement, lumber, a paved road—they had to petition Colonel E.

In his goodness, sometimes he granted them. The colonel was more than a military governor, he was a classic war lord. In Morazán south of the Torola, nothing of importance happened, nothing was ever done, without his interest and consent. Ruthless if he had to be, he turned on the faucet of his measured favors whenever he felt they could contribute to his crusade against the guerrillas. Even the proguerrilla Jesuits of San Salvador conceded that for a military commander he was merciful, and they did not claim that, like so many of his fellow colonels, his hands were steeped in the blood of past civil massacres. He was renowned throughout El Salvador as a benevolent despot of new ideas. He waged "psych-ops," building schools, clinics, roads, providing medicines, dentists, corn and sisal seed to win the loyalty of his subjects. And he had a sense of humor.

The colonel's office at the cuartel was plastered with guerrilla posters calling him LADRON, MENTIROSO, ASESINO, Thief, Liar, Murderer . . . ¡SE BUSCA! ¡RECOMPENSA $100,000! ¡TIPO PELIGROSO! WANTED! $100,000 REWARD! COULD BE DANGEROUS! . . . this last with a picture of the colonel in a painted-on mustache. He displayed the posters to me as his favorite war booty, jolly as he did so. He took off his tunic and his floppy hat, sitting down at his desk in a white T-shirt. He was nearly forty, but without the hat his pouting lips seemed less churlish and he looked like a boy.

COLONEL E: . . . Not all army commanders wage psych-ops as I do. The roots of this war are not military, but political, social, and economic. Our mission as soldiers is not only to impose security, but to remove the causes of war by improving economic and social conditions.

AUTHOR: An enlightened policy, *mi coronel*.

E: This very day I'm starting another project for displaced persons in Morazán. I'm building houses, distributing clothes, sending in doctors. Here, look at this map. I'm consolidating a whole area with projects of health, education, and reconstruction in Chilanga, Lolotiquillo, Gotera, and San Carlos. We'll expand the projects in a widening periphery to include Yoloaiquín, Cacaopera, Sociedad, Jocoro, El Divisadero, Sensembra, and Yambal. We didn't come to win the war, but to win the peace.

A: Admirable, *mi coronel.* May I make a comment?

E: *Claro.*

A: With all respect, you seem to take away with the right hand what you give with the left. What of the fires? Why do you burn so many of the campesinos' stores and crops?

E: The guerrillas burn the crops.

A: But you said you control this territory.

E: We *do.* The guerrillas slip in sometimes.

A: Ah. Then the guerrillas control only Perquín and the enclave north of the Torola.

E: They do not *control* it. It is a *zona de persistencia,* a pocket of persistence only. We can go in whenever we want.

A: I've seen many fires. Does the army never start them?

E (*displeased*): Sometimes, but seldom (*a muy pocas veces*), and it's definitely not our policy. The campesinos burn away the land to prepare for planting.

A: The water table, I'm told, has dropped seventeen feet. The riverbeds are drying up. The trees are dying. For lack of trees, the earth is so eroded that when the rains come the soil cannot hold the water. Your aid to the populace is praiseworthy, but burning out the guerrillas seems to come first. Is this a scorched-earth policy, *mi coronel?*

E: There are hot, self-combustible minerals in the earth. The fires start themselves.

In the evenings as the sun set I visited the Franciscans to tell them of my encounters during the day and to hear their comments. As I passed the grated cement of the cuartel I could see the steam and hear the soldiers taking their showers and shouting "puta." The church next door was nineteenth-century Spanish colonial, for Holy Week draped in purple, with a portal of Saint Francis preaching to the birds; the Franciscans lived comfortably in their cloister across the street, and they served cold beer. Colonel E's remark about self-combustible minerals became the joke of Holy Week for these irreverent Irish friars. "Well *of course* there are self-combustible minerals," laughed

Padre F. "Phosphorus, for example, which comes on the end of a stick. It's called a match." He told of a soldier who entered a peasant's house, politely asked for a box of matches, then burned the house down.

Padre F was droll about Colonel E ("Oh, he's a cha-a-rming man, he is"), but his bitterness, the bitterness of all the friars, toward the army and President Duarte's government was deep. "The Salvadorans have such dignity," I observed. The friars retorted that even their dignity was being crushed by the army's policy of scorched earth and stingy handouts. The government was so rotten. The enrollment at Gotera's agricultural college had declined terribly since youths refused to show their faces for fear of being press-ganged. And yes, you could buy anything in El Salvador if you had money — including exemption from military service. The poor were the cannon fodder, not the rich boys. When they stepped on guerrilla land mines, their legs were amputated by army doctors without much thought. The officers walked behind the troops, but when *they* stepped on land mines the surgeons struggled to save their limbs. (I wondered, Could the surgeons be that callous? and made a mental note to pursue the question in the capital.) Some friars seemed to favor the guerrillas. "Many of the guerrillas," said Padre F, "are Christians."

On Holy Thursday, Padre O, a young itinerant friar, clad traditionally in a coarse brown habit, took me in his truck as he toured Morazán, celebrating Masses. We went first to Cacaopera, just south of the Torola, where not so long before the guerrillas had kidnapped, then shot nine men as informers for the government and press-ganged another one hundred fifty into the People's Revolutionary Army. The good father did not allude to these barbarities, but after Cacaopera he kept stopping his truck, urging me to photograph whole hillsides of burned-out sisal. "The army," he said in soft anger. "The beans are burned, and the coffee crops, the fruits are burned, in this lovely province of my boyhood. Once we could feed ourselves . . . no longer. Each day, the desert grows."

Possibly he exaggerated the army's guilt. I knew that some campesinos did indeed burn off land for planting, just as the army torched the land to set off guerrilla land mines that would otherwise maim or kill its soldiers. Possibly the friars defamed Colonel E when they accused him of a "scorched-earth policy," yet whoever bore the greater guilt I knew that I was witnessing an ecological and human tragedy. I met a victim.

He was a tiny, shriveled man, a campesino no more than thirty who looked sixty. From Cacaopera Padre O had driven to a tumble-down adobe church in Lolotiquillo. As usual the church was mobbed with sweating campesinos and the padre's homily was prolix; as usual I slipped out for a cigarette. I sat in the shade of a gnarled tree, near a crumbling wall with an immense army poster, a rogues' gallery of foreign guerrillas — a Spaniard, a Belgian, a Moroccan, a Spanish woman, three French women — being hunted by the government. ESTOS SON LOS ENEMIGOS DE EL SALVADOR . . . MERCENARIOS COMUNISTAS QUE AYUDAN AL FMLN PARA DESTRUIR EL SALVADOR . . . WHEN YOU SEE THEM DENOUNCE THEM TO THE ARMY OR SECURITY FORCES. As the Holy Thursday Mass progressed, the shriveled campesino, who had been stalking me since my arrival, emerged from the church in a straw hat and gathered the courage to approach me beneath my tree.

"*¿Señor?*"

"*¿Sí?*"

"Are you the North American ambassador?"

"No. I have no power, no money, and no visa." My standard preemptive speech: all Salvadorans seemed to assume that any stranger was American and issued visas to the United States. "Cigarette?"

"*Gracias.* I'm Pablo. I have a problem."

"I can't solve it, Pablo."

"Last week, my farm burned down. My wife and — "

"Who set the fire?"

He sighed, suggesting fear: "*La gente.* People."

"Which people?"

"*Los niños.* Kids."

"I'm not a policeman, Pablo. Was it the army?"

He turned away his face. Was he fighting tears? "*Sí.*"

"I'm sorry, Pablo. Here's a little money for your children. There's nothing more — "

"Please. I want to work for you. I'll do anything. Listen — "

I ran away from him, back across the dirt plaza toward the shanty church, but he pursued me, grabbing my arm. "*Favor.* Please. Work. I'll go with you. *Excelencia* . . ."

"I'm not the ambassador. Leave me alone."

"*Favor* . . ."

"You little pest, go back to the church and say your prayers! *¡Basta! ¡Basta!* Enough! Enough!"

I fled into the church. Pablo did not follow me. From the dense mob,

I looked back. He stood in the plaza beneath the sun, alone and tiny, then crouched in the dust, finishing his cigarette.

Eventually Padre O drove me back to San Francisco Gotera. Later in the afternoon I left the Arco Iris and explored the outskirts of the town. I found myself on a dirt road climbing upward through rows of hovels where more refugees lived. I came to a soccer field, all red dust, where boys were playing, beside a high stone wall baking in the brilliant sun. This was an enormous structure, mounted with tile-roofed sentry towers and in their shade machine guns. At the gate, I learned the purpose of the institution. It was the Centro Penal, a prison for common criminals.

The jefe was gone for Holy Week, so it was easy for me to talk my way through the guards and clanging doors to the interior of the jail. No sooner was I inside than dozens of men crowded to the bars of a courtyard, gripping the bars, gazing, calling out greetings, as though they had granted an appointment for my appearance exactly at that moment. The guard opened a huge padlock and I passed into the cobblestoned courtyard. It was hung with laundry, threadbare jeans, underwear, white shirts, dripping in the sunshine. The men were mostly young with savage eyes, but some were old or wrinkled before their time. I sat down on a bench at the end of the yard; fifty men flocked about me. Had I come from the capital with news from the minister of justice? No, I had only been passing by, and what was this about the minister of justice? "We have a petition with the minister of justice!"

It seemed that most of the men in this penitentiary had never been brought to trial. They had simply been dumped here, abandoned, allowed to languish four, five, six, seven years or longer without being formally charged. Or if they were charged their cases were never heard. Or if their cases were heard their trials had been dropped because they were too poor to pay attorneys or to bribe their way to freedom.

I already knew that bribery was the norm in Salvadoran justice, the system so corrupt that often only cash — up to $1,000 for a campesino, much higher for a richer man — could free a prisoner, trial or no trial. (By contrast, no senior officer of the army or security forces suspected of political death-squad murders had ever been prosecuted or punished.) The men before me now were accused of homicide, rape, theft, and other common crimes. Possibly most of them were guilty, some of them seemed dangerous, yet still I thought of Jean Valjean, locked up for nearly twenty years for stealing a loaf of bread.

But what was this petition to the minister of justice? A simple request, they said, for trials. The men did not seek their liberty, only their trials, so that a judge could sentence them and liberty one day would follow. "What can I do for you?" I murmured. "I'm a foreigner. I have no power." I could intercede with the minister of justice, they pleaded, with the president of the Supreme Court, the Archbishop of San Salvador, the North American ambassador . . .

"*Claro,*" I answered weakly, "*el ministro, el presidente, el arzobispo, el embajador* . . . when I return to the capital." I tried to be polite but unconvincing, not wishing to ignite their hopes. I had been on the isthmus for half a year, nearly enough to inure me to yet another tale of misery. The prisoners pleaded on, but one of them — tall, with a shaved head — rescued me from further embarrassment. Fearful of the guard, he produced a scrap of paper and scribbled this note in English:

> Please
> I Need   your   help.
> Im   iN   prisoN   here
> The [illegible] CommΛNdΛ
> meNt   is   very   bAd
> with me.
> I'm   very   Long   oF
>   my   house.
> I   have   N'T   WorK
>   p   leAse   givme   your
>   help.
> I   need   tweN ty
>   Five   ColoNs   For
>   my   Fud
> I'm   From   Ah-uA ch
> ApAN   city.

"For food?" I asked in English.

"I'm hunger," he replied in English.

I gave him twenty colons. The guard confiscated the letter. "What does it say?" he demanded.

I translated. For the phrase "The Commandament is very bad with me," I said, "*El comandante es muy simpático con migo.*" The guard let me keep the note, and I asked him to let me out.

But the courtyard opposite was full of prisoners, too, and now they stood at the bars, almost rioting, demanding equal time. The guard opened another padlock, and I passed through. The prisoners here, it seemed from fragments of their conversation, were all accused (suspected) of murder. They had been lifting weights and weaving handicrafts—tiny black crucifixes, made of thread—until I came. The inmates of this jail—perhaps a hundred—were not, so far as I could tell, physically mistreated, and though their nutrition was primitive (mostly rice and beans, thrice a day) they seemed robust. Their families could visit them, and for their wives in matrimony or common law conjugal visitations (*visitas íntimas*) were allowed in private rooms on Sundays. Moreover, this penitentiary, like most Salvadoran institutions, and the inmates saw to this, was immaculately clean.

By now I was in the murderers' dormitory, long rows of crowded beds, double-tiered, prim, and Spartan. As the prisoners pressed about me, I noticed one youth in particular. He had a mop of black hair, a faint mustache, wistful face, biceps pronounced from body building. He wore a scrubbed T-shirt and tight, faded jeans. I pitied his wasted youth. I imagined him, a toothless old man, half a century later, still here. In his copper hands, he holds a striped kitten.

"*¿Le gustan los gatos?* Do you like cats?" he asks me.

"*Claro.* Yours reminds me of my Tabby. What's your name?"

"Mario Enrique."

"Why are you here?"

"*Homicidio.*"

"Are you guilty?"

"*Defensa propia, sí.* Self-defense."

Mario Enrique and the other prisoners drew up a neat list of their names and the length of time each had served here without trial. "Jesús Aristedes Quintanilla = 4 años . . . Rafael de Jesús Enrique = 5 años . . . Manuel de Jesús González = 6 años . . . Julio Antonio Menendez Orellana = 7 años . . ." (I have used their real names at their request.) Again I protested my impotence. Mario Enrique pressed his cat against my jaw, insisting: "Nobody else will help us." I capitulated, politely. "*Sí . . . el ministro, el presidente, el arzobispo, el embajador . . .* in the capital." With the list in my pocket, I hugged the cat and left the prison.

On the dirt road, I suffered pangs of guilt. Indeed, I had been feeling guilty all afternoon about tiny, burned-out Pablo, crouching in the dust of Lolotiquillo: I could have done more for him. I returned to the penitentiary; again the prisoners crowded to the bars. "I'll do all I can for you in San Salvador," I shouted. They cheered, and that made me feel better.

That evening, at the cloister, I discussed the case with the friars. Sister N, from the convent nearby, a bony woman in a brown veil, was visiting. I showed her the note from the inmate with the shaven head. ". . . I'm very Long oF my house . . . I need tweNty Five ColoNs For my Fud . . ." She laughed. "Oh, that's Felipe," she said. "I recognize his handwriting. He's written the same note to me several times. Felipe's a drug addict, he is. Cocaine, heroin, glue, anything he can get his hands on. He'll spend your money to get stoned. Oh, you're naive, you are."

But what of all the others? Should I not at least make inquiries of their cases in the capital? "Well, of course," Sister N said, "if you enjoy wasting your time. We've tried and tried. Officials keep telling you to come back tomorrow. Nothing ever happens. The prisoners' files are probably lost— deliberately. You'll spend your whole life at it, you will."

Walking home to the Arco Iris, I decided to forget the prisoners.

Dawn, and Good Friday. No sooner did the day begin than campesinos from all the province poured into San Francisco Gotera, swelling the population. Early in the morning, hundreds of men and youths bore the Holy Cross from the Franciscan church down to the arid Río San Francisco, then back again up the parched hills: Calvary relived. Even the landscape was similar: rolling hills of burnt umber, so evocative of Palestine.

Toward noon, Padre F and other Franciscans in brown, hooded habits led the faithful through the streets for the Vía Dolorosa. After them walked beautiful young women in black hair and white habits, then acolytes, in white habits with black cinctures, bearing brass crosses on high poles. More men followed, bearing a bier garlanded with flowers and a huge statue of Christ, robed in red velvet, crowned with real thorns, staggering beneath His heavy cross. Behind the bier marched an orchestra of soldiers in visored caps, blaring out a dirge with trumpets, tubas, and drums, courtesy of Colonel E. The colonel himself did not choose to be present, but in my mind I saw him, marching behind his mournful band, in his tunic and regalia, his pouting lips mumbling lamentations, all benevolence.

The crowd — youths, old men with parasols against the sun, young women in mantillas of lace, old women in mantillas of bath towel, multitudes of children — surged behind the orchestra. Even in the nations of Islam, I had rarely seen such fervor. The faithful *threw* themselves into these ceremonies, laughing one moment, in tears the next. "They insist upon them," Padre F said. "If we ever stopped, ah, *then* you'd see a revolution, you would."

Yet even on Good Friday, adolescent, press-ganged laughing soldiers, the cannon fodder of the state, continued to rumble through the streets in their American personnel carriers and armor-plated trucks mounted with machine guns en route to more killing missions in the region of the Torola, where they would torch more land, step on more mines, lose more limbs, or be ambushed and return to Gotera dead. Military helicopters still chopped across the cloudless sky. And even in Gotera, during the Vía Dolorosa, on the side of an umber hill, another fire raged.

4

AFTER HOLY WEEK, I returned to the capital via San Miguel, flying again through an ashen haze over fantastic volcanic cones and crater lakes. At my hotel in San Salvador, I found a telegram awaiting me: SUPLICAMOSLE POR FAVOR RECIBA NUESTROS MADRES LLEGARAN. JESUS, MARIO, MAURICIO SALUDOS. WE BEG YOU PLEASE SEE OUR MOTHERS THEYRE COMING . . .

It was signed by Mario Enrique, he of the striped cat at the penitentiary in Gotera. I brooded, and decided to ignore it. But by now I was intrigued with the Salvadoran system of justice. Soon I visited the women's prison at Ilopango, on the outskirts of the capital, not far from a volcanic lake, looking for a young woman I shall name "Marta."

I found her eventually beyond the high walls and barbed wire and male guards in the political prisoners' courtyard, all trees and twittering birds and sunshine, on a Sunday morning. She was lovely, in her early twenties, skin the color of light chestnut, smooth, swept-back chestnut hair, and dark opalescent eyes. She wore a neat dress of pink and white, and one of her legs was bandaged. In her arms, bundled in a pink blanket, she held an infant. She seemed afraid to talk, but I enticed her to a bench in the arcade, where softly she said much.

Early the previous year, not far from San Salvador, Marta had been abducted by four heavily armed men in civil dress and shoved into a van with black windows. Blindfolded, she was driven to a secret place, a cement room where for several hours the men interrogated her and accused her of working for the FMLN. Marta denied the accusation, whereupon she was handcuffed, stripped of all her clothing, and threatened with death. "Reveal your collaborators, and we will let you live," the men said. "I have no collaborators," Marta answered. "I'm not a guerrilla." The men beat her, then covered her head in a *capucha,* a tight hood much favored by Salvadoran torturers. Suffocating, with an anvil, as it were, pounding in her chest, Marta fainted. The men revived her with a bucket of ice water. She persisted in claiming innocence, so they smothered her again in the capucha, and yet again. "I'm innocent," she said. The four men removed their clothes, and, methodically, one after the other, raped her.

"I was taken then to the headquarters of the National Police. There, for five days of interrogation, I was kept naked and bound. I was kept alone, under a bright light, seated and bound to a wooden stool, without sleep and without food. I confessed to nothing."

Eventually a military judge declared Marta guilty of "political crimes" and dispatched her to Ilopango for an indefinite sentence. A month later, at six in the morning, rampaging air force troops, in full uniform and arms, invaded the prison, robbed the women, and shot Marta in the leg. Taken to a hospital for an operation, Marta was told by the doctors that she was pregnant — the result of her rape on the day she was abducted. She screamed for an abortion. The abortion was refused. In the autumn, still infirm from her leg wound, Marta gave birth to a girl at Ilopango.

This was the child, six months old now, quite healthy, a beauty herself, who sucked at Marta's breast. "The abortion . . ." Marta mused. "I'm glad I didn't have it. I love my daughter . . . I've nothing, no one else . . Who is the father? . . . How long will I be here? Will my daughter grow up in prison? . . ."

That seemed possible. On the day I visited, there were sixty-seven women and twenty-one children in the political section of Ilopango. The place seemed more a nursery, a day-care center, than it did a jail. Little girls and boys toddled about the courtyard, laughing with their mothers in the sunshine, bouncing balls, jumping rope, riding tricycles. This prison was so strange, a locked gate beyond but otherwise with no guards about.

More women appeared in the arcade, strolling in pairs. They were young, well shaped, smartly dressed, and heavily made up. Their breasts strained against tight, bright jerseys; they wore jeans that hugged their thighs and high heels. Up and down they marched, laughing, their heels clicking on the tiles, pretending not to notice me seated on my bench. Why, this was a beauty pageant. One woman in particular caught my fancy, and when I smiled she sat down to chat. She was Magdalena. Her eyes were smeared with green shadow. "Why the pageant?" I asked. "We have nothing else to do," Magdalena laughed. "At least we can keep our dignity."

No women in this jail were locked up; they gossiped in the corridors, played cards at tables, tended children, heard lectures, in the kitchen dressed fowl for Sunday luncheon. The place was spotless — the women were Salvadorans, after all — and I saw no supervision. This puzzled me. I was puzzled even more when I saw slogans and banners of the FMLN all over the walls: ¡UNIDAS PARA COMBATIR HASTA LA VICTORIA FINAL! ¡¡REVOLUCION O MUERTE!! ¡¡¡VENCEREMOS!!! Who ran the jail — the police or the FMLN?

The mystery deepened when I visited La Esperanza, Hope, the men's prison at San Luis Mariona, another suburb. This jail was much larger than the prison at Ilopango. After penetrating the first wall, you climbed a winding hill, walked past a shop that sold prisoners' handicrafts, then surrendered your passport to the guards to gain admittance to the prisoners' blocks. A body frisking, a series of locks and turnstiles, and you emerged into a huge sun-drenched concrete courtyard with basketball hoops. Men — hundreds of them — were milling everywhere. To the right was the *sector político* and eight hundred political prisoners, all accused of working for the guerrillas.

I went to Mariona looking especially for two prisoners, sons of a trade union leader, José Vladimir and Jaime Ernesto Centeno (true names), who supposedly had endured hellish tortures. I found Vladimir first, a sandy-haired, fair-skinned little fellow, very intellectual, very bourgeois. Despite his youth (he was twenty), he was already a professor of physiology and human anatomy at the Instituto Nacional. He took me into the clinic, which he tended, and locked the door. "They keep shutting off the water," he complained, demonstrating with a dry faucet. "We have hardly any water." Yet the clinic was clean, the prison was clean, the prisoners were clean, Vladimir was clean, *without water*. Vladimir sat down on the bench beside me, rolled up his shirt, ran a finger up and down his left forearm. "See the little red marks? Electronic torture; it's supposed to leave no traces, but if you look closely you can see the little red marks. They also attached the electrodes to my testicles.''

Such nightmares happened, according to Vladimir, because his father, Humberto, was so hated by the Duarte government. Humberto, an official of the telecommunications union, had been agitating for an improved labor contract when eight armed men in civil clothes invaded his house. They kidnapped him, Vladimir, and Jaime, tied their thumbs together behind their backs, thrust paper bags over their heads, and threw them into a truck. The truck took them to the cuartel of the Policia Hacienda, the infamous Treasury Police. With news of the arrest, the union threatened to halt telecommunications throughout El Salvador. Under such pressure Humberto was soon released. His sons were less fortunate.

Vladimir and Jaime (only eighteen, a Boy Scout) were delivered to the solicitude of a captain, the chief interrogator of the Treasury Police. The captain ordered the brothers separated. Jaime's ordeal resembled Vladimir's, but I continue with Vladimir's account: "I was stripped naked. My thumbs were tied again behind my back, and they put a blindfold on me. I was struck on the head, punched in the stomach, kicked in the balls. The arches of my feet were beaten with sticks. A plastic bag full of lime was tied over my head, and when I gasped for air the lime scorched my lungs. Then the electrodes, two hundred volts applied to my genitals and other soft parts of my body. I was suspended, by my thumbs, so that only my toes touched the floor. I heard children weeping. 'Your brothers and sisters,' they said. I was taken down, plunged into a tub of urine and shit, and held under until I almost drowned.''

I shuddered. "I can't believe that!" I protested. "The other tortures are terrible enough. But to be plunged into a tub of *excrement?*''

"*Sin embargo es la verdad,* but it's the truth," Vladimir insisted.

For nearly a week the Centeno brothers were not fed, and they were deprived of sleep. In rancid food, they were fed drugs that weakened their resistance. Told that their father was dying and would receive no medical attention until they signed confessions, the sons admitted to working for the FMLN. They were charged with kidnapping the chief of civil aviation, despite the testimony of witnesses that they were at school when the abduction happened, then filmed for television and forced to confess the crime to the nation.

I spoke to at least twenty other political prisoners at Mariona; all told me they had undergone tortures similar to the terrors of the Centeno brothers. Only one admitted he had "collaborated" with the FMLN. Another, once a driver at the United States Embassy and accused of "spying" on the embassy for the guerrillas, recounted the same tale of electrodes and immersion in tubs of urine and excrement, but added some interesting details. "My teeth," he said. "The Treasury Police had a special apparatus, very complicated, for sending electric charges through my teeth. They used to pull out fingernails, but now they're so eager to please the North Americans they're careful to leave no marks of torture on the body. Late one night, naked, I was taken to the precipice of Puerta del Diablo outside the city, where they held a submachine gun to my head, threatening to shoot me and push me off."

Naturally I wondered how the Treasury Police and the National Police would respond to the accusations of torture I heard incessantly at Ilopango and Mariona. I was recommended to Colonel Carlos Reynaldo López Nuila, vice minister for public security, El Salvador's chief of police. He was a short, dark man in eyeglasses; he received me in civil dress in his neat, cool office at the Ministry of Defense. He reminded me a bit of Daniel Ortega: he looked like a clerk. He did not, his critics said, act like one. Various Salvadorans of the peaceful left accused him of links, earlier in the decade, to the death squads. I opened with my usual dumb questions.

AUTHOR: What is the present state of public security, *mi coronel?*

COLONEL: El Salvador is a democracy. Our first concern is to assure the rights of each citizen. This is a personal priority of President Duarte's. We're developing a new image, a new attitude in each member of the security corps. Not simply a change of uniform, but a change *in the mind* of our men. We have new programs of education and formation — human relations, human rights, public relations.

A: Will you send any senior police or military official to trial for death-squad murders?

C: Thirty-five hundred members of the security forces have been dismissed for improper conduct and nine hundred have been tried for various crimes.

A: And senior officers, *mi coronel?*

C: To my knowledge no senior officer was ever involved in such crimes.

A: The political prisoners at Ilopango and Mariona all told me that they were tortured.

C: We've paid particular attention to this question, carefully instructed all our interrogators, established special norms of control and permanent supervision to prevent abuses . . . Our interrogation of terrorists is intense. We interrogate, wait an hour, interrogate again. Under the law, we have only fifteen days to obtain testimony to determine guilt or innocence. When you're dealing with a terrorist, you never have witnesses — they know they'll be killed — so we interrogate the terrorist. We let most of our prisoners go. We send thirty-five, forty percent to tribunals and detention. We don't beat anybody.

A: Worse than beatings, *mi coronel*. Rape, electrodes, the capucha . . .

C: The prisoners *lie*. They're dangerous. They are dedicated to acts of terrorism, without scruples. Most of them are assassins. They don't act like priests or helpless women! . . . We do not use the capucha or those other tortures. We interrogate with discipline.

A: Does the discipline include psychological torture?

C: I don't believe so. Psychological torture is practiced everywhere in the world.

A: Some prisoners, *mi coronel*, told me they have been plunged into tubs of shit.

C: *Jamás*. Never. Not even in isolated cases. When I was minister of police I visited the prisons twice a day. I would have noticed the smell. I never saw men plunged into tubs of shit, *baños de mierda*. *Jamás!* We opened the prisons, invited in priests and human rights groups. None of them said they saw tubs of shit.

The colonel was agitated, gesturing with his right arm, miming the dunking of a man as he said *"baños de mierda."*

I returned to Mariona, still unconvinced by Vladimir's account of this Satanic torture. He stood his ground. It was a Sunday, fiercely hot; the sun shone nakedly on the immense cement courtyard; the place shimmered with people. In little more than a fortnight, the population of the sector *político* had swelled from eight hundred to nearly nine hundred men. Youths mostly, well dressed, few peasants, urban middle class; their visiting parents, sisters, wives — well dressed, the bourgeoisie — mingled with them in the courtyard, opening thermos bottles and picnic baskets. That was the scene: a huge picnic. A smaller courtyard inside the political section was splashed with slogans: ¡¡FMLN — VANGUARDIA DEL PUEBLO!! . . . ENEMIES OF THE PEOPLE — THE BOURGEOISIE, THE BOURGEOIS ARMY! ¡¡IMPERIALISMO YANQUI — ENEMIGO PRINCIPAL!! . . . ¡¡VENCEREMOS!!

I knew now that these prisoners at Mariona, like the women at Ilopango, were permitted to organize their own lives and discipline. The FMLN controlled the political sections of both jails. The discipline was harsh, and it included revolutionary indoctrination. Drugs were forbidden; prisoners caught with drugs were severely punished. Like many Marxist insurrections, the Salvadoran insurgency was puritanical.

Meanwhile the pleading telegram from the abandoned common criminals at Gotera bore fruit. One evening after dark a frail woman, in her forties perhaps, showed up at my hotel. "I'm Mario Enrique's mother," she said. He of the cat. I hesitated, thinking I should dismiss her straightaway, saying that her son's case was hopeless and I could not help her. We stood face to face in the lobby; she fumbled in her shabby bag and took out a sheaf of letters. "For you," she said. "From the prisoners." I asked, "Will you come to my room, Señora?"

I was embarrassed to receive anyone in surroundings of such opulence. My hotel was the Novo, in the Colonia Escalón, the richest quarter of San Salvador; though inexpensive, my suite had two bedrooms, a kitchen, a salon, and it overlooked a swimming pool. The señora sat down on the edge of a couch; she had a certain terrified dignity. I asked, "Would you like a Pepsi Cola?"

"Just a drop. I have a weak bladder. May I use your toilet?"

I read the letters: they reeked of gracious despair. Jesús Aristedes: ". . . in the name of Our Celestial Father . . . for six years no trial . . . forgotten . . . no economic resources . . . my wife and two sons . . . Our Celestial Father . . ." Mario Enrique: ". . . your unforeseen visit . . . your generous heart . . . we brim with hope because of you . . . God is with you and now with us . . . a thousand apologies . . ." Señora emerged from the bathroom. She wore a red sweater and a black skirt; her brown hair was drawn into a bun. Her teeth were bad, and her skin was puffy. She may have been a beauty once: decay. I asked, "How did Mario get in trouble?"

"I'm not sure," she said. "He's so beautiful. His sweetheart lives with me and their little daughter . . ."

"Do you work?"

"I can't find work."

"How do you eat?"

"His sweetheart works — in a cafeteria — even on Sundays. She can't visit Mario at Gotera. It drives him crazy."

"Why don't you go to Gotera?"

"I do, on Sundays, when I can find money. Sometimes the guerrillas stop the bus. When I don't show up, Mario goes crazy."

"Have you no idea how he got in trouble?"

"It was so long ago. He was so young. At night, I think, in someone's house, he had a fight with another man . . ."

"With knives?"

"*Sí* . . . Mario only wants a trial. He could spend the rest of his life in jail."

She sobbed for a few seconds. Mario had been in Gotera for six months, but before Gotera he had been shuttled from one jail to another for five years. His mother had visited many officials since the day of his arrest, but she could pay no bribe and they would not help her. "I met the head of prisons once," she said. "In the courtyard, as he left his office. He was in a hurry. He told me, 'Tomorrow.' " I glimpsed her, this sickly, patient woman, standing in courtyards, waiting in ante-chambers, for nothing.

Some days later, I was invited to the Presidential Palace outside San Salvador, a huge place with marble balustrades built around a garden. Inside a great office, all carpets and mahogany, President José Napoleón Duarte's boon companion rose to greet me.

He was minister of culture and communications, but the title did no justice to his power. Julio Adolfo Rey Prendes was the President's eminence grise. He seemed El Salvador's suavest man — and the jol-liest. When he laughed a little goiter quivered on his neck. He was a renowned jokester and raconteur, not ashamed to pursue pretty women or to drink too much at high state functions. El Presidente's chief propagandist, adviser, confessor, and chum; they joined the Boy Scouts together, founded the Christian Democratic party together, fled into exile together. Where Duarte foundered, Rey Prendes struggled to suc-ceed: he had conducted public and secret negotiations with the guerrillas to end the civil war, endeavors so far abortive. Ray Prendes bemused me with his candor.

He admitted that some torture was still practiced in the dungeons of the National and Treasury Police and that the whole system of justice was a shambles. "I don't understand these military tribunals," he la-mented. "Confessions extracted under torture are worthless. Confes-sions signed but not seen are worthless." Some people would say anything to avoid torture, and the real culprit could escape. He knew of a man who signed twelve contradictory confessions. He mimicked a terrified man signing scraps of paper. "Oh no no no. I'm not a murderer. I'm innocent. Give me the paper! I'll sign it! Oh yes yes yes. I'm a murderer! I'm guilty. Give me the confession! I'll sign it!"

In court the judge threw out the case. "To the extent that the military still tortures, we're trying to stop it. They're beginning to realize it doesn't work." He meant physical torture. As for psychological torture, "Yes, we practice it, but so does every other country."

And yes, some judges took bribes. They were poorly paid, there were not enough of them, and the courts were so impoverished they had no typewriters. The penal code was medieval. With government and U.S. money, however, the justice system was being made more just. "Ah," I said. I handed him my list of abandoned common criminals at San Francisco Gotera. He read the list carefully, dropping his jolly face. "This is so sad," he said, and he seemed to mean it. "To be left in jail so long without hope. My wife was a criminal lawyer. She tells me of such cases."

Again, such travesties happened for want of resources. During the worst days of the death squads, eight hundred political murders a month, "we had only sixty-five detectives. They were good for nothing! So poor they had to thumb rides! They had to take the bus!" For common crimes, I could imagine the accumulation.

I pressed the Gotera case. "I'll pass this list to the president of the Supreme Court," Rey Prendes said. "I'll speak to him myself. I promise."

Señora rejoiced when I told her this news that evening. She had taken to visiting me at night, though I was never sure when she would show up. When she did not, I grew anxious. Eventually after dinner I would go out to the street, walk up and down, waiting for her. Sometimes I heard the chatter of automatic weapons, since after dark the guerrillas stole into the capital. A cement mixer and a dump truck blocked my view of the avenue beyond, but when I heard Señora's soft footsteps and saw her frail shadow in the dim lamps against the dump truck, I was calm.

In my suite I laid out food—cold ham, tomato, cookies, and bananas—for Señora to eat. She picked at it. "Why don't you eat?" I asked. "I'm not hungry," she said. "Do you have a bag? I'll take it to Mario on Sunday." Señora's was the perennial ritual of an adolescent girl seduced, beaten, and abandoned: her lover had walked out even before Mario was born. Mario's was the only life she had or wanted. She lived to visit Mario on Sundays—the visits were her food. The bus schedule from the capital the hundred miles to Gotera was not convenient. She had to leave at dawn on Sunday, and she had only two hours to pass with Mario at the prison before she caught the last bus back. "Mario goes crazy if I don't come. He's always there, squeezing the bars, waiting for me to come. We don't talk much. He hugs me." She sobbed for a few seconds. Once, only for an instant, I sobbed with her. I said, "Eat." She put my bananas and cookies in her bag: the sobs were her nourishment.

Before dawn one Sunday, I took her in a taxi to the bus station. The depot was a tumult of campesinos and their tiny children, stampeding onto buses that could not contain them, with hens, goats, and grandmothers, harassed, shrieking porters heaping luggage on the roofs, then lashing it down with threadbare rope. I fussed over Señora's ticket, and after finding her a window seat, stood outside her window still dispensing advice as the bus pulled out. "Eat the cookies!" I called after her. "They're not for Mario!" She nodded, and the bus was gone.

Soon I saw Dr. Julio Alfredo Samayoa, the minister of justice, an amiable plump man with a mouth faintly like a fish's and a remarkable resemblance to Georges Pompidou. He sat beneath a gilt ceiling and walls lined with legal books and a kitsch Alpine painting of village and lake, snow-capped mountains. Like Rey Prendes, he surprised me with his sympathy.

"But I *know* of the Gotera case," he said. "I've visited every prison in El Salvador." He produced a pile of color photographs of himself surrounded by inmates, proving his point, then held up a batch of letters from distraught families seeking trials for their sons and daughters in every corner of the country.

MINISTER: I read every letter. In the margin, I note the action.

AUTHOR: I recognize, Excellency, your strained resources, but imagine yourself in jail, without a trial, for ten years.

M: I know, it's terrible. The prisoners of Gotera did have trials, but they had no money to pay their lawyers and their cases were abandoned. I've created an office of legal assistance for just such cases.

A: Won't it be difficult to find their files?

M: No, we have a system. We can find their files in half an hour. Rest assured, I'll take action. I'll help the prisoners of Gotera to have new trials and decide their fate.

A: Thank you, Your Excellency.

M: I'll notify the mothers of the prisoners. I'll go to Gotera myself with this list of yours and see the men.

A: Thank you, Your Excellency.

M: I'll investigate. *¡Hoy mismo!* This very day!

Señora did not visit me that evening, so next day I called at her home to convey the minister's promise. I have misplaced my note on her barrio's location, but I remember climbing steep squeezed alleys in the heat of the afternoon. Open sewers trickled through the barrio but released no smell. Women scrubbed clothes on wooden horses between shacks of wood and corrugated tin. Again, there was a luxuriance of barefoot children and such a labyrinth of alleys that for minutes I lost my way. When Señora sees me at her door, she cries, "Ooooh." When I tell her about the minister, she cries, "Ooooh." We sit down at once to write Mario of the news. I counsel patience, however, and add a postscript: "Don't pray for miracles."

Señora's shack was a heap of wooden chairs and cardboard boxes, blankets, and some dry foodstuffs. Before a picture of the Virgin, and one of Mario, stood some votive lamps with no more wax. A ladder led to a loft and Mario's bed, where he had slept with his sweetheart and conceived his child. His sweetheart was at the cafeteria, working, but his daughter, about six years old, darker and less wistful than her father, came in from the alley leading a blind woman. This was Señora's mother, a hag in an apron, snowy hair, and no teeth. I lingered long enough to be polite, sipping a cup of tea and promising to pursue the Gotera case with President Duarte when he received me.

I returned to my opulence in Escalón uneasy and full of doubt. I had been encouraged by the minister's promises but not quite convinced. I kept hearing Sister N's voice: "Oh, you're naive, you are. Well, of course, if you enjoy wasting your time . . . You'll spend your whole life at it, you will." Next day, by chance, at the Hotel Camino Real, I met the minister of justice again. He volunteered that he had telephoned the director of the prison at Gotera. "Your list is exact," Dr. Samayoa said. "However, one of the inmates has escaped, and another is so violent he killed a fellow prisoner."

"Will Your Excellency now bring the remaining men to trial?"

"*Claro.*"

He seemed less zealous. Next morning, at the last moment, the palace called to cancel my audience with President Duarte. "The President is ill." Not a diplomatic illness; he canceled all of his appointments indefinitely; the man had a bad stomach and suffered chronic agony. I passed the Gotera list to the Archbishop of San Salvador and the United States ambassador; the president of the Supreme Court was too busy to receive me. Señora continued to visit me at night, and we continued to hope together for good news soon.

5

AS I WRITE THIS in New England, snow falls outside, Mozart sings softly from my stereo, and spread upon my desk are photographs of mutilated Salvadoran children. Here is a picture of a child, ten years old, supine in a garbage dump. His face and torso are disfigured by knife wounds and the bullets that sent him—I am sure of this—to Christ. The photograph is stamped by the Salvadoran Commission on Human Rights and bears a notation: "Dressed in yellow shirt, blue pants, no shoes . . . *Vestido en camiseta amarilla, pantalón azul, sin zapatos. Asesinado . . . 12 de diciembre del/84.*"

I was given this document, and others like it, by the women at the office of Mothers of the Disappeared (Comité de Madres y Familiares de Presos, Desaparecidos y Asesinados Políticos de El Salvador) situated on the Calle Oriente above the Pizza Boom. The women crowd around me, sending up sighs, pointing and mourning as I leaf through their albums of human corpses with legs, tongues, genitalia missing, faces erased by acid. Nothing has improved, they claim. Our sons are still murdered, the repression is stronger, the death squads have been reactivated.

They tell me that "on the outskirts of San Salvador, more mutilated and decapitated bodies are being found again. Selective 'disappearances' are increasing—ten in the last week. Ask any mother who walks in here—most of these atrocities are committed by the army, the National Guard, the National Police, and the Treasury Police. We have documentary proof, but we get no sympathy from your North American ambassador! A few weeks ago, a delegation of North Americans and two of us went to the embassy to talk to the ambassador. He didn't believe our statistics, and he had no interest in what we told him. He didn't *listen.* He told us that El Salvador is a democracy, with a good president, peace, and work. He told us, in perfect Spanish, 'You're liars. Your Committee of Mothers is a front for the FMLN.' "

"I've heard that accusation," I interjected.

"No, we're neutral. The only reason for the war is social injustice. The army terrorizes and kills to defend the privileged classes. The victims are the poor—our *sons*. We only seek information about our sons, trials for the guilty, and liberty. Does that make us guerrillas? We have no links to the guerrillas.''

The embassy insisted that they did: "They are not sweet old ladies." That some mothers sympathized with the FMLN was common knowledge; that they exaggerated the atrocities of the state was clear when one compared their arithmetic with the statistics of the archbishop—Monseñor Arturo Rivera y Damas, whose predecessor was assassinated in 1980.

Unquestionably, the worst horrors happened then, in the early 1980s, when the death squads so diligently produced thirty-five headless corpses a day. Since 1983, this civil carnage had gradually diminished to an inventory of corpses that varied between several a week to perhaps thirty per month. Pressure from the United States contributed to this improvement, though the most notorious killers were never punished; the moans of the torture chambers were likewise muted, though torture continued to be practiced. For the police, severing ears, tongues, and genitalia for the most part passed from fashion in favor of technology (electrodes), beatings, immersions, deprivation of food and sleep, and other techniques that left no traces on the victims' skin.

And yes, despite their denials, no doubt many of the political prisoners I met at Ilopango and Mariona were guerrillas or their collaborators, just as the FMLN instructed its followers in case of capture to claim that the police tortured them. And yes, the embassy counseled the police that torture foolishly created more guerrillas, and many prisoners escaped torture by signing confessions they never saw; but still, perhaps a quarter of the prisoners were physically tortured anyway, though at the embassy I was assured that the true statistic was "ten to fifteen percent." And yes, however diminished, the death squads—drawn from the security forces, the civil defense, various free-lance vigilantes of the radical right—still went out at night.

Thus whatever their sympathies or overstatements, the mothers moved me. How could anyone, visiting their dark warren above the Pizza Boom, hearing their histories of sons and husbands butchered in the night, turning over the leaves of their albums and those faces of mutilated children, not be moved? It is hardly possible to meet a Salvadoran, rich or poor, who has not been intimately touched by horror. In a sermon at San Salvador's cathedral, a priest tried to psychoanalyze the torturers:

"Sin has become structural. Many of these men who torture inside the barracks . . . do no more than obey orders; it is all part of the system. How many times are great torturers fathers who are so good and kind to their children, and their wives, at home? . . . How is it possible that fathers and husbands so tender at home, when they pass through the door of the barracks become so ferocious and terrible? Because the system of structural sin pushes them to it. If they did not, then others would. Some say, 'If I do not torture they will say I am a collaborator with the guerrillas and they will torture me.' It is a great chain of evil within the system of sin." One remembers Jacobo Timerman's Argentine torturer who begged Timerman's help to gain admittance for his son to an exclusive school. To consider such compartmentalized emotions — separate boxes of the brain for love and horror — is to think of Hitler. Even Hitler loved his dog.

Thus one probes for historical explanations, into the mysterious rituals of Indian darkness and tribal nights, into the violent mixture of Indian and Spanish culture that produced mass psychosis or what Jung called convulsions of the "collective unconscious." After the Castilian kings expelled the Jews and Muslims from Spain and conquered the American tropics, they sent to the new hemisphere not only the crucified Christ and His love but the terrors of the Holy Inquisition and the rapacity of the conquistadores, who enslaved and slaughtered whole civilizations in their greed for spice and gold.

This legacy of horror became entrenched in the Salvadoran psyche and lingered long after the isthmus broke the bonds of Spanish rule in the early nineteenth century. Indeed, given the peculiar conditions of the country — its tiny size, swelling population, scarcity of arable soil, the peonage of its Indians and campesinos, the avarice of its oligarchy — the legacy was exacerbated. Military tyrannies became essential to preserve the opulence of the few and to contain the restive population. In 1931, for example, an eccentric officer, General Maximiliano Hernández Martínez, mounted a coup d'état and established a military dictatorship that lasted twelve years and gripped the nation in nightmares.

General Martínez was a figure of folkloric blood lust, raving mad probably. A dabbler in the occult, he shared his delusions with the Salvadoran people as he lectured them on radio: "It is a greater crime to kill an ant than to kill a man, because a dead man is reincarnated but an ant dies forever . . . How good that children go barefoot. Barefoot they can better receive the beneficial effluvia of the planet, the vibrations of the earth. Plants and animals don't wear shoes.'' Martínez forbade further industrialization, and when a measles epidemic raged he forbade vaccinations. He had the street lamps wrapped in colored cellophane, confident that the tinted light would dispel the pestilence.

A North American diplomat, visiting soon after General Martínez seized power, wrote that ''El Salvador today is much like Russia before the revolution . . . ripe for communism. The revolution may be delayed for several years, ten or even twenty, but when it comes it will be bloody.'' In fact, a communist insurrection erupted early in 1932, and as it did the nearby volcanoes of Guatemala erupted and with them the volcano of Izalco in El Salvador's western province of Sonsonate. The air was filled with fine ash, the earth trembled, as the campesinos of Sonsonate, waving machetes, marched toward the towns. Not far from San Salvador itself, rebels attacked a telegraph office crying, ¡Viva la República Soviética! When campesinos attacked Sonsonate town, they killed perhaps one hundred people, raped, and pillaged. General Martínez responded by sending in the army and ordering a matanza — massacre.

In the shadow of Izalco volcano, groups of fifty men were bound together by the thumbs and led to the wall of the Church of the Assumption, where they were shot. Other victims were made to dig mass graves before they fell into them from the bullets of machine guns. On the roads, the National Guard shot everybody. Farabundo Martí, once General Sandino's secretary, was shot by a firing squad, but many campesinos were less lucky. They were tortured, disemboweled, tossed into the air, and caught with the tips of bayonets. Pigs and vultures feasted randomly on human corpses.

> General Ochoa made all who had been captured crawl on their knees to him seated in the courtyard of the fort. He said to them: ''Come here and smell my gun.'' The prisoners pleaded in the name of God and their children, for they had heard shots.
>
> But the General insisted: ''If you don't smell my gun then you are a communist and afraid. Who has no sin knows no fear.''
>
> The campesino smelled the barrel of the gun, and the General put a bullet in his face. He said, ''Bring in the next one.''

The matanza was effective. To this day, nearly six decades later, Sonsonate and the contiguous coffee areas of western El Salvador offer the least sympathy and support to the guerrillas of the Farabundo Martí

National Liberation Front. Perhaps thirty thousand campesinos and Indians were slaughtered in the matanza, 2 percent of El Salvador's population at that time. The late communist poet Roque Dalton wrote the epitaph of the matanza:

> All of us were born half dead in 1932
> We survived but half alive
> Each one with an interest-bearing account of 30,000
> dead compounded daily
> That continues today to charge with death those
> who continue being born
> Half-dead
> Half-alive.

The memory of that matanza helped to inspire the urban insurrection of 1979 and the FMLN's war against the government ever since. In response, the Salvadoran military resolved to repress the insurrection by fighting a "dirty war" on the Argentine model and imported Argentine officers to advise them how to wage it. The death squads were the exotic result. The logic was lucid in its cold blood: if you kill enough innocents, you can quell the wanton cities. And the death squads succeeded: the urban insurrection was crushed, though the bad seed was sown and the revolution spread to the countryside, whereupon there followed the witless massacres of civilians by the army in zones of rural combat.

Add to all of that the vagaries of U.S. policy and the changing of the guard in Washington. In late 1980, when the American people repudiated President Carter, the Salvadoran colonels had every reason to believe that his agenda of human rights had been brushed aside as well. President Reagan and General Alexander Haig swept into power announcing to the world that in their crusade against communism they would "draw the line" at the isthmus.

What did Reagan or his secretary of state — what did the American public — know or care about Salvadoran history? In their unfathomable ignorance, had Haig or Reagan any notion of the consequence of their words? The Salvadoran colonels took Reagan's election as a license to kill. The worst bloodletting of the death squads — eight hundred to nine hundred bodies a month — took place between the time of Reagan's election and the end of his first year. And it was not until more than three years after Reagan's election — December 1983 — that Vice President Bush visited San Salvador to tell the colonels to stop killing civilians.

Wherever I went in El Salvador, I asked people to explain the deepest reasons for the killing. "We learned it from the Spaniards," said some. "It's the natural consequence of capitalism," said others. "It's in our blood," said others. I was repelled by the blood argument. Salvadorans were innately no more evil than the rest of us. For every horror story I heard, I witnessed remarkable acts of love; under like conditions Salvadoran horror could happen anywhere, including the United States. "The horrors happen because the killers are never punished," a human rights official tells me. True, but still not deep enough.

When I returned to my study in Massachusetts, I burrowed into literature looking for answers. I found them, maybe, in a passage from Cardinal Newman that had been drummed into me in youth by the classical Jesuits. Newman considered the world "in its length and breadth, its various history, the many races of man, their starts, their fortunes . . . their conflicts" and then "their habits, governments, forms of worship . . . their aimless courses, their random achievements . . . the tokens so faint and broken, of a superintending design . . . the greatness and littleness of man, his far-reaching aims, his short duration, the curtain hung over his futurity, the disappointments of life, the defeat of good, the success of evil, physical pain, mental anguish, the prevalence and intensity of sin . . . that condition of the whole race . . . in the Apostle's words, 'having no hope and without God in the world,' — all this . . . inflicts upon the mind . . . a profound mystery . . . absolutely beyond human solution."

What could Cardinal Newman say to such a mystery? ". . . either there is no Creator, or this living society of men is . . . discarded from His presence . . . *if* there be a God, *since* there is a God, the human race is implicated in some terrible aboriginal calamity." So . . . back to the Fall . . . to Original Sin . . . to the Garden. As a rationale of horror it may still seem wanting, but I can suggest no other.

6

SALVADORANS OUTSIDE the prisons seemed to suffer almost as much. Misery was the norm; most people accepted it, made do, with sighs, for life was always so, a vale of tears. The guerrillas were unpopular, but nobody I met in El Salvador any longer believed President Duarte's campaign promises of peace, work, and social justice. Land reform schemes, which Duarte inherited, were ineffective but still too radical for the Salvadoran right. The superfluous poor migrated from the land to the cities, which could not contain them, and the cities teemed with bright young men and women desperate for work. Throughout the country, unemployment and marginal employment afflicted half the populace; in San Salvador, 70 percent.

I had seen similar migrations of the poor from the barren land to the tumid cities of Egypt, India, Morocco, Ghana, Congo-Zaire, and elsewhere in the great tropics. And so in San Salvador there they are, thousands of the indolent young, restless, milling, in the plaza beneath the statue of General Gerardo Barrios before the unfinished cement cathedral, selling cigarettes, sunglasses, lottery tickets. They spill over into the Plaza Martín nearby, where they sell newspapers, and into the Parque Libertad a block or two away, where they shine shoes and loiter, listening to an Evangelical, Bible in hand, preach of the Kingdom To Come. Restless, milling. Many of them do not stay. Instead they walk to the border, all across Guatemala and Mexico to the Río Grande or southern California. Today six hundred thousand of them, maybe nearly a million — at any rate more than a tenth of El Salvador's population — live in the barrios of Los Angeles, San Antonio, Miami, Brooklyn, even Boston, without documents, doing menial work, sending their savings home, and their remittances are a richer source of dollars than even coffee to El Salvador.

For all his endeavors to reduce misery, nothing Duarte did seemed to succeed. He devalued the currency, raised the minimum wage, imposed controls to fight inflation, but in such an unstable society few had confidence to invest; flight of capital continued, unemployment remained a scourge. For his modest interference with a free economy, the right — urban entrepreneurs, coffee landlords — considered Duarte a socialist. The leftist trade unions mounted massive demonstrations in the streets, demanding peace and work.

Duarte had been chosen President in 1984 in a free election, much to the relief of the Reagan administration, which has boasted of this triumph of Christian Democracy ever since. His reputation as a Christian Democrat, however, had a greater gloss abroad than among his own people. Duarte himself was said to be honest, but his government, from the cabinet to the lower bureaucracy, seemed dank with corruption. The chronic story in a poor country: a man becomes a minister, and no matter his clean intentions his family and extended family — in a society still of clans — hound him for the pearls of office. Now that Papá is a minister his loved ones at last can get rich. Papá's wife wants a new house, his children want their own cars and study in the United States, his uncles, in-laws, cousins want jobs. His life becomes unbearable until he relents and sells his ministerial favors at market value. Lower down, even a driver's license demands a bribe. And compounding the corruption of the government was Duarte's style of rule.

His critics called Duarte a megalomaniac; at the least he loathed the faintest challenge to his preeminence and chose weak ministers, though he hardly listened to them. "He's deaf," his own cronies said. His ministers drew up elaborate plans addressing social problems; the President tore them apart, deciding everything himself. His vacillations were another curse. Then Inés Guadalupe, his daughter, was kidnapped by the FMLN. The President's natural anguish as a father forced him to bargain for her liberty, but the affair strained his relations with the army and in the end made him ever more beholden to the right-wing military establishment. Upon all such trials, superimpose the civil war and the mania of the guerrillas to wreck the economy.

The FMLN controlled only enclaves of territory in Morazán and Chalatenango, but its troops and agents operated throughout the country—in Santa Ana to the west, Cabañas in the center, La Unión to the east, and elsewhere, not least in San Salvador itself. The guerrilla armies had suffered many deaths and desertions, their total strength did not exceed five or six thousand troops, but they continued to wage a terrible war of attrition. Their land mines maimed and killed not only soldiers but innocent peasants. "Our aim with the mines is to turn every road into a river of blood," boasted Joaquín Villalobos. And some months after I left Gotera and San Miguel, the guerrillas stole into those towns in the middle of the night, attacked the garrisons, and killed hundreds of soldiers.

The guerrillas burn down municipal offices, destroying precious records of campesino births, marriages, and land deeds. They levy "war taxes" on farmers and kidnap mayors; they stop buses and trucks and shoot civilian passengers who resist. They shoot civilians they suspect of collaborating with the army. Above all, the guerrillas sabotage the economy. They attack bridges, power pylons, and telephone lines, interrupt transport on the main roads, torch crops of coffee, cotton, and sugar that earn foreign exchange. They have made power blackouts in San Salvador and throughout the country commonplace. The FMLN's cold-blooded destruction costs El Salvador hundreds of millions of dollars a year and compounds the suffering of the people. Such sabotage and terror reflect a classical revolutionary strategy of inviting repression, of escalating chaos, unemployment, flight of capital, of rendering conditions throughout society so intolerable that eventually (the guerrillas hope) the masses will revolt and the government will collapse.

Before me as I write is a guerrilla poster showing Reagan bearing guns, helicopters, bags of dollars and Duarte driving across a bridge about to be blown up. Guerrillas are everywhere with guns and explosive charges, demolishing power lines, the army, Christian Democracy, the other bourgeois parties, indeed the whole infrastructure of the country: POW! The mood of the cartoon is comical, as if the devastation were wildly funny and the Salvadoran poor were not its victims. But then the FMLN, like the Sandinistas, has its own conception of the poor: the real poor support the revolution. The Farabundo Martí Front was divided into five armies; such guerrilla comandantes as Jorge Shafik Handal of the Communist Party of El Salvador, Leonel González of the Popular Liberation Forces, Roberto Roca of the Revolutionary Party of Central American Workers, and Fermán Cienfuegos of the Armed Forces of National Resistance were all hardened ideological Marxists trained variously in Cuba, the Eastern bloc, Vietnam, and Sandinista Nicaragua. Joaquín Villalobos of the People's Revolutionary Army had enjoyed similar indoctrination but was considered less theologically pure. Despite their common theology — God is the Revolution — the comandantes were riven with rivalries and internecine assassinations.

Villalobos himself ordered the execution of the renowned Salvadoran communist poet Roque Dalton in 1975 and may have shot him with his own hand. Here is Dalton's vision of the Revolution, contained in his ode to the matanza of 1932: "Let us unite the half-dead who are this country . . . / Against the murderers of the dead and the half-dead / All of us together have more death than they / But all of us together / Have more life than they. / The all-powerful union of our half-lives / Of the half-lives of all of us born half dead in 1932." Villalobos killed Dalton, or had him killed, on the pretext that he was a CIA spy; in truth, Dalton opposed him in a power struggle. Here in its turn was another world of tenuous alliance, constant treachery, and blood.

In Managua in 1983, Mélida Anaya Montes, nom de guerre Ana María, a former schoolmistress intriguing for control of the Salvadoran

Popular Liberation Forces, was murdered, stabbed eighty times with an ice pick. Her rival in the guerrilla army, Salvador Cayetano Carpio, nom de guerre Marcial, a Stalinist of the old school who doted on the doctrine of prolonged war and resisted Cuban and Sandinista tutelage of his revolution, was implicated in the murder. Old and sick, a mythic revolutionary, the Salvadoran Ho Chi Minh, Marcial railed against his converging enemies, then shot himself. Purges of Marcial's disciples throughout the FMLN soon followed.

Nevertheless, for all of their vendettas, in late 1985 the five fighting factions of the Farabundo Martí Front announced their intention to forge a single Marxist-Leninist party in El Salvador led by a "vanguard" that would wage "a twenty-year war" against "North American imperialism" and "liquidate the capitalist system." Nominally the guerrillas remained allied with non-Marxist bourgeois revolutionaries, but such allies were increasingly irrelevant and could never march in the vanguard. Nakedly, unlike Fidel Castro and the Sandinistas, who at least had the guile to dissemble before they seized power, the Salvadoran guerrillas boasted of their communism.

Earlier, together with the bourgeois revolutionaries, the guerrillas had been content to promise a political agenda that echoed the Historic Program of the Sandinistas. They promised to "liquidate the economic, political and military dependence of our country on Yankee imperialism"; to "transfer to the people, through nationalizations and the creation of collective . . . enterprises, the fundamental means of production and distribution"; and to create massive public services for health, literacy, education, and housing through "a truly revolutionary and popular power." Like the Sandinistas, they also promised to respect limited free enterprise and political pluralism. As I pore over these utopian documents today, I remember all the times I heard like promises of a socialist Elysium in so many poor nations of the world, and I think of the results. I think of Nicaragua, of Sandinista rhetoric, and the reality of that country nearly a decade after the Revolution.

Now the Sandinista model is not enough for the Salvadoran guerrillas. Relations between the fighters of Farabundo Martí and the Sandinistas had long been close but envenomed by Sandinista arrogance and reciprocal suspicion. From their rich war chest (money from kidnappings, mostly), the Salvadorans had given the Sandinistas $10 million in cash before the Triumph. Once in power, the Sandinistas repaid the debt by sending arms to their Salvadoran comrades and allowing them to establish offices for propaganda, logistics, and other purposes in Managua. Yet the Sandinistas had their own priorities; in power they were anxious about their foreign image as moderate revolutionaries, and often they counseled prudence to the Salvadorans and were niggardly with aid. Over time, the Salvadoran comandantes resented the Sandinistas' manipulations, their bourgeois compromises, and called them "chauvinistic, irresponsible, and without ethics."

Thus in resolving to forge their Marxist party the Salvadoran guerrillas looked beyond the Sandinista and Soviet models and even beyond Fidel Castro to the prolonged and victorious struggle of the Viet Cong. They gazed deeply as well into their own heroic legend, into the struggles and unyielding life of Agustín Farabundo Martí. El Negro Martí — so named for his dark looks — began his legend as a law student, devouring the doctrines of anarchists and Marxists that filled a little shelf in the library of his school. The son of a prosperous farmer, soon after World War I he was arrested in San Salvador for student agitation. Exiled, he moved to Guatemala, where he mingled with other leftist intellectuals and with them formed the Central American Socialist party. By 1927, he was in Nicaragua, a colonel in General Sandino's army and Sandino's secretary. By then Martí was a confirmed Marxist, and his ideological differences with Sandino grew so agitated that a rupture followed. Martí returned to his homeland to organize destitute workers and to help found the Communist Party of El Salvador, which looked to Moscow for inspiration in establishing a workers' state.

The new party achieved considerable success in appealing to the Indians of the western coffee plantations and to the proletariat of San Salvador. Martí preached a minimum wage, social security, the right to strike, progressive taxes, free and universal education, state ownership of transport, equality for women and Indians. Repression soon followed. Thereafter Martí's life became a fugue of street riots, imprisonments, hunger strikes, popular adulation, more repression, government manhunts, soldiers firing into mobs. Then the communist insurrection — the first in the Western Hemisphere — and the matanza of 1932. The Communist party was annihilated root and branch; Martí was shot, dumped into a nameless grave, covered with weeds. The matanza changed everything, and its ghost haunts everything; its embers glow in the guerrilla civil war. It is a garden also, ever ripe with the martyrdom of Farabundo Martí.

Knowing this, it is less difficult to grasp the implacable nature of the

Salvadoran guerrilla and why he is distinct even from his fellows in Cuba and Nicaragua. He has suffered more; victory has been denied him longer; he knows that if he is captured he will be shot or tortured horribly. Such suffering and prolonged war create their own mystique; I glimpsed that during my brief detention by the guerrillas in Morazán. Guerrillas in the field sleep hugging their rifles, with all they own beside them. They live on tortillas and beans if they can find them, in the mountains on the meat of rabbits and reptiles if they are lucky. They rarely bathe, and then only in rivers, and their bodies are covered with the bites of insects and the scars of wounds. All suffer chronic dysentery, diarrhea and blood, worms gnawing incessantly at their bowels.

Yet there was a macabre romanticism in that life, that saga of sleeping beneath the stars and never being sure you would wake up, the tough idealism and ceaseless danger. In our present time only Marx and Mohammed can inspire such violent devotion. Despite themselves the comandantes, all the elite guerrillas, loved it. It was the only life they knew. It was almost as though, like gamblers who play to lose, they hoped never to win the war or that they would never have to govern and could remain in the mountains forever. Their mission was less to liberate than to *be* guerrillas, waging the armed struggle for its own pure sake.

Destruction, also, if done long enough, makes its own mystique. Suppose the guerrillas *should* one day win the war and come to power? In 1983, on Radio Venceremos, they acknowledged that with victory they "will expel from the country all those who yielded our homeland, our resources and our power of decision to imperialist interests." Not a threat to be laughed off. A former guerrilla comandante told me that the FMLN might not even bother to expel its enemies but would shoot them in the thousands — using the Cuban model of the early 1960s. Pondering the history of the Farbundo Martí Front — knowing the special psyche of these guerrillas as compared to the milder Sandinistas, recalling the horrors they have so long suffered at the hands of the security forces, above all remembering the blood feud born of the matanza — I believe the comandante. A guerrilla victory in El Salvador would not end the killing, merely prolong it for different reasons. In power, the Martí guerrillas might make the Sandinistas look like Swedish socialists.

And yet the Salvadoran people, so bled by the war, so disgusted by both government and rebels, yearned for dialogue between Duarte and the guerrillas to give them peace. Monseñor Rivera y Damas, Archbishop of San Salvador, labored constantly as mediator to fulfill his people's wish.

When I visited the archbishop in his modest office in the city, I found him morose. I genuflected to kiss his ring, but he wore none; I addressed him in Latin, but he did not respond; he lacked Cardinal Obando's twinkle. A tall man, a learned canon lawyer, he sat in a black suit beneath a photograph of his predecessor.

Ah, his predecessor, another of El Salvador's slaughtered lambs, Monseñor Oscar Arnulfo Romero, assassinated, most probably by the extreme right — shot in the chest and face as he celebrated Mass. Since that sacrilege in 1980 Monseñor Romero has been venerated by his people, and rightly so, as a martyr-saint. The left burns incense to his memory; in the warren of the mothers above the Pizza Boom a halo hovers above the portrait of his head. His tomb in the cathedral is a people's shrine, covered with candles and flowers; miracles have been attributed to his celestial intervention. The Jesuits, who influenced him greatly — even wrote his speeches — mourn him as much.

"I have often been threatened with death," Monseñor Romero said prophetically only a fortnight before his murder. "I do not believe in death without resurrection. If they kill me, I shall rise again in the Salvadoran people. Even now I offer my blood to God for the redemption and resurrection of El Salvador. If God accepts the sacrifice of my life, if they come to kill me, I bless them that do it. Martyrdom is a Grace."
And for him a rare grace; Graham Greene reminds us that Monseñor Romero was the first archbishop to be murdered at the altar since Saint Thomas à Becket was butchered at Canterbury by the minions of Henry II in the twelfth century.

I could hardly blame his successor — burdened with such memories — for being somber. Or cautious. Monseñor Romero had railed against the army and the rich; Monseñor Rivera condemned the atrocities of both sides, but he chose his words with prudence and managed to stay alive.

The archbishop did not have much to offer me. He had coaxed government and guerrillas to the negotiating table several times, and he has done so since, but nothing of moment emerged from those encounters. Essentially the guerrillas said: Our troops stay where they are, and give us ministries in the government. Essentially Duarte replied: Lay down your arms, then we'll talk. As for the extreme right, inside and outside the army, it still aspired to total extermination of the armed left. Since the archbishop could not stop the war, he struggled as best he could to make it less brutal. "We're trying to help refugees, widows, orphans, wounded guerrillas . . ."

If only the army would abolish the death squads altogether, cease uprooting the civil populace and bombing guerrilla hospitals; if only the guerrillas would soften their economic sabotage and stop laying land mines . . . then government and guerrillas might talk with greater confidence of a political solution. Alas, the parties were so far apart . . . We sat silently for some moments as a clock ticked. "*Tempus fugit*," the archbishop said finally. I smiled at his subtle joke, and took my leave.

The war went on. The guerrillas fought with M-16 rifles, M-50 and M-60 heavy machine guns, mortars, grenades, 90 mm cannon, and (most lethally) with their land mines. This largely was American weaponry, transshipped from Vietnam through Cuba and Nicaragua or captured on the field of battle. The government forces, nearly fifty-five thousand strong, pursued the guerrillas ferociously, on the ground with rifles, submachine guns, and armored trucks, 60 mm and 81 mm mortars, M-79 grenade launchers; from the air with Hughes and UH-1 helicopters that rained machine-gun bullets, A-37 jet aircraft that dropped 500-pound and 750-pound iron fragmentation bombs on guerrilla strongholds and field hospitals.

No longer did the army massacre civilians, but since the guerrillas lived among the people in such provinces as Chalatenango, the army and air force bombed villages, destroyed houses, crops, and hospitals in rebel zones, killing civilians who got in the way. Other civilians fled, or the army relocated them in camps. Or the refugees lived in slums, along railroad tracks, without papers, work, or medicine . . .

7

THE UNITED STATES EMBASSY in San Salvador was not surrounded by a moat, but still it was a fortress in the truest sense. It stood on a noisy street, all concrete walls and searchlights, buffered by cement blocks and men with submachine guns; inside were elaborate electronics to thwart potential terrorists.

I had been warned by the Mothers of the Disappeared that I would find the ambassador — Edwin Gharst Corr — a Tartar. The human rights champions of the Americas Watch Committee were scarcely more complimentary; to them the ambassador was insensitive, dismissive of the cruelties of the army and police, an apologist for Duarte. Ambassador Corr and Aryeh Neier, the renowned vice chairman of Americas Watch, had clashed bitterly. Even Salvadorans of the right disliked the ambassador. They called him the "Proconsul," but that was predictable for any envoy with more than a million dollars a day to spend in this embattled republic. Intellectuals of the left called him *el virrey* — "the Viceroy."

I liked him. Rather a short man, he received me in shirt-sleeves and stocking feet, which he put on a coffee table as we conversed. "You're the first writer I've ever talked to on the record," he said. He was a southerner, from Oklahoma, an ex-marine, a career diplomat with traces of a drawl. He had spent much of his life in troubled places, Quito, Cali, Medellín, Mexico City, as ambassador to Bolivia and Peru, and even his enemies granted his intimate knowledge of Latin culture. I liked him precisely because as the embodiment of U.S. power he was different from so many career ambassadors. He wasn't bland or careful, he was blunt and tough, and he wanted me to know it.

AUTHOR: What are the essential U.S. objectives in this war?

AMBASSADOR CORR: The war is a means to an end — a viable, constitutional democracy in El Salvador. We want a stable, peaceful environment. The same kind of "low-intensity" conflict persisted in Colombia for decades. Only several hundred Tupamaros wrought havoc in Uruguay. We're here for the long haul. We shouldn't be overly optimistic about achieving victory . . . in a short time . . .

A: Will the United States accept a negotiated settlement — power-sharing between the Duarte government and the guerrillas — or only a military solution?

AC: We'd be delighted if, in a short time, through better execution of the war, the guerrillas were forced to the negotiating table and a reasonable settlement — or were broken militarily or politically liquidated . . . It's absolutely false to say that the U.S. doesn't favor a meaningful dialogue. But the Salvadorans understand their country far better than we do. The time and place for dialogue must be left to the constitutionally elected leaders of the country . . . El Salvador is not the Confederacy, and this is not a civil war. It's not a full-fledged insurgency. (*With excitement.*) The guerrillas are a bunch of terrorists.

Bandits and terrorists, people who shoot indiscriminately. In the fall of nineteen eighty-three they were a full military force — no longer!

A: How can you have a viable democracy when the government tortures its own people?

AC: We're not fools or blind. But El Salvador has gone from eight hundred political deaths a month to thirty a month. No doubt some torture still exists, but what you heard at Ilopango and Mariona is a distorted picture of reality. Those prisoners say that to the press. Torture is declining. It's not a policy of the police or the armed forces. They video-tape interrogations now — to assure it doesn't occur.

A: I keep hearing that the embassy doesn't listen, that it tries to discredit human rights people who talk of torture and the other sorrows.

AC (*with vehemence*): When Mr. Aryeh Neier is too adamant to admit any improvement at all, I question his ability as an observer of human rights in El Salvador. Listening is a two-way street. I sign two hundred letters a month about human rights. I've been to the refugee camps repeatedly . . .

A: Everywhere I turn, Ambassador — left, right, and center — people call this Christian Democracy a façade.

AC: It's *not* a façade. In an election today — if people faced the real alternatives and not mythic idyllic utopias — Duarte would win hands down. Democracy was never practiced purely even in Athens. We're in a *process* here.

A: We're in a morass. How do we get out?

AC: By creating — and this will take time — a viable constitutional democracy . . . We won't know if the Christian Democratic government is a success before the second or third presidential election in 1989 or 1994 . . . We are winning the establishment of democracy, so eventually the war will be won by military means or by constitutional democracy.

Later, I debated my doubts with an embassy counselor who had sat with the ambassador and me. I wondered, wasn't the country so wounded and exhausted, would it not be better, after all, to encourage President Duarte to share power with the guerrillas? Not an idea I liked, but what could be worse than the status quo?

The counselor said sure, save a few lives, stop the war today, but end with a Marxist state. An end that overrepresented the Marxist-Leninists in the settlement would not be a true end. The war would truly end only when there existed a just, honest, humane, responsive government that reflected the will of most Salvadorans; democracy would never work until they believed it could, and the people didn't believe yet. The ambassador had predicted this would take years; the counselor said "a generation." Thus the strategy of the United States looked into indefinite perspective, and that meant a material commitment for just as long. The U.S. had already spent over a billion dollars on El Salvador, and it had to be ready to spend billions more. How tragic if the next president of the United States were not to possess such resolve.

8

I SEE THE SORROWS of Central America as a religious mystery, and I believe that all human problems, in the end, are theological. I have tried to be honest, and to show that I prefer to be liberal in politics as I tend to be traditional in faith. However, Salvadoran society was so cruel, my conscience could not laugh off the alternative solutions of liberation theology and the leftist Jesuits.

I began to read liberation theology, or its first amorphous formulations, when I lived in Europe. Since World War II, a dialogue of sorts had been conducted between Marxist intellectuals and liberal Jesuits and other Christians, particularly in France. When I lived in France in the late 1960s, I followed their dialectic with fascination: imagine, reconciling Marx and Christ? I was excited and hopeful.

When I visited the Netherlands in the early seventies I sought out Marxist Jesuits. They told me that most of the structures of Western consumer society would have to be torn down to achieve true liberty and social justice. Hardly a new idea: I had heard it constantly during the student revolution in Paris, 1968: *On va construire la nouvelle société sur les cendres de l'ancienne.* Yet the focus of the Dutch Jesuits was still largely on Europe, not on the misery of the Third World. One radical Jesuit did tell me, "Jesus Christ was a saint — like Che Guevara." It seemed were I to embrace such novelties I must accept not only a convulsion of society but a Christ so demystified His divinity was dubious. He was not a Christ I cared to know. Moreover, my direct experience of the Third World — the collectivization of wealth, the good intentions of socialism smothered in slogans, bureaucracy, tyranny of the police — made me cynical of utopian solutions.

Reading Latin American liberation theology as I wandered through the isthmus, I found the divinity of Christ conveyed in a new dimension. The key text of the liberating Christ is Luke 4: 18–19: "The Spirit of the Lord is upon me, because He hath anointed me to preach the Gospel to the poor; He hath sent me to heal the broken-hearted, to preach deliverance to the captives, and recovering of sight to the blind, to set at liberty them that are bruised, To preach the acceptable year of the Lord." This is a Christ who rejects the world as it is and exhorts Christians to look for deliverance not in death but to build His Kingdom here on earth. Sin is real, Satan is real, but they fester not only in our single *selves* but even more in the collective *structures* of society that oppress the poor and produce the scandal of their misery. The Church had formally pronounced her preference for the poor at Medellín (1968) and Puebla (1979). To the theologians of liberation, such a preference meant nothing unless applied concretely to the dismal lives of the poor in such tormented nations as Brazil, Peru, Nicaragua, El Salvador.

In practice (or "praxis," to use their dearest word), this meant an innate disgust with mere tinkering, reformism, gradualism, bourgeois liberalization; it meant a transformation of all structures of society from top to bottom. The consciousness of the masses had to be raised ("*concientización*"): they had to be encouraged constantly to recognize their rights in Christ and to struggle for them as they groped toward the Kingdom of God.

Saint John Evangelist in Revelation (Apocalypse) 21: 1–4 had described that Kingdom, that New Jerusalem where God will dwell with His people: "And God shall wipe away all tears from their eyes; and there shall be no more death, neither sorrow, nor crying, neither shall there be any more pain: for the former things are passed away." Furthermore, the Kingdom should be sought here on earth. Was it enough, therefore, to progress from military dictatorships to civil democracies on the European model? No. What relevance had the forms of such democracy — periodic elections, parliaments, pressure groups, a free press, a free economy, competing parties — to the squalor of the poor? Christian liberation addressed true needs: to eat, to work, to read, to be housed, to be healthy, to have land. Classical democracy, at best, promised solutions that merely nibbled at the margins; liberation theology looked to the core.

In so doing, it looked to the debasing dependence of the Latin nations on the cruel whims of capitalism and particularly on the greed of the United States. The armies, oligarchies that governed so many Latin nations, were bound hand and foot to North American imperialism, politically and economically, and especially through the multinational corporations. As a tactic the United States might from time to time urge restraint and liberalization on the ruling elites, but their interests were essentially the same — to preserve the present system of dependency and exploitation, to the benefit of both — and to entrench the structures of sin on the flesh of the poor.

The theology of all this was centered on Christ as Liberator, but the science — the method of examining social, economic, and political reality — was largely Marxist. "For us, Marxism is a given," a Salvadoran Jesuit sociologist told me. "We all use Marxist analysis. It's beyond debate." He was a devout priest who traveled often to perform admirable pastoral work behind guerrilla lines. Of course he rejected the atheism of Marx, and like his Jesuit fellows he was selective in interpreting Marx as he borrowed from other social philosophers. Nevertheless, Marxism dominated the social thought of the Salvadoran Jesuits. *Naturalized* Salvadorans, I should add; many were Basque Spaniards.

"The principal contribution of Marxism to liberation theology is to oblige us to commit ourselves to struggle against injustice — against capitalism and imperialism which maintain the majority of people in a state of inhumanity," said Padre Ignacio Ellacuría, the charismatic rector of the Jesuits' University of Central America in San Salvador. He added that another gift of Marxism was "its ethical character . . . its revival of hope."

The Jesuits' devotion to Marxism reinforced their resentment of the Polish Pope and of the flaccid democracy embodied by President Duarte and his Christian Democrats. One evening, Padre Jon Sobrino, another Basque and one of the most renowned liberation theologians, stood outside his office at the university and vented to me his contempt for all the pretense of Duarte's government: "It's theater, staged by the United States to show the world that El Salvador is democratic. An elected president, a parliament, a free press, et cetera, et cetera. The real purpose is to get money from the U.S. Congress to continue the war and crush the FMLN." I might have qualified his argument, but otherwise I found it hard to refute.

These Jesuits did not propose that their country should slavishly copy Cuba, though they admired Cuba for its real social achievements, its independence of the multinationals and the United States. El Salvador had a free press and much misery; Cuba's press was bound, and though

Cubans were poor few were destitute. As for the FMLN, the Jesuits barely bothered to disguise their sympathy. The Jesuits' vision of the new society, it seemed to me, was born not so much in hope of Christ Liberator as in despair of the traditional governance that cursed El Salvador. They saw Salvadoran society as so unjust, American domination as so debasing, that no other new order—even of the FMLN— could be worse.

The Jesuits promoted dialogue between government and guerrillas —tirelessly they turned out essay after prolix essay, ran endless errands into guerrilla dens, struggling to discover some formula to stop the war. The war went on. They were convinced, and they may have been right, that only by dividing power between the warring sides could the country know peace. In the meanwhile the greater villains were the Duarte government and the military machine of the United States, the enemy of peace. But surely the Jesuits condemned the indiscriminate guerrilla land mines? "It's the only way they can defend themselves," said one Jesuit. "I know they respect religion," said another. "When the air force bombers come, the guerrilla comandantes pray," said a third. "I don't agree that the FMLN's desire for dialogue is purely tactical," said Padre Sobrino. "The guerrillas are not so contemptuous of the people. They're more humane than that. Who has more love for El Salvador—the army generals or the commanders of the FMLN?" Scores of the Jesuits' former students had joined the guerrillas; others joined the army, the radical right.

The Jesuits' dream was lovely in a way. Should the FMLN ever come to power, they hoped to infuse it with Christian mercy, much as the Nicaraguan Jesuits hoped to Christianize the Sandinistas. Not a Jesuit I met could quite bring himself to speak ill of the guerrillas beyond admitting they were not popular. One quoted Aquinas at me, justifying revolt against tyranny. I quoted Aquinas back at him: when the revolt becomes inordinate, the multitude suffers even more. (The ethics of tyrannicide have long bedeviled the Jesuits; when Juan de Mariana, interpreting Aquinas, justified tyrannicide in the seventeenth century and the assassination of Henri IV of France ensued, odium fell upon the whole order.) "And what about the land mines?" I insisted. "Nothing from the guerrillas is as *bad* as this government!" he answered, almost shouting.

I half agreed with him. I respected these Jesuits because they lived their principles. They lived frugally; repeatedly their residence was bombed, but they persevered. Some lived atrociously, intermingled with the poor. I remember one, a foreigner not untypical of his Salvadoran fellows. He lived in San Antonio Abad, a hot slum where most were jobless, where men walked dazed from sniffing glue, and where only weeks ago three more headless bodies had turned up. This Jesuit, call him Father Ignatius, had served in the highest councils of the Order, yet he fled new promotions to work for the poor.

And not just work for them: to *be with* them. That justified all of his discomfort, to live with them, to share their sorrows, to agonize beside them in their struggles, hour by hour, for justice. His brief was to aid refugees, and that kept him in constant motion. He was forever flying to distant reaches of the world, attending conferences, seeking converts to "the subversive Christ," preaching the utter union of the Jesuits with the poor. (I wondered, was the Jesuits' obsession with the poor an act of flagellation for their centuries of educating the rich?) In El Salvador his transport alternated between a motor scooter with no muffler and a truck with no ignition. Upon his scooter he traveled all over El Salvador, often into guerrilla territory, on his errands of grace. In Guatemala once, he was so disabled by dysentery he vomited his dentures down the toilet. He seemed to me half mad, or rather a fool for the sake of Christ.

His opinions were bitter, a constant quiet litany of rage. Unlike so many modern Jesuits he seemed to respect the Pope, but toward American power he was unforgiving. All of El Salvador's problems could be traced to the Monroe Doctrine. He loathed the cruelty and corruption of the government almost as much. He spent much time bribing officials to release refugees they suspected were guerrillas. "I must," he said. "A lesser evil. Can't see them tortured." He was awash in refugees with no papers, no money, no hope, who dared not venture from their camps for fear of the police. At a camp, one evening he celebrated Mass in a tin shed, clad only in his street clothes and an Indian stole. His homily was about liberation. "Liberation from what?" he asked his refugees. "*Del pecado* — from sin," a woman answered. "*Muy bien,*" Father Ignatius said, "*pero también la liberación de la sociedad,* but also the liberation of *society.*" The man never stopped.

Again I half agreed with him: liberation theology might foment class struggle, but with or without it there *was* a class struggle in El Salvador. Were I a Salvadoran refugee, slum dweller, campesino whose family had been slaughtered, probably I would become a Marxist zealot, even a guerrilla. The lucid side of me says no, even reincarnated you would shrink from utopian solutions. Am I sure of that? Once more, I look to my liberation theology. The books are piled on my desk: Gutiérrez, the Boff brothers, Segundo, Sobrino, Ellacuría . . . Here is Phillip Berryman, struggling to decipher Ellacuría's "The Crucified People: An Essay in Historical Soteriology": "Earlier in the essay he had quoted a long passage on the 'proletariat' from Marx, noting its 'deep religious inspiration.' The implication, not clearly stated, is that the crucified people is the bearer of salvation for the world, something like the proletariat for Marxists. However, Ellacuría differs from Marx's judgment on the *Lumpenproletariat*. Presumably what he means . . ."

Ellacuría is typical of the liberationists: great blobs of theory, erudite, fervent, mystical, Platonic, utopian, tireless, obscure, preposterously verbose. Often the only clear idea is that if you disagree you don't love the poor. The Marxism doesn't bother me — I got used to it in France — I do not even ask that the theologians learn more of economics, I pray only that Christ might miraculously make them succinct.

Liberation theology removes Original Sin from the souls of individuals and places the curse on society. It is visionary in its belief in the perfectibility of man here on earth. Finally I join with that most visionary of Jesuits, Daniel Berrigan: "Once [the liberationists] leave the Bible, they lose me . . . They show a certain contempt and fear of God as a Person. In place of the personal God, one is offered a sampling of the following (and I quote): 'Task,' 'Revolution,' 'Force,' 'Motivation,' 'Horizon,' and (yes) 'Omega Point,' and (I swear it) 'Shining Dots,' 'The Great Exclamation Point,' and . . . 'Exuberant Yes.' . . . Do we have here anything more than a flea market of little idols? . . . I hope I do not sound contemptuous of suffering and victimized people."

So do I. Most of liberation theology is murky, much of it is nonsense, but might it not contribute to making Latin society less cruel? Might it not serve as pressure, as an incentive for social justice? If so, it seems useful, and we all must cheer. Yet after months of hacking in that thick garden, I gave up. I left the liberationists in their garden and visited the army hospital in San Salvador.

The hospital was jammed with peasant soldiers, fresh from the battlefield, their feet and legs blown off by guerrilla land mines. In intensive care, naked youths, some of them unsexed, were sprawled about, nurses and physicians pumping them with blood, battling to save their limbs and lives. I remembered hearing that the doctors cared first for the limbs of officers, but here all suffering seemed equal. The mines lurk just beneath the surface of the soil. The soldier (or the campesino) steps on a blasting cap set off by sulfuric acid mixed with sugar and potassium hypochlorite. The mine beneath is tiny — two-inch plastic garden hose packed with aluminum powder, gunpowder, rocks, glass, and human excrement. An American medical officer calls the youths who have lost both limbs "bilateral amputees."

Next day, I received a letter from Father Ignatius. He told of a woman he knew whose son, a guerrilla, had just been killed. "An eyewitness, herself wounded, related how government soldiers had cut off his hands and feet, slashed his face and partially skinned him before he died. The mother, quiet and dignified in her grief, did not even know which of her sons was killed — the boy of fourteen or his brother of twelve . . ."

He wrote on, of the new and just society the survivors of such horrors were still struggling to build. Weary of his theology, of all liberation theory, of the Satanic killing on either side, I was thrust back to solitude, to my own diffidence. The liberationists insisted in the abstract on the need for ideology and taking sides, but in the concrete I could not favor either government or guerrillas. As usual, I could not *choose*. Yet inside the vast sorrow of that dwarf nation, I felt guilty, too, and my detachment needed to justify itself. In a play, I had written: "Guilt is grace." I'm not sure what that means, but still I hoped it might be true and so indulged my guilt in acts of petty charity.

As I prepared for my departure, Señora came to say farewell — at night, as usual, in my bourgeois rooms above the swimming pool. I had no further word, I told her, on the fate of Mario and the other common criminals at San Francisco Gotera. But I promised to keep trying, to seek help in Washington, and gave her money for the bus. She kissed me. I flew back to Costa Rica wondering whether those abandoned men would ever be brought to trial.

From San José and Massachusetts I wrote repeatedly to House Speaker Thomas (Tip) O'Neill and Senator Edward Kennedy, to urge them to ask the President and secretary of state to intercede with the Salvadorans. They did not reply. Maybe the case lacked glamour, merely a hundred human beings dumped and forgotten. *Well, of course, if you enjoy wasting your time . . . You'll spend your whole life at it, you will*. I received one acknowledgment, from Ambassador Corr: "You may be sure that I will discuss with high Salvadoran Government officials your list of prisoners who have been incarcerated for extremely excessive periods of time without judicial process of their cases." More appeals, more silence ever since, and an earthquake in San Salvador: a thousand people died, whole barrios collapsed.

The future of Duarte's Christian Democracy seemed as fragile. Death-squad assassinations increased, and so did guerrilla sabotage; negotiations for an internal settlement foundered yet again, and in disgust the populace voted the right wing to control of parliament. By mid-1988, President Duarte's bad stomach turned to terminal cancer, as though his illness were another metaphor for the body politic of his nation. Would the right wing assume the Salvadoran presidency? The guerrillas, predicting anarchy, hoped so.

Meanwhile, after the earthquake, I had received a letter from Señora. She was living in the street, in an open camp, sharing her bed with the rain. ". . . *pero estamos con vida que es lo mas importante y que se haga la voluntad de Dios. Mario siempre está en Gotera. En nombre del Señor Jesucristo* . . . but we're alive, which is what counts, and so goes the will of God. Mario is still in Gotera. In the name of Our Lord Jesus Christ . . ." So far as I know, to this day Mario and the other prisoners were left to rot in jail, and so much for my own little venture into liberation theology.

IV / INTERLUDE IN COSTA RICA

It was an entanglement of the childish-dreaming,
myth-making primitive mind . . . In the world of ten
thousand years ago . . . human sacrifice . . . plunder
. . . a mass of infantry holding spears . . . chariot
fighting . . . For four years and a quarter [World War
I] had lasted, and gradually it had drawn nearly everyone . . . into its vortex . . . Eight millions of people
had been . . . killed . . . another . . . twenty-five millions had died through the hardships and disorders
. . . Scores of millions were suffering and enfeebled . . .

H. G. Wells, The Outline of History

1

IN SAN JOSE as usual I retreated to my hotel room and wrote essays on the suffering I had seen. Given such confinement I saw too little of Costa Rica, the only real democracy on the isthmus. When I finished writing I ventured outside the capital to visit Central America's only real revolutionary — the man who outlawed the army.

This was José Figueres Ferrer — "Don Pepe" to his compatriots — thrice President of Costa Rica, who dissolved the nation's garrison in 1948. Costa Rica has made do with a mere police force ever since; thus her measured prosperity and bliss. I was attracted to Don Pepe by his public candor: he declared, only days before I met him, that Ronald Reagan's worst blunder was "to have been born."

My appointment took me eastward to Cartago on a wet Friday afternoon in June. The weather all over the isthmus had passed from the dry season to the Caribbean monsoon, and the rain on the highway was heavy. My driver got lost on side roads, but eventually he found Don Pepe's house halfway up a mountain. The house was a rambling chalet, and, surrounded by peaks and misty rain, it might have been in Switzerland. Indeed, Costa Rica so resembled Switzerland in its social contract that I made this theory the theme of my questions. I asked Don Pepe, how did you do it? How did you abolish war?

He was an old man, rheumatic, shuffling, very lucid, leaning on the arm of his nurse. He sat down painfully in the library and told me his story. "I agree," he said in hoarse English, "I'm a revolutionary. In the nineteen twenties, I was living in Boston, attending MIT and learning hydroelectric engineering. One day, I was standing by a bookcase and some books fell on top of me. One fell into my hands. It was *The Outline of History* by H. G. Wells. I sat down and read it. Wells called war a ridiculous relic of the past, a curse of our tribal nature. I was young and precocious, eager for great ideas, and at the time I was studying utopian socialism. Wells was a utopian, and I loved his ideas.

"Little did I know that when I returned to Costa Rica I would become commander of a revolutionary army. I went to war three times to achieve the constitutional rights denied to our people. You see, I was deeply influenced by Jefferson also. He said that when people are oppressed they have not only the right but the obligation to war and violence. I may seem to contradict myself, but no. In nineteen forty-eight, we were cheated of our electoral rights by a coalition of conservative politicians and the international communist movement. I rallied a rebel army made up mostly of students and intellectuals. We declared war on the government. Costa Rica had only eight hundred thousand people then, but two thousand died in the fighting. We won.

"I headed a temporary junta to prepare the return to constitutional rule. I was called the 'Liberator' since the day I entered San José at the head of my troops. I took advantage of my power to suppress two armies — my own and the government's. I founded the National Liberation party, and with a name like that you have to liberate. I liberated my country from armies. Before the parliament, we introduced a new constitution that legally abolished the army forever. Maybe in five hundred years we won't even need police.

"No sooner had we suppressed the army than Costa Rica was invaded from Nicaragua by the Somozas. We discovered how powerful we were *without* an army. The whole world — including the United States — offered to help us. Our citizens still had weapons, and they put up a hell of a fight. We met the Nicaraguans at the border, and even our women were on the front lines. *Everybody* wanted to fight. The Nicaraguans didn't get far. We didn't give them a chance. They withdrew in a few weeks. In nineteen fifty-five, they invaded again. We kicked them out. I was elected president the first time in nineteen fifty-three — or was it fifty-four? I forget . . ."

By now the rainstorm was torrential; thunder cracked against the peaks, and cut the lights. The President, though clearly tired, did not seem to notice. He kept stumbling on dates, yet those decades past were as near to him as the storm outside.

"FDR, Truman, Kennedy, Adlai Stevenson, I knew them all. Reagan? *No thanks*. I loved the liberal thinkers. My first American author was Emerson. Once we outlawed the army, we introduced social reform.

We nationalized banks, railroads, electricity. We secured the farms and other private property in private hands — anything that could be managed by a family. We introduced social security, free schools, and medicine . . ."

A chauffeur with his wife and two small girls entered the library to bundle Don Pepe in sweaters and raincoat. It took some time against his stiff bones. He was going down to San José to see his doctor. He kept talking.

". . . We regulated prices. With no army, we had lots of money for education and public health. We spent a few cents on revolvers for the police. This is a *utopian* society. I'm pro-gringo but not pro-Republican. I'm against the Green Berets. I don't like the present U.S. government. I'm against businessmen managing society — it should be managed by thinkers, not merchants. I'm pro-Sandinista. That doesn't mean I approve of all they do. But I hate to see a country I love — the United States — telling the Nicaraguans how to run their country. I'm a minority in Costa Rica. Do you want a ride to San José?"

We drove down the wet mountain toward the capital in the twilight, the chauffeur and his family with us, the President in front, remembering. ". . . Today we've had the heaviest rain in years. Isn't that funny, the lights went out? I electrified Costa Rica. I installed the telephone system. Nineteen twenties, I think. A model? Costa Rica as a model? For the rest of Central America? Because we have no army? Yes, but only when you have a different kind of government in the United States — one that sees us differently — otherwise there's not much hope. We're all so dependent on the United States. The United States is our biggest problem."

We dropped Don Pepe at the doctor's office, and the chauffeur drove me to my hotel. It seemed to me that centuries could pass before the other nations of the isthmus copied the pacifism of Costa Rica, though I hoped that the interregnum might be more swift. Of course, this country paid a price for its beatitude. With no army, it lacked heroism and drama. All societies should be as lucky, but they will do without the violent romance and mad poetry of such places as El Salvador and Nicaragua, not that I recommend them. Costa Rica is dull, like Switzerland. Unlike the Swiss, Costa Ricans *are* hospitable; they invite you to dinner, forgetting only to tell you the address.

I missed Señora and her nocturnal visitations. Uprooting, restless motion: the pox on my life. I looked from the balcony of my room, down to the plaza and the Opera House of San José, and fancied that I glimpsed her, moving in the crowd, as a light rain fell. Should I go back to San Salvador? No, I had other tasks, but at least my next stop would restore excitement. The day after I saw Don Pepe, at dawn, I returned to Nicaragua.

V / NICARAGUA REVISITED

In Utopia . . . there is no private property . . . Everything is under public ownership, no one has any fear
of going short, as long as the public storehouses are
full. Everyone gets a fair share, so there are never any
poor men or beggars. Nobody owns anything, but
everyone is rich — for what greater wealth can there
be than cheerfulness, peace of mind, and freedom
from anxiety?

Sir Thomas More, Utopia, *1516*

I

IT RAINED EVEN HARDER in Managua—cloudbursts of thunder and lightning that rolled in from the volcano and the lake and turned the potholed streets to rapids. To me this was summer, but Nicaraguans called it *invierno* — "winter" — for the rain. The torrents fell in the afternoons; the rest of the day the sun shone suddenly, and the air was always sodden. I was given my old room in the rear of the Siete Mares, shabby, but it was home. Electricity was cut off more often, and in the mornings for want of running water I could not shower or flush the toilet. Viktor cursed the weather and the Sandinistas and now was drunk by noon.

I had been gone from Nicaragua for nearly five months. In my absence the cordoba had tumbled in value from twelve hundred to two thousand to the dollar. The largest note was for one thousand cordobas, so I gave up packing the bills in my pocket and stuffed them instead in an airline bag. There was almost no bread, and the lines at the bakery in the Plaza de España were longer than ever, but most people abstained from bread, satisfied with tortillas when they could find cornmeal. The government had ceased its pretense of no hunger. Even the Sandinista press published reports of mismanagement in high places: twenty thousand pounds of beef allowed to rot, two hundred thousand chickens that died for no feed. Mothers telephoned the talk shows on Radio Sandino: "I can't feed my children."

Even in the rain, after luncheon in the afternoons outside the Siete Mares, barefoot filthy boys scavenged in the garbage barrel. "How many brothers and sisters have you to feed?" I ask a boy as he retrieves some rotten cabbage for his bag.

"*¡Bastante!* Enough!" he answers sharply.

"Where's your mother?" I ask, handing him some cordobas. He snatches the cordobas, without thanks. Two little girls with begging bowls wander down the road, followed by their grandmother. I fill the bowls with dry crackers. *"Gracias."* Across the road some soldier girls go on talking.

From the hotel my driver Julio took me to the slums of Las Torres, the Barrio Oriental, and then the marketplace. In Las Torres some women said, "Today we have some rice and cabbages, but no sugar, no soap, and no cooking oil. We're hungry, not starving, life has never been so harsh." At the market I found the meat vendors almost in revolt. "No meat for a week," a woman shouts at me across her empty stall.

"Whose fault is it?" I ask.

"¡El estado! The state's!"

The phenomenon of hunger fed on itself. Since the government controlled all prices and distribution, it robbed the farmers of incentives, and they refused to produce; besides, the currency was cheap toilet paper. No doubt the contra war and U.S. economic pressure worsened the crisis, but the key was declining production, and for that the Sandinistas were mostly at fault.

Palpably U.S. policy was partly responsible for Nicaragua's misery. The Sandinistas devoted half of their meager resources to defense, and if they had no war to fight they might have done much better in addressing domestic want. The closer you looked, however, the clearer it became that much of Nicaraguan suffering was caused by the government. Food supply, the whole ebb and flow of social wealth, was officially controlled by the Ministry of Interior Commerce, headed by a young comandante, Ramón Cabrales, a former mountain guerrilla illiterate in economics. He managed distribution, decided prices, licensed merchants and vendors. His ministry was to the economy what Tomás Borge's security apparatus was to the political opposition — a bureaucracy of repression, and just as feared. The ministry employed inspectors, constantly in search of illegal merchants, speculators, black-market operations, all foodstuffs and other goods sold above official prices. The ministry confiscated contraband and jailed people.

So harsh was this economy of scarcity that the black market flourished anyway. The higher the demand for scarce food, the higher the incentive to hide production from the ministry and sell it to profiteers of the *mercado negro.* Beans on the black market cost only twice the official price early in the Revolution, but now they cost more by factors of ten. So the ministry cracked down harder, which intensified black-market incentives and pushed prices and inflation yet higher as the currency was further debased.

The scarcity of food — the crisis of production — had other causes still. No modern economy, including Marxist economies, can function without a secure professional class, yet Nicaragua's professionals had largely fled. Since the Revolution, 55, perhaps 60 percent of the nation's physicians, dentists, lawyers, engineers, architects, business managers, agronomists, electricians, plumbers, veterinarians, economists, car mechanics, and repairmen for radios, televisions, refrigerators, and air conditioners had vanished and their families with them. Combined with the campesinos who had fled for other reasons, the expatriates numbered maybe more than half a million, an astonishing proportion for such a small country.

Businesses could no longer function for lack of repairmen, technicians, and spare parts, and the shortage of spare parts was aggravated by the U.S. embargo. The professionals had fled to Costa Rica, Miami, Los Angeles, San Francisco, New York City, and by hook or crook their money — and the money of the Nicaraguan rich — fled with them. At least $1 billion — more likely several billions — had migrated to Miami since the Revolution, frightened out by Sandinista economic upheavals, and still another cause of social misery inside Nicaragua. To compensate for the flight of professionals, the state had introduced technicians from Cuba, Mexico, Algeria, Bulgaria, and East Germany and was training thousands of young Nicaraguans in Cuba and the Soviet bloc, but the time lag was long, the training often inferior, and so far the effort had failed. Still the Sandinistas seemed to accept the flight of the professional middle class: they knew they could never count on its loyalty to the Revolution. For the comandantes, quixotic social transformation was far more precious than mere economic cost, however high. For this they sought a new technocracy, docile and well indoctrinated.

I visit Dr. Lino Hernández in his cavelike human rights office. Lino says that since my last visit the state security has seized another two thousand political prisoners, for a total of seven thousand, perhaps more, not counting Somoza's National Guardsmen who are still locked up. "Massive incarcerations in Chontales, Nueva Guinea, Matagalpa, Jinotega, Estelí, Nueva Segovia, and Chinandega — they're suspected of collaborating with the contras. Lately political prisoners are mixed with common criminals. At the Zona Franca and Tipitapa prisons, the criminals rob and beat the political inmates with the connivance of the police. In León a leader of the Social Christians was beaten to death by the state security. We know of twenty-six new 'disappearances' . . .''

Soon I read an affidavit from an elderly bourgeois who had been interrogated by Comandante Lenin Cerna, Tomás Borge's right hand and director of the state security:

> The soldier of rank ordered me to undress. He punched me on my chest, followed by several kicks. He asked me, "Do you know who I am?" I answered that I did not. Then he told me, "I am Comandante Lenin Cerna, and you are going to die right here!" He put his pistol to my right temple . . .
>
> Comandante Cerna attacked me, punching and kicking me all over my body and saying, "Why are you attacking the Revolution? Why don't you respect the comandantes? Why do you make fun of the heroes and martyrs?" I replied that in the Parents Meeting I had spoken on the "New Education" and that I had, in fact, said that the system was dehumanizing. It was based on hatred between brothers, warmongering, and the dissolution of the family, as well as attacks on the Church. I told him that Comandante Borge affirmed that "the Revolution is love" — and I could not see why they were so upset because we Christian parents were proclaiming an education based on love.
>
> Comandante Cerna ordered that I be handcuffed with my arms behind my back. The handcuff had a cutting edge, and as they made me kneel in front of him and they pushed me backwards, the edge cut my back. As I reclined thus on the handcuffs, he placed his boot on my ribs . . .

This scene, though unpleasant, lacks the Satanic dimension of Salvadoran torture. After reading dozens of such testimonies — after talking directly to former captives — it seemed to me typical of Sandinista interrogation of political prisoners in Managua. Lino insisted that interrogations in the provinces were more brutal. I believed him, but still I concluded that compared to other torturers on the isthmus the Sandinistas sinned less. I agreed with Ambassador Z: "For the fine arts of horror, the extreme right will never fail you."

Yet I agreed as well with Virgilio Godoy, the erudite ex-minister: "The Sandinistas don't use death squads. They practice psychological torture, but physical torture is not the norm. Foreign journalists want to see mutilated bodies. That's not the way the Sandinistas do things. They don't need to. They control and intimidate the entire population through the press, the party, the schools, the economy, and the state security.''

Indeed, it was not only their harsh justice, their thousands of political prisoners seized often for cause in the midst of war, but the broader reality of Sandinista rule that made me so sad for Nicaragua—obsessive controls, obstinate incompetence, a ruined economy, growing hunger. Even President Ortega, of all people, publicly reproached the deficiencies of his government. The per-capita income of Nicaraguans, he conceded, had fallen to what it had been nearly a decade before the Triumph. I suspected it was truly lower. ''We cannot,'' the President added, ''blame everything on the war.''

2

I RESUMED MY CAMPAIGN to see Tomás Borge. At INTERPREN, the government bureau for foreign correspondents, I was cheerfully handed some new forms, the Solicitud de Entrevista, Request for Interview, and other papers, which took an hour to fill out. The first form was four pages long and asked fifty-one questions.

What was my mother's maiden name and my residential telephone number in the United States? The date of my marriage, the nationality of my wife, and the birth dates of my children? List all your studies, all your academic degrees, and all languages you speak. Whom have you ever worked for? List all names and dates. What is your business telephone? Which foreign countries have you visited? Which foreign countries have you worked in? What positions have you held? Areas of specialization? Outstanding aspects of professional activities? Countries previously visited on professional assignments? Previous visits to Nicaragua? Specify all dates. What is your migratory status? Provide dates. What is your present migratory classification? List your memberships in societies or institutes. Provide the full names and addresses of three Nicaraguans whom you know personally. Name the topics you intend to write about in Nicaragua. Explain the subjects you intend to write about in Nicaragua. What will be the themes of your writings on Nicaragua? Add observations.

I imagined myself a Nicaraguan, petitioning for a ration card or a bag of cement. The first form was merely my request for accreditation. I had another to fill out for my Solicitud de Entrevista with Comandante

Borge. Under TEMAS A TRATAR (Subject) a notation followed in English: "Please be especific." I knew that Borge had a sense of humor, so I wrote "Bureaucracy in the Kingdom of God." No, I reflected, the form will never leave this office, and I tore it up to fill out another.

I handed the forms to a blithe girl in a gringo T-shirt—ST. PATRICK'S HIGH SCHOOL RA! RA! RA!—and duly paid my $25 U.S. for accreditation. She glanced at my Solicitud de Entrevista. "I'm sorry," she said. "Comandante Borge's not seeing people." Someone else said, "He's going on vacation—to Cuba." I returned to the Siete Mares to read his speeches.

They were marvelous, arias of language that somehow avoided bombast for their rhapsody. ". . . And the capitalists, regardless of their conceptions of the Nicaraguan workers and peasants, must identify with the patriotism of the peasants and workers if they are to remain in Nicaragua. The Sandinista Front is the vanguard of the Revolution. The Sandinista Front is the vanguard of all Nicaraguan patriots. The Sandinista Front is the vanguard of the workers and peasants. The Sandinista Front is the living instrument of the revolutionary classes, the guide leading toward a new society." (*Applause*.) ". . . And here, near the tomb of Carlos Fonseca, we should like to speak a little to our brother and tell him . . . Carlos, listen to how your bones, your strong and beautiful bones, march on under the fulness of the sun, stepping on the ruins of the old and putrefied society, knocked down by the stone fists of these men and women. Carlos . . . the anger, the tenderness, the burning coals, the hopes belong to you. Maker of flintstones, brother, tamer of wild horses. Carlos . . . your dreams have come true." (*Prolonged applause*.)

Now and then in the fog of rhapsody a fact shone through. ". . . The big majority of guerrillas who won the war aren't administrators. Many of them learned to read in the course of the struggle. Our Revolution has a very big shortage of scientifically trained personnel. The people who were in the trenches and in the mountains were not the gentlemen with the Harvard educations but the illiterate peasants and workers. Could we put a competent businessman in charge of a strategic area? Of course we could, but a businessman who hates the Revolution? We'd rather give the job to a country bumpkin . . ."

No matter, the bumpkins had the guns. Once Borge pointed to a soldier's rifle. "That," he said, "is power. Never abandon it." I understood. From adolescence, he spent most of his life fighting in the mountains or locked in Somoza's jails. Amnesty International called him the world's most tortured man. After the tables were turned and he took over the secret police, even his friend Graham Greene said of him, "I would not want to pass the night in one of his prisons." An American who watched him at a Sandinista rally was as spellbound as the Nicaraguans. "Borge is tiny, but a real presence. He speaks in grand, intricate religious metaphors, rolling the words about his mouth, luxuriating in them. For emphasis he will describe a great arc with his left arm and the rest of him will follow, his head turned to the side (like a rock drummer, transported by his rhythm), the words and phrases cascading, torrential: '. . . We need peace as fish need water and birds need open spaces to build their flights. But peace is one thing and subjugation quite another. If peace is like corn, liberty is like air. If peace is the land, liberty is the light. We love peace, my brothers, as we love life, but we love liberty infinitely more than life, and for that we say: *Patria Libre o Morir*.'. . ."

He was talking, of course, of the war against the contras. The American continues: "In that moment, I sensed something: the man missed the mountains. He was more at home with romance than reality. Reality meant the day-to-day running of the Revolution, the bureaucratic angling, the niggling decisions about allocating toilet paper, the slow strangulation of his dream."

Yet that was the enchantment of Nicaragua: the weird dreaming, wild visions, madhouse fragrance, heads full of theory, cupboards bare, poetry at war with squalor. Borge was more than a policeman, a thug who tortured people, he was a mystic: ". . . Carlos . . . here is our working class, your working class with its calloused hands and shining eyes, standing at attention, faithful to you until victory, until blood, until death. Here is your working class — comrade postman, street seller of candies and of splendors. We are gatherers of your resurrection. We are not frightened by phantoms, by mummies, by imperialism, we are not afraid of the Cains. We, Carlos, beloved brother, we are your thirst and the riverbed of your working class. Today we say to you, we are running toward a new society, toward the total elimination of the exploitation of man by man. *¡Patria Libre o Morir!*" (*Ovation. Chants of* "*¡Poder Popular! People's Power! People's Power!*")

During that torrential winter-summer, the usual rumors in Managua of an imminent U.S. invasion had receded, but not the rage of the Sandinistas at the atrocities of Reagan's Freedom Fighters. The counterrevolutionaries were hardly waging war at all, as ever they seemed like simple terrorists, not true guerrillas; they went on attacking schools and clinics, murdering civilians, raping women, but they seldom engaged the army face to face. More and more, in the highlands of Jinotega near the Honduran border, their favorite weapon was becoming land mines, and the victims were mostly helpless peasants.

My conscience twitched. I had met too many land-mine victims in El Salvador to remain indifferent. In my nightmares — a gray jerky silent film — I still saw the mutilated peasant youths in the army hospital in San Salvador.

The contras' land mines were planted on a lesser scale, but the sin was the same. The contras' sabotage, their economic and human wreckage, was not so vast as the crimes of the Salvadoran guerrillas, but the principle was constant. If I recoiled from Marxist land mines in El Salvador, then — much as I disliked the Sandinistas — I had to recoil from contra sabotage and land mines in Nicaragua because the victims were innocent civilians. From Managua that winter-summer I watched the debate in the U.S. Congress for another $100 million for the contras, and I had to disapprove.

Comandante Borge agreed with me. As an orthodox Marxist he had anticipated the counterrevolution, and once it happened his scorn grew claws. The contras were mercenary lice, Yankee cockroaches, CIA baboons. Cardinal Obando kept harping, "Talk to them." Oh yes, said Borge, "When the rivers of Nicaragua run backward." The other comandantes were as adamant but with less pith. As for Reagan's visions of a contra victory, Borge was at his best: "*El Presidente Reagan tiene todo el derecho del mundo a tener sueños eróticos, con su imaginación llega al orgasmo.*" Reagan had every right to his wet dreams.

Stimulated by Borge's rhetoric, I drove downtown to *La Prensa* for a chat with its chief editor, Pablo Antonio Cuadra. Don Pablo was an elderly bourgeois, all bones, a long neck, black spectacles, part owl, part giraffe. He was probably Nicaragua's finest living poet.

Here are his images of Sandinista Nicaragua:

> *Vivo en un país entristecido*
> *por los cultivadores de fusiles.*
> *Cualquier cosa se peinsa*
> *con los testículos:*
> > *Arriba, . . .*

> I live in a land made so sad
> by men who reap rifles

And decide things
with their balls:
                        Above,
faces yesterday full of grace
or dreams, now vacant
their eyes fixed on the gun.
"Homotextuals" fix on Marx
What does the seer say
Why are corpses such the rage?
In such a scheme of things the Good God has no place
But happiness oh yes
And weeping
And gnashing teeth. Dream
heavens and they will burn away your hell.
My Land of country folk
Infested with soldiers! My Land
once gurgling poems now
Mouthing slogans! My Land
oozing children
condemned to die.
What hope may we ever feel
Bent on our knees? We grow old
all by ourselves. We cry out
in the void: Manuel!
Ramón! Félix! Federico!
But our sons
                        have vanished . . . !

. . . *¿Qué esperanza sentamos*
en nuestras rodillas? Envejecimos
en la soledad. Estamos llamando
en el vacío: ¡Manuel!
¡Ramón! ¡Félix! ¡Federico!
Pero nuestros hijos
                        han partido . . . !

I visited Don Pablo on a bad day, but lately all days went badly at
La Prensa. The bulletin board outside sagged now with new articles
that Borge's censor, the intractable Captain Blandón, had refused permission to publish. A forbidden headline: DESPUES DE 7 AÑOS DE REV-
OLUCION EL PUEBLO GRITA: ¡NO HAY COMIDA! AFTER 7 YEARS OF

REVOLUTION THE PEOPLE CRY: WE HAVE NO FOOD! Inside, before I confer with Don Pablo, a young reporter tells me, "Just as I predicted. Now we can't even print Cardinal Obando's *name*. Now we're censored *twice* a day."

Within a windowless room, Don Pablo was as gloomy but with defiance. I had with me his renowned essay on Rubén Darío and the mysterious duality of the Nicaraguan character, the *"dos-en-mi-mismo, two-in-myself,"* the ceaseless war of soul and flesh, the mystic and the sensual, joy and anguish, love and hate, life and death. I wondered, did this not hint of necrophilia? Don Pablo put aside his journalist self, put on his poet self, took my question, and wrapped it in macabre lyricism. Fair enough for me to convey his thought in free verse.

> A Venezuelan poet asked me,
> "Why does such a happy people
> have such a bond with
> death?

> Revolution or death
> Democracy or death
> Free fatherland or death?"

> I told him, For us, death is like a
> wife.
> We have a conjugal union with
> death.

> How did we learn to love death?
> A thousand years ago, under the Nahuatl,
> we learned the cult of death, and
> human sacrifice. And ever since
> we have kept the cult of
> death.

> The Sandinistas took our cult of
> death, and made it
> worse. Their symbol is the
> Raised Rifle. All must serve the
> "Armed Rebirth." Tomás Borge, on the morrow of the
> Revolution, when asked what the
> Revolution needed most, replied
> "Arms, arms, more arms."

Our peasants are rooted in the
earth, but the earth should belong to the
peasant, not to the
Revolution. He wants to go to
market, talk all day to his
friends, haggle in his own
society. Force, selling to the faceless
state, is against his
nature. It's not
Nicaraguan.

Sandinista priests, some Jesuits, are
deluded. Saint Paul preached the
"New Man," but new men in
Christ, not new men in
politics. I told the brothers Cardenal their
marriage of
Marx and
Christ is
unnatural. The Church has chosen for the
poor, not chosen for the
state. Not chosen for the godless

"Vanguard." Oh, that myth, that
men who bore arms in the
mountains were thus
anointed to
govern!
God didn't give them
brains, and neither can the
Revolution.

For Nicaragua,
Sandinismo is a form of
suicide.

3

I DROVE OUT of the city to the Curia to call on Cardinal Obando.

Relations during recent months between the Sandinistas and the official Church had grown venomous. Miguel D'Escoto, foreign minister and defrocked Maryknoller, had walked hundreds of miles across Nicaragua on a "Vía Crucis," Way of the Cross, to protest the crimes of the contras. For the Cardinal's silence on the contras, Father D'Escoto had labeled him a "traitor . . . an accomplice in the assassination of our people," and called on him "to repent his sins." If he did not, the foreign minister threatened to "excommunicate" the primate from the Popular Church, a riddle, since His Eminence was not a member.

The Cardinal replied by citing the First Epistle of Saint Peter and comparing D'Escoto to Satan: "Be sober, be vigilant; because your adversary the Devil, as a roving lion, walketh about, seeking whom he may devour." Again, the primate appealed for negotiations between the Sandinistas and the counterrevolution. "We appeal for those who are dying, whether from the Sandinista Front or from the other side, because they are Nicaraguans and we love them all." The Sandinistas: "We will *never* talk to the contras."

Before the primate received me, I paused to chat with Monseñor Bismark Carballo, the Cardinal's spokesman and right hand, by now my friend. I liked him for his easy laughter; he kept a comic photograph on his desk of John Paul II, fingers and thumbs around the infallible eye sockets, staring googly at the camera. Monseñor Carballo was one of the most interesting men in Nicaragua; even the Sandinistas found him fascinating. In fact, they photographed him naked and ran the film on television.

It took me six months to gather courage to ask the young monsignor about that incident: I did so now. His face darkened. He was an attractive man, more sensuous than handsome, with a lush mane of very black hair and those full lips and nostrils that suggest Indian blood. Whenever I met him I recalled Somerset Maugham's portrait of a youthful priest in prewar France: "There was the quick fire of the South in his aspect and I asked myself what urgent faith, what burning desire had caused him to abandon the joys of common life, the pleasures of his age and the satisfaction of his senses, to devote himself to the service of God."

Monseñor Carballo sometimes wore black or gray clericals about the Curia, but just as often he favored smart boots, Calvin Klein jeans, Sergio Valenti shirts. Priests are often afraid of women, yet I have rarely met a man as much at ease with them. He drifted in and out of offices at the Curia, telling jokes, laughing, chatting with young nuns, the Cardinal's matronly secretary, or with any of the many women who came to call on His Eminence. Whenever he visited an academy or the Catholic Youth, the girls went crazy, giggling, squealing, cheering him as they might a rock idol—especially since the incident.

That had happened several summers ago, three years after the Sandinistas seized power. Relations between the Revolution and the Roman Church had soured: the Pope condemned the Popular Church, and then the auxiliary bishop of Managua was beaten by a Sandinista mob. Monseñor Carballo explained:

"My parish is San Miguel en la Brisa, and there was a Charismatic Catholic woman living there. This woman insisted that I go to lunch at her house. I went at midday on a Wednesday. The moment I entered the house I met a man, a civil person with a pistol, who ordered me to remove my clothes.

"I did, and the man beat me on the head. I tried to defend myself. Two policemen entered the house. By this time, the woman was naked also. I was dragged outside, still naked, to a military car. A television crew was waiting at the door of the house."

I asked, "What was the naked woman doing?"

"I don't remember the details. I was taken to the police station and released to the papal nuncio. Later, from two members of the state security we learned that the incident had been staged by the Ministry of Interior. Until today, the Sandinistas use the pictures in an army recruitment film to discredit the Church. Tomás Borge set me up."

On the front pages of *Barricada* and *El Nuevo Diario*, Managua, August 13, 1982, are large photographs: Monseñor Carballo, naked, is seen struggling with a bigger man inside the doorway of a house and being dragged away outside by two policemen. A black X conceals his private parts. The incident backfired on the Sandinistas. Thereafter, the monsignor's Sunday Mass was thronged, and he became a lion to his people.

It is assumed that Monseñor Carballo never forgave Tomás Borge and the Sandinistas for his embarrassment. It is surely true that after the incident, for all his youth, he became even more conservative than the Cardinal in faith and discipline, more hostile to priests who favored the Revolution. He was dissecting the Marxist Jesuits when Josefa, the Cardinal's secretary, summoned me to see His Eminence.

In that monastic office beneath the Velázquez *Crucifixion,* the primate—severed by the state from nearly all communication with his people—was nonetheless in pithy humor.

CARDINAL: . . . Not all Nicaraguan Jesuits are Marxist. The Jesuits of Granada are very balanced.

AUTHOR: But the Jesuits of Managua attract the most attention.

C: Oh, the Managua Jesuits, almost all are Marxists. They think the only solution for poor countries is socialism. For them, liberation means Marxism. In theory, that's very romantic. In practice . . . look at Nicaragua today.

A: But Eminence, they do reject the atheism of Marx.

C: Marx's atheism doesn't interest them, only his sociopolitical project, and they've identified with that. If you point out to them that Nicaragua's condition is much worse, they refuse to recognize it's worse. They blame everything on imperialism.

A: Can't the Pope influence them?

C: They don't much respect the Pope. They oppose me because they work for the Sandinistas and I'm not identified with the deterministic state, *estado determinado.* They have all the means of communication at their disposal, and I have none . . . It was easy for Father Fernando Cardenal to tell you there is no Marxist instruction in the secondary schools—to lie to you—because he's a Marxist. A certain Jesuit offered a young Jesuit *Das Kapital* as an ordination gift. Another presented a machine gun. Both gifts were accepted. In 1979, Father César Jerez [rector of the Jesuit university] wrote an article calling Tomás Borge a saint.

A: But their goals are benign. They do want to help the poor.

C: For them Nicaragua is a laboratory, and we are all their little guinea pigs. *Por ellos Nicaragua es un laboratorio, y somos todos sus pequeños conejillos de Indias.* Religion is not their first priority. Their first priority is politicosociological; religion comes later. They think they can Christianize the Sandinistas, but on television and in the other media the Sandinistas go on ridiculing religion—the Pope, the Mass, the Holy

Virgin, Christian matrimony — and their goal is to eliminate religion. About that the Jesuits remain silent, or they insist that Marxism respects religion.

A: This quarrel is more than religious, Your Eminence, it's also political. The Jesuits attack you because you refuse to condemn the contras.

C: We're against all violence. In Nicaragua, however, we have no objective information because all information is manipulated by the Sandinistas. We should denounce all injustice, but if we spoke against the contras our words would be twisted.

A: Your critics — including your critics in the United States — find your position too subtle. Surely Your Eminence is aware of the contras' atrocities?

C: I don't say that the contras are angels. It's very difficult to know reality. When I was at the United Nations recently, the Sandinistas said I endorsed the one hundred million dollars for the contras, but I made no such declaration. As a pastor I don't say yes or no.

A: May we focus on the legitimacy of violence by either side? Aquinas allows proportionate violence against tyranny under strict conditions. As a principle, is the contras' violence justified?

C: I'm a pastor. In Rome, Cardinal Ratzinger has reaffirmed Aquinas's justification of violence as a last resort — but such a decision is left to the Christian conscience of the layman. As a pastor, I must remain independent.

A: You have always been the mediator of Nicaragua's quarrels. Does that dictate your silence?

C: We need peace, a sincere dialogue for reconciliation, between the government and all elements of the opposition — including the armed opposition.

A: You mean with the contras. The Sandinistas say *never*.

C: That's their present position, yes.

A: How long can Nicaragua go on like this? How serious is the hunger outside Managua?

C: It's terrible, everywhere, and the hungriest are the most poor. How can people live without bread? Have you been to the market, Edward?

A: The other day.

C: No meat, eggs, or cheese. No system of distribution. Cattle all over the country, but meat can't enter Managua. Cheese they make in one province, in the next you can't find cheese.

A: Does Your Eminence visit the market?

C: The other day, out in the country. No medicines, no basic foods, hardly any corn, beans, tomatoes, lettuce, pipián. Imagine, it used to be you could buy twenty pipián for twenty cordobas. Now five hundred cordobas can't buy a single pipián.

A: Forgive me, Eminence. What is *pipián*?

C: A small squash. People use it to make soup.

I returned to the Siete Mares marveling how perfectly Nicaraguan: you meet a Cardinal and discuss vegetables. The next day, I met a Jesuit and discussed utopia.

He was Padre R, a theologian of UCA, the Jesuit university, that academy beneath Sandino's red and black flag, where the sides of buildings were splashed with portraits of Sandinista martyrs and slogans promising death to the Yankee invader. A slight man, all Vandyke beard and black spectacles, Padre R helped to publish *El Tayacán,* the popular tabloid of the liberationist Jesuits, full of well-wrought cartoons and didactic bubbles that identified Christ with the Revolution. He was close to the foreign minister and other clerics, frocked and defrocked, inside the government. I told the father that I still could not quite understand how the Revolution and the Kingdom of God converged. He drew me a sketch:

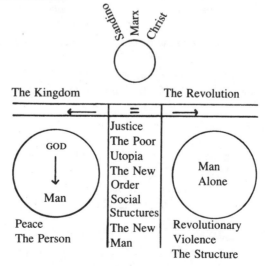

Padre R explained that "the Kingdom of God is utopian. Sandino, Marx, and Christ converge in the Revolution and in the New Nicaraguan Man." Utopia is born as the New Man—once abandoned in his misery—struggles to remake social structures, which means conversion and redemption of the person. The Kingdom of God is realized in a radical new social order, utopia. God and man are reconciled—man is no longer alone—because the human person has achieved peace through social justice.

"The Kingdom of God and the Revolution are the same. The New Man prefers the way of peace, not violence. Sometimes, however, he finds revolutionary violence necessary. We're not perfect. There *is* a class struggle between the rich and poor, but it's a sociological problem. I don't care for theories but for *facts*."

In another age, Lytton Strachey found the doctrine of papal infallibility charming for "its very exorbitance. Not because he satisfies the reason, but astounds it, men abase themselves before the Vicar of Christ." One is tempted to such sarcasm toward the theologian's utopia—until one remembers that for nearly two centuries the Jesuits achieved utopia in Paraguay.

In the early seventeenth century, a company of visionary Spanish Jesuits, enamored of the primeval culture of the Guarani Indians, prevailed on Philip III of Spain to create the Reductions of Paraguay. These colonies of baptized aborigines were destined to become a self-governing Christian republic, based on the pure communism of the Gospels. The Jesuits, far from holding native custom in contempt, saw themselves as merely the tutors and trustees of Indian welfare, which they had been called to lead toward the Kingdom of God.

From the first establishment of the Reductions, the Jesuits insisted on the freedom of the Indians and their isolation from the greed and slave-running of imperialists from Portugal and Spain. Hounded by Brazilian slave hunters, the Jesuits led the Guarani through thick rain forest, across endless lakes and mountain ranges, deeper and deeper into primeval nature in quest of their divine Kingdom. These migrations, fragrant today with the aroma of myth, resulted in scores of new Reductions remote in the wild, where scores of thousands of aborigines were baptized into Christ and flourished as free men.

Yet the Jesuits never rested: the jungles beckoned still. "The Fathers," writes a Jesuit historian, "crossed turbulent streams and treacherous swamps, faced death from ravenous animals, poisonous snakes and savage humans. They carried with them only their breviaries and their cross-topped staffs. Once the nomads were settled on the Reductions, time and again the wild children of Nature ran away, and the Fathers had to follow after them.'' Polygamy and other vices of the savages, the sinister power of the sorcerers, were eventually vanquished. Thirty Jesuits were martyred; others died of fever.

The civilization of the Reductions blossomed in planned villages, advanced farming, cattle raising, carpentry, masonry, blacksmithing, schools, hospitals, painting, and sculpture. The Jesuits' churches were gilded temples rich with vestments and plate; sports, printing presses, drama, and orchestras flourished; Indians played Italian masters on the violin. Land and property became the common possession of the tribes, yet some private ownership was permitted, and commerce was structured to abolish greed. Even Voltaire, prince of cynics, revered the Reductions: "Laws were there respected, morals were pure, a happy brotherhood bound men together; there was abundance everywhere."

In the latter eighteenth century, the Reductions were destroyed by slave hunters, the imperial greed of Spain and Portugal, and the Holy Inquisition. The Indians were expelled with the fathers, and the Jesuit republic reverted to jungle. Of the Reductions today, only ruins and memories remain, enough to suggest that utopia is possible.

I thought of the Reductions as Padre R doodled more sketches on his pad. "I don't care for theories but for *facts*." I was tempted to mention a few. I wished to ask, "How do you reconcile your Kingdom with the hunger in Nicaragua? With the terrible failures of the Revolution and the Jesuits' constant excuses? Are you like the other Jesuits? Do you blame everything on the United States?" But Padre R was not the kind of priest I could bully. He believed every word he said and glowed with Christlike fire. No Marxist Jesuit ever touched me more. I asked, "Does your family live in Nicaragua?"

He looked up from his sketch. I could see his pain. "I come from a family of privilege," he said. "Professionals. Bourgeois. They owned farms. They have left Nicaragua."

The campus clock struck noon. Padre R had to celebrate a student Mass. "Would you like to come? There won't be many students." Walking to the chapel he said, "My friend Miguel D'Escoto went too far in threatening to excommunicate the Cardinal. The divisions in the Church are a scandal. We must reconcile! We're committing suicide!"

4

AT THE SIETE MARES, in the midst of thunderstorms late one night, Viktor was having a crisis. The Sandinistas, fed up with his drunkenness and disappearances, had asked the Czechoslovak Socialist Republic to call him home. I sympathized with the Sandinistas: however badly they needed hydraulic engineers, Viktor was not of much use.

No, I sympathized with Viktor, as he sat at a table in the Chinese restaurant, surrounded by bottles of Flor de Caña and several of his girls, crying he could not go home. The girls were as tearful, four of them, young girls wide at the hips in tight jeans, one in rainwear, another with negroid lips, her copper fingers caressing his very blond head. The disheveled restaurant, beer bottles, and abandoned food beneath the painting of the Sacred Heart echoed with their regrets. Who would care for them when Viktor was gone? Who would feed them, buy them clothes and beer? Who would give them flowers? When Viktor saw me he staggered to his feet and stuffed a package of Parliaments into my shirt pocket.

In a blur of Spanish and broken English he told me, "I love Nicaragua. *Chicas pesos soy libre.* Girls money I'm free. Oh, oh. In Prague, no laugh. Drink the beer, Edward?" He sat down, dealt cards to the girls. A soldier with a pistol sat drinking beer in the corner, minding his own business. His T-shirt said, CONTRA LA BURGUESA Y IMPERIALISMO POR EL DESARROLLO DE LA REVOLUCION. Viktor rose again, lurched at the soldier, slightly tore his shirt. The soldier flared and touched his gun. Viktor sat at the soldier's table, dealing him dollars, crying out in English, "Oh, oh. Fuck the communism."

5

AT DAWN, some blond men came to put Viktor on an airplane for Havana, I supposed en route to Prague. I watched him walk sadly, soberly, to a black Skoda and vanish behind opaque glass. Then I took to the road myself, heading toward Chontales, contra country.

Somehow I found comfort in my constant motion, the next mountain, valley, village, new people, new problems with no solutions; compulsive, drugged, I couldn't stop. Yet I took little pleasure in my companion.

I mean Julio, my driver. He had been recommended to me by American friends in Costa Rica, and I had used his services since my first arrival in Managua. He was a stumpy, smooth-faced man, somewhere in his thirties, uneducated but very glib, so tending to fat that he did not so much walk as roll forward. Julio's taxi was an old, tiny Datsun, and like most automobiles in Nicaragua it was falling apart. The paint had eroded, like the floorboards, and I could see the road rushing beneath; the seat springs chewed my trousers. But the taxi was Julio's castle and once inside it I became his hostage. He never stopped talking.

As a petty capitalist with his taxi and a small house, Julio had to pay taxes to the Sandinistas, and he hated them to the point of philosophy, summed up constantly in his favorite phrase, "*El capitalismo . . . capitalism is the exploitation of man by man. El comunismo . . . communism is the exploitation of man by the state.*" He repeated these equations day and night, often at the top of his voice. When not philosophizing, Julio mooched. Would I lend him fifty thousand cordobas? Would I buy him a color television at the dollar shop? Would I bring him razor blades, shaving cream, a new carburetor, and a can of red paint from Costa Rica? Would I get him a visa for the United States? Despite his wife and several children, in Managua he would sometimes pick me up with a whore in the front seat. I told him to stop; he never did. In the provinces, whenever we entered a new village, he told all and sundry who I was. I told him to stop; he kept doing it. Ten, twenty times I decided to dump Julio, but he was the devil I knew. "*El capitalismo . . . el comunismo . . .*"

We sputtered toward the heart of Nicaragua. In Matagalpa city the Sandinistas were celebrating Carlos Fonseca's fiftieth birthday, but nobody showed up for the festivities. In the park little girls danced forlornly in the rain to an audience of me. A banner: CARLOS, WE'LL SING YOUR SUBVERSIVE SONGS! WE'LL WORK TODAY AND REST TOMORROW! Onward through Boaco province to Chontales, south by southeast, through sudden bursts of sun and rain, herds of cattle and cowboys on horses constantly crossing roads, campesinos living under thatched roofs that reminded me of Africa, rolling meadows and steep mountains that in this wet season when the sun shone were so Arcadian, so green.

In Juigalpa, the capital of Chontales, I lodged at the Hotel Mayales, behind the cement cathedral and around the corner from the bingo parlor and the bishop's palace. The Mayales was Juigalpa's best; like most Isthmian buildings its exterior was flush with the sidewalk, and one had to enter to see its lovely garden, where ducks and kittens cohabited in the frond. That, however, was the limit of its charm; I shaved from a crude basin in the courtyard and ran through the courtyard in the driving rain to a toilet that never worked. Another family hotel; the Señora proposed to put Julio and me in the same room, an ordeal I could not face. He snored, talked in his sleep, and I could not bear the proximity of his fat body and the smooth tires he piled by my feet. I slept alone, in a filthy cubicle next to Julio's, and I could hear him snoring.

In the morning after breakfast, I fled Julio to sit in the Parque Central facing the cathedral. Soon I was approached by a mustachioed little fellow with threadbare sneakers and a volume of Rubén Darío. "I'm Maximo," he said. From that name I might have thought of Roman emperors were it not for Maximo's way of talking, a delightful singsong that ended all vowels in soprano and reminded me of a comic Mexican I had heard on the radio as a child. Of course Maximo had no money, he had not eaten in a day or two, and his hotel was the park. "I'm from Managua," he said. "I came to Juigalpa to find work."

Unhappily, Maximo had no papers, since he had fled to Costa Rica to avoid serving in the Sandinista army and was terrified of prison should he apply for new ones. That meant no ration card either, a real problem because he had a sweetheart and three infant children in Managua with a fourth on the way. Another bother, his sweetheart had lost her birth certificate and so no ration card for her. "*Es igual,*" said Maximo. "There's no work or food anyway. I used to buy *hamburguesa* on the street. No hamburguesa now. I might find a tortilla, a cup of coffee, if I had some pesos . . ."

I handed him some cordobas, and again I was struck by the natural and gracious way Nicaraguans — and poor Central Americans generally — accepted money. He — they — said *gracias* softly, with no fuss. Never did anyone refuse for pride; no reason to. Except in Honduras, never did I see servility, only dignity, a tacit reciprocal admission that the giver had means, the receiver did not, and seize luck softly when it comes your way.

I invited Maximo to luncheon at the Mayales; anything to escape eating with Julio. After luncheon I offered to rent him a cubicle in the hotel, but he refused with horror. Registering in a hotel meant registering with the police. He would sleep in the rain, thank you. Yet for several days thereafter, until he returned forlornly to Managua, Maximo came faithfully to the hotel to see me if I was there, to await me if I was out. At the hotel he was never idle; he sat alone in a corner of the courtyard, squatting with his ankles crossed, writing me long letters.

Rarely did he hand one over; he was never satisfied with his compositions, and after completing several pages in his notebook, he would rip them out, crumple them, and toss them away. The pages scattered in the wind and rain to the nooks of the courtyard and past the ducks and kittens in the lush garden. After Maximo left, I scavenged about and collected them. Even with a magnifier they were not easy to decipher. Maximo wrote in a microscopic hand, had no notion of grammar, and his spelling was deplorable. But certain words and phrases, recurring again and again, reveal the mind of that little vagabond.

". . . *pobresa* . . . poverty . . . *falta* . . . want . . . *nesecidad*, need . . . *techo*, shelter . . . *pueblo*, people . . . *repuñante como es el marxismo*, Marxism is so disgusting . . . *empleo*, work . . . *futuro* . . . *régimen militar* . . . *quiero la libertad* . . . *libertad* . . . *libertad* . . . *libertad* . . . I want freedom freedom freedom freedom." Had Tomás Borge or Ernesto Cardenal, those philosopher-kings of the Revolution, ever seen such letters no doubt they would have sneered at them. Maximo was a delinquent, a draft dodger, and no matter he was penniless, not of the "true" poor. Nobody belonged to the people simply by being poor, nor were the people necessarily the majority. The true poor, the true people, were revolutionaries, and revolutionaries never mocked the Revolution. For Christian revolutionaries, according to Ernesto's *Gospel,* "the poor of Jesus Christ are the poor who practice love. The bourgeois poor, the poor opposed to revolutionary changes, are not the poor of the Gospel."

Poor Maximo!

Poor Chontales. Chontales was a great ranch, with cows, bulls, sheep, and goats grazing in valley after valley, yet in the restaurants of Juigalpa there was little meat, or the meat had the taste of string, and that jawbreaking meat was always heaped with raw cabbage. In the markets, vegetables were scarce or too costly for the poor, except for cabbage, mountains and mountains of cabbage. The poor would never starve if they lived on cabbage.

I have written heretofore that the Nicaraguan people were hungry though not starving, but in the hovels around Juigalpa I found families that suffered from incipient famine. They lived in huts with thatched roofs, shacks sinking in mud, where myriad naked infants toddled about, or in more humble habitations of logs and twigs at the mercy of the wind. Such dwellings teemed with new families, desperate people only recently descended from the mountains in search of food. I remember one woman and her many children amid their mud and sticks, with some scraps of rotting meat, a few tortillas, and a bag of sugar—their food for a week. "We eat three or four times a week," she said. "The government does nothing for us. We have no papers."

Radio Sandino, Radio Revolución, Radio Insurrección broadcast incessant appeals to the populace: WORKERS, FARMERS, PATRIOTS IN THE WAR ZONES, PRODUCE MORE! The people of Chontales seemed to be deaf. In response to every crisis, the state imposed new regulations and seized more private farms, but even the meekest of the campesinos passively resisted the leaden hand of bureaucratic socialism and produced less. Some campesinos told me bluntly, "We don't want land reform." Others were wary, sullen toward the government but unwilling to vent their feelings for fear of *orejas,* "ears," spies. They spoke out by not working, barely growing more than enough for their own hunger. What remained of the bourgeoisie, the people who read *La Prensa* and kept portraits of Cardinal Obando in their offices, were vehement.

Some lawyers, small merchants, leaders of the local opposition parties gather one night to meet me: "The contras are our only hope to save us from communism. Go anywhere in Chontales, north to Boaco or eastward through Zelaya to the sea, you'll find sympathy for the contras in all classes, among the most poor, even among soldiers forced to serve in the Sandinista army. The contras are active only miles from Juigalpa, in Juste, in Santo Tomás, Santo Domingo, Cuapa, Acoyapa, San Pedro Louago, and in La Libertad, where Cardinal Obando was born. Whenever they descend from the mountains and pass by farms, the campesinos feed them gladly. Then comes the state security, dragging the campesinos off to prison, interrogation, and torture. We know of fifteen hundred new political prisoners in the last few months. Ninety percent of the people in Chontales oppose this government. We want the quickest way out. We all look to the United States. Will your Congress be so cruel and stupid as to refuse the contras weapons and money to save us from communism?"

One bourgeois, more rhapsodical than the rest, shouts: "Send us your airplanes, your paratroopers, and your bombs. Better a North American invasion now. I'd rather see my own house blown up, for the sake of my sons and future generations of Nicaraguans. Anything—to save us from communism."

The Sandinistas had a large army camp on the outskirts of Juigalpa and even a command post that faced the central park. That lovely shady place, with a bandstand built in better times and a statue of Mother Nicaragua giving suck, was always thronged with soldiers, loitering on the benches or lining up, queuing in long columns, then mounting East German IFA trucks for missions to the countryside to kill or capture rebels. In Julio's junk heap or in more robust vehicles in the blessed company of others, I followed the trucks at a distance or encountered them from time to time on the muddy dirt roads of Chontales between Juigalpa and Santo Tomás, between Santo Tomás and Acoyapa, between Santo Domingo and La Libertad, and on the narrow tributaries of the long road to Rama in the province of Zelaya toward the sea.

The contras roamed the countryside in small bands of men and boys rarely more numerous than eight or ten. They had trudged from the Honduran border in the north for fifty days, martial equipment laden on their backs, across unmerciful terrain, and in Chontales they took shelter in the mountains, living on squirrels and snake meat. These were the troops of the Jorge Salazar Command, a permanent insurgency force in Chontales numbering several thousand. From time to time they were resupplied by air drops from planes flown by American mercenaries out of El Salvador and Costa Rica. When the insurgents descended from their lofty caves, they attacked buses and collective farms, cut electricity and telephone lines, shot civilians occasionally, but they had yet to interrupt Sandinista arms convoys rolling to the interior on the road from Rama.

Wherever the contras emerged, the Sandinistas in their armored land units and HIP and HIND helicopters kept them from massing, confined them to small clusters, roving and running constantly. To Chontales and other central provinces more Soviet weaponry poured in, rifles, mortars, howitzers, minelayers, armored trucks, SAM missiles, multiple rocket launchers, armed transport helicopters, Cuban technicians who tutored the Sandinistas and flew with them on missions. Sandinista conscripts were known to pursue the enemy without zeal, but in the vanguard were always the BLIs, the elite counterinsurgency battalions, deeply indoctrinated, high in morale, superbly armed.

Yet however harassed the contras, they persevered in the wild and maintained their presence in Chontales, not least from the sympathy of the conservative Catholic peasants. Some of the insurgents' allies were catechists, teachers of the faith, Delegates of the Word, and that further poisoned the state's hostility to the Church. In no corner of Nicaragua did the counterrevolutionaries enjoy such a solid social base or such a wide support network. The peasants fed them, warned them of army movements, hid them in homes and forest. The Sandinistas knew this, and their response was ruthless. And *efficient*. They were bumpkins in economics, not in matters of security. Once guerrillas themselves, they knew all the tricks of intelligence, of harboring fugitives, of "safe houses," all the clandestine means of keeping insurgents supplied and fed.

Thus in central Nicaragua and especially in Chontales the army mounted increasing sweeps throughout the countryside in search of contras and their collaborators. Often they arrested four hundred, five hundred people at a time, including whole villages, in their unyielding campaign to crush the insurgent support network. The army swept up the suspects, and in tandem came Borge's men of the state security, in charge of jails and interrogation.

The Sandinistas seized the innocent with the guilty, but such arrests had the intended effect of intimidating the larger populace against helping the guerrillas in the future. As their methods of intelligence grew more sophisticated, their interrogations harsher, the Sandinistas kept the rebels weak. Yet the contras kept coming in, the supply drops increased as the months passed, and the insurgency continued. All this was done against that verdant landscape, those sudden bursts of sun and thunder, shepherds and horsemen and hills of olive, another garden.

6

ONE MORNING I went to Cuapa, in the hills some miles outside Juigalpa. Only months before, the contras had attacked Cuapa, shot up a collective farm, and killed some people, but today a fiesta was in progress.

In fact, since the campesinos so rarely worked, the fiesta had been going on for a week. It was focused, like so many bucolic celebrations, on the parish church, firecrackers, bullfights, beer, and guaro. There was a slight anomaly about the parish church, named for Saint Francis of Assisi, whose feast is not celebrated until October. But years ago the parish patron had been Saint John the Baptist, whose feast fell conveniently now in June, so everybody celebrated *that*. In the murky bars between thatched roofs and earthen floors, indolent young cowboys prepared for the processions by quarreling over women and getting drunk. A soft rain fell on Cuapa.

Toward noon, the religious feast unfurled. The Bishop of Juigalpa, in full pontificals, celebrated Mass and preached, then the multitude poured out of the church and the firecrackers started, volleys of rockets that men and boys released from the steps against the rain. The faithful marveled at the noise, huddled beneath umbrellas, and headed toward the forest bearing a statue of the Virgin, who had her own grotto.

No ordinary grotto. A year after the Revolution, the Virgin had descended from Heaven and appeared near the river, between a bower of trees and a pile of rocks, to a campesino called Bernardo.

Bernardo de Cuapa was the impoverished sacristan of the parish church, a small wizened man with a thatch of graying hair, much given to melancholy, thoughts of death, and constant recitation of the mysteries of the rosary. In the forest one April afternoon, as he completed his devotions, he saw a flash of lightning, then brilliant illuminations and a dazzling cloud. Rays of splendor beamed in all directions; a woman of extraordinary beauty descended on the cloud and stood amid the stones and flowers in the grove. She was barefoot, wore a long white robe, a mantle trimmed with gold, and a ribbon of unearthly colors tied to her cincture. Her hands were crossed on her breasts. She said, "*Soy la Madre de Jesús.* I am the Mother of Jesus." She told Bernardo to instruct the people to love one another, to work for peace, to recite the rosary constantly. She warned that Nicaragua would suffer terribly if the people did not heed her message and deeply change.

Thereafter, Bernardo saw the Virgin in the same grove on the eighth day of each month until October. He described the visions as "celestial feasts." The Virgin was not always alone. In June, she brought with her the first Christians, vested in luminous white, the first Dominican Fathers, the first Franciscan Fathers, angels, archangels, and colored lights. She spoke of the glory of her Son, then ascended with her companions to Heaven on her blinding cloud.

For subsequent encounters Bernardo was pursued by pilgrims, who saw great circles of colored light dancing between the earth and sky but not the Virgin.

Bernardo: "She is standing on the heap of stones above the flowers."

Pilgrims: "We see only a shadow."

Bernardo: "O Lady! Appear to them so they may believe! They don't believe! They say I see the Devil! Let them see you, Lady!"

The Virgin did not reply. She lifted her hands to her breast, her lovely face went pale, her brilliant garments turned to gray, she became the Dolorosa as in Holy Week and for the pilgrims' unbelief she wept. Wildly, Bernardo sobbed.

Bernardo: "Forgive me, Lady! It's my fault! You're angry with me! Forgive me! Forgive me!"

The Virgin: "*Yo no estoy enojada.* I'm not angry. I mourn for their hardness of heart. Pray, Bernardo, pray they'll change."

In her final visions the Virgin warned of heavy crosses the Nicaraguan people would have to bear and then repeated, over and over, "*No vayan a la violencia, no vayan nunca a la violencia.* Do not turn to violence, never turn to violence. Change! *Soy la Madre de todos ustedes, pecadores.* Sinners, I am the Mother of you all."

Then, for the last time, through the branches of a cedar tree the Lady was lifted to Heaven on her dazzling cloud.

As at Fatima and Lourdes, the faithful, the lame, and the crippled came afterward to Cuapa, to the river and the tiny grotto beneath the trees, seeking visions, cures, and miracles. By December 1981, thousands and thousands of believers would converge on Cuapa on a single day, young and old, mostly the poor, women in wheelchairs pushed by Boy Scouts, the multitude crying and sobbing, waving their arms at the empty sky beseeching signs. None appeared. Bernardo went about his life, still singing the Lady's song. Rome was wary of his visions; miracles take centuries to consider, and the Holy See was in no hurry.

The Sandinistas were less patient. Visions of the Virgin were not on their agenda, and they ridiculed Bernardo on television and in their newspapers, as did the fathers of the Popular Church, though if the Virgin had endorsed the Revolution or quoted Karl Marx, or if Bernardo had seen visions of Sandino, perhaps they would have blessed him. Bernardo was obviously not of the "good" poor. The Sandinistas sent goons to Cuapa to beat him up, then in the press accused him of sodomy. They hounded him out of Cuapa, and he vanished into the faceless proletariat.

The campesinos of Cuapa still mourn for Bernardo, still pray and plant flowers in his grove, but once the processions trickled out, the Holy Virgin was forgotten in the fiesta. Now the rain beat harder on my face. The bullfights started. The stadium, built of sticks and branches, faced the church; between church and stadium, women sold watery ice cream cones and hundreds of bottles of beer (odd, during such scarcity), not the weak Toña beer but the tasty Victoria brew. In the stands, a brass orchestra announced the corrida as in Spain. Small laughing boys in straw sombreros sat on the wooden fence around the immense ring; from houses nearby, beautiful, small laughing girls in their Sunday dresses watched through latticed windows as in Andalusia. The adults were as childish in their rejoicing, in their zeal to ignore their government, forget privation, delay their work another day. *¡Fiesta!* I thought: such fun, such a handsome, carefree folk.

The bullfight was unorthodox, without killing and never cruel. Men drove great-horned white and black bulls into the arena, not so much a ring as a vast pudding of mud where the beasts trod ankle-deep. Cowboys in straw hats, muddy jeans, and boots chased the bulls on horseback, taunting them with blunt sticks. Shirtless youths waved flags at the bulls, then jumped on their backs and rode them roughshod as they swigged bottles of beer and guaro. When the bulls bucked them off, the daredevils rolled in the mud, howling with pleasure and drinking still.

Near me stood another youth, draped in a huge red flag, swigging a bottle of beer and hesitating at the edge of the ring, as though fearful to chance the bulls. "I need another beer," he told me.

We strode to a vendor beneath the stands, where he drank three. He said, "I'm Antonio," but otherwise he watched the bulls, talking and laughing only about them. His white T-shirt, dripping wet in the chilly drizzle and splattered with mud, clung to his torso. He was lithe and good-looking, with flared nostrils and bronze skin, but his classic face was flawed by an ugly scar high on his temple (a stab wound?) and at the center of his mouth was a sick gray tooth. Eventually his attention wandered from the bullfight, and when I told him I came from the United States he revealed his fondest wish: a swimming pool. He would own one when he was rich, in the United States. "Do you live in Los Angeles?" he asked. "*¿Hay piscina en su casa?* Do you have a swimming pool?" With such a yearning, Antonio was not of the "good" poor, either.

Now he tired of our conversation and turned to someone else, asking for guaro. He swigged at the stranger's bottle until the stranger demanded it back. It was raining hard as Antonio, waving his red flag, stepped into the ring.

He had no skill; with the others, he sloshed in the mud, but when a bull approached him he shied away, dragging his sodden flag. Once or twice he tried to mount a bull, but hardly had he touched the beast he was shaken off. Yet even as he waded in the mud, Antonio's movements were somehow graceful. I turned away to look for Julio to drive me home.

Finally, as the rain became torrential, I found him beneath a tree. Julio had trouble starting the car, but as he did a misty shadow rapped on my window.

It was Antonio, his boots and jeans caked with mud. He wanted a ride to Juigalpa. Where was his red cape? I wondered. "A bull's wearing it," he said. As we left Cuapa, rolling over hills and valleys, the rain ceased abruptly and the sun burst out. Antonio chattered on, boasting of his daring with the bulls, but I was silenced by the beauty of the landscape.

We stopped the Datsun on the crest of a hill, and it seemed that the whole of Chontales lay at our feet. In the fading afternoon the sky was mauve, and a cloud, shaped like a winged horse, galloped weirdly in slow motion across the mountains. In a valley, puffs of smoke ascended from a village. I fetched my binoculars from the Datsun and looked more closely. Some soldiers were entering the houses, emerging with campesinos whose arms were raised. The campesinos were collected on an open field, and a hut was burning. Another sweep, I thought. I handed the binoculars to Antonio, and he said, "*Sí*. I've done them."

"You're a soldier?"

"*Sí. Soy militar.*"

"Why aren't you fighting the contras?"

"I'm on leave."

"So. You're a Sandinista."

"I hate the Sandinistas. They came to my house and dragged me off, put me in the army. I'm leaving Nicaragua. I'm going to the States."

"When?"

"Any day now."

"You have to finish your patriotic military service."

"Fuck my patriotic military service. I'll desert."

"They'll shoot you."

"They'll have to catch me."

"How will you get to the States?"

"I'll take an airplane."

"You'll never get a visa."

"You'll get me one."

"Impossible."

"I'll walk."

I believed Antonio. Millions of Mexicans, hundreds of thousands, possibly millions, of young Central Americans had already walked to the borders of Texas and California, and most of them had slipped through. Surely this is one of history's great migrations, Biblical in resonance, and in time epic poetry will be written of it. Not everybody cared to walk. Wherever I traveled on the isthmus, I was entreated by poor and middle class to get them visas to the United States. My protests that I was a private citizen and had nothing to do with visas made no difference: I was a North American, and I could arrange the matter.

Antonio thought so, too. He lived nearby in Juigalpa, and he reappeared to press his case. Usually in the evenings when I emerged to the street, there he was, awaiting me in the little park that faced my hotel. He was not always sober; he carried with him those plastic sucking bags of clear guaro, and his childish brain could never grasp why I did not care to drink it with him. Often he was boisterous, but he could be quiet, too, and one night he sat with his back against a wall, closed his eyes, and told me what he saw.

His fantasy was not complicated. Unlike the visions of Bernardo de Cuapa, there were no dazzling clouds or dancing colored lights. Nor even, for so sensuous a youth, erotic thrills. No girls, no rock music, no friends seemed to share his heaven. As a child he had gone swimming in Lake Nicaragua not far away and hated it: the lake was dirty and the beach was covered with dead fish. He had seen pictures of swimming pools in magazines and films. His fantasy was only of himself, smiling at his reflection in a swimming pool. Were there not even trees around the pool? I wondered. Antonio saw no trees.

Somehow he had a passport. It was my assignment to get him a visa in Managua, and he would leave for Managua with me. My protests were futile, and he kept returning in the evenings to the little park.

One morning, I met him by chance in the street. He wore a green T-shirt, army boots, and camouflage pants; he sat on some stone steps near the apse of the cathedral, holding his head between his hands, his sculpted face moist with sweat. "Are you sick?" I asked.

"*Sí.*"

He lifted his upper lip, and I saw that the gum around his gray tooth was infected and turning white. "You need a dentist," I said. From his pants pocket he took out a prescription. "I can't pay for it," he said.

Nearby was a state clinic, a Sandinista slogan splashed on the wall: A LOS ENEMIGOS DEL PUEBLO, VIGILANCIA REVOLUCIONARIA. We walked down a long corridor to a window where an elderly man was dispensing pills to soldiers. For civilians there were no pills, only for soldiers. Antonio surrendered his scrap of paper, and for an envelope of pills I paid a thousand cordobas, about forty-five cents U.S. Outside the clinic, Antonio scooped up rainwater from the gutter and swallowed half the pills.

Again he lifted his lip, and again I marveled at the whiteness and decay. I thought, in ten years he will have no teeth.

7

LATER THAT DAY, I saw the Bishop of Juigalpa emerge from the precincts of the cathedral escorted by a pair of cowboys on horseback. Monseñor Pablo Antonio Vega was a short man, bald and thick, wearing eyeglasses and a white soutane. He paused by the corner of my hotel, just up the street from his palace, to bid the cowboys good-by. One of them leaped from his saddle, commanding his horse to genuflect to the bishop. The horse went down on both front knees. The bishop laughed and clapped his hands. I thought, he is like a medieval prince. Even the horses kneel to him.

I approached him and in my reverent way with bishops addressed him in Latin and kissed his ring. He said, "Will you stay in my house?"

During my several days there, I saw more than I expected. Monseñor Vega was in the closing battles of his war with the Sandinistas.

With the internal secular opposition so feeble, Monseñor Vega deferred only to Cardinal Obando as the most vigorous antagonist of the state. In fact he was more vehement, condemning the Sandinistas with the kind of language that from his lofty height the Cardinal cared not to use. As president until recently of Nicaragua's bench of bishops, Monseñor Vega had negotiated for years with the Sandinistas on church affairs. For a while they preferred him to Cardinal Obando and boasted that he was a "man we can talk to." They invited him to offer prayers at President Ortega's installation in 1984, where they seated him beside Fidel Castro. But the Monseñor was already disillusioned and, from bitter experience, claimed the Sandinistas could not be trusted. They promised much, he said, signed any scrap of paper for tactical advantage, then broke their word. They *lied*.

The Sandinistas now found the bishop an easier target than the popular and illustrious Cardinal. The Sandinista press published page after page of ridicule and denunciation, claiming that he had endorsed the counterrevolution. Certainly the bishop was elusive about the matter, even more so than the Cardinal. On his trips to the United States, he met openly with procontra foundations, and though he stopped just short of bestowing public blessings on the rebels, his sympathies seemed unmistakable. Moreover, his repeated public appeals for negotiations between the government and the insurgency, like the appeals of Cardinal Obando, were dismissed by the Sandinistas as seditious and impossible.

The bishop's residence, ugly cement on the outside, on the inside was full of alcoves, books, and flowers. Despite the scarcities, he served an abundant table, and in lieu of aperitifs he offered cheese bits and Dutch beer. He had taken a diploma in sociology at Québec and spoke fluent French, so usually we conversed in that tongue. Several comely girls, sisters and half Chinese, managed his household and cooked his meals. He seemed embarrassed by the celestial visions of Bernardo de Cuapa and urged his people to shun magic, to commune with the Virgin by living Christian lives. He had a quiet sense of humor and was more intellectual than Monseñor Obando, but he lacked the Cardinal's mischievous irony and pith.

The Sandinistas were harassing him, he said. He led me to the window. "Do you see that man on the red motorcycle? Secret police. There is another man at the corner by your hotel, and a third in the bingo parlor across the street. They spy on me constantly." Yet when we drove in his pickup truck throughout Chontales on his pastoral rounds, we were not followed. Perhaps some campesinos informed on him. The bishop, dressed in soutane and a brown golf cap, stopped often to give them rides in the rear of the truck, and the numerous passengers banged on the roof of his cabin when they wanted to jump off. In the road the mothers held up their children for his blessing and then went about their business. I said, "What a marvelous people, Monseigneur."

"You noticed," he mused. "They ask of life only one thing—to be left alone. They'd prefer no government at all, but this one?" How these campesinos hated working for the state, tilling land of the state's or of their own whose crops the bureaucracy took from them under the vigilance of the police. After years of euphoric illusions, revolutionary myths, and dreadful hardship, the Nicaraguan people knew that dogmatic ideology could never satisfy their needs.

No doubt the contras had violated human rights, but the sins of the Sandinistas were much worse. The comandantes talked of free speech as though it were candy to be given children, not man's natural right. The people had been robbed of their right to speak, to work, to worship free of the violence of the state. "This new dictatorship crushes man and thrusts a helmet of silence over his head," the bishop continued. The Sandinistas warned constantly of a North American invasion, but Nicaragua had already been invaded by their beloved friends, Cuba and the Soviet Union.

Nicaragua had exchanged one form of imperialism for another, and for that the Roman Church shared some responsibility. The Church had led the battle against Somoza; the bishops' condemnation of the dictator caused the U.S. Congress to cut off money, and Somoza rightly blamed them for his downfall. But the bishops were fallible men: how could they have known that the future would be worse?

Monseñor Vega wove variations on themes of tyranny, on the doctrines of Aquinas, on the people's right to insurrection as a last resort. The Church had always taught man's right to self-defense. "When a man is tryrannized by the state, when the state strips him of all his liberties, subjects him to terrible violence, he has the right to rebel." Insurrection was justified against Somoza; now it was not for the Church, but for the people in their collective conscience to decide their fate. If the Theology of Liberation endorsed rebellion against tyrannies of the right, should it not do likewise against tyrannies of the left?

We were headed from the countryside back to Juigalpa, passing more soldiers in East German trucks, on the hunt no doubt for new contras or embarking on another sweep. Over the garden of Chontales the sun disappeared again, and we drove in a raw drizzle. And I thought: this man is begging for trouble.

"There's no ideological difference between Ortega and Borge, as you so often hear," he continued. "All the comandantes are hardened Marxists, devoted to the consolidation of a totalitarian state. Their weapons are force and deceit. I dealt directly with the comandantes, and I know them too well. They can't, they won't, they'll never change."

He recounted an exchange with the Pope during John Paul's visit to

Nicaragua in 1983, after Daniel Ortega had harangued His Holiness at the airport and the Sandinista mob—angry that the Pontiff did not condemn the contras—drowned out his homily with chants of *"¡Poder Popular! ¡Poder Popular!* People's Power! People's Power!"* Tomás Borge signaled to the Sandinista cadres when to shout and when to quiet down. The Cardenal brothers, at the time still priests in good standing, likewise raised their fists and roared, *"¡Poder Popular!"* A Sandinista nun screamed *"¡Puta!"* at the Pontiff.

The Pope: "How do you explain this?"

Monseñor Vega: "It's for the best."

The Pope: "I am angry and confused and I cannot understand you."

Monseñor Vega: "The Sandinistas showed Your Holiness—and the whole world—their true face. They will never change."

When we reached the bishop's residence, a layman hurried out and told him, "Monseñor, soldiers and the state security are after us again. They followed the nuns to market, abusing them with threats and filthy words."

It was late afternoon. We went inside. Eventually we heard drums and trumpets not far away. The pretty Chinese girls ran with excitement up the marble stairs; the bishop and I followed to watch the parade from the upper floor. As I gazed down at the street and saw the band, the red and black banners, I realized this was a Sandinista demonstration directed against my host. I could hardly call it menacing; only weird. Several hundred men and women—soldiers and civilians, girls in school uniform—marched impassively by, crying slogans softly, almost like sleepwalkers.

What ensued was more chilling. A man stood opposite on the steps of the bingo parlor and through a megaphone provided a list of contra atrocities, blasphemies against the Pope, and threats of death against the bishop. Two elegant wooden coffins were placed at the bishop's doorstep—one for him, the other for Cardinal Obando.

Coolly the bishop watched the demonstration through a window curtain. I asked, *"Qu'en pensez-vous, Monseigneur?"* He said, *"Ces gens-là ne sont pas de mon peuple.* Those are not my people."

I raised my camera, and from across the street a man took my picture as I took his picture. The bishop said, "They will claim you are the CIA agent living in my house."

8

HE SAID IT WITH GOOD HUMOR, but his troubles were sufficient, so in the morning I left his house. At the Mayales, Julio rushed to me, waving his fat arms. "Don Eduardo! Don Eduardo! The state security has come three times to see you!"

Toward noon a young captain from Tomás Borge's ministry appeared in the courtyard and as we sat at a table questioned me politely. He pored over my passport, studying each visa microscopically, making little notations in his book.

CAPTAIN: Why are you staying so long in Chontales, Meester Edward?

AUTHOR: I enjoy your mountains, *mi capitán*.

C: What were you doing in Cuapa?

A: Watching the bulls.

C: Why did you visit the Capuchin Fathers in Rama?

A: They're North Americans.

C: On your way back from Rama, why did you turn off the road and visit Paesilla and Muelle?

A: To buy cigarettes.

C: Twice?

A: There were no cigarettes in Paesilla.

C: What did the campesinos tell you in Boaco?

A: That your ministry asks many questions.

C: You visited Monseñor Vega at ten o'clock on Tuesday morning.

A: I did not meet the Monseñor until Thursday afternoon. I assume you know that, *mi capitán*.

C: What do you think of the Monseñor?

A: I enjoyed his Dutch beer, *mi capitán*.

He scribbled in his book. Julio sat uncomfortably at the next table, avoiding my glances, pretending to read his newspaper. How I loathed thesc martial governments. Finally the captain returned my passport.

"All for now, sir," he said. "May I recommend that you do not prolong your visit to Chontales? You may begin to find that our, ah, mountains do not agree with you. Anything else I can do for you, Meester Edward?"

"Can you get me an appointment with Comandante Borge?"

The captain laughed and went his way. I turned to Julio hiding behind his newspaper.

I: "The Sandinistas aren't that efficient, Julio. They never followed me in the street or in the car. You talk a good game, but when you meet a policeman, you cave in. You told the captain of all my movements, didn't you?"

Julio: "Who, *me?*"

9

THAT EVENING, I saw Antonio again in the little park. He was in gray jeans, a white shirt, half drunk. In the streetlight he showed me his bad tooth. The gum was swollen slightly and oozed pus. "*Pulsando*. It's throbbing," he said.

He had two plastic bags of guaro and began sucking one. "We're going to Los Ranchos."

"I'll go, Antonio," I answered, "if you'll stop drinking. Can't you throw away the guaro?"

In the Parque Central, where women sold crisp tortilla crusts filled with slop, I made him eat, then we walked down the street and uphill past a cinema to Los Ranchos. The disco served only beer, but Antonio hid his bags of guaro beneath his shirt and we slipped in. The place was a huge oval shed, with a dance floor in the center, very dark but for flashing lights, without a band but deafening with recorded pop. It was full of girls, more girls than men, since young men were away in the army or avoided discos for fear of spontaneous recruitment.

We sat in a dim nook, at a table as far as I could manage from the blaring music. Antonio continued to suck guaro, to see his dream. ". . . happy in the States . . . the pool . . . *mi piscina* . . ." I could see his vision also, this savage youth smiling at his reflection in the water. He asked, "When are we going to Managua?"

"Antonio, why don't you dance?"

"Managua."

"The state security has told me to leave Chontales. I'll leave tomorrow. I'll meet you at noon, in the little park."

"*¿Palabra?*"

"*Palabra*. My word."

"And the visa?"

"I'll try."

Antonio staggered from the nook, pressing his rotting teeth. He approached one group of girls, and then another, but they turned their backs on his drunkenness and refused his invitations to dance. He reached the dance floor, crowded with couples beneath the flashing lights, throbbing with drums and Hispanic sound, and danced alone.

A man's voice sang, something about *la luna . . . si la luna se va . . . rayo de luna . . . sino mañana adiós . . . rayo de luna . . .* As I watched Antonio, I knew that if he ever reached my country it would devour him, that in his weakness and ignorance he would end and very soon in some barrio of Florida or California as a drunkard, a gigolo, or a junkie . . . *rayo de luna . . . sino mañana adiós . . .* Would it not be better after all if his dreams were dashed and he remained in this garden to rot more slowly? I hoped he would never walk through Mexico to the border. I glimpsed him, still dancing in his private pool of light, pressing his tooth.

At dawn, with only obnoxious Julio, I returned to Managua.

10

DURING MY ABSENCE from the capital, my friend Don Pablo Antonio Cuadra received an interesting letter: "*Estimado Señor Director:* On superior orders I hereby notify you that effective at once the newspaper *La Prensa* is closed for an indefinite time. With nothing to add, may I take this occasion to assure you of my respects." It was signed by Captain Blandón and duly stamped by the Ministry of Interior.

The day before, the United States House of Representatives had authorized another $100 million, mostly in military assistance, to the contras; the bill was sent to the Senate, whose blessing seemed certain. The open secret of *La Prensa*'s sympathies and its refusal to condemn the insurgency were to the Sandinistas acts of treason. In its last issue, never published, the newspaper compounded its sins by calling for national "dialogue," a code word of Cardinal Obando's for negotiation with the counterrevolution, more evidence of perfidy.

The Sandinistas had already silenced scores of other independent newspapers and radio stations. *La Prensa* was the last and most important. With its suppression, now only the vanishing private sector, the weak political parties, and the Roman Church remained to resist the state, and none had newspapers. Unquestionably the Church was the stoutest rock: the Sandinistas knew it, so — more bluntly than ever — they besieged the rock.

Monseñor Bismarck Carballo, the Cardinal's youthful counselor, was abroad in Europe and Miami during the week of *La Prensa*'s misfortune. The Sandinistas told him he could not come home. Since the prelate was so anti-Sandinista, the decree of exclusion had a clear political motive; even more, it was a personal stab at the primate since he and Carballo were so close. I heard eventually that exile in the United States was breaking the blithe monsignor's heart. He could hardly bear to live away from his homeland, his parish, and his Cardinal. However, his exile was only a rehearsal.

A day or so after my return to Managua, Monseñor Vega drove from Chontales to the capital to give a news conference at the International Press Club. I was bothered still by the death threats from the bingo parlor, the wooden coffins at his doorstep in Juigalpa. Since my return to Managua I had heard rumors that the Sandinistas might assault him on the road or make him disappear. At the entrance of the press club I approached the bishop and told him so. "They're after you, Monseigneur," I said, hoping he would modulate his words. "*On verra,* we'll see," he replied cheerfully and then sat down in a crowd of cameras and foreign and Sandinista journalists.

The man threw caution to the wind and rain, repeating essentially all he had told me in Chontales, more daringly. He recited the sins of the Sandinistas, evoking again the doctrines of Aquinas and the people's right of revolt. "It is unjust if people can rebel against one kind of dictatorship but not against the other." The Sandinistas seized on these remarks and howled.

Next morning, *Barricada* splashed a cartoon of Monseñor Vega worshiping the American flag. INSOLENTE PROVOCACION, said the headline: "Vega blesses contra crimes, welcomes invasion." VEGA CONFIRMS HIS TREASON! added *El Nuevo Diario*. A morning later, less than a week after the coffins were placed at his doorstep, Monseñor Vega was summoned to the state security at Juigalpa and deported to Honduras. "He does not deserve to be Nicaraguan," the government announced.

John Paul II, who was visiting Colombia, protested that the deportation "evokes the dark ages." On Sandinista television, as Monseñor Vega's face was intermixed with human corpses, Ernesto Cardenal hissed, "Judas, Judas, Judas." Later I met Ernesto and asked him if his commentary was not a bit strong. "After all, Padre, he is your bishop." Ernesto laughed and handed me a photocopied sheet of paper. "Not a bit," he twinkled. "Look at that paper. Saint Jerome said that Peter was a bishop but so was Judas, that Judas was not a real bishop, not even a Christian. Too strong? Much stronger a bishop who supports the mercenaries, the massacres of men, children, and old women. Judas!''

Some weeks after his expulsion, I met Monseñor Vega in Guatemala City and asked him what happened. ''I was summoned by the state security early in the morning,'' he said, ''and taken to the jail outside Juigalpa. They have seven hundred political prisoners in that place, mostly campesinos, and they call them contras. Two hundred prisoners were seized that week, my people, some my Delegates of the Word. They keep them in underground cells and torture them. They seemed to think I was a contra general, because on the baseball field they had two helicopters waiting, one for me, the other for my armed guard. We flew to an artificial lake, then changed course, turned north over the mountains. I did not protest—to what purpose? I told the crew, 'You have my blessing.' They smiled maliciously. A physician rode with me. He was most polite. He asked, 'How is your health?' I thought, 'They are going to push me out.'

''We landed at a military base in Madriz district in the north, full of soldiers. Immediately I was put in a jeep, surrounded by military vehicles, and driven to the frontier at El Espino. The officer handed me a passport, and he told me, 'Monseñor, you must seek another country, since you can no longer live in Nicaragua. You must go and live with the contras or with Reagan.' I replied, 'You can deport my body from Nicaragua but not my heart.' A trailer truck came along, I hitched a ride in the cabin, then entered Honduras on foot. I had almost no money, and not even my toothbrush. I don't regret a word I said. I miss my people painfully.''

The closing of *La Prensa* and the exile of the hostile prelates were state decisions that required the unanimous agreement of the comandantes. No outsider knew how, exactly, the comandantes achieved consensus in their secret councils. One heard rumors of violent debate and even of fisticuffs, but intense debate behind closed doors is true of any politburo. Supposedly Tomás Borge and Bayardo Arce as the "radicals" engaged in devious games for power against the "moderate" Ortega brothers and Jaime Wheelock, but ideologically their differences were of nuance. All of the comandantes as Marxist-Leninists were devoted to the supremacy of the revolutionary vanguard (which they embodied) and to the doctrine that the class struggle is the locomotive of history. The comandantes were very inbred, and not only ideologically. They had known and slept with each other's wives in the old days before marriage and the Revolution; they shared the same dreams and phobias. Whatever their personal frictions, they had closed ranks in recent years and remained remarkably united in the face of Reagan's malice.

Comandante Borge was especially resolved to close *La Prensa;* Comandante Arce warned Monseñor Vega well in advance that if he persisted in his hostile declarations he would be kicked out. Following the U.S. House's vote to renew armed assistance to the contras, all of the comandantes gambled that disgust with the contras in Western Europe and in much of the United States would allow them to close *La Prensa* and expel the clerics without high cost. They gambled shrewdly. Protest throughout the world for the silenced *La Prensa* was rather mild, and outside Nicaragua only Rome seemed really to care about the banished ecclesiastics. Inside Nicaragua, everyone wondered: will they expel Cardinal Obando?

On the Sunday afternoon following Monseñor Vega's misadventure, I called on the Cardinal in his garden. Josefa hastened out of the large house and said, "Isn't it all so terrible? What will they do to us next?" The afternoon was sunny-cloudy and very warm. I waited in the garden, admiring the orchids, until I noticed the Cardinal, in white and scarlet, standing near the palm and frond. He was not reading his Office, did not seem to be praying, perhaps only meditating. His hands rested on his paunch, and his dark Indian features were impassively composed. Even in affliction the man was cool. He noticed me at last, and we chatted in the garden.

The Church was being crucified, he said matter-of-factly. "We are being cut off from the Nicaraguan people. What can we do without newspapers and radio? Now the Sandinistas have expelled my brother bishop, and they are threatening the other bishops and terrorizing the laymen who work in the parishes. They are choking us off. Everywhere I go, I am followed by the secret police. The turbas, the Sandinista mobs, will attack me next. The persecution will get worse. We shall continue to resist."

If I expected him to be sentimental about the loss of the young monsignor, to mourn the exile of his spiritual son, I should have known better; the Cardinal was never sentimental, even in distress. He said simply, "Father Carballo was in charge of communications." That was the crucifixion: being cut off, not only from a friend but from his people. I suggested that he should not travel, the comandantes might keep him out. He said, "I'll think it over." He brooded for a moment. "There are voices in the Vatican trying to silence me."

"Whose voices, Eminence?"

He was silent.

"Will they succeed?"

"No, the Pope is very tough."

"So is Your Eminence."

He remained impassive. I returned to the Siete Mares. I had other events to brood upon that weekend. In Jinotega province, near the Honduran border, the contras had just killed thirty-four civilians — most of them women and small children, some of the women with child — by another land mine. The innocents had been riding in a truck, over a mountainous dirt road vital to their peasant lives. The Sandinista press that Sunday was lurid with enormous photographs, horrific pictures of infant corpses and tiny coffins. The headlines roared: THIS IS THE WORK OF THE VEGAS . . . THESE ARE THE CRIMES BLESSED BY THE BISHOP.

I wondered, were the contra land mines also manufactured of sulfuric acid mixed with sugar, gunpowder laced with rocks, glass, and human excrement? That night, my dream resumed, the same gray jerky silent film full of mutilated peasant soldiers, bilateral amputees. Maybe such dreams resulted from my poor diet: I was living largely on crackers and beer. Aldous Huxley once wrote that malnutrition causes chemical changes in the brain which can induce mystical experience. If not mystical, I was sadly at the mercy of my phantoms and miserably confused. *Morally* confused.

To me the Sandinistas were repugnant, and I shared the social values of *La Prensa,* the bourgeois intellectuals, the liberal parties of the secular opposition, and of Cardinal Obando. Yet none of them had ever denounced land mines or other atrocities of the counterrevolution, and my dilemma was compounded. I began to sympathize again with the moral outrage of the Sandinistas and then to see the metaphysics of the civil war as an endless corridor, mirror facing mirror. It was not enough to say that both sides were wrong and the United States as well. I needed to take another step, which I could not do, and my sorrow about the land mines led me nowhere. I went back to bed, and my jerky film.

I I

FROM MY JOURNAL: Without Viktor, the Siete Mares is not the same, and at night the Chinese restaurant is even drearier. I miss his roistering, his girls, and his noisy card games. This afternoon, however, I received a visit from another friend.

It was Maximo, the little vagabond, still carrying his Rubén Darío. He had returned from Chontales to Managua before I did, and he came to me here in my shabby room with his *compañera,* sweetheart, and her younger sister. They sat on my unmade bed, marveling at the cool breezes of the air conditioner (only one blackout today), which for them seems magical.

Veronica, Maximo's woman, is a mess. She is twenty but looks twice that and is several months along in her fourth pregnancy. Her hair is drawn into a bun, her slippers are falling apart, there is a wide hole in her red jersey. She speaks well. I ask her who is watching their three infant children. "My mother," she says. What did she feed the children this morning? "They didn't eat this morning. Last night we had tortillas and a little rice." Did she often wake up with no food for the children? "These days, *sí.*"

Maximo sits beside her, their hands entwined. He is still looking for a job. He asks me cheerfully, "Eduardo, did you ever wake up in the morning without a crust of bread and not a peso in your pocket?"

I am embarrassed. I answer, "No, Maximo, I never did. But I've been through the world and at least I know what you mean."

Anita, Veronica's sister, is a beauty. She is fifteen, her soft hair falls in tresses across her shoulders, her breasts have not fully ripened. I wonder, will Anita resemble her sister in five years? I ask her, "What will you be doing in five years?"

"I'll be married," Anita says, "to some nice man in some nice place far away from Nicaragua."

VI / GUATEMALA

I went back to the hotel to bed and began to read *Dr Thorne*, "There is a county in the west of England . . . very dear to those who know it well. Its green pasture, its waving wheat, its deep and shady . . . lanes . . ." Trollope is a good author to read in a foreign land — especially in a land so different from anything one has ever known as this . . . A cockchafer came buzzing and beating through the room and . . . one felt the excitement of this state . . . I remembered the confessor saying to me in Orizaba, "A very evil land." One felt one was drawing near to the centre of something — if it was only of darkness and abandonment.

Graham Greene, The Lawless Roads

I

ANGRY, UNFULFILLED for having failed again to meet Tomás Borge, I flew from Nicaragua over Honduras and El Salvador to Guatemala City. I lingered in the capital long enough to see some diplomats and officials, then headed west by northwest toward the Indian highlands and Lake Atitlán.

The tourist books quote Aldous Huxley as calling Atitlán "the most beautiful lake in the world." In fact, he said the opposite: "Lake Como, it seems to me, touches the limit of the permissibly picturesque; but Atitlán is Como with the additional embellishment of several immense volcanoes. It is really too much of a good thing. After a few days in this impossible landscape, one finds oneself thinking nostalgically of the English home counties."

Huxley is one of my favorite writers, but I disagreed with him about Lake Atitlán. It may indeed be the most beautiful place on earth, and its splendor did not make me yearn for less. The lake, fifty square miles of it, was formed a hundred million years ago by some fantastic volcanic convulsion. The three volcanoes, one named for Saint Peter, rise above the southern shore, and to the north a mountain range completes an enclosure all purple-green. Thick jungle covers the slopes of the volcanoes. The mountains soar, but already the lake laps the vegetation at a level that exceeds five thousand feet, and perhaps the thin air helps the water achieve such various color. In the mornings, when the wind blows up from the Pacific sea, the waters are a restless but mild blue. They turn to deeper blue when the sky is cloudless, then blend to gray when the evening fog rolls in. At dawn, at sunset, in the middle of the day, one glimpses conflicting hints of emerald, lapis lazuli, gentle red, deep crimson.

The lake is sprinkled with tiny islands, and along their shores loons that millennia ago ceased to fly paddle like ducks and dive for fish. The periphery of the lake is barbarous with wildflowers — coffee berries, very red, rose mallow hibiscus, bougainvillea that suggest magenta. Most of the villages that surround the lake are named for the Apostles — Saint Mark, Saint Luke, Saint John, Saint James, Saint Peter, Saint Paul. These villages are accessible only by boat, but the voyage is rewarded by the lake itself and by the rich Indian culture beyond the docks.

Three tribes, with distinct languages and woven costume, descendants of the nations of the Tzutuhil and the Cakchiquel, inhabit the shores of the lake, the men tilling their fields for corn, the women weaving cloth in their adobe houses and thatched huts. Until recently guerrillas infested the volcanic jungles, venturing into the villages and inciting rebellion, so as a precaution the Guatemalan army plied the waters of the lake, marched through the forests on the slopes, and invaded the villages and hamlets, massacring thousands of Indians at random.

As I began my holiday at Lake Atitlán, however, massacres were the memory of others and remote from my jaded mind. For nine months I had been traveling constantly on the isthmus or writing in sealed rooms, my diet these last weeks in Nicaragua had been dreadful, I was hungry and exhausted. For days at Panajachel, a resort on the lake, I devoted myself to eating. As in El Salvador, one could get anything in Guatemala if one had the money. The meats here were not so tasty, but I rejoiced in soup, bread, and sweet pies. The weather was glorious, and I loved the sun and the spray of the motorboats on my face. At night, I watched video tapes of bad American films in a hippie bar.

Yet as the days went by in such calm and beauty, I grew restless again. I began to agree with Huxley, to feel vaguely bored even in that garden and nostalgic for something else. I began to read again.

One of my books was Graham Greene's *The Lawless Roads*, written five decades ago as a "personal impression of a small part of Mexico at a particular time, the spring of 1938." Greene's journey through revolutionary Mexico lasted only five weeks, but that was sufficient for a harrowing evocation of what he called "the fiercest persecution of religion anywhere since the reign of Elizabeth." Much of the drama happened in the state of Chiapas, hardly a hundred miles due north from where I sat. The book has serious flaws. Greene's world-weariness, already well ingrained, can become disingenuous and oppressive. But the core of the book is marvelous, as fresh today as when he wrote it.

The Lawless Roads abounds in ruined churches, hunted, murdered priests, the grieving faithful, visions of the saints and of the Holy Virgin. It contains the essence of the mordant Greene style and his obsessive theological motifs. Here is all the raw material of *The Power and the Glory*. Between the lines, one can watch Greene's rich mind at work, foreshadowing the errant sexuality and reluctant martyrdom of the whiskey priest. And the narrative seethes with the vagaries of nature, with violent rainstorms, stabs of lightning in the valleys, as Greene generously shares with us his fantastic dreams and nightmares.

Here is the early, politically conservative Graham Greene: "What possible hope had the worker that conditions would ever reach the old capitalist level in *his* lifetime? Oh, how weary one gets of this fight to help future generations! I wandered from church to church seeking help for myself, not for an unborn soul." And the early, devoutly orthodox Graham Greene: "I have no sympathy with those who complain of the wealth and beauty of a church in a poor land. For the sake of another peso a week, it is hardly worth depriving the poor of such rest and quiet as they can find in the cathedral . . . In a church the democracy is absolute. The rich man and the poor man kneel side by side for Communion; the rich man must wait his turn at the confessional."

As I read this book, I realized that I was more comfortable with the younger Greene than with his elderly successor. Greene opened *The Lawless Roads* by quoting Cardinal Newman's classic lamentation about Original Sin: "Either there is no Creator, or this living society of men is in a true sense discarded from His presence . . . *if* there be a God, *since* there is a God, the human race is implicated in some terrible aboriginal calamity." In his autobiography of 1971, Greene writes that "in January 1926 I became convinced of the probable existence of something we call God, though now I dislike the word with all its anthropomorphic associations and prefer Chardin's 'Noosphere' . . . With the approach of death I care less and less about religious truth." Hence today his bewildering distinctions between belief (which he has lost) and faith (which he retains), his denunciations of John Paul II as a "horror," his zeal for Nicaragua's Popular Church, and his rapport with such crackpots as Padre Ernesto Cardenal. No doubt Greene's admiration of the Sandinistas is conditioned by his distaste for American policy, and fair enough: I mean simply that I miss his old theology.

The Lawless Roads rekindled my lust for new experience, making me unsatisfied with mere beauty and yearning again for the stark excitement I had known in Morazán and Chontales. Not enough that his book resembled familiar provinces; it drove me farther, toward a similar drama some miles north of Atitlán, still in Guatemala but just next door to Mexico, in the Indian department of El Quiché, more precisely in the "Triangle of Death."

I set out for the Triangle in early August. It was rough reaching that remote dominion high in the Sierra los Cuchumatanes. From Santa Cruz del Quiché, the capital of the province, I took a bus early in the morning. The distance to the Triangle was not sixty miles, but the ascent was steep and winding and the road had nearly ceased to exist. The bus had no gears, or what remained of the gears required the driver to stop every few miles to make repairs. I sat smothered among smelly human beings and their cackling poultry. The journey took all day.

From the frigid heights, the blue mountains dropped to plateaus planted with corn and wheat, then into squeezed valleys watered by angry streams. In this topography, earthquakes were a part of life; dormant volcanoes blew off their peaks, then remained in permanent eruption; at intervals the earth steamed. These western highlands, extending from Guatemala City to the border of Mexico, were the home of the Mayan Indians, not that the Indians governed it. Entering the district of Quiché I saw a sign: BIENVENIDOS A QUICHE, TIERRA DE HOMBRES VALIENTES, DONDE EL PUEBLO Y EL EJERCITO HAN DICHO NO A LA SUBVERSION COMUNISTA. At last, in late afternoon, from the slope of a mountain, I saw in the farthermost nook of a long valley my destination of Nebaj.

Nebaj (pronounced Ne-*bak*) was the Triangle's chief town, and now I was in the homeland of the Ixil (Ee-*sheel*) people. The Triangle, in size about four hundred square miles, was bounded by Nebaj and the towns of Chajul and San Juan Cotzal. The people were overwhelmingly Ixil, but commerce was controlled by *ladino* Guatemalans whose tongue was Spanish and whose ancestry mingled Spanish with Indian blood. The Ladinos, the minority in Guatemala, were culturally elite and ran the country. Nebaj offered but one lodging, the pension of Las Tres Hermanas, run by three elderly Ladino sisters.

The rooms were rudimentary, built around a flower garden full of hens and geese, a huge sink with icy water in the open air, where you washed and shaved, and then an outhouse where you held your nose as you soothed nature. My bed was horizontal wooden slats heaped with coarse blankets, and how I needed them. The nights at that altitude were cold, the rain lashed down and the wind howled.

At dawn, in the kitchen by the wood stove, the elderly sisters were waiting with steaming coffee, scrambled eggs, beans, and fresh hot bread. Luncheon and supper were just as good, thick soups, garnished fowl, and fruit puddings. The sisters were pious virgins, but other women at that hotel did not share their virtue.

The whores came on weekends — three hideous girls in blue jeans, metal stiletto heels, and brown doll faces smeared green and orange. They stayed in one little room, at the corner of the garden by the gate and the dirt road, where all day long they received their trade in groups of three. Their customers were soldiers, dwarfish youths in olive Israeli uniforms who waited beneath the covered walk outside my room to escape the rain.

The putas never bothered me. The Indian women — barefoot in red skirts and woven turbans, babies lashed to their backs, selling cloth — were another matter. They infested the garden and the covered walk. It was never enough to tell them you were not interested, no, no, no, you didn't want cloth. You gave them a quetzal to feed the children and politely asked them to be gone, but they kept coming back, unrolling the cloth, into the dining room, the kitchen, lying in wait for you to emerge from the outhouse, even pushing through the broken latchkey of your room, standing over your bed and unrolling the cloth. Finally, you fly out of bed into the dirt road, pursued by children.

Two Ixil children in particular attached themselves to me — Gaspar, about twelve, and Jacinta, no more than four, his sister. Gaspar was round-faced under a black cap he never removed. He wore rubber boots, but Jacinta, angelic in Ixil costume, was barefoot until I bought her shoes. Gaspar spoke good Spanish, touted his talents as a guide, and even produced torn pieces of paper, his references in English: "Give these children a chance. The history of Guatemala is sad, and so is theirs. They are far from their home village, and their parents are dead."

Gaspar took me everywhere, often with Jacinta trailing behind. We walked from Las Tres Hermanas up the dirt road to the main plaza and the white adobe church, the steps of the church seething with children, watching men in fantastic colored masks and costumes enact a mysterious pageant. Inside, the floor of the church was covered with pine needles, the saints as elaborately dressed up as the prancing masked men. The celebrations had started for the Feast of the Assumption more than a week away, explained Gaspar. The plaza was a panoply of tents, bazaars, games of chance, men and boys playing saxophones, trumpets, and marimbas in the relentless drizzle. Nearby, in the vestibule of the priest's house, hundreds of war orphans were being fed lunch, their only meal of the day. From the cuartel behind the church, a hundred soldiers in Israeli combat gear, Galil automatic rifles slung over their shoulders, marched in formation around the plaza then back to the garrison, chanting a martial song.

We repaired to the outskirts of the town and the immense public hospital. It was five years old but so clean and gleaming, so modern in architecture and equipment, I might have thought it was built yesterday. Room after enormous room, corridor after corridor, ward after endless ward, consulting chambers, operating chambers, in-patient, out-patient, emergency department, ambulance garage, maternity section, pediatrics department, dentistry department, radiology department, isolation ward, psychiatric ward, intensive care, on and on. The hospital was empty.

It was spooky, so deserted that in the psychiatric ward when I screamed "Crazy! Crazy!" my screams echoed down the halls. The hospital had no medicine, no physicians, no nurses, and no patients. It had been built during the dictatorship of General Fernando Romeo Lucas García to make kickback money for the general and his friends — according to the new minister of the interior, who received me later in the capital. "Under General Lucas, six hundred million dollars was stolen," he told me. "What the Somozas stole in Nicaragua in forty-five years, the Lucas crowd stole in less than four." In Guatemala, 20 percent of the populace consumes 70 percent of the proteins; the rate of infant death ranks with the world's highest, and the infants die of bronchitis, stomach convulsions, and diarrhea.

Gaspar led me next to a *polo de desarrollo* in the hills called Xemamatze. These *polos,* "poles of development," were in theory model villages, strategic hamlets partly inspired by the Vietnam War and set up by the military dictatorships on Israeli advice. The army had re-gathered many Ixil from their remote villages in the mountains in its campaign to isolate the Indians from the Ejército Guerrillero de los Pobres, the Guerrilla Army of the Poor.

Inside a wood cabin, we found a young costumed woman squatting before her loom, weaving cloth with delicate geometric patterns, dancing images of birds and beasts, surrounded by her brood of children. Gaspar translated from Ixil to Spanish. Nobody would buy her beautiful cloth, she said, and she had no electricity, no drinking water, nothing to feed her six children but tortillas, chili, and salt. Her husband was on the Pacific coast, picking berries on a spice plantation for pesos to buy them food. Their ancestral lands lay high on the mountain, only miles away, but they could not return because they feared the government soldiers and the Guerrilla Army of the Poor.

Nearby, at a schoolhouse, technicians from the new civilian government were vaccinating infant children against measles, diphtheria, whooping cough, but their patients were scarce. Few mothers dared to bring their children for inoculation because they feared the army would inject them with poison.

Gaspar led me up the mountain, through the drizzle and the rolling mist, to a bull farm. That day the bulls were being castrated, then bound by their four hoofs. A bull was dragged from the pen, across the road to the slaughterhouse. Palomino, nearly golden, he was lashed down by taut rope above an open drain for his blood. A woman in red Ixil costume and several men with machetes and dull knives hovered about; I expected them to dispatch the beast, as a matador would, with a stab above the neck, or perhaps to chop off his head, but it did not happen.

Instead, a man crudely chopped out his heart. The Ixil woman plunked the beating heart into a plastic bucket, and a white dog licked at the trickle of blood. Even without his heart, the bull struggled to stay alive. I do not mean mere twitching. He breathed and strained against his bonds for about five minutes. Then he gave a great final jerk, a heaving sigh, and lay still. Even in death his eyes shone as huge green gems. I thought they simply caught the light, so I moved about, but his eyes continued to glow. Even as the rest of him was hacked to pieces, his green eyes shone.

As my days passed in the Triangle, I realized that what happened to the bull had already happened to the Ixil Indians.

2

FROM THE BULL FARM, Gaspar and I descended the mountain to the town, to the garrison behind the church. At the sentry post I scribbled a note of self-introduction and prevailed on the guard to take it to the comandante. Shortly I was invited to pass inside the barricade of brick and sandbags, but as I climbed the steps of the cuartel an officer marched out to confront me. "I'm sorry," he said, wagging his finger. "I cannot speak to you. If you have any questions about military matters you must address yourself to the Ministry of Defense in Guatemala City. I have no authority to talk to you.''

He was a trim Ladino, dark with a mustache, his face running slightly to fat, smartly uniformed in a crested beret, polished boots, camouflage greens, a trench jacket against the cold. "No authority, no authority.''

AUTHOR: Are you the commander of this garrison?

COMMANDER: At your service.

A: A pity you can't talk to me, *mi comandante*. I had hoped to go out on one of your patrols—against the Guerrilla Army of the Poor.

C: Ha ha! There are none! Everything is quiet in this district. I can't talk to you. No authority! Ha ha! You're a good journalist.

A: You're a perceptive soldier.

C: What's your name?

A: Edward. And yours, *mi comandante?*

C: Marco Antonio.

A: Ah. Marcus Antonius. A Roman emperor. Forgive me. A Roman triumvir and military governor.

C: *Sí.* Marcus Antonius! *¡Emperador Romano!* I like that. Ha ha! I don't like that. The Roman Empire was decadent. The United States is the new *imperio romano!*

A: I am told that the mayor does not matter, that you, *mi comandante,* command three thousand troops, that you are the real ruler—the military governor—of the Triangle.

C: Ha ha! Who said that?

A: Your subjects.

By now a number of his officers and men were squeezed in the cuartel door, spilling out onto the cement steps, eavesdropping. Evidently the comandante enjoyed jousting with a North American before his troops. He had a habit of cocking his head, thrusting up his chin, his hands on his hips, a little like Mussolini, yet somehow the pose was charming. His constant laughter was an eruption, beginning deep within his trench jacket and ending in a high pitch.

C: Mr. Edward! Have you seen a model village?

A: Just now, *mi comandante.*

C: Stupid, evil people call the polos concentration camps, but you know better, don't you, Mr. Edward? The people are at liberty. They can come and go from the polos as they please. Is that not true?

A: There seemed to be free movement, yes.

C: The army is the *friend* of the people. Everything is calm. The guerrillas are in the mountains, very far from the people. Ha ha! The people *love* the army.

A: And the accusations in the world press, *mi comandante?* That the army massacred the Ixil throughout the Triangle?

C: The people died in *combat* — between the army and the guerrillas. Why does no one mention the brave *soldiers* killed in combat? You don't believe those lies in the *New York Times* — that the army massacred the people? The army is the protector of the people! We are here to protect the people! We are the guardians of the national values of Guatemala — *patriotismo, honor, lealtad* [loyalty], *sacrificio, responsabilidad, justicia, esperanza* [hope], *trabajo* [work], *la fuerza de voluntad* [the power of will], *y sobre todo la disciplina* [and above all discipline]. Ha ha! What do you think of the national discipline of the United States?

A: We have a problem.

C: Drunkards, drug addicts, sexual promiscuity.

A: It's better in Guatemala?

C: You are the Roman Empire. You ruled the world, and now you're falling. Guatemala needs arms to crush communist subversion, but you're afraid to give them. We need economic aid, but without your conditions. Your country stinks with corruption. All the problems of Central America start in the United States. We don't want your American way of life in Guatemala. I know what I'm talking about, Mr. Edward. I was trained by the American military.

A: But you're wearing an Israeli uniform.

C: Ah, Israel! Israel is another matter! Now *there's* a country! Ha ha! Strong family values! Independent — even from you. Ha ha! Nobody pushes them around.

We were distracted by the xylophone sound of a marimba and the approach of a procession from up the street. Ixil men filed past in the drizzle, bearing on their shoulders a crowned statue of the Virgin, garlanded in lace and pink robes and followed by cultic saints as resplendent in green, gold, and blue. The men were members of a *cofradía,* a confraternity devoted to veneration of the Virgin and mysterious tribal divinities. The comandante tugged at my elbow. "Look, Mr. Edward! See how everything is normal here! The people have their religion, their processions, look how they are happy."

"You're a Catholic?"

"Ha ha! Oh no. No, no, no. Ha ha! I'm Evangelical. Born again."

"But you're smoking."

"A sin. I'm not completely cured of vice. Ha ha! I respéct the Catholic Church. I don't like all those ceremonies. *Jesucristo es el hijo único de Dios,* Jesus Christ is the only Son of God, and that is enough. The Catholics don't respect legitimate authority."

The procession was disappearing in the rain. The comandante sent volleys of Writ after it — Saint Paul's Epistle to the Romans, chapter 13 — and the verses rolled out: "Let every soul be subject unto the higher powers, the powers that be are ordained of God. Whosoever therefore resisteth the power, resisteth the ordinance of God: and they that resist shall receive to themselves damnation. *Porque los magistrados no son para temor al que bien hace, sino al malo. ¿Quieres pues no temer la potestad?* But if thou do that which is evil, be afraid; for he beareth not the sword in vain: for he is the minister of God, a revenger to execute wrath upon him that doeth evil. Ha ha!"

Gaspar led me back to the plaza and the church steps, where the prancing men in colored masks and costumes were still engaged in their occult pageant. The masks, with carved beards and flowing wigs, were surmounted by two-cornered hats and brilliant plumage; the costumes were of red, green, and blue, woven gold brocade, puzzling geometric patterns and great black staring eyes sewed on. The men uttered muffled sighs and expostulations from behind the wooden masks, but mostly their drama was a mime: strangulations, lashings, sword fights with swords of real silver, stabs, recumbent bodies, pretended deaths.

Still I understood too little and looked about the plaza at the throng of Ixil faces to read their response. They were stoic. The Ixil women were handsome and well formed, but the men seemed stunted and rather ugly. The Ixil had endured much, but they never complained. Gaspar was confused in explaining the pageant, so I asked an old man in a black jacket and a straw hat. "It goes back centuries," he said, "starting with the Spanish conquest. It is the story of our people's suffering." In Guatemala, especially in the Triangle, the flower of horror unfolds slowly.

3

THE HORROR BEGAN to unfold from the hour in the early sixteenth century when the Spaniards landed on the isthmus. The Ixil, like all the Maya, before the conquest lived in sophisticated settlements, not cities so much as centers of ceremony, and around them they tilled the land. They were artists and scientists as well, in sculpture, mathematics, and astronomy. The Maya were a populous race, but they were reduced by the enslavement and carnage of imperial Spain. In the mid-sixteenth century, a Dominican missionary wrote to Charles V in Madrid protesting the "slaughters, violences, injuries, butcheries and beastly desolation" inflicted by the conquistadores upon the Indians and lamenting that millions of the Maya had been killed. These depredations inspired the infamous *leyenda negra,* the Black Legend, which in looking back was not a legend at all.

In a bizarre foreshadowing of today's model villages, the sixteenth-century Spanish uprooted the Indians from their tribal settlements and collected them into concentrated towns and villages called *congregaciones.* Yet even worse than the uprootings, enslavements, and massacres were the diseases of the Old World that the conquerors brought with them. Measles, mumps, smallpox, typhus, unknown to the Indians before the conquest, infested them now in epidemics and pandemics. In the region of the Sierra los Cuchumatanes, including the Triangle, from the day of the conquest until 1680, the Mayan population fell more than 90 percent. By the early nineteenth century, during a plague of typhus, bands of orphaned children wandered aimlessly about, crying and begging for bread. A friar wrote of his remaining flock as "birds without a nest, flying all over the countryside without belongings, and naked. Oh, what suffering!"

For many centuries, perhaps millennia, before the conquest, the Mayan Ixil possessed a rich oral culture that mixed animism, ancestor worship, and human sacrifice. At the summit of the universe sat Q'esla Kub'a-l, the supreme god, and beneath him a married couple, Kub'a-l and Kuçuç, the sun and the moon. Lesser deities were the gods of the wind, the cloud, and the storm. Ghosts lived in rivers, mountains, and caves. The sun, like a third eye, shone forth from the chests of huge divinities. The greater gods were so magnificent that lesser ones carried them across the sky on chariots.

The Spanish friars, confronting the Ixil gods, struck hard rock. The Ixil resisted conversion, so the friars had to settle for suppressing human sacrifice and allowing the Indians to merge their idolatry with the rubrics of Rome. The tribal gods were baptized with the names of Christian saints. Kub'a-l and Kuçuç became Jesus and the Virgin Mary. In the chapels and the streets, the hybrid cult flowered in the cofradías. The

Ixil still worshiped graven images in their secret caves. They loved incense and guaro, and during their feasts and processions drunkenness commingled with religious rite.

The Ladinos of Guatemala looked down upon the Ixil as ignorant, inferior, children of witchcraft, if not subhuman. Ladino contempt made the Ixil natural victims of Guatemalan politics and justified new pogroms that resulted eventually from upheavals in the capital and the wild misjudgments of U.S. policy.

In 1951, an idealistic officer, Colonel Jacobo Arbenz Guzmán, was elected Guatemala's President. Mildly leftist, President Arbenz the following year introduced a moderate law of agrarian reform, which respected the principle of private property and expropriated only uncultivated portions of large plantations. In a society overwhelmingly rural, the reform benefited about one hundred thousand poor peasant families and affected less than two million acres. The Guatemalan right resisted the reform—and so did the United Fruit Company.

United Fruit—displeased because the law had confiscated four hundred thousand acres of the company's uncultivated land and modestly increased its minuscule taxes—mounted a propaganda assault in the United States against the Arbenz government as communist in character and dangerous to the American national interest. The polemic fell on friendly ears in Washington, where, in 1953, John Foster Dulles had become secretary of state and his brother Allen director of the CIA.

Ignoring the nuances of Arbenz's mild socialism, heedless of Guatemala's foul poverty, maniacal in his anticommunism, John Foster Dulles conspired with his brother to overthrow Arbenz and replace him with a government that would undo land reform. To fill the role of president, the CIA found a disaffected Guatemalan colonel, Carlos Castillo Armas, and trained his troops in Nicaragua with the connivance of the Somozas. Some communists at lower levels of the Arbenz government provided Dulles with moral pretexts. The CIA told big lies, dropped leaflets from airplanes, broadcast reports of fictitious battles, and sowed panic among the Guatemalan people. The Dulles coup succeeded swiftly. Following a few bombardments from the sky, the army deserted President Arbenz, and Castillo Armas seized power in July 1954.

The new President rescinded the agrarian reform and restored all expropriated property to United Fruit. He banned the banana workers' federation. Labor organizers were mysteriously murdered. At the CIA's behest, a National Committee of Defense Against Communism drew up a secret list of thousands of suspected "communists." A Preventive Penal Law Against Communism decreed the death penalty for various "crimes"—including labor union activities commonplace in the United States—that could be construed as "communist." The secret police prospered.

Such repression, which barely foreshadowed the terrors to come, was predictable when the Dulles brothers decided to depose Arbenz. Guatemala to this day has not recovered from the CIA coup. Throughout the rest of the isthmus and Latin America at large, the coup identified the United States with reaction. It confirmed anti-Americanism as the only respectable posture of progressive forces, and it encouraged other right-wing despotisms in the region to flourish with full confidence of Washington's blessing. Arbenz's success might have strengthened liberal and democratic movements elsewhere throughout Central and South America, but his overthrow helped to make Marxist revolutions—as in Cuba and Nicaragua—inevitable.

In 1957, Castillo Armas was assassinated. In the early 1960s, the Guatemalan guerrilla movement was born. It was composed of young, visionary soldiers whose goal was democratic government and who in the beginning had no Marxist associations. In 1962, President John F. Kennedy, naively fascinated by theories of counterinsurgency, made another of those North American state decisions that resonated with such tragic consequence for the Guatemalan people. He approved a "pacification" program aimed at the rebellious eastern provinces. The pacification included marginal works of mercy such as digging wells but focused on generous assistance—T-33 jets, C-47 transports—to the Guatemalan military.

Yet the insurgency, though briefly crushed, refused to vanish. In late 1962, the guerrillas regrouped in FAR, the Rebel Armed Forces, and began a new insurgency in the mountains of the northeast. By 1966, at the bidding of his generals, the powerless civilian President Julio César Méndez Montenegro accepted President Lyndon Johnson's offer of Green Berets to save democracy in Guatemala. Under their tutelage, the army pursued the guerrillas with new efficiency, but that success was not enough for the Guatemalan colonels. They added another twist—death squads. In the cities and throughout the countryside these paramilitary assassins joined the security forces in orgies of blood against civilian critics of the state—students, labor activists, campesinos.

Stephen Schlesinger and Stephen Kinzer—in *Bitter Fruit,* their admirable study of the CIA coup and its consequences — write that "the extent of American involvement in the carnage is difficult to quantify, but it was substantial." U.S. aircraft, flying from bases in Panama, dumped napalm on guerrilla bases, and the Green Berets trained the Guatemalan military not only in guerrilla warfare but in techniques of interrogation. The U.S. Office of Public Safety over several years trained thirty thousand members of the national police.

From late 1966 until 1978, a succession of military dictatorships produced unprecedented feats of state violence — tens of thousands dead — and most of the victims were the mutilated corpses of civilians. An immense earthquake in 1976 killed twenty-five thousand Guatemalans and left hundreds of thousands homeless. In 1977, President Jimmy Carter suspended all U.S. economic and military aid to Guatemala as punishment for its abuse of human rights. The colonels retained their friendships in the Pentagon, however, and an American surrogate stepped into the breach. Israel became Guatemala's new source of weapons, equipment, and military advice. And the worst was yet to happen.

In 1978, yet another military dictator, General Fernando Romeo Lucas García, assumed the presidency in a rigged election, and, according to Schlesinger and Kinzer, "the scale and breadth of the terror that now enveloped Guatemala became difficult to grasp." Senior ministers of the present civilian government told me that under Lucas García the toll of political murders rose to fifty bodies a day, worse even than El Salvador's zenith of thirty-five. It was not sufficient to crush the remnants of the armed left. The purpose of the Guatemalan death squads, linked intimately to the army and directed from the Presidential Palace, was nothing less than to destroy the nation's political center.

No one with an education seemed immune. Lawyers, professors, students, trade union leaders, journalists, poets, priests, catechists, campesinos, politicians, schoolteachers were kidnapped, tortured, mutilated, then dumped by the roadside in city and country alike. Then — and to this day — there were no political prisoners in Guatemala — only political corpses. As in El Salvador, the carnage was propelled by its own logic. With the center eliminated, the nation would be reduced to the cruel choice of a communist revolution or the prevailing military dictatorship. But it would be false to describe that choice as simply between the extreme left and the extreme right. In their carnage the military rulers had passed beyond the ordinary classifications of political philosophy. They had become, in a word, Nazis.

The terror was extremely lucrative. With their grip on the state exchequer, General Lucas García and his cronies inside the army and the reactionary commercial sector launched superfluous industrial and hydroelectric projects rich in the rewards of graft. Like the Somozas, General Lucas loved real estate and acquired ranches and plantations that rolled for miles and thousands of acres. For the right price, other lords of plantations could be confident of military protection. Throughout the rest of Guatemala, the standard of life fell far below the level achieved during the period of Arbenz's presidency.

This was especially true throughout the province of Quiché and the Ixil Triangle, not that life there was ever rich. In the mid-1970s a new insurgency had been born in the mountainous jungles of the northern Quiché—the Guerrilla Army of the Poor. The insurgents were both Ladino and Indian, but they aspired to an Indian base. They promised the Indians complete equality and mixed a Marxist critique of capitalism with appeals to Mayan values. They believed that Indians were potentially the greatest revolutionary force and that the path to power might eventually run through the western highlands.

Their first operation was the murder of a plantation lord. The army responded swiftly, sending in helicopters and parachuting troops from American C-47s. But the rebellion spread, from the jungles of the north deeper into the mountains and heartland of the Quiché, into contiguous provinces, into the heights and valleys of the Ixil Triangle.

Many Indians joined the insurgency, seduced at first by wild promises. The guerrillas promised them land, livestock, money, houses, trucks, the redistributed wealth of the rich if they would rally to the war against the state. They led Indian families high into the mountains and made them work land; the insurgency reached the towns, which it enveloped. Within several years the Guerrilla Army of the Poor controlled most of the Triangle, and at the zenith of its dominance the government was reduced to a redoubt around the garrison of Nebaj. The war was always bloody, the guerrillas committing their own full share of murders and executions, but nothing to compare with the savagery of the government that ensued.

Under the dictatorships of General Lucas García and his successor, General Efraín Ríos Montt, a devout born-again Evangelical, the army considered every Ixil a guerrilla. Here is a random list of state atrocities that stays inside the Triangle and ignores the rest of Guatemala's agony. August 1980: the army gathers residents of San Juan Cotzal and shoots sixty male villagers. September 6, 1980: the army attacks Chajul, bombing the convent, beating and interrogating residents, and killing at least thirty-six. April 15, 1981: forty to one hundred campesinos are massacred in the village of Cocob near Nebaj. April 3–5, 1982: soldiers kill most of the residents of Chel, Juá, Amachel, and Mangal near Chajul. During much of this time, President Reagan was urging Congress to restore military aid to Guatemala.

I met some of the survivors. The Ixil mayor of San Juan Cotzal told me that "the army would come, surround a village, and burn it down with all the men, women, and children still inside. If anyone escaped, soldiers would shoot the burning victim as he ran out of the village. Within sixty square miles of Cotzal municipality alone, the army killed seven thousand people."

Within the area of Nebaj, perhaps twenty thousand people were killed or "disappeared" or fled. The army dropped huge quantities of bombs, machine-gunned villages from helicopters, rained gasoline on crops, houses, people, setting them aflame. From throughout Quiché, scores of thousands of terrified Indians fled across the border into the Mexican state of Chiapas, and most of them remain there, still too frightened to return. It was not uncommon for the army to invade a village and shoot every third man. In some villages the women were raped, the men beheaded, the children dashed to death against the rocks of riverbeds. I could never be sure of the tales of cannibalism. In San Salvador, Father Ignatius, who knew Guatemala well, told me earnestly of this incident: An army officer collected the Indians of a village, seized an infant child, with a machete chopped him lengthwise into halves, and ate his brains. Here is a fragment of one Indian woman's experience:

> My name is Rigoberta Menchú. I was born in the region of Quiché . . .
> One of my brothers was a catechist. The other was secretary for a cooperative in the village; that was his only crime. They kidnapped him, and he spent sixteen days in the hands of the army. He was only fourteen years old. They ripped off his fingernails, cut off his tongue, then destroyed the soles of his feet and burned his skin. One day the army circulated a notice throughout our communities ordering everyone to come to one of the villages the following day to witness the punishment of some guerrillas. At eight A.M. a military truck arrived. They made about twenty men get off the truck; men who no longer looked human, and among them was my little brother. He was so disfigured . . . catechists and my little brother.
> They lined up the prisoners, dressed like soldiers. The captain in

command gave a speech which he constantly interrupted to tell his squad to keep the prisoners on their feet. They hit them with their rifle butts to make them stand, but they would just fall down again. When he finished the speech, the captain said that all subversives would be treated this way. And when he gave the order to undress them, they had to cut off the uniforms because the blood from the wounds made the uniforms stick to their bodies. They tied them and piled them up together, then the captain ordered his soldiers to pour gasoline over them and set them on fire. I was looking at my brother. He didn't die right away, nor did the others. Some screamed; others could no longer breathe so they didn't scream, but their bodies were writhing. The soldiers left shouting, "Long live the army! Long live President Lucas! Death to the guerrillas!" My mother was still hugging my brother's body . . .

My mother died three months later. The military chief raped her and tortured her as they did my brother. They made her suffer a long time, to make her talk about the guerrillas. When my mother was in the throes of death, the army commander ordered that they feed her intravenously and that they give her food. They revived her, and when she recovered her strength, they tortured her again. They placed her under a tree in the middle of the countryside, and her body became infested with worms, because we have a fly there that settles on wounds and immediately lays eggs. The soldiers kept guard over her body day and night to make sure that none of us tried to free her. She resisted a long time and then died under the sun and in the cold. They didn't let us recover her body. The troops stayed until the vultures and dogs ate her . . .

As a woman, I have decided not to marry or have children. According to our traditions this is unacceptable; a woman should have children. But I could not endure it if what happened to my brother should happen to one of my children. From time to time I wish my mother had never given birth to me. I don't want a boyfriend because it would be one more reason to grieve. They would kill him for sure. The only thing I can do is to struggle, to practice that violence I learned in the Bible. I don't believe that the Bible can be used to explain everything. As I told a Marxist colleague who was surprised that a Christian like me wants to make revolution, neither does Marxism contain all the truth . . . I am not the only orphan . . .

Today there are perhaps two hundred thousand war orphans in Guatemala. By the reckonings of various human rights groups, at least one hundred thousand Guatemalans have met violent death since the Dulles coup. In a lifetime of traveling the world, even in the heart of Africa, I have never come so close to martial cruelty on such a scale. This carnage lasted until the middle of this decade, only fifteen hundred miles from the border of Texas, and few North Americans even knew of it. How many would have cared? One morning I paid a Ladino pig farmer to drive me in his truck from Nebaj to Chajul and San Juan Cotzal, the other towns of the Triangle.

From my journal: "Not long out of Nebaj, both before and after the Río Chixoy o Negro, Raúl the pig farmer began pointing out to me where various Ixil *aldeas,* hamlets, had stood before the army burned them. I saw nothing but valleys, trees, and bush. "But where *are* they?" I asked. "*¡Por ahí! ¡Por ahí!* Over there! Down there!" he kept repeating, pointing up or down. Of the crimes there was no trace. Raúl went on pointing, to at least ten places along the sides of hills where hamlets, villages had sprawled. The army had not merely burned, it had brought in bulldozers to demolish and plow under. Perhaps once or twice I did see, high on a green hill, the wreckage of a house."

On Israeli advice, the army regrouped many of the surviving Indians into the *polos de desarrollo,* where supposedly they would live and work the land under the protection of the government, free from guerrilla contamination. But the strategic hamlets have centralized their squalor and for some time seemed no more than open-air prisons, the "concentration camps" that their critics called them. These strategic hamlets evoke the larger issue of Israeli assistance to Guatemala's martial governments — possibly the most chilling chapter of Israel's links to rightist military dictatorships in the Third World.

Starting in the dictatorship of General Lucas García, Guatemalan troops have killed at least thirty thousand Indians in the western highlands, and they killed them mostly with light Uzi submachine guns, very popular with the soldiers because they seldom jam, and with heavier Galil assault rifles. Guatemalan officers have been trained extensively in counterinsurgency in Israel, which has also provided them with aircraft. "In fact," writes the author-academic Victor Perera, "Israeli advisers, in the guise of agricultural aides, helped to devise General Ríos Montt's 'beans and rifles' counterinsurgency strategy. The beans and rifles program included the formation of the Vietnam-style strategic hamlets; the systematic scorching of Indian homes and fields; and the subjugation of hundreds of thousands of highland Indians, who were forced into so-called civil defense patrols. Patrol members are still routinely coerced into doing the military's bidding by denouncing and executing their own neighbors as 'communist guerrillas.' "

A liberal specialist on Central America, Perera is himself Guatemalan and Jewish. During his travels throughout the highlands of Quiché, he saw army bivouacs that uncannily resembled Israeli field stations. "The counterinsurgency special forces were outfitted like Israeli soldiers in Lebanon or the Sinai, with Israeli radio equipment, battle gear, mortars, Galils, and helmets. Even the field kitchens were Israeli." As a friend of Israel, Perera was dismayed because the strategic hamlet program was partially based on the armed kibbutzim along Israel's borders: "The military is attempting to implant in Guatemala a distorted replica of rural Israel but with a labor force that would be Indian rather than Arab or Sephardi."

Israeli electronics equipment and technology have been of considerable assistance to Guatemala's military intelligence. In the annex of the National Palace, Israeli technicians helped to install a computer with the names and files of thousands of "subversives." In 1980, the Israeli labor federation Histadrut wrote to Prime Minister Menachem Begin proposing that Israeli arms sales to Guatemala be stopped, decrying human rights abuse in Guatemala as "an affront to all humanity." Begin did not care; Israel was making allies and money.

To the Guatemalan colonels, the Roman Church was as expendable as the Indians. Ever since Vatican Council II and the Conference of Medellín, the Church had become identified with social justice and structural change. Her theological challenge to military dictatorships, though muted in Guatemala, made her an enemy to the colonels. The Guatemalan bishops were divided in their counsel, but in provinces such as Quiché, catechists and priests sided with the impoverished population. Thus they were guerrillas and had to be killed.

In the diocese of Quiché alone, during the terror of Lucas García, three priests were murdered, hundreds of catechists were tortured, shot individually or massacred with other Indians, kidnapped in the deep night and disappeared forever. The Bishop of Quiché persisted in defending his people's rights, then barely escaped an ambush intended for his murder. Throughout Guatemala, at least twenty priests were murdered. Scores of others, and scores of nuns, were forced into hard exile, as was the Bishop of Quiché.

It was sobering to reflect that this butchery of the Roman Church was done by the fascist right, not by the Marxist left. In Sandinista Nicaragua, the minions of the state closed the Church newspaper, silenced the Church radio, beat up pious laymen in prison, deported priests and a bishop, chased naked monsignori down the street. But could the sins of the Sandinistas compare to this? In Nicaragua, priests were kicked out; in Guatemala, they were machine-gunned. I called on the former Bishop of Quiché, returned from exile.

He was a lean gray man in eyeglasses, now the auxiliary bishop of Guatemala City, sitting in the colonial archbishop's palace next to the neoclassical cathedral, all massive stone and marble. From his breast pocket he removed a ballpoint pen, and on the back of an envelope calmly wrote out for me the names of sixteen murdered priests whose identities he remembered.

I asked, "Monseñor, what was the great lesson you learned from the years of darkness?"

"This is all so complicated. This is all so sad. Any government has the right to defend itself. Our military governments did this by 'dirty war.' But the problem is ideological on both sides, because the guerrillas embrace violence, too, as the only means to end injustice and solve society's problems. So a cycle was born, and you've seen the result. Flight of capital, destruction of resources, unemployment, agony, death everywhere. The bishops of Nicaragua condemned Somoza, and Nicaragua is *worse* off now. I know all the Jesuits' theories of 'self-defense' and 'just war,' but nothing can justify wars that make things worse. So here is the lesson. Guerrilla wars don't work."

The army has a secret weapon against guerrilla wars of the future. Since the (incomplete) subjugation of the Ixil Triangle, the military has promoted other cults to compete with the "subversive" Church of Rome. I mean the cults of puritan, fundamentalist Evangelism.

Throughout Guatemala a quarter of the populace have defected from Rome to the Evangelicals, and in the Triangle the figure may be nearly half. In Nebaj alone there are thirteen fundamentalist temples. One enters them from the rain, boots oozing from the muddy road, to sit beneath roofs of leaky tin and hear a lot of shouting. The Pentecostal charismatics scream their prayers, speak in tongues, wail, rock, and enter trances.

They have not much else to fill their time. All of these sects forbid drinking, smoking, gambling, card playing, soccer, dancing, brawling, wife beating, adultery, fornication, playing or listening to the marimba, and worshiping Ixil idols in the house. They read the Bible constantly, interpret it very narrowly, utter constant thanksgiving and praise to

God. Men, women, and small boys rise in the congregations to declaim their testimonies of answered prayers, of newly pure and transformed lives.

They have no social doctrines, only personal salvation; their creed speaks not to forms of government, the sadness of the world, only to the soul. They do not seem to resent the army, since whosoever rules this world, this country, this Triangle is of no concern to them; their terrestrial journey is so very brief as they look to the Beyond. Everything is written out in Scripture, just as the comandante told me. Let every soul be subject unto the higher powers, the powers that be are ordained of God, and they that resist shall receive to themselves damnation . . .

The Evangelicals have mounted a great assault against the culture of the Catholic Ixil—easygoing, too fond of music, feasts, fireworks, dancing, and getting drunk. Each believer is expected to spread the creed, to purify the old customs, to destroy the witchcraft and the pagan idols. An enfeebled culture suits the army's purpose. The army may expect no challenges to its rule from the Evangelicals, with their absorption in the next life, their meekness, as the Ladinos entrench their dominance. Many Ixil convert to Evangelism because Catholicism is so suspect and as simple self-defense. Favors, jobs, and food can flow from meekness.

Fear still infests the whole Triangle. The government may control the roads and towns, but the Guerrilla Army of the Poor continues to dominate the slopes and caves of those lofty mountains. The government army has grown more cautious, hesitating to climb the mountains, preferring to lie in wait for the guerrillas as they descend the slopes for food and pick them off. The insurgents still control hundreds of families high in the mountains. Now the Ixil are disenchanted with the Guerrilla Army of the Poor, with all the promises of a richer life, so more and more refugees, whole families, starving and in rags, the children with those orange tufts of hair, the blight of kwashiorkor, straggle down from the sierra and cast themselves on the mercy of the state. But neither the army nor the civil agencies have food or shelter for them, so many stay hungry. All over the Triangle the civil government has erected signs, PAZ Y DESARROLLO, Peace and Development, but there is no development, no public works, no industry at all.

The war of graffiti goes on. The guerrillas: ¡VIVA EJERCITO GUERRI-LLERO DE LOS POBRES! The government: ARMY OF THE POOR—THIEF, ASSASSIN, DECEIVER OF THE PEOPLE! In San Juan Cotzal, the Ixil mayor, a little man with a brown mustache, received me sitting at a steel desk in a long, bare room. Unemployment in Cotzal, he said, was 95 percent. Most of his people lived on tortillas, chili, and salt. In the model villages there was no work, either, so families drifted out of the villages and hamlets to the plantations of the Pacific coast.

"They go to the coast for some months, not to earn money," he said, "but only to survive. They go to avoid death by hunger. Whole families go to the plantations to pick coffee, sugar, cotton, and cardamom. Their wages are low, they work twelve hours a day, and the cost of their food is deducted by their masters.

"They live under roofs without walls, exposed to the storms and disease. They have no doctors. A family of father, mother, and six children may leave here for several months and return with a few centavos and three children. The other children have perished on the coast."

4

I RETURNED EVENTUALLY to Guatemala City to look more closely at the new civilian government.

In 1983, born-again General Ríos Montt was overthrown and succeeded by still another military dictator, General Oscar Humberto Mejia Victores, who swore oaths to respect human rights, then allowed death squads to return to the cities and continued Ríos Montt's campaign of killing Indians in the highlands. The murders were not of the same mythic scope: General Romeo Lucas García still wears those laurels. At last, in 1986, a young and charismatic Christian Democrat, Marco Vinicio Cerezo Arevalo, assumed the presidency after a free election. Vinicio — even his enemies call him Vinicio — installed Guatemala's first legitimate government in thirty-two years.

Vinicio did not come to power comfortably. The colonels, nudged all too slowly by the United States, only agreed to free elections when they stared their disastrous economy in the face and realized that their incompetence could not govern Guatemala forever. After years in the wilderness as leader of the Christian Democrats, having thrice escaped the death squads by a hair, Vinicio developed a keen sense of what a civilian president of Guatemala might accomplish. Philosophically, he tended to the left, but he knew that the reactionary economic oligarchy would not countenance land reform, so he did not advocate it. Above all, Vinicio recognized that the army—freed of the nettles of civil administration—would retain ultimate power.

On taking office, he forged a tacit social contract with the army. The military would be left untouched, he seemed to say, would retain its authority and privileges, if it allowed him respectable political space. The army must allow him certain clear preserves—to direct foreign policy, to pursue development and modest social change. The army must forswear future coups and let him govern. In exchange, the army would not be punished for its past crimes.

This implicit bond supposedly maintains the fragile balance of power in Guatemala today. Sadly limited by the army and the reactionary rich—including landowners who will kill to prevent agrarian reform —Vinicio hoped to creep in small steps toward democracy and social justice.

"We're not revolutionaries, we're realists," his ministers told me. "What we have undertaken to do we cannot do *de la medianoche a la mañana*, between midnight and dawn. Our chief task is to take measures and create institutions that will prevent the past from repeating itself. We can't afford to be impetuous. In the face of a violent and backward oligarchy, we must proceed step by prudent step. Otherwise we'll pass into history only as another failure. Ours is a government of transition, to prepare the way for real democracy. Our aspirations may be modest now, but we are struggling to start an *irreversible* process toward democracy, development, and social justice. We can't achieve our goals even in five years."

Given the recent reign of horror, I sympathized with this argument. Should Vinicio fall, should he push the colonels too far, too fast, should they abandon him and again seize total power, the result would be chilling not only for the Guatemalan people but, by example, for the whole isthmus. Like El Salvador, Guatemala needs probably a generation of unmolested civil rule before it can even begin to make the ordinary life of slumdwellers, campesinos, and Indians significantly better. If Vinicio succeeds in reducing unemployment by 10 percent in five years, he will have achieved much.

I recognized equally the trenchant counterargument, common to North American liberal intellectuals and moderate Guatemalan leftists. The United States encouraged Guatemala's return to civilian rule only because at last it saw that military solutions were not working. The

United States did not want real democracy for Guatemala, for any nation of the isthmus, but only the trappings—elected presidents and parliaments, free press, free enterprise, and so on—as a cover for its true purpose. That purpose was a continuance of Guatemala as a U.S. economic colony, if not a banana republic, with real power entrusted to the army to protect U.S. strategic interests through counterinsurgency. Thus, a sort of "democratic fascism" would do for Guatemala.

Given the dreadful U.S. record, the counterargument seemed plausible. Nevertheless, I saw no choice but to embrace gradual change. To Vinicio's experiment in Guatemala—whatever its weakness—I saw no rational alternative. To redeem the future, he had to forget the past.

Or was my reasoning false? The past hounded him. Human rights groups kept demanding an accounting of their vanished relatives and punishment for the assassins; Vinicio kept maneuvering to evade them. Nor did the killing stop. During Vinicio's first year, at least a thousand new corpses turned up. Many seemed the victims of common crime, but others were killed apparently for political reasons. Various partisans of human rights claimed that G-2, military intelligence, was still directing political murder from the attic of the National Palace. The truth was elusive. Did the army high command still order deaths or merely tolerate free-lance assassins in uniform? No one, including Vinicio, could be sure. It was at least clear that retired military officers, miscellaneous ex-policemen, and rightist vigilantes still roamed with impunity, killing for profit, for political motives, or settling old scores.

During the second and third years of Vinicio's presidency his grip on power has seemed even more tenuous. Murders and disappearances, clearly political in character, directed as before at critics of the military, continued and went unpunished. The army resumed its "sweeps" in the Indian highlands. Renegade government troops tried briefly to mount an insurrection against Vinicio in 1988. And the guerrillas, though few, would not vanish. At Playa Grande, at the edge of the northern Quiché, they killed and maimed more soldiers—with land mines.

5

I HAD AN ODD MEETING with General Héctor Alejandro Gramajo Morales at the National Palace, that pile of Florentine wedding cake and marble. General Gramajo was then the army's chief of staff; now he is minister of defense. He is not merely more powerful than Vinicio, he may be the true ruler of Guatemala. As I entered the palace, I paused to watch a disturbance in the plaza. Campesinos were demonstrating, demanding work and bread. Families of the disappeared also demonstrated, holding aloft bright red banners and great white boards stuck with thousands of tiny photographs of their deceased: OH, GIVE US BACK THE BODIES OF OUR SONS! OH, BRING THE BUTCHERS TO JUSTICE!

Inside the palace, General Gramajo's cavernous office was a haze of blue and mahogany. The general was a stocky, good-looking man in a tunic that left his elbows bare. He was easy to talk to, and I remarked on his youthful appearance. "Oh, I'm going gray," he laughed, and boyishly bent his head to ruffle the hair at the nape of his neck. He had been trained in the United States.

His remarks were a less merry, more bureaucratic version of the comandante's speech in Nebaj. The army, said the general, had largely defeated the subversives, and now it would win the hearts and minds of the Indians in the highlands — not least because it was working inside the constitution, with respect for law and the democratic process. Possibly some isolated individuals, some now retired officers, had been guilty of excess, but as an institution the army *never* committed crimes. The army was the protector of the people, the guardian of Guatemala's democratic values, of the people's liberty, sovereignty, and patriotic symbols. "The army is the strongest pillar and the stoutest column of the state. The people must have confidence that in this mission the army will never change — that the army is eternal."

I mentioned my visit to the Ixil Triangle. The general asked for my impressions. "Very sad, *mi general*," I answered. "The army has, shall we say, pacified the roads and towns, but the Triangle is full of widows and orphans."

"And the model villages?" he asked. "Are they concentration camps?"

"I can't call them that, at least during the time I saw them. People seemed free to come and go."

"You see?"

"However, *mi general*, however. The people in the model villages, throughout the Triangle, are destitute. They have no work."

The general cried out and slammed his hand on the side of his chair. Oh, his sadness, his pain, his desolation for those poor Indians! Amiably he continued, "Work for the population is the responsibility of the civil agencies." I said, "*Mil veces gracias, mi general,*" and bowed out of that blue and mahogany haze. For days thereafter I looked more deeply into the army.

In a population of eight million, the army had multiplied rapidly in recent years to maybe forty thousand men. The elite corps of officers originated mostly in a province of the southeast — Chiquimula, next door to Honduras. Chiquimula was largely Ladino in blood, more educated, sophisticated, developed, richer than the Indian highlands of the west. The Chiquimula military loathed the Indian languages, all Indian culture, and regarded the Maya as backward and pagan. More Ladino officers had converted to Evangelical Christianity because the Roman Church defended Indian rights and objected particularly to the *kaibilies* — the special counterinsurgency forces that had so excelled in slaughtering Indians.

The several Chiquimula officers I met all talked like General Gramajo and the comandante at Nebaj, another native of Chiquimula. The army is eternal: the protector of the people, the guardian of the national values of Guatemala, the strongest pillar of the state! Small wonder that by accretions since the Dulles coup, these few thousand Ladino officers have become a caste unto themselves. The army runs its own bank, its own investment fund, officers dabble in industry, real estate, rural plantations, and become very rich. The Guatemalan army has evolved into a paragovernment, a state within a state. It employs its own economists, sociologists, geologists, agronomists, chemists, historians, and, as we know, philosophers. They have their own plans for the future of Guatemala. No surprise that Vinicio, if he survives, must proceed slowly.

The Chiquimula officers indoctrinate their troops, even the Indian troops, in their own exotic values. Through self-hypnosis, crowd hypnosis — convincing oneself, then one's troops in the field, that the Indians were subhuman — they moved without discomfort to the next step, mass slaughter. Here is an army sign I saw at Sacapulas, in Quiché, on the road to the Ixil Triangle:

> *Solo el que lucha*
> *Tiene derecho a vencer.*
> *Solo el que vence*
> *Tiene derecho a vivir.*

> Only those who struggle
> Have the right to win.

Only those who win
Have the right to live.

Hitler could have said that; perhaps he did. It could be said as easily
by the Marxist left. Any Guatemalan army officer will protest, "We
have done *nothing wrong.*" His voice will rise; he may even shake his
finger in your face. "And don't you, North American, don't you *dare*
lecture us on how to civilize our Indians."

I never tried. Little or none of this horror might have happened were
it not for the willful interventions of the United States. One must visit
Guatemala and mingle with its people to understand the scope of the
evil that the American government unleashed.

6

I WILL TRY to transcend the horror by reliving my last day with the
Ixil in the Triangle.

For a fortnight before the Feast of the Assumption, the Triangle's
survivors flowed into Nebaj; as the feast grew near the celebrations
grew manic. The cofradías sponsored dances in rainswept garages full
of throbbing couples, saxophones and tinkling marimba, prodigious
consumption of guaro, Gallo beer, corn liquor, and corrosive sugar-
cane rum. These were knockdown affairs that littered the floors with
drunken bodies; recumbent bodies were as common in the streets; such
was the cult. Not all of the festivities were alcoholic. The Boy Scouts
entered manhood by being dunked in a tank of water before the church,
and on the municipal basketball court the new Princess Ixil received
her robes and crown.

But the best event was the great parade, which passed in review
before the Ixil mayor and the comandante on the steps of the town hall.
As people milled about anticipating the excitement, the comandante
noticed me in the crowd snapping pictures and he walked over, waving
his finger. "Tch. Tch. You took my picture. Military regulations, Mr.
Edward. Tch. Tch."

"Sorry, *mi comandante.*"

"I am not a comandante. I am a servant of the people."

"*Claro, mi comandante.*"

"See the happiness of the people. They have everything they want.
They can go to the credit bank for easy loans. Ah, Mr. Edward, will
you never understand? Ha ha!"

He returned to the dais to give a speech, something about discipline is love. The festivities began, small barefoot boys running foot races, the mayor presenting trophies amid wild applause, women selling their eternal cloth, children vending pink and yellow cotton candy, and drunks falling down. Trumpets and drums, tubas and marimbas, and the entire youthful population of the Triangle paraded by — from Chajul and San Juan Cotzal and San Felipe Chenla and Ax'tumbal and La Pista and the model villages of Pulay and Las Violetas and Xemamatze and from high in the mountains at Salquil Grande.

On and on they came, thousands, tots in yellow shirts, boys in blue uniforms and girls in white and red Ixil costume, school banners, scores of beating drums, Princess Ixil waving from her float, turbaned women wielding staves, the prancing men in their fantastic wooden masks, hundreds of Boy Scouts in berets and starched uniforms marching in military formations and saluting the comandante.

For once he was right: they *were* happy, at least today. Like Salvadorans on Good Friday, the Ixil threw themselves into these ceremonies. And they never complained. If the horror was an unfolding flower, then so was the resurrection and indomitable vivacity of this people. Somewhere during his journey to the heart of darkness, Joseph Conrad suggested that fear always prevails. Of the Ixil he might have said, "Fear lingers, life prevails."

VII / NICARAGUA. L'ENVOI.

Be patient towards all that in your heart remains
unsolved. Try alone to love the questions.

Rainer Maria Rilke

I

I FLEW FROM GUATEMALA CITY back to Managua. The garbage barrel was gone from the sidewalk outside the Siete Mares. "Too many children were getting into it," said a waitress in the Chinese restaurant.

I had been away from Nicaragua for about two months. Electricity and water were still harshly rationed, but the weather was milder. It rained, with less ferocity. In Washington, the United States Senate had just ratified the pending $100 million in mostly military assistance to the contras. The cordoba had weakened further and was selling now at 2,500 to the dollar. Comandante Jaime Wheelock would soon announce that during the previous year inflation had reached 2,600 percent. At his human rights office, Dr. Lino told me that political prisoners in Chontales had risen by five hundred and that the number throughout the country stood at seven thousand. Everyone in Managua spoke of the nation's exhaustion and wondered when something would snap.

I watched Sandinista television and saw Tomás Borge give a speech. He addressed a crowd of apathetic militants of the CDS, civilian Sandinista defense committees, pleading for more efficiency, higher production, a war against the black market. "What are your most urgent tasks?" he shouted at the crowd. "Defense! Production! Revolutionary vigilance!" they shouted back by rote.

As always, Borge was eloquent, rolling the words around his tongue, creating that great arc with his arm, the rest of his dwarfish form following after, the language torrential. ". . . *Somos dueños del porvenir y del canto de los gallos,* We are masters of the time to come and of the rooster's song, we are masters of the seeds, of the honeycombs, of the udders of the cows, we are masters of our self-respect and valor, *somos dueños de nuestra dignidad y nuestro coraje . . .*"

Yet today he screamed so much he left me a little cold. I thought: this is the closest I will ever come to Tomás Borge. I had given up trying to reach him through the Sandinista bureaucracy and despaired of ever meeting him before leaving Nicaragua.

One evening after dinner I met Ambassador Z in the Intercontinental bar. The place was full of Arabs, chattering in their own tongue. From their dialect I concluded they were Libyans. When Z arrived we retreated to the corner and ordered chilled Russian vodka.

z: What's the chief thing you've learned in Central America, Edward?

A: Something I already knew. That I hate military dictatorships. Of the right or left. The right kills; the left controls, making life unlivable. For the ordinary campesino, life — assuming he survives — may be even worse in Guatemala than it is here.

z: If that's so, it's largely the fault of the United States.

A: In Guatemala? Definitely.

z: In Nicaragua, too.

A: Of that I'm less sure. From the beginning of the Revolution, most of the Sandinistas' woes seem self-created. In their mania to control, they provoked inevitable resistance — the contras, the Church, the entrepreneurs. Nicaraguans who wearied of resistance, the technicians the Revolution needed most, fled the country. For the poor souls who remain, to get beyond grammar school they must submit totally. You want a ration card? Stay in good odor with the police. You want to be a writer? Get a recommendation from the Sandinista Youth. You need a tractor? Join the Sandinista collective. Of course there's something to be said for the Cuban model — health, education, and work — but what of the cost to the human spirit?

z: So it's a bad government. Nicaragua has always had bad government. This one is mild, I insist, as communist dictatorships go. Like any Marxist government, this one has gambled that for the sake of a better future the present generation must be sacrificed. The Sandinistas by a natural process might have evolved into something more benign if you Americans had left them alone. They might have gone the way of Hungary or Yugoslavia, but your policies have forced them into repression. You've slowed down the evolutionary Marxist process by years and maybe decades.

A: Which means more repression.

z: The longer the war continues, the harder life will become for

Cardinal Obando and the bourgeoisie. The Sandinistas will be more and more tempted to Draconian and Stalinist solutions.

A: Unless there's a popular insurrection.

z: That will *never* happen. Borge is too efficient. You Americans are such bullies. I wouldn't mind if you were smart bullies. If your present policy doesn't win, if you merely pick and bleed, you'll make things even worse when the contras are defeated and you end up with nothing.

A: But when Reagan leaves the White House, I should imagine that any future president will abandon military solutions and settle for a containment policy.

z: That's the best you can hope for. But for a long time, future U.S. presidents will be picking up the pieces of a policy disaster. What will you do? Build a Berlin Wall? In the end, once Reagan is gone, assuming the Soviets don't send troops here — they're not that stupid — I suspect that you Americans will walk away from Nicaragua as Reagan walked away from Lebanon.

A: That's the distant future. For the near future — you've seen the economy — something must snap, and soon.

z: It may, but even if the country starves the Sandinistas will never relinquish power and they will never share power. This vodka is getting warm.

Early next morning I drove to the Curia to bid adieu to Cardinal Obando beneath the Velázquez *Crucifixion.* I was sad for my farewell to this stout Indian prince, for whatever his imperfections I was fond of his person and admired his defiance of the state.

Stubbornly he repeated his proposals for negotiation between the Sandinistas and the counterrevolution, impervious to my objections that the government would not accept them. "A dialogue," he insisted, "a sincere dialogue, a real dialogue for reconciliation, not a tactic by either side." Again he declined my invitation to condemn the contras: they were Nicaraguans like the Sandinistas and he loved them all. As for the future of the Church, she would continue to struggle through the pulpit and the family against the odious monopoly of the state.

"God will somehow help us. We pray for the richness of the free man who is given the chance to make choices. Bread without liberty is bitter, and now the people have no bread. We face a long struggle, and our strategy is to survive. We know we shall, for we have the promise of Christ 'unto the consummation of the world.' But today we are the Church of Silence." He sighed, as though resigned to indefinite

Sandinista rule. "Only God knows how long we shall walk in silence. Marxism-Leninism will remain with us for many years."

He escorted me to the antechamber, where I kissed his ring, and he was gone. Riding back to the city I reflected on the Cardinal's realism about long Sandinista rule. Even should the Sandinistas fall, most improbable, in the schools and army they had indoctrinated a new generation of Nicaraguan youth in Marxist values, estranging many from the traditional values of the Church. Whatever happened, the Church faced a fierce struggle to retain the allegiance of the young. I wondered what would happen inside the Roman communion itself, so divided in Nicaragua between the conservative authority of the Cardinal and the sandinismo of the People's Church.

I reflected on the Marxist Jesuits. Most Nicaraguan Jesuits were not Marxist; they were traditional fathers who taught the young, ministered to the poor, looked with reserve and anger at the Revolution. But it was the Jesuits of Managua — at their university, at the Historical Institute, at the National Assembly — who were famous. They were erudite true believers so identified with the Revolution they had lost their independence. They insisted on their "critical distance," and supposedly when they sat with the comandantes behind closed doors they dissected the errors of the Revolution freely. In public, you saw no evidence of critical distance. Their publications, in Spanish and English for audiences abroad, were verbose apologies for everything the Sandinistas did. Apparently they paid this price for the sake of influencing the Revolution on the inside.

They distressed me most when I challenged them about Sandinista abuse of human rights. Some, like Padre César Jerez, danced around the question, but others practiced pure denial. It is not necessary to defend the mistreatment and torture of political prisoners who do not exist. Here is Padre Jabier Gorostiaga, once director of national planning, now an economic tutor of the comandantes: "Dr. Lino Hernández doesn't verify his figures. Hundreds of political prisoners? Absolutely false. Seven thousand political prisoners? A lie. I have no evidence he works for the CIA, but it would not surprise me."

As for the convergence of the Revolution and the Kingdom of God, not all of these Jesuits pretended that such convergence would ever be complete. On a scale of A to Z, if the Revolution improved the life of Nicaraguans from A to F or G, their theology would be vindicated. Alas, since the Revolution Nicaraguan life had not advanced;

it had regressed, and badly. U.S. aggression was partly to blame, but equally or more so was the flight of capital, the technicians, and the middle class. Sandinismo was a social and economic failure, and in their sociological theology the Marxist Jesuits were identified with the disaster.

In private, some had the honesty to hint at their embarrassment. As for inside influence, the comandantes no doubt were sentimental toward these revolutionary clerics and grateful for their applause, but their real influence seemed minimal. If the Marxist Jesuits had truly kept their independence, their critical distance, they might have remained credible. They are discredited by the Revolution's mess. Such is the fate of court theologians.

The same is true of the Popular Church at large, not only because it is unpopular but because like most such movements on the edge of schism it will eventually fade away. If Rome has learned anything during two millennia, it has learned how to cope with schisms. In France after the Bastille a "Constitutional Church" was established that venerated the Revolution as Uriel Molina and Ernesto Cardenal genuflect to General Sandino. Rome played a waiting game and eventually crushed the French schismatics. That is the kind of game that Rome plays best, and against such institutional craft the Molinas and the Cardenals are no match. They are fashionable today, but tradition will devour them.

Soon I would be leaving Nicaragua, and I thought above all of the Nicaraguan people. If I had no faith in Marxist Jesuits, I would never lose faith in this strange race. They were disorganized and sensual, inefficient and voluble, too romantic and often lazy, but they had redeeming qualities. Even the most unschooled had an esthetic view of life; it was not by chance that Nicaragua was a nation of poets. Almost by collective wish, they created poetry from the dissonance and sorrow of their daily lives, because they preferred the metaphors of fantasy to the harsh facts of living. They loathed complexity and wanted life to be simple. They yawned when the Sandinistas talked of "technifying" life because they wished to work little. They lacked the concentration to be good scholars, and they laughed at everything, especially at themselves.

They were a people of deepest faith. They resisted the Popular Church not only because they favored the poetic, bleeding Christ but because in their collective intuition they sensed that the demystified practical

Christ was another Sandinista. They had no mind to substitute that Saviour for the old one. The people were wise. Theirs was not the wisdom of the efficient tractor factory, and they needed tractors, but they sensed early in the Revolution that Marxism was Somoza's fascism in a different form. The Sandinistas sought to liberate the poor by restructuring all society, but the people resisted because communism offended their free nature. They had their own kind of communism. They excelled in love and friendship, sharing generously with one another to survive relentless want. In war or peace, with the Sandinistas or without them, they faced a desolate future.

In the decrepit Datsun Julio drove me closer to the center of Managua. On a wall: ¡SOMOS EL PUEBLO ORGANIZADO! ¡FUERA LOS TRAIDORES! ¡VIVA SANDINO! I erred in calling the graffiti to Julio's attention, since it set him off again: ". . . *el capitalismo . . . el comunismo . . .*" We stopped at an intersection for a red light, and a cortege of military vans and cars sped past us. I glimpsed a familiar face—Tomás Borge's. Julio: ". . . *el capitalismo . . . el comunismo . . .*" I: "Shut up and follow Borge."

At a distance we followed the cortege up some hills toward the old country club. Other cars as well were converging on the gate; when we reached the gate the guard merrily waved us through as though we were expected. We proceeded up the drive through the disused golf course to a modern building, a convention center. People were assembling on the steps, and in their midst Borge, in military dress, greeted his admirers. Then he went inside. I followed him.

The convention hall was full, and the multitude rose to its feet to applaud the minister. He took his place at the center of the dais between Vice President Sergio Ramírez and Comandante Lenin Cerna, director of the state security. The luminaries sat beneath this legend: FIRST SEMINAR ON PENITENTIARY SYSTEMS IN THE AMERICAS. I found a seat in the front row.

Delegations from Mexico, Panama, Costa Rica, Cuba, South America, Canada, the United States, and Europe were intermingled with Nicaraguans throughout the air-conditioned, timbered hall. Amid prolonged rhythmic cheering, Borge rose to speak. He heaped scorn and humor on President Reagan, to delighted laughter, but he had another purpose also—to prove that he ran an ideal penal system in Nicaragua. ". . . rehabilitation . . . legal forms . . . human dignity . . . high morale . . . enlightened methods . . . society transformed . . . prisoners who pick coffee, build houses, work productively . . . archetype of a human penitentiary system . . . renewal of man . . . Carlos Fonseca . . . blood . . . corn . . . dawn . . .''

He had barely tested his wings; now he took off. It was not enough, he cried, to establish a model penal system. He wanted to abolish jails altogether in that blissful future when society would overflow with liberty and justice. Until such time, ''we have constructed nine new penitentiaries, excellently equipped, which all of you are invited to visit.'' His peroration was sublime.

''Nosotros tenemos una confianza infinita en los hombres. We possess a boundless belief in men. One day in the history of mankind, when the threat of nuclear apocalypse lies in the rubbish heap, we shall have no need of armies, police, or prisons. On that blessed day there shall be no forbidden fruit, nor vanity, nor selfishness, nor social difference, only the kingdom of life, of moral beauty, of love. Let us seize for ourselves, if we dare, a grain of sand to build this paradise on earth, *ese paraíso terrenal.*''

Torrential applause. This was vintage Borge, the Borge who could move the unbeliever. Yet surprisingly he was upstaged by one of Somoza's goons. Two dozen former National Guardsmen had been brought in their blue prison uniforms from one of Borge's model jails, and they sat under guard in the audience listening to the minister of the interior's oration. Anastasio Somoza II's personal bodyguard, an erstwhile master sergeant, a huge brute in his blue jumper, strode to the podium and read a prepared speech.

He thanked Borge for his imprisonment. This minion of Somoza was confined now to a *granja de régimen abierto,* an open prison farm, where he had been rehabilitated and reeducated. ''I am a new man,'' he said humbly, ''different, with a new outlook on life. I am a shoemaker, farmer, I operate a hydraulic press, and I paint primitive pictures. This is not propaganda.'' Speaking as well for hundreds of other imprisoned somocistas he added that under revolutionary confinement ''we are protected in our rights and our human dignity. At all places and at all times, our physical, mental, and moral integrity has been supremely respected.'' Then he marched up to Borge and shook his hand.

A woman all in white sang a passionate ode to peace. A man with a guitar sang a passionate ode to Tomás Borge, reliving Borge's torture in Somoza's jails and redeeming those terrors with the Triumph.

"... *la tortura* ... *el pueblo* ... *la violencia* ... *corazón* ..."
The assembly rose to sing the Sandinista hymn.

> *Adelante marchemos compañeros*
> *Avancemos a la Revolución* ...
> Wrapped in the banner red and black
> Free fatherland, victory or death.

> Sons of Sandino
> Don't sell out, don't surrender
> Fight on against the Yankee
> Enemy of mankind.

> *Adelante marchemos compañeros* ...

The assembly adjourned for luncheon. I followed Borge. Halfway through the hall he paused to greet Somoza's men in their blue prison garb. As they shook his hand and mumbled words they seemed respectful, subdued, and sad. On the steps of the convention center, Borge embraced a fair-skinned man in black clericals whom he had lauded in his oration—Padre Uriel Molina, uncrowned pope of the People's Church. The minister became engulfed in the crowd, and I nearly lost him. Ah, there he was, entering the dining hall.

A woman stood at the door checking invitations. I did not even carry a credential on my lapel; she gave me a queer glance, but I pretended not to notice her and she let me pass. The dining hall was elegant, all silverware and linen. I milled with the guests, drinking cold beer. Eventually I saw Comandante Lenin Cerna, sitting at a table alone. Then I saw Borge, sitting at the next table talking to two young men in civilian dress. Such an embarrassment of riches. I sat down beside Borge.

I mumbled my name and shook his hand, but he was in the middle of a sentence and his handshake was perfunctory. His young guests were Guatemalans, and he was expatiating to them about the virtues of his open farms. "Our prisoners live, sleep, and work under no guard, no surveillance whatsoever. This is remarkable. You must admit, really, this is remarkable. And remember, many of these men are serving very severe sentences. There are no walls or fences, they could just walk out, but they never do."

He orchestrated his words with body language, rolling his torso as he spoke. When he said, "They could just walk out," he opened and closed his fists. "Their only guard is our total confidence in their conduct." Borge began glancing at me from behind his tinted spectacles, wondering who I was. "We have seven such open farms, and not a single case of escape. Imagine, *compañeros,* each three months the prisoners can visit their families for a week. Imagine! We've never seen an infraction of our rules!" There had been no security checks at this convention, either. I thought: if I were violent, if I had a gun, I could shoot Borge dead right now. He glanced at me again, and his eyes met mine. "We have confidence, *compañeros,* so much confidence in our system. The farms reflect our humane and Christian principles." Abruptly he got up and left the table.

Luncheon was served — no wine, but more cold beer, sweet rolls, salad, lobster Newburg in the shell, and iced fruit cocktail in a great orange rind. It was the most delicious meal I was ever served in Nicaragua. I kept my eye on Borge. I was not done with him. He ate little if at all; he kept circulating among the tables, shaking hands and greeting people. Finally, after dessert, I saw my chance. I rose, walked across the room, and trapped him between two long tables.

"*¿Mi comandante?*"

There ensued a sort of dance. He turned on his heel and walked the length of the tables, but by that time a group of people had blocked the exit. He turned back to me, and we danced a little tango as I blocked the other exit. I am of medium height: I towered over the rotund, bespectacled policeman in his khaki tunic.

AUTHOR: *Mi comandante,* human rights people tell me of seven thousand political prisoners in your jails.

BORGE: They say eleven thousand.

A: They talk of beatings, torture, and inhuman conditions in your jails.

B: Calumnies.

A: How many political prisoners have you?

B: We have no political prisoners in Nicaragua. We have only National Guardsmen and counterrevolutionaries.

A: How many?

B: Four thousand.

A: Of those, how many are counterrevolutionaries?

He was clearly annoyed. He motioned to walk past me, but I crowded him with another question. I had him at last, and no escape, *mi comandante.* The space between the tables was my open farm. Some aides sat there, and he turned to one, snapping his fingers.

B: How many are counterrevolutionaries?

AIDE: One thousand.

B: One thousand.

A: I'm concerned about the conditions in your jails.

B: You can visit the jails and see the conditions for yourself.

A: Will you arrange my visit to El Chipote, *mi comandante?*

Angry, he moved again to brush past me. By now the aides were murmuring, restive like their master, so from my open farm I allowed Borge to escape. Soon I flew to Costa Rica and home to the United States.

2

HOME TO THE BIG LAND of the Boston Red Sox and their death wish and Ivan Boesky and his odes to greed. "Greed is all right, by the way. I think greed is healthy. You can be greedy and still feel good about yourself." I suffered cultural shock, not in going to Central America but in returning to the United States. And consider this:

"The . . . city became frantic in its effort to explain something that defied meaning. Power seemed to have outgrown its servitude and to have asserted its freedom. The cylinder had exploded, and thrown great masses of . . . steam against the sky. The city had the air and movement of hysteria, and citizens were crying, in every accent of anger and alarm, that the new forces must at any cost be brought under control . . . A traveler in the highways of history looked out of the club window on the turmoil . . . and felt himself in Rome, under Diocletian, witnessing the anarchy, conscious of the compulsion, eager for the solution, but unable to conceive whence the next impulse was to come or how it was to act."

That is not some living sage, lamenting the Washington of the Iran-contra affair and Lieutenant Colonel Oliver North, it is Henry Adams describing his return from Europe to the United States in 1904. Yet how perfectly Adams prophesied the mood of my fatherland as the focus of attention shifted now from Central America to the anarchy of policy in Washington.

Shortly after I left the isthmus, the American mercenary Eugene Hasenfus was shot down over southern Nicaragua on a supply mission to the contras, his links to Colonel North and the National Security Council were unveiled, and President Reagan's Central American policy began to unravel.

As more and more secrets were revealed, the American public marveled at Colonel North's industry. He was indefatigable in keeping the
contras armed and fed, in flouting laws to the contrary, in dissembling
to Congress and the secretary of state. After his dismissal from the staff
of the National Security Council in November 1986, he seemed to grow
more candid. Here is a fragment of his testimony to a joint committee
of the Congress in July 1987:

Q: Is it correct to say that following the enactment of the Boland
Amendment, our support for the war in Nicaragua did not end and that
you were the person in the United States Government who managed it?

COLONEL NORTH: Starting in the spring of 1984, well before the Boland
proscription of no appropriated funds made available to the Department
of Defense and the CIA etc., I was already engaged in supporting the
Nicaraguan resistance and the democratic outcome in Nicaragua. I did
so as part of a covert operation. It was carried out as early as the spring
of '84, when we ran out of money and people started to look in Nicaragua, in Honduras and Guatemala, El Salvador and Costa Rica for some
sign of what the Americans were really going to do . . . And yes, it was
carried out covertly . . . in such a way as to ensure that the heads of
state and the political leadership in Nicaragua — in Central America —
recognized the United States was going to meet the commitments of the
President's foreign policy. And the President's foreign policy was that
we are going to achieve a democratic outcome in Nicaragua and that our
support for the Nicaraguan Freedom Fighters was going to continue, and
that I was given the job of holding them together in body and soul. And
it slowly transitioned into a more difficult task as time went on and as
the CIA had to withdraw further and further from that support, until
finally we got to the point in October when I was the only person left
talking to them . . .

Q: Colonel North . . . you've admitted before this committee that
you lied to representatives of the Iranians in order to try and release
the hostages, is that correct?

CN: I lied every time I met the Iranians . . .

Q: And you've admitted that you lied to the Congress, is that correct?

CN: I have.

Q: And you've admitted that you lied in creating false chronologies
of these events, is that correct?

CN: That is true . . .

Q: Can you assure this committee that you are not here now lying to
protect your Commander in Chief?

CN: I am not lying to protect anybody, Counsel. I came here to tell the truth. I told you that I was going to tell it to you — the good, the bad and the ugly . . . I committed, when I raised my right hand and took an oath as a midshipman, that I would tell the truth, and I took an oath when I arrived here before this committee to tell the truth, and I have done so, painful though it may be for me and for others. I have told you the truth, Counsel . . .

As Colonel North's tearful testimony progressed, on the ground in Nicaragua the contras were actually fighting a little better. With their $100 million, with their new rifles, grenade launchers, mortars, howitzers, and air drops, they attacked not only collective farms, they even engaged the Sandinista army occasionally. With their new Redeye missiles, they shot down several Sandinista helicopters. Thousands of contras more penetrated deeply to the interior, into such favored provinces as Chontales, where they wrought increasing havoc. They struggled to wreck infrastructure — bridges, electric power, telephone communications, road and river transport — thus compounding the misery of the Nicaraguan people as the Marxist insurgents reaped similar sorrow in El Salvador. After all, other people's sorrow was the beauty of proxy warfare. What did Ronald Reagan and the dying CIA director William Casey care for mourning Nicaraguans so long as no American blood was shed and they could nibble at the edges of Soviet power?

Why, the contras even seized fragments of territory along the Honduran border as big as postage stamps. They seized no cities, ports, or enclaves. The Soviet Union reinforced the Sandinista army. The popular insurrection the contras yearned for never happened. They killed and maimed more innocent civilians with American Claymore land mines.

As for the Nicaraguan economy, by the end of 1986, the cordoba sold illegally at 4,000 to the dollar. By June of 1987, at 7,000; by August at 12,000; by January 1988 at 45,000. The government was running out of paper for printing money; projections for inflation in 1988 ran to 10,000 percent. Columns of decrepit automobiles stretched for miles waiting all day for tiny rations of fuel; telephones and factory machinery ceased to work for want of power, ruining the machinery; the government spent 60 percent of its resources on the war. Finally, in February 1988, the Sandinistas reformed the currency by dropping three zeros from the nominal value of the cordoba and circulating new bills, but even that solution seemed ephemeral.

The Sandinistas had sworn oaths on Sandino's head that they would never talk to the contras and denounced as traitors, mercenary lice, CIA baboons all Nicaraguans who ventured they should do so. Tomás Borge would accept negotiations with the counterrevolution when the rivers of Nicaragua ran backward, and he loved the laughter when he reviled Ronald Reagan for his wet dreams. Nevertheless, in the summer of 1987, when President Oscar Arias Sánchez of Costa Rica proposed such negotiation, the Sandinistas acquiesced. As the months passed, one realized they had not much choice. Their economy was collapsing; the Soviet Union had no mind to finance their failures forever; hard cash from Europe was drying up; the U.S. Congress would renew military aid to the counterrevolution unless the Sandinistas sought peace.

During months of desultory maneuvering, it became obvious that only an eminent mediator could bring the warring sides together. Who other than Borge's "Antichrist," Padre Miguel D'Escoto's "accomplice in the assassination of our people," the bête noire as well of the U.S. religious left for his silence on the contras? For weeks, President Ortega visited Cardinal Obando every day, reinstating him in his classic role as arbiter of the quarrels in the Nicaraguan family.

In late 1987, when I saw the photographs of the Cardinal shaking hands with President Ortega on the steps of the papal embassy in Washington, Foreign Minister D'Escoto standing behind them gazing sheepishly at the Cardinal's face, I wondered about the primate's thoughts. After all, only yesterday the good father was threatening to excommunicate His Eminence. Yet as I reviewed the notes of my conversations with the primate, in retrospect his strategy was clear. Had he condemned the contras, had he taken the Sandinistas' side in the civil war as the Catholic left insisted he morally must do, he would have destroyed his credibility as mediator once both sides wearied of the war and were ready to talk. The Sandinistas had said they would *never* talk to those mercenary assassins. But the Cardinal, so shrewd, patient, cunning, so schooled in the convulsions of his people's character, knew that in politics all oaths are ephemeral and that if he stood his ground against anathemas and kept insisting on negotiation one day it might happen. He was the only mediator the contras trusted, and both sides — he knew — would eventually need him again.

In early 1988, having brought the enemies together, the Cardinal was dismissed as mediator by President Ortega as the Sandinistas and the contras talked directly. The contras also had little choice. They were running out of arms and food, the Sandinistas with their superior Soviet weapons were chasing them across the border of Honduras, and they recognized that in the wake of the Arias initiative the U.S. Congress was not disposed to give them guns. In the meanwhile, the Sandinistas had allowed *La Prensa* to resume publishing, Radio Católica to resume broadcasting, they had rescinded the state of emergency, and released some political prisoners. In 1987, they had allowed the exiled ecclesiastic Monseñor Bismark Carballo to return to Nicaragua. (Monseñor Vega of Juigalpa was also invited to return, but he refused "until Nicaragua has democracy.") In the contra sanctuary in Honduras, Colonel Enrique Bermúdez had told me that "even if all U.S. aid stops, we will go on fighting." That was not to be, at least in March 1988, when at Sapoá in southern Nicaragua the contras signed a limited truce with the Sandinistas and Cardinal Obando added his signature as witness.

Forty to fifty thousand Nicaraguans were dead in seven years of civil war; in 1987 alone twenty Nicaraguans a day had been sacrificed in a populace of three million. President Reagan, distressed that the Sandinistas remained in power and that his Freedom Fighters had fought so inconclusively, at least could be consoled with a qualified and dubious policy success. His support of the counterrevolutionaries had pushed the Sandinistas into negotiation to liberalize their rule, the stated objective of U.S. policy. Yet at such cost! Whatever concessions the Sandinistas might make as the decade closes, they might well have made in 1981 under the pressure of shrewd diplomacy and without the toll of fifty thousand human corpses.

As for the content of a permanent peace in Nicaragua — should it ever come — I am reluctant to dabble in prophecy. By mid-1988, only a temporary truce had been concluded and no permanent solution had been achieved. In June 1988 the negotiations collapsed. No doubt subsequent negotiations will be as tormented, protracted, full of crisis, veering again toward collapse if they do not founder altogether, resume and founder yet again. Conceivably with failure the contras might resume the battle.

Any settlement will perforce confirm the Sandinistas in power. The contras have demanded free elections, free schools, complete liberty of the press, an independent judiciary, guaranteed property rights, a permanent role for private enterprise, an end to the military draft, and removal of the army from control by the Sandinista party. In their ensemble the demands are a pipe dream, and they can only represent a maximum initial proposal. During the bargaining the Sandinistas might well be pushed to significant concessions, but the total result will still be marginal.

The Sandinistas will allow limited press freedom, limited property rights, limited private enterprise. They will allow parties of the opposition to compete for public office within constraints. They may soften somewhat their monopoly of education, but they will never surrender control of the army and the police. On the contrary, they plan to *increase* their army. I doubt also they would permit a non-Sandinista to assume the presidency of Nicaragua with true executive power over the army and the police. To ensure that the substance of the Revolution endures, the Sandinistas will never significantly share power. So much for avoiding prophecy.

3

DURING THE TWILIGHT of Ronald Reagan's presidency, I have imagined a meeting with his successor:

THE NEW PRESIDENT: Can I trust the Sandinistas?

AUTHOR: No.

P: Why?

A: Look at their history, Mr. President. They make concessions only for tactical reasons. They'll sign any scrap of paper, resume making mischief, and in this country they can always take cover behind the religious left. If you make a deal with them — and I hope you'll try — demand proof of compliance.

P: What's the basic deal?

A: Inside Nicaragua, you'll have to let them keep their Revolution. This won't be easy, but we should encourage the Sandinistas toward evolutionary Marxism. With sticks and carrots, we should nudge them as best we can away from the Cuban model toward the models of Yugoslavia and Hungary — less bureaucracy, more private incentives, a real role for the middle class, with the press and the Church as free as possible.

P: Is it achievable?

A: Not for many years. Successful socialism supposes something to distribute, and in Nicaragua there's nothing left. Just to prevent the economy from regressing further — let alone regaining the levels of

Somoza—Nicaragua will need at least half a billion dollars of aid per annum indefinitely.

P: Oh, we can't afford that.

A: Maybe with Spain and the other West Europeans we could start with tentative amounts and see how the Sandinistas behave, especially toward their neighbors. Once they settle with the contras, they'll be desperate for normal economic relations with us.

P: What should I send them first?

A: Food. For the Nicaraguan people. Irrespective of concessions from the Sandinistas. We should never make starvation a weapon of our diplomacy.

P: What about the external Sandinista threat? Everybody tells me I should contain them.

A: You should, but containment will be expensive. You'll be expected to build up Honduras, El Salvador, and Guatemala into viable democracies, and that will take more than money. The Sandinista threat of subversion to the rest of the isthmus has been overdrawn. Who would want to copy such failure? As for the Cubans and Soviets, of course they must go home. That's basic, and the Sandinistas know it. The whole point of containment is to make the cost of mischief prohibitive to the mischief-maker. The Sandinistas have a fixation on a U.S. invasion—from *any* president. Remember the marines. For a solemn commitment from us never to invade, the Sandinistas might concede much.

P: You mentioned money for the other countries.

A: I wouldn't be extravagant.

P: I can't be extravagant.

A: Flashy solutions like the Alliance for Progress will get swallowed in the corruption of the politicians. We pump money into unstable societies and they stay unstable. If the governments of the isthmus reduce unemployment by 10, 15 percent in five years, they will be doing well. The focus of our aid should be to create work.

P: How?

A: I don't know. We should avoid big programs with armies of rich and conspicuous experts. We should be generous, we should share our resources, but how we do that without creating futile bureaucracies is a riddle we have not learned to solve. Essentially, Central Americans must reform their own sinful structures and solve their own problems. We should encourage our banks to be liberal in rescheduling Central

American debt, forgiving loans wherever possible, including Nicaragua's. We should somehow allow most illegal Central Americans in the United States to stay. Without their remittances, their families at home will starve. This is heresy to the left, but millennial solutions always fail and revolutions almost always make things worse. The most the poor can hope for is gradual and incremental change. I pray it will be faster, but I'm full of doubt. The riddles are economic, but more deeply cultural. How do you redeem overnight a culture sunk in guaro and sexual bondage? With luck, stability, intelligent help from us and Western Europe, maybe in twenty years, maybe in forty, the poor will truly be better off. With luck, in twenty years the poorest nations of the isthmus may achieve the level of Portugal and Yugoslavia in the 1960s.

P: That's not much.

A: It's better than going backward.

4

ON THE DAY before I left Nicaragua, I was suddenly informed that Bayardo Arce Castaño, one of the nine comandantes on the National Directorate and with Tomás Borge the most ideological, would receive me that evening at party headquarters. Throughout the day I hastened about Managua, seeking more of Comandante Arce's personal history.

He was the son of a bourgeois journalist, and as a student he had worked as a reporter at *La Prensa*. While at the newspaper he was recruited into the Sandinista underground; he moved to León, then into the northern highlands, where he organized logistics for the early guerrillas. During the Sandinistas' final offensive against Somoza, he became chief political officer for the Northern Front and with the Triumph assumed his laurels as a Comandante de la Revolución. Bayardo Arce seemed to incarnate all the romance and legend of the Revolution — all the guerrillas who lived on roots and snake meat and risked mountain leprosy for a noble cause.

I passed an hour that afternoon with a bitter leader of the opposition who had sat for several years with Arce in the Sandinista government and knew him well: "Bayardo is without scruples. He envisions a Nicaragua governed by the ghost of Lenin. He's intelligent, a man of many levels, and — like Borge — has a vast talent for telling lies."

Later, a lovely young woman of the comandante's acquaintance said that "Bayardo is dashing and reckless, a radical Marxist. Lately he's lost some of his power to President Ortega, but he runs the party so he's still strong. He got drunk and gave some silly press conferences, and for a while the other comandantes told him to shut up. He drives a Mercedes and chases women."

The Mercedes did not prejudice me against the comandante or make me less certain that he loved the poor. I remembered a friend of President Sadat's who told me, "Anwar wants every Egyptian to be rich. He wants every Egyptian to live in a palace and to drive a Mercedes. But if every Egyptian can't, he'll take them for himself."

At sunset Julio drove me from the Siete Mares to a park near the football stadium and party headquarters. "Wait for me," I told him. "Don't run off." The party building was modern and well maintained, the interior all new carpets and polished wood. Trim young Sandinista officers in perfect khaki passed me in the corridors bearing documents.

Comandante Arce kept me waiting in his conference room, windowless, too brightly lit, with a red and black Sandinista banner and enormous portraits of Carlos Fonseca and General Sandino. I thought black thoughts again about government by soldiers, but when the comandante appeared he disarmed me. As he strode toward me in the long room, he displayed the swift, feral movements of a cat, and I glimpsed him in the mountains, all claws and stealth, ready to pounce in ambush. No less martial for his chic sports jacket, he was gracious, youthful, bearded, reminding me of Che Guevara. He said, "Ah! I saw you Wednesday evening at the *New York Times* party."

"But we did not speak, *mi comandante.*"

"I'm a guerrilla. I never forget a face."

I shan't forget his — beneath a thick mane of dark hair, he had a full mouth and darting black eyes still too wary to be civilized. Most of his comments were worthless, the sort of propaganda that appears in *Barricada*. He was amusing once or twice. He kept saying "Rocky Reagan" — I think he meant "Rambo Reagan." He was certain that were Marx or Lenin alive today they would be Sandinistas. "Gorbachev, too, if he lived in Nicaragua. If Rocky Reagan lived in Nicaragua he'd be a contra." He was interesting on one topic — the revolutionary vanguard, which with the eight other comandantes he embodied.

"Until Somoza's time Nicaragua never had a revolutionary political party. There were other parties that opposed Somoza, but we Sandinistas were the first to advocate a revolution. If leaders of other illegal parties were caught, they had only to serve six months in jail. If *we* were caught, we faced thirty years in jail—when Somoza didn't shoot us. We realized then that not all Nicaraguan patriots were ready to shed their blood, to profess as we did, 'Free Fatherland or Death.'

"Thus those of us ready to give our lives became a group, objectively different from others who served the cause but were not willing to shed their blood. Some of them served in air-conditioned offices. We militants took up arms, in the cities and in the mountains. The people respected us, admired us, believed in us, and finally followed us into battle. Logically, from our group rose the vanguard."

This was the heart of the matter. One had to fight as Bayardo Arce did, endure terrible hardship in the mountains or (as Tomás Borge did) ghastly torture in the jails, to be worthy to govern. "I did not fight the Revolution in an air-conditioned office. I gave up everything. I abandoned my family, my job in journalism, my economic future, for a dangerous life in arms. It was logical that people should hold me more worthy of respect, follow me as a man of consequence."

The vanguard was essential because the Nicaraguan people were not naturally revolutionary. In conception the Nicaraguan vanguard was not wholly Leninist. It borrowed selectively from other revolutions, including Cuba's. It was Che's call that the comandantes heard as well, and he called from the mountains, where the will of the masses would be regenerated, among the ferocious streams and savage beasts, where the vanguard would be born and the mysterious will of the people would find its voice. In power, the vanguard would educate the people in their future, define their deepest wishes better than the people could themselves, and make the people free to choose what the vanguard would decide was best for them.

When I emerged from party headquarters, Managua was blacked out. In the dark I looked for Julio, but he had disappeared. Angrily I decided to walk home, but in the maze of streets I got lost. In a slum somewhere I passed a church, glimpsed the candles flickering, heard the wails and lamentations. *Rosa mística, Torre de David, Torre de marfil, Casa de oro.* I must have walked in circles because an hour later I passed the football stadium and was back at party headquarters. Julio was there, with a new whore in the front seat.

Too tired to protest, I climbed in back and told him to take me home. The Datsun would not start. Julio got out and cursed, lifted the hood, tinkered with the engine, but he had no flashlight and his repairs seemed pointless.

His whore was a handsome mulatto woman from the Atlantic coast. She spoke some English and tried to engage me in conversation.

"How was your meeting with the comandante?" she asked.

"Fascinating," I said. I added bitterly, thinking of all of them, in Honduras and El Salvador, in Guatemala and Nicaragua, "*Sí, mi comandante, claro, mi comandante, gracias, mi comandante.*"

My outburst seemed to puzzle her. In the darkness she turned her body to me.

"Tell him to give us more milk," she said.

Santurce, Puerto Rico
Newton Centre, Massachusetts
March 1987–May 1988

EPILOGUE

I returned to Nicaragua—for several weeks—in August 1988.

During my absence, the drama of Nicaraguan life had significantly evolved. In their management of the economy, the Sandinistas had—desperately—grown rather more pragmatic. They had relaxed some of their controls over prices and distribution and were struggling to stifle the black market by allowing the new cordoba to float freely at its real value against the dollar. Amazingly, in the marketplaces of Managua and in the provinces that I visited in the south and center of Nicaragua once again, food—basic grains, rice, beans, corn, cooking oil, fish, fowl, meat, and soap as well—were considerably more abundant. The government had even suspended rationing.

Unfortunately, the new pragmatism, welcome though it was, after years of mismanagement and ideological rigidity seemed too little and too late. Estimates of inflation—tragically high even by the calculations of Sandinista economists—ran to 12,000 percent and higher for 1988 by the calculations of independent Nicaraguan economists. The cost of the basic basket of food had risen at least 7,000 percent since 1981. Even these statistics were exponential as the rate of inflation geometrically compounded itself week by week, month by month, into stratospheric projections that no one really could predict.

Months earlier, the economic ministries had been reorganized and consolidated as the Sandinistas endeavored to undo their chronic errors and introduce efficiency. The new cordoba, established at ten to the U.S. dollar in February, was inexorably weakened by persistently declining national production. Brushing aside Marxist theory and reverting to orthodox economics, the Sandinistas hoped that by allowing the cordoba to depreciate they would render farm exports more attractive to foreign markets and earn greater quantities of foreign exchange. However, the opposite consequence ensued. As the new cordoba dropped dramatically in value, the cost of essential imports soared, and the populace suffered even more. Years of controlled prices and distribution had wrought such havoc, so enfeebled production, that the damage seemed impossible to repair.

From ten cordobas to the dollar in February the currency had depreciated to about four hundred to the dollar in August. Thus the familiar fate of the old cordoba—from seven to the dollar under Somoza to the tens of thousands until early 1988—had resumed its terrible chaotic cycle with the new currency as well. One can imagine the effect on the Nicaraguan people. I had thought that when I departed Nicaragua in late 1986, the suffering of the people could hardly grow worse, and I was wrong.

The abundance of food in the marketplace was due, not to higher production in the public or the private sectors, but to the penury of the populace. If food was plentiful, the multitude had no means to buy it, and it remained heaped in the marketplace, untasted. Unemployment had risen to new levels that afflicted at least half the workers and peasants; wages had risen to only insubstantial fractions of the swift inflation. The average wage of an urban worker varied between three and four thousand cordobas per month at best—perhaps $10 if he were lucky—barely enough to feed a family of seven for two or three days. Heretofore people scrimped and went without: now, many starved.

Nicaragua is not like Somalia or Ethiopia, lunar lands of arid desolation devoid of vegetation; in the languorous rhythm of Nicaraguan life, many of the poor manage to cope. In the countryside, the campesinos pick mangoes from the trees, grow fruits and vegetables on their tiny plots of land, barter between themselves for other necessities without recourse to money. Even in the slums of Managua, wherever the shacks of the poor are surrounded by parcels of land however tiny, people pick fruit from the tropical bush and plant tomatoes and various edibles that in some measure assuage their hunger. Alas, for too many of the squeezed urban poor there is no such land to scratch upon, and for them the hunger gnaws.

As always, I wandered in the worst slums, and the condition of infant children especially appalled me. For months—the Sandinista press made no effort to conceal it—an epidemic of diarrhea had been raging among the children. Before they had suffered from malnutrition: now I saw more evidence of kwashiorkor, arms and legs as thin as toothpicks, bellies distended from hunger and parasites, the roots of their hair turning yellow and orange, their little cribs of sticks and branches foul from diarrhea. The diarrhea is an initial symptom: dehydration follows, and then death. Each week, hundreds of children throughout Nicaragua — perhaps thousands, nobody really knew — were dying from diarrhea. The hospitals were largely empty of medicine, and now the state hospitals that still stocked some medicine made the patients pay for it. Mothers told me that they were charged a thousand cordobas for injections of their infants — a new tax that few could afford, so the infants went without medication as well as food, and more perished.

The exodus of skilled and educated Nicaraguans increased. As of 1986 upward of 55 percent of the nation's technicians — engineers, physicians, electricians, car mechanics, on and on — had despaired of life under the Revolution and fled the country. Now the percentages were higher, and the evidence was dismaying as I read the classified sections of *La Prensa* and the Sandinista press as well. People were putting their houses, automobiles, all of their possessions up for sale and getting out. And not only the bourgeoisie — the poor also, insofar as they owned anything at all. As I motored through Managua and the provinces, repeatedly I found that friends — the poor and the once better off — had migrated in the meanwhile to Costa Rica, Honduras, California, and — above all — to Miami. The social impact of the growing "brain drain" seemed ever more deep, for the migration was happening just as the Revolution strained to be more pragmatic and it needed skilled hands crucially.

I have stressed the new economic pragmatism of the comandantes, but in the greater scheme of things — in the practice of state policy as a whole — such pragmatism proved to be largely an illusion.

We know that earlier in the year the Sandinistas signed a truce with the contras that — despite sporadic violations by either side — had largely held and was repeatedly prolonged. Shrewdly, with precise design, the comandantes used the truce to eliminate the contra support network in the central provinces and to consolidate their military dominion throughout Nicaragua. From their perspective, they can hardly be blamed for doing so. Yet what struck me more than anything during my return to Nicaragua — quite as much even as the plague of infant diarrhea — was the proliferation of soldiers through town and country-side alike. Soldiers were *everywhere*.

By the government's own admission, in a populace of three million the active military force had increased in 1988 to eighty-five thousand troops, by far the largest army in Central America. By the calculations of the political opposition and foreign military attachés in Managua, the true figure of active forces ran from one hundred fifteen thousand to one hundred twenty-five thousand men with at least as many in reserve. The government's rationale was its fear that before he left office Ronald Reagan would indeed invade Nicaragua; despite all the talk of peace negotiations and force reductions Humberto Ortega, the minister of defense, had yet to disavow his objective of military forces of six hundred thousand men by 1995 — or a fifth of Nicaragua's present population.

Wherever I traveled — throughout Managua, on the back dirt roads near Granada and Lake Nicaragua, through the hills and valleys and towns of Boaco and Chontales in the center of the nation, there they were — soldiers, soldiers, more soldiers. Perhaps they were so visible because the fighting had largely ceased and they had descended from their redoubts in the mountains to mix with — and intimidate? — the population. On the country roads, many troops trudged on foot or hitched rides. In the towns and cities, they roared past incessantly in jeeps and huge East German trucks, coming and going — where?

The misfortune for Nicaragua was that these legions of men in uniform produced nothing — they only consumed. By universal account, now 62 percent of the state budget was devoted to maintaining and strengthening the army. The army was a Moloch, and what little the nation had — cement, medicine, construction equipment, spare parts, gasoline, much of the food — the army devoured. For the civil populace, the new pragmatism in economics was laudable for its intent, but the heart of the matter was the size of the army and its own ceaseless hunger.

Not that the army was serene in its ubiquity or free of trouble. The migrations from Nicaragua so prevalent in the civil populace were even more contagious among youths of draft age. When the army came to press-gang, many youths simply ran away — to the mountains, to Costa Rica, to Honduras and Mexico if they could make it. Campesinos in Boaco and Chontales told me that the army was inducting boys of fourteen, thirteen, even ten. The army waited for the youths to emerge from cinemas, invaded their homes at night, surrounded whole barrios, even held their parents hostage until they surrendered for service. Similar incidents occurred in Managua and other cities.

And then the shootings — new to my ears since I had not heard of such incidents during my previous visitations even as the contra war raged. More and more, the army and the state security were shooting youths who resisted or fled from forced recruitment. These incidents, according to campesinos and townspeople I met in Boaco and Chontales in central Nicaragua, had become quite common. I shall repeat one incident told to me by an activist of the political opposition in Boaco province, which I have no reason to disbelieve since he did so in the presence of several men and women who also knew the victims personally and who confirmed his account.

On July 19, 1988, the ninth anniversary of the Triumph, a fiesta was in progress in the countryside near Boaco town. The army arrived in trucks, on another mission of forced recruitment. A youth of twelve tried to flee on a horse; he was shot dead. Five of his brothers, ages eleven to twenty, were summarily executed at the same fiesta together with a family domestic for a total of seven dead from the same household. The Sandinista commander justified the killings by denouncing the father of the youths, a Conservative activist, as *"el hombre más reaccionario de Boaco."* Later, I approached a grieving member of the family in Boaco town, but he declined to talk to me for fear of further reprisals.

In Managua, I raised the incident with a high Sandinista official. He said, "When we hear of such shootings, we investigate. The offenders are referred to the military courts. The human rights situation in Nicaragua is far from perfect, but tortures and killing are not a policy. If incidents happen, they are punished with the full force of law."

Campesinos of Boaco and Chontales told me otherwise: the culprits were never punished. Such killings, I suspected, were part of the state's policy to intimidate the young into military service by setting grim examples. These examples in their turn were pieces of a larger mosaic of repression coldly conceived and carried out in most of Nicaragua.

For all the new pragmatism in the marketplace, campesinos were still forced to join the detested state cooperatives. Campesinos in Boaco told me of a "concentration camp" about forty miles from Boaco town where six hundred families, uprooted from their own farms, were forced to live and work the land and were not allowed to leave. In the cities, the Sandinistas were hard at work encouraging schisms and fragmentation of the numerous parties of the political opposition. This classical tactic of divide and rule was not confined to the conservative and center parties — but was even applied to the Communist Party of Nicaragua.

The Sandinistas were nervous. Their high officials and their newspapers acknowledged great popular discontent, but they were resolved that the anger of the masses for the chaos of the economy would never crystallize into effective political revolt — and as usual their countertactics were effective. They turned repression on and off as they might a faucet — jailing opposition leaders for a time, closing *La Prensa* for another fortnight, silencing Radio Católica anew — relaxing their grip when passions cooled but ready to be harsh again should the fragmented opposition threaten to coalesce.

Dr. Lino Hernández, that valiant champion of human rights in Nicaragua, told me that despite their promises of more freedom and their erratic relaxation of various other controls, the Sandinistas still held about six thousand two hundred political prisoners (not counting former National Guardsmen) and that in the provinces prisoners accused of collaboration with the contras were still tortured. The comandantes' drive to eradicate the contra presence in Chontales, to crush once and for all the remnants of popular support for the counterrevolution, was unyielding and largely a success. Lino himself, a year earlier, in August 1987, fell victim again to Tomás Borge's revolutionary justice. Accused of attacking a policeman, he was beaten, jailed for nearly a month in a foul cell, and for a fortnight resisted his jailers by refusing to eat.

As for the future, the Sandinistas and the opposition waited in painful suspense for the election of the next President of the United States. Under either Democrats or Republicans, the contras as an effective military force against the Sandinistas seemed doomed. The Sandinistas hoped openly for a victory of the Democrats, and some high Sandinistas even fantasized that Michael Dukakis as President would pay them reparations of more than a billion dollars to atone for the crimes of Ronald Reagan and to reconstruct Nicaragua. As for George Bush, they considered him less fanatical than Reagan and hoped they could strike some sort of bargain even with a Republican White House.

Certainly a bargain on external security issues between the Sandinistas and the United States — with either the Democrats or the Republicans — still seemed possible. But I see no reason to revise my view that the Sandinistas will continue to entrench their rule and to refuse to share effective power. President Ortega and Comandante Bayardo Arce stated in August, "We have reached the limit of our flexibility." I see no reason to disagree with President Arias of Costa Rica that "the Sandinistas are less afraid of the contras than they are of freedom and democracy."

Whoever is elected to the U.S. presidency, I foresee tormented relations between the United States and Sandinista Nicaragua indefinitely. This not least because the conservative wings of both the Republican and Democratic parties will not cease to complain of a Marxist abscess in the heart of the isthmus and the Sandinistas' continued commitment to "internationalism" (reiterated by President Ortega on July 19, 1988), which translated means enduring support for revolution throughout the Latin tropics and opposition to U.S. hegemony.

I continue to meditate on the Nicaraguan poor and to wonder who bears the greater blame for their misery. Throughout this book I have repeatedly denounced the cruelty of the United States and the dreadful suffering it has caused by its support of the contras and its pursuit of a military solution. Yet in revisiting Nicaragua I regret that my earlier reproaches of the Sandinistas were not stronger and that I may have failed to be vigorous enough in showing how much harm the Revolution has wrought upon the Nicaraguan people.

I complete this Epilogue in my shabby room at the Siete Mares as the Isthmian monsoon drenches the night outside with greater ferocity than I have ever seen, more hovels of the poor are washed away, and in the garden of Nicaragua more infant children die of diarrhea.

A few days ago, at the Jesuit university, I sought out Padre R. You will remember this saintly Jesuit doodling for me a sketch that demonstrated the identity of the Revolution and the Kingdom of God, and how Sandino, Marx, and Christ converged. Now he told me, "The Revolution has turned our economy to ruin . . . We don't need ideologues to manage the economy, we need pragmatists . . . I have reconciled with Cardinal Obando and assembled other Jesuits at my table to dine with him . . . Nicaragua must *not* become another Cuba . . . One of my own students was seized by the state security in Estelí and tortured with lighted cigarette butts . . . Above all, Nicaragua must have freedom."

In April, Tomás Borge summoned to his house the director of an independent radio station whose broadcasts had displeased him. With his own hands, Borge attacked the man, and in *La Prensa* a photograph appeared of the unfortunate gentleman with lesions on his mouth. Yet still I loved Borge's rhapsodies: "Tomorrow, some day soon, an unknown sun will shine to illuminate the land that our heroes and martyrs promised us. A land with rushing rivers of milk and honey where every fruit will flourish, except the fruit of discord, and where man will be the brother of man . . ."

I have looked everywhere for the Revolution's other philosopher-king, Father Ernesto Cardenal. Alas, Ernesto had a falling-out with President Ortega's wife, and in an economy measure some months ago his Ministry of Culture was abolished. Ernesto was fobbed off with a supernumerary new title. One of his friends told me he had returned to his commune in Lake Nicaragua to write poetry. Another told me that no, he had seen Ernesto only yesterday driving about Managua wearing his eternal black beret. It did not truly matter that I failed to find Ernesto, for I knew the message of his poetry, past, present, and future: "The Revolution is love."

Managua
August 1988

NOTES

NOTES (INCLUDING SELECTED BIBLIOGRAPHY)

I / THE CONTRAS. . . HONDURAS

page

6   Americas Watch: *Human Rights in Nicaragua: 1985–1986* (New York: The Americas Watch Committee, 1986), pp. 86–93.

7   *Psychological Operations in Guerrilla Warfare:* See "Taylalan," *Psychological Operations in Guerrilla Warfare: The CIA's Nicaragua Manual,* trans. from the Spanish, with essays by Joanne Omang and Aryeh Neier (New York: Random House, Vintage Books, 1985).

15 Bermúdez: My conversations with Bermúdez took place near the Nicaraguan border on November 19 and 20, 1985. They are, of course, abbreviated here.

19 Successive Honduran governments: For the history of Honduras, see Vilma Laínez and Victor Meza, "The Banana Enclave," *Ariel* XIII, no. 256, Tegucigalpa (May 1973), pp. 5–26, trans. by Annie Street, cited in *Honduras: Portrait of a Captive Nation,* Nancy Peckenham and Annie Street, eds. (New York: Praeger, 1985).

19 Beaulac: Willard Beaulac, *Career Ambassador* (New York: Macmillan, 1951).

19 Around the turn of the century: *Psychological Operations in Guerrilla Warfare,* essay by Joanne Omang. Among other features, the manual advises the contras on how to "neutralize" (kill) civilian adversaries. It also states: "An armed guerrilla force always carries with it implicit terror because the population, without saying it out loud, fears the arms can be turned against them." In his essay, Aryeh Neier, vice chairman of the Americas Watch Committee, described the document as a "manual for terrorists" which adds the United States "to the list of rogue nations practicing international terrorism."

22 For further information on the U.S. international police power, see the essay on the Monroe Doctrine by Dexter Perkins, professor emeritus of American Civilization at Cornell University and author of a history

of the doctrine, in the *Encyclopædia Britannica* XV, 1961, pp. 735–38. See also "The Legacy of Monroe's Doctrine," by Gaddis Smith, Larned Professor of History at Yale, *The New York Times Magazine*, September 9, 1984.

22   Nebulously considered "subversive": See *Militarismo en Honduras: El Reinado de Gustavo Alvarez, 1982–84*, Serie: *Cronologías*, no. 2 (August 1985), Tegucigalpa, Centro de Documentación de Honduras (CEDOH), published by Victor Meza, a disenchanted leftist now refreshingly nonideological and one of Honduras's best-informed intellectuals.

23   Alvarez: See Christopher Dickey, *With the Contras: A Reporter in the Wilds of Nicaragua* (New York: Simon & Schuster, Touchstone Books, 1987).

23   Negroponte: Following similar comments on former Ambassador Negroponte in an article of mine on Honduras in the *New York Review of Books* ("The Country of Nada," March 27, 1986), the *Review* published an angry letter from Mr. Negroponte in its edition of June 12, 1986, stating (among many other objections) that his relationship with General Alvarez "was never as chummy as Sheehan's article would suggest. My dealings with Alvarez were correct, relatively infrequent and very much on an equal footing. Anyone who personally knew both of us can attest that it would have been totally out of character for Alvarez to accept a role subordinate to the United States Ambassador."

The distinguished political columnist and author Stanley Karnow, an old friend of Ambassador Negroponte's (and of mine), wrote in the same number of the *Review* that "Sheehan should have stuck to the issues, rather than personalizing his criticism with cheap shots."

In reply, I wrote that Ambassador Negroponte *was* an issue, and that if I mentioned him in unfavorable terms it was because his performance in Honduras had been so controversial: "My description of [his] tenure . . . was . . . based on conversations with a cross section of opinion, Honduran and foreign, inside Honduras. These included at least half a dozen American and other Western correspondents with long experience in that country, several respected Honduran journalists, human rights activists, several academics and lawyers, three senior Western diplomats from countries friendly to the U.S., an official of an important government ministry, two former cabinet ministers, several churchmen both Honduran and American . . . Mr. Karnow is of course correct in suggesting that Ambassador Negroponte was executing higher administration policy in turning Honduras into a U.S. base. But both the style and substance of Mr. Negroponte's performance seemed offensive to many Hondurans I talked to.

"Whatever his more positive accomplishments—and despite his protestations to the contrary—he is remembered in Honduras mainly for his close association with the despotic General Gustavo Alvarez Martínez, whose cruel reign under U.S. tutelage marks one of the darkest periods of modern Honduran history."

In 1988, General Alvarez returned to Honduras and was held by court order under house arrest pending charges against him of murder and other human rights abuse (Associated Press, April 19, 1988).

28   AIDS: See Sam Dillon, "Troops, streetwalkers transform Honduran town near U.S. camp," *Miami Herald*/International Edition, April 11, 1986. Dillon wrote: "Americans recently have been targeted with a string of ugly accusations . . . Charges that American soldiers have sexually abused young boys [in Comayagua] and have sparked an AIDS epidemic, cannot be confirmed."

41   Blindfolded, shackled, and tortured: See *La Prensa*, Managua, Nicaragua, January 8, 1986, for further details of this incident. See also Padre J. Guadalupe Carney, *To Be a Revolutionary* (San Francisco: Harper & Row, 1985). Father Carney, an American Jesuit, is believed by his family to have been captured during a joint counterinsurgency operation directed by the U.S. military in 1983 during the reign of General Alvarez, then interrogated, tortured, and killed at the El Aguacate air base in Olancho. His body has never been found. His family's fears were confirmed by a former Honduran army interrogator, Sergeant Florencio Caballero, in an interview in the *New York Times*, May 2, 1987. "The American priest was killed," Caballero stated.

42   "So easy": Author's free translation. The Spanish verses are from two poems, "De niño a hombre" and "La ciudad de los niños," from the collection *Los pobres* by Roberto Sosa, Colección Salamandra (Poesía) (Tegucigalpa: Editorial Guaymuras, 1983).

44   Committees for Civil Defense: On February 23, 1988, Reuters reported from London: "Amnesty International said today that death squads attached to a secret military unit appear to have reemerged in Honduras and could be responsible for three killings in January. 'Reports during 1986 and 1987 of bombings and intimidation campaigns suggest that such units may have been reactivated and are once more deployed against individuals singled out for their outspoken opposition to government policies,' AI said."

46   Drug deals: The *Los Angeles Times* reported on February 13, 1988, that the most senior officers of the Honduran military were "suspected of protecting Colombian drug traffickers who use [Honduras] for transshipping cocaine into the United States, Reagan administration officials said yesterday. 'How can we compete with that kind of money?' [a State Department] official asked. 'Even the CIA doesn't have that kind

of money.' " On the same date the *Boston Globe* reported U.S. senator John F. Kerry's investigation into a possible "contra connection with drug money and allegations that link some of the [drug] cartel's vast profits to the US-backed rebels in Nicaragua."

47 "Financial": The annual report for 1985 was published under the bilingual title *"Nuestra misión es ser una empresa lider /* Our mission is to be a leading company" by the Corporate Offices, Kativo Chemical Industries, S.A., Apdo. 4178 — Telex 2122 San José, Costa Rica.

50 *"La Historia de Honduras"*: This is the entire text of the poem "Secreto militar," from *Secreto Militar* by Roberto Sosa, Editorial Guaymuras, Tegucigalpa.

50 Idle gossip: See *La Tribuna,* Tegucigalpa, December 12, 1985.

50 López: General López was interviewed by Mike Wallace on "60 Minutes," CBS-TV, March 29, 1987. In this interview, López confirmed that contra death squads had been operating in Honduras.

51 The money economy: For a different view, see the "Appendix to the Report of the National Bipartisan Commission on Central America" (or "The Kissinger Report") (Washington, D.C.: U.S. Government Printing Office, March 1984), authorized by the ambassador's boss (President Reagan): "Per capita income is . . . under $600 and in the countryside is probably well under $200. According to the [Honduran] government's own figures, 57 per cent of Honduras's families live in extreme poverty, lacking sufficient income to cover the cost of the basic basket of food . . . And social conditions have deteriorated further . . . The housing shortage has tripled over the last 20 years."

My interview with the U.S. ambassador, John A. Ferch, by his agreement, was on the record. (Normally comments by U.S. diplomats are not on the record.) The text here was included in my "Country of Nada" in the *New York Review of Books*.

II / NICARAGUA

55 Sandinista hymn: Author's translation.

59 Palestinians: See my "A Proposal for a Palestinian State," *The New York Times Magazine,* January 30, 1977.

63 Ortega's speech: The full text of Ortega's speech was translated in Tomás Borge, Carlos Fonseca, Daniel Ortega, Humberto Ortega, and Jaime Wheelock, *Sandinistas Speak* (New York: Pathfinder Press, 1982).

66 Sandino manifesto: This translation of Sandino's first political manifesto was published in *Tricontinental,* Havana (July–August 1984). It is reprinted in *Nicaragua: The Sandinista People's Revolution, Speeches by Sandinista Leaders* (New York: Pathfinder Press, 1985).

69 The Sandinista National Liberation Front: Translation from the Spanish by Will Reissner, reprinted in *Sandinistas Speak.*

71 Fonseca's severed head: Shirley Christian confirms that Fonseca's head was brought to Somoza on page 33 of *Nicaragua: Revolution in the Family* (New York: Random House, 1985). The rest of the incident, possibly embroidered, was related to me by a Sandinista official in Matagalpa during my first tour of Nicaragua's provinces in January 1986.

Miss Christian's two chapters on General Walker, General Sandino, the Somozas, and the origins of the FSLN, pages 3–33, drawing from dozens of sources in Spanish and English, may be the most informative short essay in English on those subjects. In addition to the basic Sandinista documents cited in my narrative or in my notes above, I have consulted Neill Macaulay, *The Sandino Affair* (Chicago: Quadrangle, 1967), probably the definitive history in English of General Sandino. For a basic work in Spanish on Sandino by a man who knew him, see José Román, *Maldito País* (Managua: Editorial Unión, 1983). For an insight into Jaime Wheelock Román's ideological speculations, cited in my narrative, see (if you can endure his turgid prose) his *Imperialismo y Dictadura* (Mexico City: Siglo Veinteuno, 1975) and his *Frente Sandinista: Hacia la Ofensiva Final* (Havana: Editorial de Ciencias Sociales, 1980).

For information and basic texts on Sandinista ideology, I have also consulted David Nolan's rich work, *FSLN: The Ideology of the Sandinistas and the Nicaraguan Revolution* (Coral Gables, Fla.: Institute of Interamerican Studies, University of Miami, 1984).

See also Peter Rosset and John Vandermeer, eds., *Nicaragua: Unfinished Revolution, The New Nicaragua Reader* (New York: Grove Press, 1986): Henri Weber on General Walker on page 141, and the verse of Rigoberto López Pérez, assassin of President Somoza García, cited by Edmundo Jarquin and Pablo Emilio Barreto on page 163.

80 Dr. Alejandro Bendaña: My conversations with Dr. Bendaña took place initially at the government press office on December 17, 1985, then at the Foreign Ministry on December 23, 1985.

84 Today, for us: Tomás Borge, *Carlos, el Amanecer Ya No Es Una Tentación* (Havana: Ediciónes Casa de las Americas, 1980), cited in Nolan, p. 121.

86 Ortega speech: See "Daniel ante los marchistas: Política USA es de genocidio," *El Nuevo Diario,* Managua, December 20, 1985, p. 1.

89 Conference of Medellín: For the basic texts, see *Los Textos de Medellín y el Proceso de Cambio en América Latina* (San Salvador: UCA Editores, 1977/85).

90 Puebla: For the basic texts of the Puebla conference, see *PUEBLA: La evangelización en el presente y en el futuro de América Latina, Tercera Conferencia General del Episcopado Latinoamericano* (San Salvador: UCA Editores, 1979/85).

91 Karl Marx: Karl Marx and Friedrich Engels, *Manifesto of the Communist Party*, III (London, 1848), *Great Books of the Western World* 50 (Chicago: *Encyclopædia Britannica*, 1952), p. 430.

91 Children's new textbooks: The juvenile lessons cited were given to me by various teachers in Nicaraguan schools during my tour of the provinces in January 1986. A nun in Estelí, obliged to teach these slogans, told me: "Just listen to the Sandinista radio. All the slogans you hear are exactly what we must teach the children."

93 "The Antichrist": Christian, p. 205.

94 Monseñor Obando: See Stephen Kinzer, "Nicaragua's Combative Archbishop," *The New York Times Magazine*, November 18, 1984, a basic document on Cardinal Obando's background. I have combined parts of it with other research, including personal conversations with the Cardinal. See also Chris Hedges, "Vatican II reforms gave rise to liberation theology," *Dallas Morning News*, March 2, 1986.

97 Padre Uriel Molina Oliu: For further details of Padre Molina's background, see Christian, pp. 30 and 203–34 passim, including details on his foreign financing.

97 M-19: See Chris Hedges, "A Clash of Wills: Radical Priests in Nicaragua," *Dallas Morning News*, March 3, 1986; the article also gives details on Molina's financing.

102 Tomás Borge letter: Letter published in Father Molina's magazine, *Amanecer, Boletin del Centro Ecuménico Antonio Valdivieso*, no. 28–29, Managua (July–August 1984), pp. 34–35. Author's translation.

102 Human rights commission: The full name is Comisión Permanente de Derechos Humanos de Nicaragua. Dr. Hernández is the executive secretary of CPDH.

102 Borge's secret police: The official chief of state security is Comandante Lenin Cerna. I have described Borge as head of the security in the general sense, since Cerna and all security officials report to Borge as minister of interior.

102 Procontra committee: PRODEMCA, The Committee for Democracy in Central America, headed by Penn Kemble.

105 El Chipote: See also Stephen Kinzer, "Ex-Inmates Cite Harsh Managua Jail," *New York Times*, August 24, 1986.

108 Rare crucifixes: See Christian, p. 205.

110 Borge publicly denied he was a Marxist: See Borge quotation, Nolan, p. 97.

110   To fifteen hundred: Officials of the independent Permanent Commission
      on Human Rights of Nicaragua (CPDH) told me that "in 1979, after
      the Revolution, under a fanatical Sandinista officer, three hundred peo-
      ple were killed in Granada. The officer was later sent to Cuba but never
      punished. Various 'special measures' were carried out between 1979
      and 1981, and between 1982 and 1985. People were discreetly 'dis-
      appeared' and killed. The total number of victims may have reached
      seventeen hundred. Luis Carrión, vice minister of interior, and Tomás
      Borge, were ultimately responsible."

111   The American ambassador: The ambassador at the time was Harry E.
      Bergold, Jr.

114   *Nicaragua: Through Our Eyes:* The newsletter, undated, was sold and
      distributed during the peace vigil outside the U.S. Embassy in Managua
      in late 1985 and for several months in 1986.

116   Biafra: See my "Death Watch in Biafra," *The Saturday Evening Post,*
      June 19, 1968.

118   We will be new, love: Gioconda Belli, in *Nicaragua in Revolution:
      The Poets Speak,* Bridget Aldacara et al., eds. (Minneapolis, Marxist
      Educational Press, 1980), p. 275, cited in Nolan, p. 1.

119   "They're members of a cult": See Chris Hedges, *Dallas Morning
      News,* March 4, 1986.

119   Useful idiots: Ibid.

119   Waugh: Evelyn Waugh, *Robbery Under Law: The Mexican Object
      Lesson* (London: Catholic Book Club/Chapman & Hall, 1939/40),
      p. 11. This book was never published in the U.S.

120   Ambulances into Nicaragua: Some of these ambulances from the brigade
      were finally imported. Later, I saw them at the Ministry of Health in
      Managua.

121   León: For further vivid detail of the fighting in León, see Dickey, pp.
      52–53.

122   Rubén Darío: For Darío's life and poems, see Justino Blanco Z., *Rubén
      Darío: Biografía y Poesías* (Mexico City: Editorial Olimpo, 1963). The
      verses in English, e.g., "month of roses," are from Lysander Kemp's
      translation of 1965. Pablo Antonio Cuadra's essay "Rubén y la dual-
      idad" may be found in his classic *El Nicaragüense,* décima edición
      (Managua: Ediciónes El pez y la serpiente, 1981), pp. 22–30. See also
      Stephen Kinzer's essays in the *New York Times Book Review,* January
      18, 1987, and in the *New York Times,* May 14, 1985.

123   "Each morning": Dickey, p. 93.

127   "We must educate": Primary school texts were given to me by Father
      Cardenal, minister of education. The secondary school basic text on
      Marxist-Leninist philosophy was shown me by a high school girl in

León, and I photocopied it. The statements on education by Tomás Borge and Father Cardenal are quoted in *1984: Nicaragua* (San José, Costa Rica: Libro Libre, 1985), in the essay "Situación de la Educación," by Xavier Zavala, pp. 151–77. A photocopy of Father Cardenal's letter of March 4, 1980, stating "schoolhouse for political formation," may be found on pp. 174–75.

128   "Under Somoza": For a perceptive analysis of the failure of Sandinista agriculture, see Forrest D. Colburn, *Post-Revolutionary Nicaragua: State, Class and the Dilemmas of Agrarian Policy* (Berkeley: University of California Press, 1986).

130,   Bernanos: The quotations of Georges Bernanos are abstracted from *The*
132   *Diary of a Country Priest* (New York: Macmillan, 1937). The translation is by Pamela Morris from the French, *Journal d'un curé de campagne*.

135   The Holy See: *Miami Herald*, January 25, 1986.

135   Barricada: *Barricada*, January 3, 1986.

136   "They squeeze": Author's conversations with Cardinal Obando on December 15, 1985, and January 9, 1986.

137   Salaries of Jesuits: See Joseph P. Fitzpatrick, S.J., "The Strange Marxism of Nicaragua," *America* magazine (Jesuit), June 8, 1985, p. 464.

140   Thomas Merton: For a detailed account of the Merton-Cardenal friendship, see Michael Mott, *The Seven Mountains of Thomas Merton* (Boston: Houghton Mifflin, 1984), pp. 302, 305, 426 passim.

140   David Nolan: Nolan, pp. 74–75, citing Cardenal in his *El evangelio en Solentiname*, 4 vols. (Managua: Editorial Nueva Nicaragua, Ediciónes Monimbó, 1983), I.

141   As thyself: Ernesto Cardenal, *El evangelio en Solentiname*, I, 95. Author's translation.

141   Everybody dresses: Ernesto Cardenal, *In Cuba* (New York: New Directions, 1974), p. 7.

142   Comandante: Excerpt from Cardenal's *Libre*, translated by Stephen Kinzer, cited by Chris Hedges, *Dallas Morning News*, May 6, 1985.

142   "Obsessive, like love": Ernesto Cardenal, cited in Nolan, p. 123.

142   Fernando Cardenal: All the quotations of Fernando Cardenal are excerpted from his conversation with author, January 16, 1986.

142   Saint Paul: Colossians 3:9–11: "Lie not to one another, seeing that you have put off the old man with his deeds; And have put on the new man, which is renewed in knowledge after the image of Him that created him." Phillip Berryman writes: "The phrase 'the new man' has a particular resonance for some Latin Americans since Che Guevara and other Marxists also speak of a revolutionary 'new man' (a few are sensitized enough to add 'and woman')." See Berryman's *Liberation Theology, Essential Facts about the Revolutionary Movement in Latin*

America and Beyond (New York/Philadelphia, Pantheon/Temple University Press, 1987), p. 59. This book is a useful guide to liberation theology.

144   "Marxism . . . crucified": These seven sentences are taken from Pedro Monzon's interview with Ernesto Cardenal in *Sábado Gráfico,* Madrid, 1978, which I have translated directly from a photocopy of the newspaper page on which the interview was published. The page does not contain an exact date.

144   Ernesto Cardenal: Author's conversations with Ernesto Cardenal, January 17 and September 19, 1986. Excerpts from both conversations are combined in this account.

145   Borge letter: Borge's letter to Cardenal was published in *Amanecer,* no. 34–35 (March–May 1985), p. 28. Author's translation.

146   *Filosofía marxista-leninista:* This is the same text referred to on page 127 of my narrative and page 326 of these notes, published by Editorial Progreso, Moscow, 1982. On this point Fernando Cardenal told me on January 16, 1986, that "an international campaign of calumnies is being waged against Nicaragua, claiming persecution of priests and that our education is Marxist. *Show me*—page by page—*where* it's Marxist . . . It's true that in our universities Marxism is studied, but *not* in our secondary schools."

146   Konrad Lorenz: See my "Conversations with Konrad Lorenz," *Harper's,* May 1968, and in *Exploring Psychology* (New York: Crowell, 1973), pp. 404–20.

149   Egypt: See my "The Birth Pangs of Arab Socialism," *Harper's,* February 1962. This essay, though critical, in retrospect was too optimistic for the future of Arab Socialism and of President Nasser.

III / EL SALVADOR

154   Operación Héroes de Joateca: See *El Mundo,* San Salvador, April 10 and 15, 1986, for more detail of this military campaign.

162   In an army sweep: This may have been the massacre reported by the Lawyers Committee for International Human Rights, "Justice Denied," New York, June 19, 1985, pp. 62–65: "For approximately two weeks in mid-December 1981, soldiers from the Atlacatyl Battalion . . . took part in a search-and-destroy operation in Las Toriles, La Joya, Meanguera, Cerro Pando, El Mozote" and other villages in Morazán. "The Human Rights Commission of El Salvador has estimated the number of deaths to be 926"—and another human rights group reported that "the number of civilian deaths exceeded 1,000."

166   Shot nine men: See the *New York Times,* November 4, 1984.

166   "Scorched-earth policy": When I returned to San Salvador I protested
       to the U.S. Embassy about the army's burning policy in Morazán. A
       senior embassy official told me: "I checked with the cuartel in San
       Francisco Gotera after your question. The army does burn some crops.
       They burn in front of their troops to detonate plastic land mines. They
       don't want to burn crops around established villages. This is a delicate
       problem. It is not a scorched-earth policy, but a situation of war, yes."

173   Marta: "Marta's" testimony, repeating essentially the same story, was
       given under her real name to the Comité de Madres y Familiares de
       Presos, Desaparecidos y Asesinados Políticos de El Salvador, "Mon-
       señor Oscar Arnulfo Romero," San Salvador, in late 1985 or early
       1986, an undated document in my possession. I have given her a
       fictitious name here because she requested anonymity.

175   The Centeno brothers: The Centeno brothers told essentially the same
       story to *The Guardian,* a leftist newspaper published in New York City.
       See Charles Kernaghan, "Duarte Lets Loose on Labor," *The Guardian,*
       February 19, 1986, p. 15, for more detail, especially regarding the
       labor dispute between ANTEL, the state communications agency, and
       ASSTEL, the telecommunications workers' trade union. I interviewed
       the Centeno brothers at La Esperanza prison on April 10, 1986 and
       Vladimir individually on April 27, 1986. See also *Settling into Routine:
       Human Rights Abuses in Duarte's Second Year . . . El Salvador* (New
       York and Washington: The Americas Watch Committee, May 1986),
       pp. 97–104, for further detail of the Centeno brothers' case. On the
       immersion torture, Americas Watch is less explicit: "At night, the
       brothers were separately put in a concrete water basin (*pila*) which
       was filled with filthy water and urine. It was about one meter wide and
       long, and one meter deep. They were forced to sit in the *pila,* and were
       ducked into the water to the point of near drowning" (p. 99). In March
       1988, Humberto Centeno was arrested again (AP and the *Boston Globe,*
       March 12, 1988).

177   López Nuila: Author's conversation with Colonel López Nuila, April
       29, 1986. See also *El Mundo,* March 21, 1986, and *El Salvador News-
       Gazette,* April 7–13, 1986, for the vice minister's comments on security
       officials dismissed or brought to trial and his explanations why no senior
       officials had been prosecuted.

178   Insurgency was puritanical: The Salvadoran minister of justice, Dr.
       Julio Alfredo Samayoa, in a conversation with the author on April 22,
       1986: "I permit the FMLN organizations and prisoners to organize their
       own lives at Mariona and Ilopango. There are Mafias in those prisons.
       They have their own discipline. They don't permit drugs. We tolerate
       and accept them if they don't violate our prison regulations."

COPPES, the Comité de Presos Políticos en El Salvador, governed the political sections of the prisons and was widely known to be dominated by the FMLN. However, in December 1987, after an amnesty that released 400 prisoners, the political section of the Mariona prison was disbanded and the remaining inmates were transferred to other jails throughout the country. See the *Los Angeles Times*, December 25, 1987.

180   Rey Prendes: Author's conversation with the minister, in English, April 17, 1986.

182   Samayoa: Author's conversation with the minister on April 22 and 24, 1986.

183   The Treasury Police: See *Human Rights in Nicaragua*, p. 55: "Credible reports indicate that torture was practiced by all three security forces, the National Police, the Treasury Police, and the National Guard, as well as by the other armed forces, during the . . . period . . . July to December 1985."

184   "Sweet old ladies": *New York Times*, February 2, 1985.

184   Common knowledge: Ibid.

184   Quarter of the prisoners: A senior U.S. correspondent in San Salvador, citing confidential sources in the police, told me that "20 to 25 percent of political prisoners are physically tortured." A senior official of the U.S. Embassy, agreeing that physical torture was still practiced, allowed only the "10 to 15 percent."

184   Warren above the Pizza Boom: On May 28, 1987, "a powerful bomb destroyed" the mothers' "office, injuring four people and causing considerable . . . damage," *Letter to the Churches*, published in English by the Pastoral Center, Universidad de Centroamerica, San Salvador, June 1–15, 1987.

185   Sin has become: Americas Watch, pp. 55–56.

185   Timerman: Jacobo Timerman, *Prisoner Without a Name, Cell Without a Number* (New York: Knopf, 1981).

187   All of us were born: Most of the material on the dictatorship of General Hernández Martínez and the matanza of 1932 is drawn from Robert Armstrong and Janet Shenk, *El Salvador: The Face of Revolution* (Boston: South End Press, 1982), pp. 25–32. The general's radio lectures were related by Roque Dalton in his *Las Historias Prohibidas del Pulgarcito* (Mexico City: Siglo Veinteuno, 1974), pp. 125–26. The "smell my gun" episode was cited in Lilian Jimenez, *El Salvador, Sus Problemas Socio-Economicos* (Havana: Casa de las Americas, 1980), p. 119. The Dalton poem is entitled "Todos."

188   Cardinal Newman: John Henry Cardinal Newman, *Apologia Pro Vita Sua*, VII, "General Answer to Mr Kingsley," 1864 (New York: Random House, Modern Library, 1950), pp. 240–41.

190   Duarte : For interesting details on Duarte's problems with the economy, see James LeMoyne, *New York Times*, February 10, 1986, and Tim Golden, *Miami Herald*/International Edition, May 2, 1986. Inés Guadalupe Duarte was kidnapped in September and released in October 1985 in exchange for wounded guerrillas.

190   "Our aim with the mines": Villalobos on Radio Venceremos, 1985, cited by Hedges, *Dallas Morning News,* August 4, 1985.

190   Hundreds of soldiers: More than 250 government soldiers died in the guerrilla attack on the cuartel of San Miguel on June 12, 1986; an American military adviser was also killed. The guerrillas destroyed helicopters and captured a large arsenal. See *Barricada,* the *New York Times,* and the *Miami Herald* for June 20, 1986.

191   "Let us unite": Dalton, "Todos."

191   A CIA spy: *Excélsior,* Mexico City, March 10, 1980, cited by Gabriel Zaid in his "Enemy Colleagues: A Reading of the Salvadoran Tragedy," translated by David Pritchard in *Dissent,* February, 1982, pp. 13–40, a fascinating essay on the divisions in the guerrilla movement. For more detail of Dalton's murder, see also Armstrong and Shenk, p. 71, and *Newsweek,* July 15, 1985.

192   "Liquidate the capitalist system": See LeMoyne, *New York Times,* December 22, 1985, and January 5, 1986. On the irrelevance of the FMLN's non-Marxist allies, see Hedges, *Dallas Morning News,* May 21, 1985. See also my "The 'Clean' War," *The New York Review of Books,* June 26, 1986: "The FMLN's declarations [on a single Marxist-Leninist party] are an embarrassment to the Revolutionary Democratic Front (FDR), the civilian wing of the rebel cause headed by such non-Marxists as Guillermo Ungo of the National Revolutionary Movement (MNR) and Rubén Zamora of the Popular Social Christian Movement (MPSC). Though Ungo and Zamora represent the FMLN internationally [they have no real power and] and in captured correspondence [Hedges, above] Ungo and Zamora complained in 1984 that the FMLN leaders did not consider their alliance 'a strategic one.' "

192   Historic Program: Platform of the Democratic Revolutionary Front, April 1980, cited in Armstrong and Shenk, Appendix 2, pp. 254–59.

193   "Chauvinistic": See Hedges, *Dallas Morning News,* May 21, 1985.

193   Farabundo Martí: See Thomas Anderson, *Matanza: El Salvador's Communist Revolt of 1932* (Lincoln: University of Nebraska Press, 1971), Chapter 2.

194   A former guerrilla comandante: Miguel Castellanos, chief of the Popular Liberation Forces (FPL) in San Salvador from 1982 until he defected to the government in 1985, with whom I had three lengthy meetings. Of these encounters I wrote in the *New York Review of Books,* June

26, 1986: "Skeptical at first, I checked [Castellanos's] information with a variety of sources and finally found it persuasive."

195 Essentially Duarte replied: See my El Salvador essay, the *New York Review of Books*, ibid., for specifics of the FMLN and government negotiating positions.

198 Ambassador Corr: Author's conversation with Ambassador Corr, on the record at author's request, April 23, 1986.

200 Luke 4: 18–19: King James version. More modern versions read thus: "The spirit of the Lord is upon me; therefore, He has anointed me. He has sent me to bring glad tidings to the poor, to proclaim liberty to captives, recovery of sight to the blind and release to prisoners, to announce the year of favor from the Lord." The passage is originally from Isaiah. Christ read it in the temple (v. 17).

201 The principal contribution: Both quotations in the paragraph are from a public speech by Father Ellacuría on November 9, 1985, in San Salvador.

204 Berryman: Phillip Berryman, *The Religious Roots of Rebellion: Christians in Central American Revolutions* (Maryknoll, N.Y.: Orbis Books, 1984), pp. 392–93.

204 Berrigan: Daniel Berrigan, S.J., *The Mission: A Film Journal* (San Francisco: Harper & Row, 1986), pp. 145–46.

IV / INTERLUDE IN COSTA RICA

209 "To have been born": *La Nación*, San José, May 26, 1986. President Figueres publicly retracted the remark in a paid advertisement in *La Nación* on June 1, 1986.

V / NICARAGUA REVISITED

215 Twenty thousand pounds: For beef and chicken stories, see *Barricada*, *El Nuevo Diario*, and *La Prensa*, May and June 1986, passim.

216 Nicaraguan suffering: The U.S. trade embargo, imposed on Nicaragua in May 1985, provided the Sandinistas with a rhetorical excuse for social hardship, but Sandinista economists privately admitted its marginal effect. Though most direct commerce between the U.S. and Nicaragua had stopped, some trade was still conducted through third countries, and much of the remainder was absorbed by Western Europe, Japan, and Canada. Most Nicaraguan coffee was sold to West Germany, most cotton to Japan. See June Erlick, *Miami Herald*, May 12, 1986, and Alan M. Feld, *Forbes Magazine*, August 25, 1986.

217 At least $1 billion: Economists at Western embassies in Managua estimate this as a minimum of the flight of capital since the Revolution;

the true figure may be several times as much. With so little money for capital investment, creation of new jobs is impeded; the high unemployment in Nicaragua resembles the ratios throughout the isthmus.

217   The flight: The figure of 55 percent of professional emigration was given me by Dr. Carlos Quiñonez Torres, president of the Confederación de Asociaciones Profesionales de Nicaragua (CONAPRO); the percentage probably rose by 1988. Dr. Quiñonez added: "Ninety-five percent of government projects were given to Cuban, Bulgarian, Soviet, and East German engineers, depriving Nicaraguan engineers of work . . . The Sandinistas have discouraged the practice of private medicine, and Nicaragua's best doctors have fled." He estimated the total of expatriate Nicaraguans since the Revolution at 700,000 to 900,000 — "almost 25 percent of the population gone." The government angrily denied that the rate of emigration resembled such high figures.

218   The soldier of rank: The prisoner was Sofonia Cisneros Leiva, 60, head of the Unión Nacional de Asociaciones de Padres de Familia de Colegios Cristianos, a type of parent-teachers association. The quotation is abstracted from his affidavit to the International League for Human Rights. See "Report on Human Rights Defenders in Nicaragua," International League for Human Rights, New York, July 1986, pp. 174–75.

219   "We cannot": See Stephen Kinzer, *New York Times,* February 22, 1986. Ortega said: "There is inefficiency on the part of ministers, and mistakes are creating a political and social problem for us. We lack sufficient contact with the daily reality of the Nicaraguan people." After indirectly deploring the economic impact of the war he added, "We can't blame everything on the war. We also have a certain responsibility here." Kinzer called the President's admissions "extraordinary."

221   People's Power: Borge's speeches are quoted from *Nicaragua: The Sandinista People's Revolution* and *Sandinistas Speak.* Other remarks and speeches are from Nolan and the American observer cited, Joe Klein, "Nicaragua at the Turning Point," *Rolling Stone,* October 10, 1985.

222   The contras' land mines: See Kinzer's articles in the *New York Times* of February 20 and July 19, 1986, and the Amnesty International and Americas Watch reports of 1986–87 on contra land mines, their other atrocities, and human rights abuse by the Sandinistas.

222   *"El Presidente Reagan":* Borge's interview with Gregorio Selser, *Barricada,* January 15, 1986.

223   *¿Qué esperanza sentamos . . . ?:* From "1984," by Pablo Antonio Cuadra, published in *1984 Nicaragua,* p. 9. Author's translation.

226   "Be sober": 1 Peter 5:8.

226   "We appeal": See the *New York Times,* March 28, 1986, and my "Battle for Nicaragua: Church, Cardinal, and Comandantes," *Commonweal,* May 9, 1986.

226   Maugham: W. Somerset Maugham, *The Razor's Edge* (Philadelphia: Doubleday/ Triangle, 1944–46), p. 236.

227   Monseñor Carballo: See Christian, pp. 228–31, for more detail. Miss Christian wrote: "The episode . . . was generally blamed on Interior Minister Borge and the Cubans serving as internal security advisers."

229   Cardinal Ratzinger: Joseph Cardinal Ratzinger, Prefect of the Sacred Congregation for the Doctrine of the Faith, or "Holy Office." Cardinal Ratzinger reaffirmed the teaching of Aquinas in his second Instruction on liberation theology, April 1986. In *Populorum Progressio,* his Encyclical of 1967, Pope Paul VI had written (30, 31): "A revolutionary uprising [could be justified] where there is manifest, long-standing tyranny which would do great damage to fundamental personal rights and dangerous harm to the common good of the country." This was a direct distillation of Aquinas's doctrine on revolt against tyranny cited at the head of my chapters on El Salvador.

230   Cardinal Obando: Author's conversation with Cardinal Obando on June 18, 1986. I have interpolated several relevant sentences from another conversation with him on September 16, 1986.

231   Papal infallibility: Lytton Strachey, *Eminent Victorians,* essay on Cardinal Manning (London, 1918; reprinted New York: Capricorn, 1963), pp. 94–95.

232   "The Fathers": Martin P. Harney, S.J., *The Jesuits in History: The Society of Jesus Through Four Centuries* (New York: America Press, 1941), pp. 244–48, 299–303.

232   Voltaire: Voltaire is cited in the essay on the Reductions in *A Catholic Dictionary,* Donald Attwater, ed. (New York: Macmillan, 1931–39). The Reductions were the subject of Roland Joffe's marvelous 1986 film, *The Mission,* with Jeremy Irons, Robert De Niro, Daniel Berrigan, S.J., script by Robert Bolt.

236   "The poor of Jesus Christ": See Nolan, p. 112, and Cardenal, *El evangelio en Solentiname,* I, 178.

237   New political prisoners: In Zelaya department, between Chontales and the Caribbean Sea, the American Capuchin fathers told me: "We are willing to live and work under a communist government. We spend much of our time with this one trying to liberate political prisoners. The Sandinistas get whatever information they need from their prisoners." The Capuchins added that, from the numbers of prisoners in Zelaya, they calculated "far more than 7,000 political prisoners in all of Nicaragua" in mid-1986.

238   Armed transport helicopters: See the *New York Times,* July 7, 1986.

239   Jails and interrogation: Later, in Managua, I met Sub-comandante Alvaro Guzman, chief of Nicaragua's penitentiary system and one of Tomás Borge's senior aides. Describing the joint army and Interior Ministry "sweeps" of Chontales, Boaco, Zelaya, and other provinces in search of contras and their collaborators, Guzman told me: "The army makes the sweeps, but with the army are officials of the state security. When the army catches counterrevolutionaries, they are turned over to us for imprisonment and interrogation. There are no army jails. Running jails and questioning counterrevolutionaries is the job of the state security. We're very efficient at it." I believed him.

239   Contras had attacked Cuapa: In August 1985.

241   The Virgin and Bernardo: Testimony of Bernardo Martínez of Cuapa, *Revista del Pensamiento Centroamericano,* Managua, early 1980s, pp. 7–21, my photocopied pages undated. For Sandinista attacks on Bernardo de Cuapa, see *Barricada* and *El Nuevo Diario,* 1980–81 passim.

245   Bench of bishops: The official name is La Conferencia Episcopal de Nicaragua.

246   Seditious and impossible: See *Nuevo Diario* and its supplement *Nuevo Amanecer Cultural,* Managua, June 14, 1986, and *Nuevo Diario* and *Barricada,* June and July 1986 passim, for Sandinista attacks on Monseñor Vega. The conservative procontra groups in the U.S. were PRODEMCA and the Heritage Foundation.

247   "There's no ideological difference": See also the *New York Times,* October 25, 1984.

248   John Paul's visit: The details of Sandinista conduct starting with my reference to Tomás Borge were related to me by a (non-Sandinista) Jesuit who was present at the Pope's Mass. In Managua I reviewed the entire video tape of the event, and it seemed to confirm his account.

251   An interesting letter: The letter was dated Managua June 26, 1986, the day of *La Prensa*'s closing. Author's translation.

251   More evidence of perfidy: See the *New York Times,* June 28, 1986.

252   *Barricada . . . El Nuevo Diario:* See page 1 of both newspapers, July 3, 1986.

252   Deported to Honduras: On July 4, 1986.

252   "Evokes the dark ages": *Miami Herald*/International Edition, July 7, 1986.

253   "Not a bit": Author's conversation with Cardenal, September 19, 1986.

255   "Trying to silence me": Possibly one of the "voices" was Agostíno Cardinal Casaroli, the papal secretary of state. Cardinal Casaroli favors accommodation between the Holy See and communist regimes and was known to advocate a more conciliatory approach to the Sandinistas.

Several pro-Sandinista Jesuits praised his attitude in talking to me, and a Western diplomat in Managua told me that "the Popular Church wishes Cardinal Casaroli were Pope."

255   "We are being cut off": Conversation at the Cardinal's residence, July 6, 1986.

255   "This is the work of the Vegas": See *Nuevo Diario*, July 6, 1986, and *Barricada*, July 4 and 6, 1986. The land mine atrocity occurred July 2 near the village of El Cuá, Jinotega. See also the *New York Times*, July 19, 1986.

255   Huxley: Aldous Huxley, *The Doors of Perception* and *Heaven and Hell* (London: Penguin/Chatto & Windus, 1959).

VI / GUATEMALA

257   Epigraph: Graham Greene, *The Lawless Roads* (London/New York: Penguin/Heinemann, 1939/82). Citations appear throughout.

259   Huxley: Aldous Huxley, *Beyond the Mexique Bay* (London: Triad Paladin/Chatto & Windus, 1934/84), p. 82.

261   Autobiography: Graham Greene, *A Sort of Life* (New York: Simon & Schuster, 1971), p. 168.

261   Greene's admiration of the Sandinistas: See John Bank, "Graham Greene on U.S. Involvement in Central America," *St. Anthony Messenger* (Cincinnati), October 1987, pp. 18–26.

264   Minister of the interior: The minister of the interior was Juan José Rodil, an intimate of Christian Democratic President Vinicio Cerezo. His official title was ministro de gobernación.

264   20 percent of the populace: The data are UNICEF's.

269   In a bizarre foreshadowing: See W. George Lovell, *Conquest and Survival in Colonial Guatemala* (Kingston, Ontario: McGill–Queen's University Press, 1985).

269   Religious rites of the Ixil: See Benjamin N. Colby and Pierre L. van den Berghe, *Ixil Country: A Plural Society in Highland Guatemala* (Berkeley: University of California Press, 1969).

270   Restored all expropriated property to United Fruit: A Pyrrhic victory. United Fruit eventually broke up in an antitrust action by the U.S. Department of Justice and sold its property in Guatemala.

271   The CIA coup: See Stephen Schlesinger and Stephen Kinzer, *Bitter Fruit: The Untold Story of the American Coup in Guatemala* (New York: Doubleday, Anchor, 1982/84. See also Jim Handy, *Gift of the Devil: A History of Guatemala* (Boston: South End Press, 1984), and Walter LaFeber, *Inevitable Revolutions: The United States in Central America* (New York: Norton, 1983/84).

271 The Guatemalan military: Schlesinger and Kinzer, pp. 241–42.
272 Thirty thousand members: Ibid., pp. 246–47.
272 "The scale and breadth": Ibid., pp. 250–51.
272 In a word, Nazis: Amnesty International concluded that from 1966, the beginning of the great horror, until the closing months of the Lucas dictatorship fifteen years later, more than 30,000 Guatemalans were "abducted, tortured and assassinated." Other estimates are higher. See *Guatemala: A Government Program of Political Murder* (London: Amnesty International, 1981).
274 Military aid to Guatemala: For full chronology, see Jonathan L. Fried et al., eds., *Guatemala in Rebellion: Unfinished History* (New York: Grove Press, 1983), pp. 326–32.
274 Nebaj: The estimate of 20,000 comes from the present parish priest of Nebaj.
275 Rigoberta Menchú: Her story is from "Uno más Uno," translated by Javier Bajaña and Jonathan Fried, Mexico City, May 29, 1982, cited in *Guatemala in Rebellion*, pp. 194–201. Rigoberta Menchú's father died horribly also, during a notorious incident at the Spanish Embassy in Guatemala City in 1980; the police stormed the embassy and thirty-nine dissidents and Spanish diplomats burned to death inside. In exile, Señorita Menchú belonged to the Unitary Representation of the Guatemalan Opposition. In April 1988, she returned to visit Guatemala under an amnesty. She was briefly arrested and then released. See the *Boston Globe,* April 19 and 20, 1988.
276 At least thirty thousand Indians: Some human rights activists estimate the number of Indians killed at 45,000 and higher, but, as always, I prefer to err on the side of cautious statistics.
277 Perera: See Victor Perera, "Uzi Diplomacy," *Mother Jones,* July 1985; "The Lost Tribes of Guatemala," *The Monthly,* Berkeley, September 1985; and *Haaretz,* Tel Aviv, November 1985.
277 Israeli arms sales: On Israeli involvement with the Guatemalan military, I also consulted Guatemalan journalists, Western military attachés in Guatemala City, Guatemalan army officers, and concerned Israelis. Perera cites Amnesty International as a source of information on the Israeli computer in the annex of the National Palace.
277 Priests were murdered: I collected data on the persecution of the Church from clergy and laity in Nebaj, Santa Cruz del Quiché, the Lake Atitlán region, and Guatemala City.
281 "We're not revolutionaries": The summation is mainly from Juan José Rodil, minister of the interior.
282 Political murder: See Allan Nairn and Jean-Marie Simon, "Bureaucracy of Death: Guatemala's civilian government faces the enemy within," *The New Republic,* June 30, 1986.

282   Second and third years of Vinicio's presidency: See the *Boston Globe,* December 7, 1987, and March 17 and May 1, 5, and 12, 1988. Regarding the abortive military rebellion, on May 29, 1988, Julia Preston reported in the *Washington Post:* "The story told in the hallways of the National Palace is that President Vinicio Cerezo plans to use the pistol he always packs to put a bullet between the eyes of any army officer who comes to tell him he has been overthrown in a coup. 'I wasn't elected to be thrown out by force,' Cerezo said in an interview . . . He denied ever threatening to shoot a soldier, but added, 'I have said that to defend this office I will resist to the end.' "

284   General Gramajo: Author's conversation with General Gramajo, August 29, 1986.

VII / NICARAGUA. L'ENVOI.

289   2,600 percent: *New York Times,* November 9, 1986.

289   *"Somos dueños":* See *Barricada,* September 8, 1986.

292   "God will somehow help us": Author's conversation with Cardinal Obando, September 16, 1986. See also *New York Times,* September 4, 1986.

292   Their publications: See *Envío* in English, 1984–86, and *Update,* distributed by the Intercultural Center of Georgetown University, Washington, D.C., 1984–86, both published by the Jesuit Instituto Histórico Centroamericano, Managua.

294   The Nicaraguan people: I am grateful to Professor Edgardo Buitrago, director of the Museo Archivo Rubén Darío in León, for suggesting some of these reflections on the Nicaraguan people.

296   Respectful, subdued, and sad: See *Barricada* and *Nuevo Diario,* September 17, 1986, for a full account of the seminar. I appeared in a photograph on page 1 of *Barricada* taking Borge's picture as he greeted the somocista prisoners.

297   "We have confidence": Borge made similar comments on the open farms in his *Barricada* interview with Gregorio Selser.

298   "Greed is all right": Boesky was quoted in the *New Oxford Review,* Berkeley, March 1988, p. 18; the quotation originated in the *New York Times,* 1987.

298   The . . . city: Henry Adams, *The Education of Henry Adams* (New York, Modern Library, 1918/31), pp. 499–500.

300   Colonel North: North's testimony before the joint House-Senate committee investigating the "Iran-contra" scandal is taken from the *New York Times,* July 8, 10, 1987. For further background on the failures of U.S. Central American policy, see Roy Gutman, *Banana Diplomacy:*

The Making of American Policy in Nicaragua, 1981–1987 (New York: Simon & Schuster, 1988).

300 Claymore land mines: See Reuters, February 5, 1988, and the *Boston Globe*, February 6 and March 3, 1988.

300 Reformed the currency: See the *New York Times*, June 7, 1987; the *San Juan Star*, August 31, 1987; and the *Boston Globe*, February 1, 15, and 21, 1988.

302 In June 1988: See Julia Preston, *Washington Post*, June 12, 1988. In mid-June 1988 the contras again sought military aid from the Reagan administration. See the *Boston Globe*, June 15, 1988.

303 *Increase* their army: "The Defense Minister, Humberto Ortega, said today that the government plans to more than double its military forces in about seven years . . . He said the military will increase its personnel from 250,000 to 300,000 within the next six months and, conditions permitting, to 600,000 by 1995." Associated Press, Managua, December 12, 1987. The 600,000 figure would represent a fifth of Nicaragua's present population.

307 Comandante Arce: Author's conversation with Comandante Arce, September 19, 1986.

307 The vanguard: See Nolan on "Vanguard Elitism," pp. 119–21.

EPILOGUE

309 Independent Nicaraguan economists: Much of the economic data in this Epilogue is drawn from the author's conversation on August 24, 1988, with an economist at the Instituto Centroamericano de Administración de Empresas (INCAE), an independent business and management institute in Managua associated with Harvard University.

311 Epidemic of diarrhea: See *Barricada*, August 18, 1988, p. 4; and *El Nuevo Diario* and *Barricada*, summer of 1988, throughout. Also *La Prensa*, August 15, 1988, p. 5.

311 *La Prensa* and the Sandinista press: See the classified sections of *La Prensa* and *El Nuevo Diario* throughout July and August 1988.

312 Eighty-five thousand troops: Statements during January and February 1988 by the president of Nicaragua's Central Bank reported by the *Los Angeles Times* and other U.S. news organizations.

313 When the army came to press-gang: The incidents related to me by campesinos in Boaco and Chontales were confirmed by Dr. Lino Hernández, executive secretary of the independent Commission on Human Rights in Nicaragua, in conversations in Managua on August 15 and 28, 1988.

313 "When we hear": Author's conversation with Dr. Alejandro Bendaña, director general of the Foreign Ministry, August 23, 1988. He added,

"For the most part, the deliberate killing of civilians is still done by the contras."

314   Schisms of the political opposition: For example, see *Barricada* and *El Nuevo Diario*, August 15, 1988, p. 1.

314   Great popular discontent: Author's conversation with Dr. Bendaña at the Foreign Ministry, August 23, 1988. He said, "The enormous economic discontent does not translate into political opposition to the government." He added, "The economy is in terrible condition and it affects everybody . . . There has been mismanagement and we can't blame everything on the war . . . We can effectively address the hunger and infant diarrhea when we have a political settlement and peace." See also *Barricada*, August 23 (p. 2) and August 28, 1988 (p. 2), for discussion of Sandinista agricultural problems.

314   Repression: See the *New York Times*, July 10, 11, 12, 13, 15, 17, and 18, 1988.

314   Human rights: See also *Human Rights in Nicaragua: August 1987– August 1988* (New York and Washington: The Americas Watch Committee, 1988).

This report confirms in detail many of the claims I have cited of recent human rights abuse in Nicaragua. The report states (p. 4), "We have obtained evidence suggesting a pattern of serious abuses committed by government forces in remote areas . . . instances in which members of the [state security] have reportedly kidnapped and murdered individuals . . . they suspect of collaboration with the contras." Pp. 9– 10: "Americas Watch is concerned about cases of summary executions . . . in . . . Boaco, Chontales, Zelaya Sur and . . . Matagalpa and Jinotega." On pp. 124–26, the report speaks of murders, mutilations, disappearances, and a decapitation in Matagalpa province committed by government troops. Pp. 134 et seq. describe forced recruitment of underage youths and shooting of fugitives and draft resisters. Pp. 144–62 detail continuing murders and atrocities against civilians committed by the contras.

It should be noted that, continuing a long-standing disagreement, Americas Watch (pp 108–109) questions the credibility of the estimates of Dr. Lino Hernández's Permanent Commission on Human Rights about numbers of political prisoners in Nicaragua. Americas Watch considers those estimates to be exaggerated. Dr. Hernández repeatedly defended his estimates to me, insisting they were based on interviews with prisoners' families and former prisoners themselves, and on other factual data.

314   To reconstruct Nicaragua: Virgilio Godoy, leader of the opposition Liberal Independent party and a former minister in the Sandinista gov-

ernment, told me that the Sandinistas expected Dukakis, if elected, to pay Nicaragua "$1.4 billion in reparations for the contras and to reconstruct Nicaragua."

315 "We have reached": See the *New York Times,* August 7, and *Barricada,* August 16, 1988.

315 Arias: President Arias was interviewed on the MacNeil/Lehrer News Hour, August 12, 1988.

316 Lesions on his mouth: The victim was José Castillo Osejo, director of Radio Corporación. Borge attacked him on April 29, 1988. See *La Prensa,* April 30, 1988, p. 1.

ACKNOWLEDGMENTS

I wish to thank the hundreds of individuals, Central Americans or otherwise, under their real or disguised names, who talked to me, helped me, and have appeared in this book.

Additionally I should like to thank Frederick and Sandra Morgner, of the Literatura de Vientos Tropicales; Michael Drudge of the Voice of America; and Armando Icaza, of the United Nicaraguan Opposition, all of them residents of Costa Rica, for their assistance and advice. Thanks also to Tim Golden of the *Miami Herald.*

For assistance in Honduras, may I especially thank Mimi Lara of NBC; Victor Meza of the Centro de Documentación de Honduras; and Juan Ramón Duran, an eminent journalist.

For Nicaragua, I am grateful to Susan Clyde and Alberto Fernandez of the USIS; to David Oliver, an American journalist; and to the staff assistants of the *New York Times* bureau, Managua.

For El Salvador, I am grateful to Donald R. Hamilton of USIS; to Ricardo Stein of the Fundación Salvadoreña de Desarrollo y Vivienda Minima; Jemera Rone of the Americas Watch Committee; Catherine Matheson of the BBC; Morgan Powell of the *Chicago Sun-Times*; and Ana Maria de Perez, public relations officer of the presidency.

For Guatemala, I am grateful to Julio Santos, President Cerezo's chief spokesman, and to his staff; to Lucie Hood of UPI; to Julie Gianelloni of USIS; to Andrés Fajardo, then of Harvard University; to Victor Perera, the Guatemalan-American author; and to W. George Lovell, the Canadian author.

In the United States, I am grateful to Professor Jorge Dominguez of Harvard University; to Martin Nolan and Thomas Gagen of the *Boston Globe;* to Peter Steinfels, then editor of *Commonweal;* and to Robert Silvers, editor of the *New York Review of Books,* who sent me copious literature on Central America when I was on the isthmus. Thanks also to Peter Matson, president of Sterling Lord Literistic, Inc., New York, my literary agent; and to Michael C. Janeway, executive editor of Houghton Mifflin Company.

Finally, in a special category, may I express my deepest thanks to James LeMoyne and Stephen Kinzer of the *New York Times;* to Chris Hedges of the *Dallas Morning News;* and to Sharon Stevenson and Elena Caldera Greenhill of NBC, Managua. Their invaluable guidance and assistance during my difficult year in Central America deserves more than mere acknowledgment.

All responsibility for the content of this book, of course, is exclusively my own. I apologize to any helpful person I may have neglected by inadvertence, and may I emphasize that I have purposely omitted numerous helpful sources for fear of embarrassing them.

All literary quotations wherever necessary have been reprinted by permission.

INDEX

ABOUT THE AUTHOR

Edward R. F. Sheehan has had a varied career as a journalist, diplomat, novelist, academic, and playwright. He was a foreign correspondent for the *Boston Globe*, then press officer at the American embassies in Cairo and Beirut. He has contributed articles to leading publications, notably to the *New York Times Magazine*, from Europe, Africa, and the Middle East. In 1973, he won the Overseas Press Club Award for distinguished interpretation of foreign affairs, and was subsequently a Fellow at the Center for International Affairs at Harvard University. In 1976, his revelations in *Foreign Policy* about Henry Kissinger's diplomacy in the Middle East, based on secret State Department documents and expanded in book form, caused an international sensation.

Mr. Sheehan's play *Kingdoms* was produced at the Kennedy Center in Washington and at the Cort Theatre on Broadway. The eminent critic Clive Barnes named it one of the Best Plays of 1981.